WESTERN EUROPE

EUROPE

phrasebook

Mikel Edorta Morris Pagoeta

Izaskun Arretxe

Rob van Driesum

Chris Andrews

James Jenkin

Paul Hellander & Tassos Douvartzides

Seán Ó Riain

Sally Steward

Isabel Moutinho

Katie Graham

Western Europe phrasebook
   2nd edition

Published by
   Lonely Planet Publications
   Head Office: PO Box 617, Hawthorn, Vic 3122, Australia
   Branches: 150 Linden St, Oakland, CA 94607, USA
                  10a Spring Place, London NW5 3BH, UK
                  1 rue du Dahomey, 75011 Paris, France

Printed by
   Craft Print Pte Ltd, Singapore

Cover Photograph
   Detail of frieze, Villa dei Misteri, Pompeii, Campania.
   Photograph by Rob Flynn

Published
   April 1997

National Library of Australia Cataloguing in Publication Data

Pagoeta, Mikel Morris
   Western Europe phrasebook
   2nd ed.
   Includes Index.
   ISBN 0 86442 516 3.

   1. Europe, Western – Languages – Conversation and phrase books –
   English. I. Andrews, Chris. Western Europe phrasebook. II. Arretxe,
   Izaskun. III. Driesum van, Rob. IV. Title. V. Title: Western Europe
   phrasebook. (Series: Lonely Planet language survival kit)

   418

Contents

Acknowledgements

The Basque chapter was written by Mikel Edorta Morris Pagoeta. Izaskun Arretxe wrote the Catalan section. Dutch was written by Rob van Driesum, with thanks to Doekes Lulofs, and Chris Andrews wrote the French chapter, with thanks to Lou Callan. James Jenkin wrote the German chapter, with assistance from Edward and Alex Scharaschkin, and thanks to Al Sharifian. The Greek chapter was put together from manuscripts by Paul Hellander and Tassos Douvartzides, with assistance from Markella Callimassia and Christoula Nicolaou. The Irish and Welsh chapters were written by Dr Seán Ó Riain, and Italian was written by Sally Steward. Isabel Moutinho wrote the Portuguese and Spanish chapters, with thanks to Sally Steward. Scottish Gaelic was written by Katie Graham. Thanks to Seán Ó Riain for the information on Esperanto.

The editors of this book were Sally Steward and Lou Callan. Penelope Richardson was responsible for design, and the front cover design is by David Kemp. Thanks to Dan Levin for computer assistance, and Lachlan Wheeler for proofreading assistance.

From the Publisher

For ease of pronunciation, we have used a simplified phonetic translation, based on the International Phonetic Alphabet. While this can only approximate the exact sounds of each language, it serves as the most useful guide for readers attempting to speak the various words and phrases. Refer to the Pronunciation section in each chapter for a description of the sounds particular to that language. In the phonetic translations, *zh* represents the sound of 's' as in 'measure'. Bold is used to indicate word stress, that is, you emphasise the syllable that appears in bold. As you spend time in a country, listening to native speakers and following the rules offered here in the pronunciation sections, you should be able to read directly from the language itself.

Some languages in this book have masculine, feminine and sometimes neuter, forms of words. The different forms are separated in the text by slashes and/or the bracketed letters (m), (f) and (neut), when appropriate. Many words share the same form, so no indication of gender is required.

Several of the languages in this book have both formal and informal ways of speech, which means that for one word in English you may find two in the other language, one being the polite, formal, word and the other being more casual, informal. For the purposes of this book the formal way of speech has been adopted throughout, as this will ensure that at least you will not offend anyone by using the more intimate speech. In instances where the informal is commonly used, we have included it, indicated with the letters (inf).

BASQUE

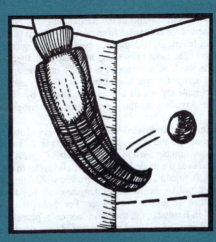

BASQUE

Basque

Introduction

No one knows the origins of the Basque language but that has not stopped some eccentrics from declaring that it is related to the Sioux language, to Japanese, even to the language of the Atlanteans. The most interesting, and plausible, theory is that Basque is the lone survivor of a family of languages which extended across Europe many hundreds of years ago and was almost completely wiped out and supplanted by such Indo-European invaders as the Celts, Germanic tribes and the Romans.

Basque has intermingled with the languages of its invaders and neighbours, and this is amply reflected in its vocabulary. The Basque number system, like that of the Celts, is based on scores and even the name for 20, 'Hogei', is similar to the Welsh word for 20, 'ugain'. Basque has borrowed words directly from Latin and, unlike the Romance languages, it has kept these words more or less as they were. For example, 'body' is 'gorputz' in Basque, from the Latin 'corpus'; 'peace' is 'pake' from the Latin 'pace' (the Latin 'c' was always pronounced as a 'k').

Basque is spoken by about 700,000 people throughout The Basque Autonomous Community (BAC), Navarre, and Iparralde (aka the French Basque Country). Although Basque is primarily spoken in small towns, it is being spoken more and more in the larger cities, especially among young people.

Centuries of neglect and marginalisation, combined with two centuries of French republicanism and 40 years of Spanish fascism, pushed Basque to the brink of extinction. But in 1979 it was declared the co-official language, along with Spanish, in the BAC and Navarre (Basque still lacks official recognition of any kind in France). Today, most of the children in the BAC are being taught in Basque at school, there is a Basque TV channel, and there are dozens of local municipal channels which feature it prominently or exclusively. There are Basque-language rock bands and rap singers. Even Microsoft Windows 95, Word and Explorer have Basque versions.

Although speaking Spanish or French in Basque-speaking towns might be expected from a foreigner, those who at least make an attempt to speak Basque are lionized and even sometimes invited for a drink.

Pronunciation

The stress in Basque is generally on the second-last syllable. Vowels are pronounced as in Spanish or Italian:

g	always hard, like 'g' in 'get' or 'Gary'
h	silent in the Spanish Basque Country; pronounced in the French Basque Country
j	generally pronounced as 'y'; or as in Spanish – a guttural sound like the 'ch' in Scottish *loch* or German *nacht*.
j	as 'tt', the American pronunciation of 'ghetto' or 'butter'
rr	a rolled r as in Spanish or Scottish
x	mostly pronounced as 'sh' as in 'ship'
tx	as 'ch' as in 'church'
ts	pronounced more or less like a soft 'ch'
tz	as the 'tz' in 'Blitz' or 'Ritz'
z	as the 'ss' in 'Mississippi'

Greetings & Civilities
Greetings & Goodbyes

Hi!	*kai-sho*	Kaixo!
Good morning.	*e-goo-non*	Egun On.
Good afternoon.	*ah-**rrah**-chahl-de-on*	Arratsalde On.
Good evening.	*ah-**rrah**-chahl-de-on*	Arratsalde On.
How are you?	*sair mo-**doos**?*	Zer moduz?
What's up?	*sair **be-rree**?*	Zer berri?
Fine and you?	*on-ghee e-tah soo?*	Ongi eta zu?
Fine, thank you.	*on-ghee, es-ke-rree-**kahs**-ko*	Ongi, eskerrik asko.
Goodbye.	*a-**goor***	Agur.
See you later.	*ghe-ro **arr**-te*	Gero arte.
Take care.	*on-do ee-**beel**-(y)ee*	Ondo ibili.

Civilities

Please.	*me-se-des*	Mesedez.
Thank you.	*es-ke-rree-**kahs**-ko*	Eskerrik asko.
Excuse me.	*barr-**kah**-too*	Barkatu.
You're welcome.	*es o-**rre**-gah-teek*	Ez horregatik.
Mr Agirre	*a-**ghee**-rre yow-na*	Agirre Jauna
Mrs Agirre	*a-**ghee**-rre ahn-**dre**-ah*	Agirre Andrea
Hey!	*ai-**soo**!*	Aizu!

Small Talk

What's your name?		
no-la ee-se-nah doo-soo?		Nola izena duzu?
My name's John		
John ee-se-nah doot		John izena dut

I'm pleased to meet you
pos-ten nais soo e-sah-goo-tze-ahz   Pozten naiz zu ezagutzeaz.

I'd like to introduce you to ...
... owr-kes-too nai nee-soo-ke   ... aurkeztu nahi nizuke.

Where are you from?
non-go-ah sah-rah?   Nongoa zara?

I'm from ...	... nais	... naiz.
Australia	ows-**trah**-lee-a-ko-ah	Australiakoa
England	een-**gah**-lah-te-rra-ko-ah	Ingalaterrakoa
Ireland	eerr-**lahn**-dah-ko-ah	Irlandakoa
New Zealand	se-**lah**-dah	Zeelanda
	be-**rree**-ko-a	Berrikoa
Canada	kah-**nah**-dah-ko-ah	Kanadakoa
Scotland	es-ko-**see**-ah-ko-ah	Eskoziakoa
the USA	es-**tah**-too	Estatu
	ba-**too**-e-tah-ko-ah	Batuetakoa
Wales	**gha**-les-ko-ah	Galeskoa

NB See our note in the Irish chapter about other countries.

Useful Phrases

How do you say that in Basque?
*no-lah e-**sah**-ten dah*   Nola esaten da hori
(h)o-ree e-oos-kah-rahs?   euskaraz?

I don't know.
*es dah-**keet***   Ez dakit.

Where's the toilet, please?
*ko-**moo**-nah, non dah-**gho**?*   Komuna non dago?

At the end.
  *ahs-**ke**-ne-ahn*   Azkenean.
On the left.
  *es-**kairr**-tah-rah*   Ezkertara.
On the right.
  *es-**koo**-bee-tah-**rah**/*   Eskubitara/
  *es-**koo**-mah-tah-**rah***   Eskumatara. (Biscay Basque)
Straight ahead.
  *soo-sen soo-**sen**-e-ahn*   Zuzen-zuzenean.

Food

The Basque Country has a reputation for having some of the best food in the world. There are high-class restaurants, smaller restaurants, bars serving food, and cider houses – sagardotegi (*sa-**garr**-do-te-ghee*). The coast, of course, is best known for its seafood.

Eating Out

Waiter!
  ai-soo   Aizu!
A little bread, please.
  *o-**ghee** peesh-kah baht,*   Ogi pixka bat, mesedez.
  me-se-des
a bottle of wine
  *bo-**teel**-(y)ah baht arr-**do**-ah*   botila bat ardoa

salad	*en-**chah**-lah-dah*	entsalada
vegetables	*ba-**rahs**-kee-ahk*	barazkiak
chips (French Fries)	*pah-**tah**-tah free-**hee**-too-ahk*	Patata frijituak

Meat & Seafood

angler	*shah-po-ah*	xapoa
chop	*choo-le-tah*	txuleta
clams	*cheerr-lahk*	txirlak
cod	*bah-kail-yo-ah*	bakailaoa
hake	*le-gah-tzah*	legatza
ribs	*kos-teel-yahk*	kostilak
	sai-es-kee-ahk	saiheskiak
squid	*shee-pee-roy-ahk*	xipiroiak
steak	*she-rra*	xerra

kokotxak *(ko-ko-chahk)*
area around the neck of the fish, considered to be the best part

Desserts

cheese	*gahs-tah*	gazta
ice cream	*ee-sos-kee-ah*	izozkia
sheep's curds	*mah-mee-ah*	mamia

At the Bar

I'd like ...	*nai noo-ke*	... nahi nuke.
a beer	*ga-rah-garr-do-ah*	garagardoa
a beer (draught)	*kah-nyah baht*	kaina bat
a red wine	*ahr-do bel-tzah*	ardo beltza
a rosé	*ahr-do go-rree-ah*	ardo gorria
plain coffee	*kah-fe oo-chah*	kafe hutsa
coffee with a dash of milk	*ka-fe e-bah-kee-ah*	kafe ebakia
coffee and milk	*kah-fes-ne-ah*	kafesne
water	*oo-rah*	aura

Signs

ERRETZEA DEBEKATUA	*NO SMOKING*
HIRIAREN ERDIALDEA	*CITY CENTRE (on buses)*
ANDREAK/JAUNAK	*LADIES/GENTLEMEN*
EDARITEGIA	*BAR*
EMAN BIDEA	*YIELD (GIVE WAY)*
ERTZAINTZA	*BASQUE POLICE*
IRTEERA	*EXIT*
KONTUZ!	*CAUTION!*
LURSAIL JABEDUNA	*PRIVATE PROPERTY*
SARRERA	*ENTRANCE*
SARTZEA DEBEKATURIK	*NO ENTRY*
UDALTZAINGOA	*MUNICIPAL POLICE*

Looking for that town on the map and can't find it? Maybe the Spanish or French was painted out or perhaps you have an old map with the old Spanish or French name. Here's some help.

Arrasate	*Mondragon*
Bilbo	*Bilbao*
Donebane Garazi	*St. Jean-Pied-de-Port*
Donebane Lohitzune	*St. Jean de Luz*
Donestebe	*Santesban*
Donostia	*San Sebastian*
Hondarribia	*Fuenterrabia*
Iruñea (or Iruña)	*Pamplona*
Lizarra	*Estella*
Soraluze	*Placencia de las Armas*

Colloquial Expressions
Reading Graffitti

The Basque Country is thoroughly politicised and this is reflected on the walls:

Presoak kalera!	Free the prisoners!
.... askatu!	Free ....!
Askatasuna!	Freedom!
Gora ....!	Long Live (the) ...!
... herria zurekin!	...., the people are with you!
Herriak ez du barkatuko	The people shall never forgive
Amnistia Osoa!	Total Amnesty!
Intsumisioa!	No Military Service!
... kanpora!	... go home!
Nuklearrik ez!	No nukes!

Some Clichés

Here are a few clichés guaranteed to bring you a chuckle:

Gora gu 'ta gutarrak!
*go-rah goo tah **goo**-tah-rrahk*
    Hurray for us!

Euskal Herrian beti jai.
*e-oos-**kahl** e-**rree**-ahn be-tee **hai***
    The Basque Country's always partying.

Aupa Erreala!
***ow**-pah e-**rre**-ah-lah*
    Hurray for Real Sociedad! (the Donostia football team)

Aupa Athletic!
ow-pah Athletic!
   Hurray for Athletic! (the Bilbao football team)

Gero arte Bonaparte.
Agur Ben Hur.
***ghe**-ro **ahrr**-te bo-nah-**pahrr**-te*
*a-**ghoor** be-**noor***
   See you later alligator.
   In a while, crocodile.

Basque Words in English

jai alai   'merry festival' – from the name of a handball
               court and now designating the fast-action sport
               of Basque handball

silhouette   'place of holes' – from the Frenchified surname
               of a Basque man (spelt Zilueta in modern spell-
               ing) who invented the art

CATALAN

CATALAN

Catalan

Introduction

Catalan is one of the nine Romance (or Neo-Latin) languages, along with French, Italian, Portuguese and Spanish. It is spoken by up to 10 million people in the north-east of Spain, a territory that comprises Catalonia proper, coastal Valencia and the Balearic Islands (Majorca, Minorca, Ibiza). Outside Spain Catalan is spoken in Andorra, the south of France and the town of Alguer (Alghero) in Sardinia. In the Spanish areas mentioned above, Catalan is an official language along with Spanish. Despite the fact that almost all Catalan speakers from Spain also speak Spanish, they will usually appreciate it when visitors attempt to communicate, in Catalan. For most of them it is their mother tongue. Catalan has a rich form of expression and its culture has produced painters such as Dalí, architects such as Gaudí and great writers such as Mercè Rodoreda.

Pronunciation

Vowel sounds vary according to whether they occur in stressed or unstressed syllables.

a	stressed, as the 'a' in 'father'; unstressed, as in 'about'
b	pronounced as 'p' at the end of a word
c	hard before 'a', 'o', and 'u'; soft before 'e' and 'i'
ç	like 'ss'
d	pronounced as 't' at the end of a word
e	stressed, as in 'pet'. Unstressed, like 'e' in 'open'
g	hard before 'a', 'o' and 'u'; like the 's' in measure before 'e' and 'i'

h	silent
i	like the 'i' in 'machine'
j	like the 's' in 'pleasure'
o	stressed, as in 'pot'; unstressed, like the 'oo' in 'zoo'
r	as in English in the middle of a word; silent at the end
rr	rolled
s	as in English at the beginning of a word; as 'z' in the middle of a word
v	pronounced as 'b' in Barcelona; as 'v' in some other areas
x	usually pronounced as in English but sometimes as 'sh'

There are a few odd combinations you should know:

l.l	repeat the 'l'
tx	like 'ch'
qu	like 'k'

Greetings & Civilities

Top Useful Phrases

Hello.	*Hola!*	Yes/No.	*Sí/No.*
Goodbye.	*Adéu/Adéu-siau.*	Excuse me.	*Perdoni.*

May I/Do you mind?	*Puc/Em permet?*
Sorry. (excuse me, forgive me)	*Ho sento/Perdoni.*
Please.	*Sisplau/Si us plau.*
Thank you (very much).	*(Moltes) Gràcies.*
That's fine/You're welcome.	*De res.*

Greetings

Good morning.	*Bon dia.*	How are you?	*Com estàs?*
Good afternoon.	*Bona tarda.*	(Very) well.	*(Molt) bé.*
Goodnight.	*Bona nit.*	Not too bad	*Anar fent.*
See you.	*A reveure.*	Awful.	*Malament.*

CATALAN

CATALAN

Language Difficulties

Do you speak English?	*Parla anglès?*
Could you speak in Castillian please?	*Pot parlar castellà sisplau?*
I speak a little Catalan.	*Parlo una mica de català.*
I understand some Catalan but I don't speak it.	*Entenc una mica de català però no el parlo.*
I (don't) understand.	*(No) ho entenc.*
Could you write that down please?	*Pot escriure-ho, sisplau?*
What is this called in Catalan?	*Com es diu això en català?*

Getting Around
Finding Your Way

Excuse me, where is ...?	*Perdoni, on és...?*
the bus station	*l'estació d'autobús/autocar*
the city centre	*el centre de la ciutat*
the post office	*Correus*
the train station	*l'estació de tren*
Tourist Information	*l'oficina de turisme*
the square	*la plaça*
the street	*el carrer*

Small Talk
Meeting People

What is your name?	*Com et dius?* (informal)
	Com es diu? (formal)
My name's ...	*Em dic ...*
I'd like to introduce you to ...	*Voldria presentar-te ...*
I'm pleased to meet you.	*Molt de gust.*
I'm here on holiday/ business/studying.	*Sóc aquí de vacances/de viatge de negocis/estudiant.*

How long are you here for?	*Quant de temps et penses quedar?*
(We're) here for (... weeks)	*(Ens) quedarem (... setmanes).*
Where are you from?	*D'on ets?*
Where do you live?	*On vius?*
I live in ...	*Visc a ...*
How old are you?	*Quants anys tens?*
I am ... years old	*Tinc ... anys.*
What (work) do you do?	*A què et dediques?*
I'm a/an (student/waiter).	*Sóc (estudiant/cambrera/cambrer).*
I'm unemployed.	*Estic a l'atur.*
Do you have a girlfriend/boyfriend?	*Tens xicota/xicot?*
I'm single.	*Sóc soltera/solter/.*
I'm married.	*Sóc casada/casat.*
I have a partner.	*Tinc parella*
What do you like doing?	*Què t'agrada fer?*
I like swimming and going to the cinema.	*M'agrada nedar i anar al cine.*
I don't like working.	*No m'agrada treballar gens ni mica*

Going Out

What are you doing this evening/this weekend?	*Què fas aquesta nit/aquest cap de setmana?*
Would you like to go out somewhere?	*Vols sortir amb mi?*
What time shall we meet?	*A quina hora quedem?*
Where shall we meet?	*On quedem?*
Hope to see you again soon.	*Espero veure't aviat.*
I'll give you a call.	*Ja et trucaré.*

CATALAN

Signs

OPEN/CLOSED	OBERT/TANCAT
BUDGET HOTEL	HOSTAL (Hs)
CUSTOMS	DUANA
INFORMATION	INFORMACIO
DO NOT TOUCH	NO TOCAR
EXIT	SORTIDA
EMERGENCY EXIT	SALIDA D'EMERGENCIA
GUESTHOUSE	PENSIO (P)
TOILETS	SERVEIS
YOUTH HOSTEL	ALBERG JUVENIL
MOUNTAIN LODGE	REFUGI DE MUNTANYA

Accommodation

Is there a campsite/hotel near here?	Hi ha algun càmping/hotel a prop d'aquí?
Do you have any rooms available?	Hi ha habitacions lliures?
How much is it per night/ per person?	Quant val per nit/persona?
It's fine, I'll take it.	D'acord, me la quedo
I'd like to pay the bill.	Voldria pagar el compte.
I'd like ...	Voldria ...
a single room	una habitació individual
a double room	una habitació doble
to share a dorm	compartir un dormitori

Food

breakfast	esmorzar
lunch	dinar
dinner	sopar

Eating Out

first course/entrée	*primer plat*	dessert	*postres*
second/main course	*segon plat*	a drink	*una beguda*

I'd like the set lunch.	*Voldira el menú del dia.*
The bill, please.	*El compte, sisplau.*
What will you have?	*Què volen prendre?*
I'll have a/an ...	*Jo prendré ...*
It's on me.	*Pago jo.*
Cheers/Good health!	*Salut!/Força al canut!*
	Bon profit!

Typical Catalan Dishes

calçots	shallots, usually served braised with an almond dipping sauce. A seasonal delicacy.
coca	a dense cake, especially popular during St. Joan (John) celebrations, when it is decorated with candied peel or pine nuts
crema catalana	a light crème caramel
ensaïmada mallorquina	a sweet mallorcan pastry
escalivada	roasted red peppers in olive oil
escudella i carn d'olla	a Christmas dish of soup and meatballs
fuet	a thin pork sausage, native to Catalunya
mel i mató	a dessert of curd cheese with honey
mongetes seques i butifarra	haricot beans with thick pork sausage
pa amb tomàquet i pernil	crusty bread rubbed with ripe tomatoes, garlic and olive oil, often topped with cured ham
sobrassada	spreadable red sausage, speciality of Majorca

CATALAN

Drinks – Nonalcoholic

almond drink	*orxata*
black coffee	*cafè sol*
coffee with a little milk	*tallat*
coffee with milk	*cafè amb llet*
mineral water	*aigua mineral*
soft drinks	*refrescs*

Drinks – Alcoholic

a beer	*una cervesa*	muscatel	*moscatell*
champagne	*cava*	ratafia (liquer)	*ratafia*

a glass of ... wine		*un vi ...*	
red	*negre*	rosé	*rosat*
white	*blanc*	sparkling	*d'agulla*

Shopping & Numbers

Can I help you?	*Què desitja?*
I would like to buy ...	*Voldria comprar ...*
How much is this?	*Quant val això?*

1	*un, una*	4	*quatre*	7	*set*	10	*deu*
2	*dos, dues*	5	*cinc*	8	*vuit*	100	*cent*
3	*tres*	6	*sis*	9	*nou*	1000	*mil*

Expressions Unique to Catalunya

rauxa	impulse
seny	intuitive common sense
déu n'hi do	a fair amount
Això rai!	No problem!
Quin tip de riure!	What a laugh!
Força Barça!	Go Barça! (Barcelona Football Club)

DUTCH

DUTCH

Dutch

Introduction

Most English speakers use the term 'Dutch' to describe the language spoken in the Netherlands, and 'Flemish' for that spoken in the northern half of Belgium and a tiny north-western corner of France. Both are, in fact, the same language, the correct term for which is Netherlandic, *Nederlands*, a West Germanic language that is spoken by about 25 million people worldwide.

The differences between Dutch and Flemish are similar to those between British and North American English: despite some differences they're very much the same language, with a shared literature.

Netherlandic is also spoken in Surinam in South America, in the Netherlands Antilles in the Caribbean, and among a dwindling group of colonially educated elders in Indonesia. Afrikaans, spoken in southern Africa, is a descendant of 18th century Netherlandic. In North American history, the term 'Dutch' referred to the sizeable group of German immigrants, the 'Pennsylvania Dutch'. The term was a corruption of *Deutsch*, which means 'German'. The Dutch resent being confused with Germans, and the two languages, despite common roots which make it relatively easy for a speaker of one to learn the other, are as different today as Spanish and Portuguese.

When travelling in the Netherlands and Flemish-speaking Belgium, you'll find that virtually everyone speaks English to some degree, and will use it. Don't let that put you off. Like almost anywhere else in the world, an effort to speak the local tongue will always be met with goodwill. If they still insist on speaking English, it's because they want to ease communication rather than deny you the chance of speaking their language.

The Netherlandic pronunciation used here is based on *Algemeen Beschaafd Nederlands* (ABN), or 'General Cultured Netherlandic', the Dutch/Flemish equivalent of 'BBC English'. This is used in education and generally in the media, and is understood, if not always used, by everyone.

Like many other languages, Netherlandic gives its nouns genders. There are three: masculine, feminine and neuter. When talking about people, you'll often find masculine and feminine versions. For example, 'student' is a male student, 'studente' a female student. These versions are rendered in the text here with the masculine first. When a noun is preceded by a definite article ('the'), masculine and feminine forms take the article **de**, pronounced *der*, while neutral forms use **het**, *ert*. The indefinite article ('a/an') is **een**, *ern*.

Netherlandic also has a formal and an informal version of the English 'you'. The formal is 'U' (written with a capital letter and pronounced *ü*); the informal is 'je' (pronounced *yer*). Netherlandic has become less formal in recent years and 'U' is no longer commonly used to address people the same age as you, let alone younger, whether you know them or not. But people who are older, especially if you don't know them, should still be addressed with 'U'. Flemish tends to be slightly more formal than Dutch.

Pronunciation
Vowels

Single vowels are pretty straightforward, with long and short sounds for each vowel. Compound vowels are a little more complicated.

DUTCH

Letter/s	Pronunciation Guide	Sounds
a	*ah*	short, as the 'u' in 'cut'
a, aa	*aa*	long, as the 'a' in 'father'
au, ou	*ow*	both are pronounced the same, somewhere between the 'ow' in 'how' and the 'ow' in 'glow'
e	*eh, er*	short, as 'e' in 'bet', or as 'er' in 'fern'
e, ee	*ay*	long, as the 'ay' in 'day'
ei, ij	*ey*	as the 'ey' in 'they'
eu	*er*	this combination sounds the way the British queen would pronounce the 'o' in 'over' if she were exaggerating.
i	*i*	short, as the 'i' in 'in'
i, ie	*ee*	long, as the 'ee' in 'see'
o	*o*	short, as in 'pot'
o, oo	*oh*	long, as the 'o' in 'note'
oe	*oo*	as the 'oo' in 'zoo'
u	*er*	short, similar to the 'er' in 'fern', or the French *de*
u, uu	*ü*	long, like the *ü* in German *über*
ui	*er*	there's no equivalent sound in English. For those who speak French, the *eui* in *fauteuil* comes pretty close, so long as you leave out the slide towards the *l*.

Consonants

ch & g	in the north, a hard 'kh' sound as in the Scottish *loch*. In the south, a softer, lisping sound.
j	as 'y' in 'you'. Occasionally, especially with borrowed words, a 'j' or 'zh' sound, as in 'jam' or 'pleasure'.

DUTCH

r	in the south, a trilled sound. In the north it varies, often occurring as a back-of-the-throat sound as in French or German.	
s	usually the 's' in 'sample'. Sometimes a 'zh' sound as in 'pleasure'.	
v	at the start of a word, almost like an 'f'	
w	a clipped sound, almost like a 'v', when at the beginning or middle of a word. At the end of a word it is like the English 'w'.	

DUTCH

Greetings & Civilities
Top Useful Phrases

Hello.	*dahkh/hah-loh*	Dag/Hallo.
Goodbye.	*dahkh*	Dag.
Yes/No.	*yaa/nay*	Ja/Nee.
Excuse me.	*pahr-don*	Pardon.
Sorry. (excuse me/ forgive me)	*so-ree*	Sorry.
Please.	*ahls-tü-bleeft/ ahls-yer-bleeft*	Alstublieft/ Alsjeblieft.
Thank you.	*dahnk ü/yer (wehl)*	Dank U/je (wel).
Many thanks.	*vayl dahnk*	Veel dank.

May I? Do you mind?
  mahkh ik? vint ü/vint yer heht ehrkh?   Mag ik? Vindt U/vind je het erg?

That's fine. You're welcome.
  daht is khoed. khayn dahnk   Dat is goed. Geen dank.

Greetings

Good morning.	***khoo-der mor-khern***	Goede morgen.
Good afternoon.	***khoo-der mid-dahkh***	Goede middag.

| Good evening. | **khoo-dern aa-vont** | Goeden avond. |
| Good night. | **khoo-der nahkht** | Goede nacht. |

How are you?		
hoo khaat heht meht ü/yer?		Hoe gaat het met U/je?
Well, thanks.		
khoot, dahnk ü/yer		Goed, dank U/je.

Forms of Address

Madam/Mrs	mer-**vrow**	Mevrouw/Mevr
Sir/Mr	mer-**near**	Meneer/Mr
Miss	yer-frow	Juffrouw
companion	reys-kher-noht	reisgenoot (m)
	reys-kher-noht-er	reisgenote (f)
friend	vreent	vriend (m)
	vreend-**in**	vriendin (f)

Language Difficulties

Do you speak English?
spraykt ü/sprayk yer ehng-erls?
Spreekt U/spreek je Engels?

Does anyone speak English?
spraykt ee-mahnt ehng-erls?
Spreekt iemand Engels?

I speak a little Netherlandic.
ik sprayk ern bay-tyer nay-der-lahnts
Ik spreek een beetje Nederlands.

I don't speak …
ik sprayk khayn …
Ik spreek geen …

I (don't) understand.
ik ber-khreyp heht (neet)
Ik begrijp het (niet).

DUTCH

Could you speak slowly please?
*kernt ü ahls-tü-**bleeft**/kern
yer ahls-yer-**bleeft** lahng-
zaamer **spray**-kern?*

Kunt U alstublieft/kun je
alsjeblieft langzamer
spreken?

Could you repeat that?
*kernt ü/kern yer daht
hehr-**haa**-lern?*

Kunt U/kun je dat herhalen?

How do you say …?
hoo zehkht ü/zehkh yer …?

Hoe zegt U/zeg je …?

What does … mean?
*waht ber-**tay**-kernt …?*

Wat betekent …?

Small Talk
Meeting People

What is your name?
hoo hayt ü/yer?

Hoe heet U/je?

My name is …
ik hayt …

Ik heet …

I'd like to introduce you to …
*mahkh ik ü/yer **vor**-stehl-
lern aan …*

Mag ik U/je voorstellen
aan …

I'm pleased to meet you.
***aan**-kher-naam*

Aangenaam.

Nationalities

Unfortunately we can't list all countries here, but try saying the
name of your country in your language, as many country names
have a similar pronunciation in Dutch. Listed here are the places
where Dutch is predominantly spoken.

Where are you from?
*waar komt ü/kom yer
vahn-**daan**?*

Waar komt U/kom je
vandaan?

DUTCH

I am from …	*ik kom ert …*	Ik kom uit …
Belgium	**behl**-*khee-yer*	België
Flanders	**vlaan**-*der-ern*	Vlaanderen
Holland,	**hol**-*lahnt,* **nay**-	Holland,
Netherlands	*derlahnt*	Nederland

Age

How old are you?
hoo owt behnt ü/behn yer?   Hoe oud bent U/ben je?
I am … years old.
ik behn … yaar owt   Ik ben … jaar oud.

Occupations

What (work) do you do?
*waht **doot** ü/**doo** yer (vor*   Wat doet U/doe je (voor
wehrk)?   werk)?

I am a/an …	*ik behn ern …*	Ik ben een …
artist	**kern**-*ster-naar*	kunstenaar
business person	**zaa**-*kern-mahn*	zakenman (m)
	zaa-*kern-vrow*	zakenvrouw (f)
doctor	**dok**-*ter*	dokter
engineer	*in-zhin-**yer***	ingenieur
farmer	*booer*	boer
journalist	*zhoor-nah-**list***	journalist (m)
	*zhoor-nah-**list**-er*	journalister (f)
labourer	**ahr**-*bey-der*	arbeider (m)
	ahr-*beyd-ster*	arbeidster (f)
lawyer	*aht-voh-**kaat***	advocaat (m)
	*aht-voh-**kaat**-er*	advocate (f)
mechanic	*mon-**ter***	monteur

nurse	*ver-**playkh**-er*	verpleger (m)
	*ver-**playkh**-ster*	verpleegster (f)
office worker	*kahn-**tor**-wehr-ker*	kantoorwerker
scientist	*way-tern-**skhahp**-per*	wetenschapper
student	*stü-**dehnt***	student (m)
	*stü-**dehnt**-er*	studente (f)
teacher	*lear-aar*	leraar (m)
	*lear-aar-**ehs***	lerares (f)
waiter	*oh-ber*	ober (m)
	sehr-vear-ster	serveerster (f)
writer	*skhrey-ver*	schrijver (m)
	skhreyf-ster	schrijfster (f)

DUTCH

Religion

What is your religion?
*waht is üoo/yer **khots**-deenst?* — Wat is Uw/je godsdienst?

I am not religious.
*ik behn neet ray-lee-**khee-ers*** — Ik ben niet religieus.

I am …	*ik behn …*	Ik ben …
Buddhist	*boo-**dist***	boeddhist
Catholic	*kah-toh-**leek***	katholiek
Christian	*kris-tern*	christen
Hindu	*hin-doo*	hindoe
Jewish	*yohts*	joods
Muslim	*mos-lim*	moslim

Family

Are you married?
*behnt ü/behn yer kher-**trowt**?* — Bent U/ben je getrouwd?

DUTCH

I am single/married.
*ik behn on-kher-**trowt**/ kher-**trowt***

Ik ben ongetrouwd/ getrouwd.

How many children do you have?
***hoo**-vehl **kin**-der-ern hayft ü/hehp yer?*

Hoeveel kinderen heeft U/heb je?

I don't have any children.
*ik hehp khayn **kin**-der-ern*

Ik heb geen kinderen.

I have a daughter/a son.
*ik hehp ern **dokh**-ter/ern zohn*

Ik heb een dochter/een zoon.

Is your husband/wife here?
is üoo/yer mahn/vrow heer?

Is Uw/je man/vrouw hier?

Do you have a boyfriend/ girlfriend?
*hayft ü/hehp yer ern vreend/vreend-**in**?*

Heeft U/heb je een vriend/vriendin?

brother	*brooer*	broer
children	***kin**-der-ern*	kinderen
daughter	***dokh**-ter*	dochter
family	*faa-**mee**-lee*	familie
father	*vaa-der*	vader
grandfather	***khroht**-vaa-der*	grootvader
grandmother	***khroht**-moo-der*	grootmoeder
husband	*mahn*	man
mother	***moo**-der*	moeder
sister	***zer**-ster*	zuster
son	*zohn*	zoon
wife	*vrow*	vrouw

Useful Phrases

Sure.	*zay-ker*	Zeker.
Just a minute.	*ern oh-khern-blik-yer*	Een ogenblikje.
Wait!	*wahkht!*	Wacht!
Good luck!	*(vayl) sük-sehs!*	(Veel) succes!

It's (not) important.
   heht is (neet) ber-lahng-reyk   Het is (niet) belangrijk.
It's (not) possible.
   heht is (neet) moh-kher-lerk   Het is (niet) mogelijk.

DUTCH

Signs

EMERGENCY EXIT	*NOODUITGANG*
ENTRANCE	*INGANG*
EXIT	*UITGANG*
THIS WAY TO	*RICHTING*
FREE ADMISSION	*GRATIS TOEGANG*
HOT/COLD	*WARM/KOUD*
INFORMATION	*INFORMATIE,*
	INLICHTINGEN
NO ENTRY	*VERBODEN TOEGANG*
NO SMOKING	*VERBODEN TE ROKEN*
OPEN/CLOSED	*OPEN/GESLOTEN*
PROHIBITED	*VERBODEN*
RESERVED	*GERESERVEERD*
TELEPHONE	*TELEFOON*
TOILETS	*WC's/TOILETTEN*
MEN	*HEREN/MANNEN*
WOMEN	*DAMES/VROUWEN*

DUTCH

Getting Around

What time does ... leave/
arrive?

> *hoo laat ver-**trehkt**/*
> *ah-ree-**veart** ...?*

Hoe laat vertrekt/
arriveert ...?

the (air)plane	*heht **vleekg**-terkh*	het vliegtuig
the boat	*der boht*	de boot
the bus	*der bers*	de bus
the train	*der treyn*	de trein
the tram	*der trehm*	de tram

Finding Your Way

Do you have a guidebook/
local map?

> *hayft ü ern **reys**-khits/kaart*
> *vahn heht kher-**beet**?*

Heeft U een reisgids/kaart
van het gebied?

Where is ...?
> *waar is ...?*

Waar is ...?

How do I get to ...?
> *hoo kom ik in ...?*

Hoe kom ik in ...?

Is it far from/near here?
> *is heht vehr/dikht-**bey**?*

Is het ver/dichtbij?

Can I walk there?
> *is heht ter **loh**-pern?*

Is het te lopen?

Can you show me (on the map)?
> *kernt ü/kern yer heht (op*
> *der kaart) **aan**-wey-zern?*

Kunt U/kun je het (op de
kaart) aanwijzen?

Are there other means of
getting there?

> *kahn ik ehr op ern **ahn**-*
> *derer mah-**neer** koh-mern?*

Kan ik er op een andere
manier komen?

I want to go to …		
ik vil naar … khaan		Ik wil naar … gaan.

What … is this?	**wehl**-*ker … is dit?*	Welke … is dit?
street	*straat*	straat
suburb	**vor**-*staht*	voorstad

Directions

Go straight ahead.	*khaa rehkht-**dor***	Ga rechtdoor.
Turn left …	*khaa links-ahf …*	Ga linksaf …
Turn right …	*khaa rehkhts-ahf …*	Ga rechtsaf …
at the next corner	*bey der **vol**-khern-**dehr** hook*	bij de volgende hoek
at the traffic lights	*bey heht **stop**-likht*	bij het stoplicht
behind	**ahkh**-*ter*	achter
far	*vehr*	ver
in front of	*vor*	voor
near	*dikht-bey*	dichtbij
opposite	*tay-khern-**oh**-ver*	tegenover

Buying Tickets

TICKET OFFICE	KAARTVERKOOP

Excuse me, where is the ticket office?	
*pahr-**don**, waar is der **kaart**-ver-kohp?*	Pardon, waar is de kaartverkoop?

Where can I buy a ticket?	
*waar kahn ik ern **kaart**-yer koh-pern?*	Waar kan ik een kaartje kopen?

I want to go to …	
ik vil naar … khaan	Ik wil naar … gaan.

DUTCH

Do I need to book?
*moot ik ray-zehr-**vear**-ern?*   Moet ik reserveren?
You need to book.
*ü/yer moot ray-zehr-**vear**-ern*   U/je moet reserveren.
I'd like to book a seat to …
ik wil khraakh ern plaats   Ik wil graag een plaats
*ray-zehr-**vear**-ern naar …*   reserveren naar …

I'd like …	*ik wil khraakh …*	Ik wil graag …
a one-way ticket	*ern **ehng**-ker-ler reys*	een enkele reis
a return ticket	*ern rer-**toor***	een retour
two tickets	*tway **kaar**-tyers*	twee kaartjes
tickets for all of us	*kaar-tyers vor ee-der-**ayn***	kaartjes voor iedereen
a student's fare	*ern stü-**dehn**-tern-tah-**reef***	een studenten-tarief
a child's/ pensioner's fare	*ern kin-der/sehs-tikh **plers** kor-ting*	een kinder/ 60+ korting
1st class	*ear-ster **klahs***	eerste klas
2nd class	*tway-der **klahs***	tweede klas

It is full.
heht is vol   Het is vol.
Is it completely full?
*is heht hay-ler-**maal** vol?*   Is het helemaal vol?
Can I get a stand-by ticket?
kahn ik ern stand-by ticket   Kan ik een stand-by ticket
krey-khern?*   krijgen?

Air

ARRIVALS	*AANKOMST*
DEPARTURES	*VERTREK*
CHECK IN	*INCHECKEN*
CUSTOMS	*DOUANE*
LUGGAGE PICKUP	*BAGAGE*

Is there a flight to …?
is air ern vlerkht naar …?
Is er een vlucht naar …?

When is the next flight to …?
wah-near is der vol-khern-der vlerkht naar …?
Wanneer is de volgende vlucht naar …?

How long does the flight take?
hoo-lahng dürt der vlerkht?
Hoelang duurt de vlucht?

What is the flight number?
waht is heht vlerkht-ner-mer?
Wat is het vluchtnummer?

You must check in at …
ü moot in-tyehk-ern bey …
U moet inchecken bij …

airport tax	*lerkht-haa-vern-ber-lahst-ing*	luchthavenbe lasting
boarding pass	*in-stahp-kaart*	instapkaart
customs	*doo-aa-ner*	douane

Bus & Tram

BUS/TRAM STOP	*BUSHALTE/TRAMHALTE*

Where is the bus/tram stop?
waar is der bers-hahl-ter?
Waar is de bushalte?

DUTCH

Which bus goes to …?
   wehl-ker bers khaat naar …?   Welke bus gaat naar?
Does this bus go to …?
   khaat day-zer bers naar …?   Gaat deze bus naar …?
How often do buses pass by?
   hoo vaak komt der bers?   Hoe vaak komt de bus?

Could you let me know when
we get to …?
   kernt ü/kern yer mer laa-   Kunt U/kun je me laten
   tern way-tern wah-near   weten wanneer we in …
   wer in … aan-ko-mern?   aankomen?
I want to get off!
   ik vil ert-stahp-pern!   Ik wil uitstappen!

What time is the … bus?	*hoo laat is der … bers?*	Hoe laat is de … bus?
next	*vol-khern-der*	volgende
first	*ear-ster*	eerste
last	*laat-ster*	laatste

Train

TRAIN STATION	*TREINSTATION*
TIMETABLE	*VERTREKTIJDEN*
PLATFORM NO	*PERRON/SPOOR NO*

Is this the right platform for …?
   is dir heht yer-ster pehr-ron   Is dit het juiste perron
   vor …?   voor …?

The train leaves from platform …
*der treyn ver-**trekt** vahn pehr-**ron** …*

De trein vertrekt van perron …

dining car	**ayt**-waa-khon	eetwagon
express	**snehl**-treyn	sneltrein
local	**stop**-treyn	stoptrein
sleeping car	**slaap**-waa-khon	slaapwagon

Passengers must …
*pahs-sah-z**heers** moo-tern …*

Passagiers moeten …

   change trains
   oh-ver-stahp-pern
   overstappen

   go to platform number …
   *naar pehr-**ron** ner-mer …*
   naar perron nummer …

Metro

Which line takes me to …?
wehl-ker leyn brehngt mer naar …?

Welke lijn brengt me naar …?

What is the next station?
*waht is het **vol**-khern-der staht-**shon**?*

Wat is het volgende station?

Taxi

Can you take me to …?
kernt ü mey naar … brehng-ern?

Kunt U mij naar … brengen?

Please take me to …
*brehng mey ahls-tü-**bleeft** naar …*

Breng mij alstublieft naar …

How much is it to go to …?
***hoo**-vayl kost heht naar …?*

Hoeveel kost het naar …?

DUTCH

Instructions

Here is fine, thank you.
heer is khood, dahnk ü
Hier is goed, dank U.

The next corner, please.
*der **vol**-khern-der hook,
ahls-tü-**bleeft***
De volgende hoek,
alstublieft.

The next street to the
left/right.
*der **vol**-khern-der straat
links/rehkhts*
De volgende straat
links/rechts.

Stop here!
stop heer!
Stop hier!

Please slow down.
*reyt ahls-tü-**bleeft**
lahng-zaam-er*
Rijd alstublieft langzamer.

Please wait here.
*wahkht heer ahls-tü-**bleeft***
Wacht hier alstublieft.

Useful Phrases

The train is delayed/
cancelled.
*der treyn is ver-**traakht**/
ahf-kher-lahst*
De trein is vertraagd/
afgelast.

How long will it be delayed?
***hoo**-lahng is heht
ver-**traakht**?*
Hoelang is het vertraagd?

There is a delay of … hours.
*ehr is ern ver-**traakh**-ing
vahn … ür*
Er is een vertraging van …
uur.

Can I reserve a place?
*kahn ik ern plaats
ray-zer-**vear**-ern?*
Kan ik een plaats
reserveren?

How long does the trip take?
hoo-lahng dürt de tokht?
Hoelang duurt de tocht?

Is it a direct route?
*is heht ern **rehkht**-strayk-ser ver-**bin**-ding?*
Is het een rechtstreekse verbinding?

Is this seat taken?
*is day-zer plaats ber-**zeht**?*
Is deze plaats bezet?

I want to get off at …
*ik vil **ert**-stahp-pern bey …*
Ik wil uitstappen bij …

DUTCH

Car & Bicycle

DETOUR	OMLEIDING
FREEWAY	AUTOWEG/ AUTOSNELWEG
GARAGE	GARAGE
GIVE WAY	GEEF VOORRANG
MECHANIC	MONTEUR
NO ENTRY	VERBODEN IN TE RIJDEN
NO PARKING	VERBODEN TE PARKEREN
NORMAL	NORMAAL
ONE WAY	EENRICHTING
REPAIRS	REPARATIES
SELF SERVICE	ZELFBEDIENING
UNLEADED	(EURO-)LOODVRIJ

Where can I hire a car?
*waar kahn ik ern **oh**-toh **hü**-rern?*
Waar kan ik een auto huren?

DUTCH

Where can I hire a bicycle?
  *waar kahn ik ern feets
  hü-rern?*   Waar kan ik een fiets huren?
daily/weekly
  pehr dahkh/wayk   per dag/week

Where's the next petrol
station?
  *waar is heht **vol**-khern-der
  behn-**zee**-ner-staht-**shon**?* Waar is het volgende
                                     benzinestation?
Please fill the tank.
  vol, khraakh.   Vol, graag.
I want … litres of petrol (gas).
  *ik vil … **lee**-ter
  behn-**zee**-ner*   Ik wil … liter benzine.
Please check the oil and water.
  *kon-tro-**lear** ahls-tü-**bleeft**
  oh-lee ehn **waa**-ter*   Controleer alstublieft olie
                                     en water.
How long can I park here?
  ***hoo**-lahng kahn ik heer
  pahr-**kear**-ern?*   Hoelang kan ik hier
                                     parkeren?
Does this road lead to …?
  *khaat day-zer wehkh
  naar …?*   Gaat deze weg naar …?

air (for tyres)	*lerkht (vor **bahn**-dern)*	lucht (voor banden)
battery	***ahk**-kü*	accu
brakes	***rehm**-mern*	remmen
clutch	***kop**-per-ling*	koppeling
driving licence	***rey**-ber-weys*	rijbewijs
engine	***moh**-tor*	motor

lights	**likh**-tern	lichten
oil	**oh**-lee	olie
puncture	lehk-ker **bahnt**	lekke band
radiator	raa-dee-**yaa**-tor	radiator
road map	**way**-khern-kaart	wegenkaart
tyres	**bahn**-dern	banden
windscreen	**vor**-rert	voorruit

Car Problems

I need a mechanic.
*ik hehp ern mon-**ter** noh-dikh*
Ik heb een monteur nodig.

What make is it?
wehlk mehrk is heht?
Welk merk is het?

The battery is flat.
*der **ahk**-kü is laykh*
De accu is leeg.

The radiator is leaking.
*der raa-dee-**yaa**-tor lehkt*
De radiator lekt.

I have a flat tyre.
ik hehp ern lehk-ker bahnt
Ik heb een lekke band.

It's overheating.
*heht raakt oh-ver-ver-**hit***
Het raakt oververhit.

It's not working.
heht wehrkt neet
Het werkt niet.

Accommodation

CAMPING GROUND	CAMPING
GUESTHOUSE	PENSION
YOUTH HOSTEL	JEUGDHERBERG

DUTCH

Finding Accommodation

I'm looking for …	*ik zook …*	Ik zoek …
Where is …?	*waar is …?*	Waar is …?
a cheap hotel	*ern khood-**kohp** hoh-**tehl***	een goedkoop hotel
a good hotel	*ern khood hoh-**tehl***	een goed hotel
a nearby hotel	*ern hoh-**tehl** dikht- **bey***	een hotel dichtbij

What is the address?

*waht is heht ah-**drehs**?*   Wat is het adres?

Could you write the address, please?

*kernt ü/kern yer het ah-**drehs** op-skhrey-vern, ahls-tü-**bleeft**/ahls-yer-**bleeft**?*   Kunt U/kun je het adres opschrijven, alstublieft/alsjeblieft?

Booking a Room

Do you have any rooms available?

*hayft ü **kaa**-mers vrey?*   Heeft U kamers vrij?

I'd like to book a room.

*ik vil khraakh ern **kaa**-mer **boo**-kern*   Ik wil graag een kamer boeken.

for one night/four nights

*voor ayn nahkht/tway **nahkh**-tern*   voor één nacht/twee nachten

from tonight/Tuesday

*vahn-ahf vahn-**aa**-vont/ **dins**-dahkh*   vanaf vanavond/dinsdag

I'd like (a) …
   ik wil khraakh (ern) …   Ik wil graag (een) …

single room	*ayn-pehr-**sohns**-kaa-mer*	eenpersoonskamer
double room	*tway-per-**sohns**-kaa-mer*	tweepersoonskamer
room with a bathroom	*kaa-mer meht baat-kaa-mer*	een kamer met badkamer
to share a dorm	*ern **kaa**-mer **day**-lern*	een kamer delen
bed	*beht*	bed

We want a room with a …
   *vey **vil**-ern ern **kaa**-mer meht* …   Wij willen een kamer met …

bathroom	***baht**-kaa-mer*	badkamer
shower	*doosh*	douche
TV	*tay-ler-**vee**-see*	televisie
window	*raam*	raam

I'm staying for … *ik bleyf* …   Ik blijf …

one day	*ayn dahkh*	één dag
two days	*tway **daa**-khern*	twee dagen
one week	*ayn wayk*	één week

At the Hotel

How much is it per night/
per person?
   ***hoo**-vayl is heht pehr nahkht/per per-**sohn**?*   Hoeveel is het per nacht/per persoon?
Can I see it?
   kahn ik heht zeen?   Kan ik het zien?

Are there any others?
*zeyn ehr **ahn**-der-er?*　　　Zijn er andere?

Are there any cheaper rooms?
*zeyn ehr khoot-**koh**-per-er*　Zijn er goedkopere kamers?
***kaa**-mers?*

Is there a reduction for
students/children?
*is ehr ray-**derk**-see vor*　　Is er reductie voor
*stü-**dehn**-tern/**kin**-der-ern?*　studenten/kinderen?

Does it include breakfast?
*zit ehr ont-**beyt** bey*　　　　Zit er ontbijt bij inbegrepen?
*in-ber-**khray**-pern?*

It's fine, I'll take it.
heht is khood, ik naym heht　Het is goed, ik neem het.

I'm not sure how long I'm
staying.
*ik wayt neet **zay**-ker*　　　　Ik weet niet zeker hoelang
***hoo**-lahng ik bleyf*　　　　ik blijf.

Where is the bathroom?
*waar is der **baht**-kaa-mer?*　Waar is de badkamer?

Is there hot water all day?
is ehr der hay-ler dahkh　　　Is er de hele dag warm
*wahrm **waa**-ter?*　　　　　　water?

You May Hear

Do you have identification?
*hayft ü lay-khee-tee-**maat**-*　Heeft U legitimatie?
see?

Your membership card, please.
*üoo **lit**-maat-skhahps-kaart,*　Uw lidmaatschapskaart,
*ahls-tü-**bleeft***　　　　　　alstublieft.

Sorry, we're full.
so-ree, wer zeyn vol

How long will you be staying?
***hoo**-lahng bleyft ü?*

How many nights?
***hoo**-vayl nahkh-tern?*

It's … per day/per person.
*heht is … pehr dahkh/pehr pehr-**sohn***

Sorry, we zijn vol.

Hoelang blijft U?

Hoeveel nachten?

Het is … per dag/per persoon.

Requests & Complaints

Can I use the telephone?
*kahn ik der tay-ler-**fohn** kher-**brer**-kern?*

Do you have a safe where I can leave my valuables?
*hayft ü ern klers waar ik meyn **waar**-der-vol-ler **sper**-lern kahn **laa**-tern?*

May I use the kitchen?
*kahn ik der **ker**-kern kher-**brer**-kern?*

Please wake me up at …
*wehk mer ahls-tü-**bleeft** om …*

The room needs to be cleaned.
*der **kaa**-mer moot wor-dern **skhohn**-kher-maakt*

Please change the sheets.
*ver-**skhohn** ahls-tü-**bleeft** der **laa**-kerns*

Kan ik de telefoon gebruiken?

Heeft U een kluis waar ik mijn waardevolle spullen kan laten?

Kan ik de keuken gebruiken?

Wek me alstublieft om …

De kamer moet worden schoongemaakt.

Verschoon alstublieft de lakens.

DUTCH

Is there somewhere to wash clothes?
is ehr ehr-kherns om klear-ern ter wahs-sern?
Is er ergens om kleren te wassen?

I can't open/close the window.
ik kahn heht raam neet oh-pern/dikht doon
Ik kan het raam niet open/dicht doen.

I've locked myself out of my room.
ik hehp mer-zehlf ber-tern-kher-sloh-tern
Ik heb mezelf buiten-gesloten.

The toilet won't flush.
der way-say/heht twah-leht trehkt neet dor
De WC/het toilet trekt niet door.

I don't like this room.
day-zer kaa-mer ber-vahlt mer neet
Deze kamer bevalt me niet.

It's too small.	*heht is ter kleyn*	Het is te klein.
It's noisy.	*heht is lah-wai-ikh*	Het is lawaaiig.
It's too dark.	*heht is ter don-ker*	Het is te donker.
It's expensive.	*heht is dür*	Het is duur.

Checking Out

I would like to pay the bill.
ik wil khraakh ahf-ray-ker-nern
Ik wil graag afrekenen.

I am/We are leaving now.
ik ver-trehk/wey ver-trehk-kern nü
Ik vertrek/wij vertrekken nu.

address	*ah-dres*	adres
name	*naam*	naam
surname	*ahkh-ter-naam*	achternaam
room number	*kaa-mer-ner-mer*	kamernummer

Useful Words

air-con	*air-kon-di-shernt*	air-conditioned
bathroom	*baht-kaa-mer*	badkamer
bed	*beht*	bed
blanket	*day-kern*	deken
clean	*skhohn*	schoon
dark	*don-ker*	donker
dirty	*smir-erkh*	smerig
double bed	*tway-per-sohns beht*	tweepersoons bed
electricity	*ay-lehk-tree-see-teyt*	electriciteit
excluded	*ehks-klü-zeef*	exclusief
fan	*vehn-tee-laa-tor*	ventilator
included	*in-klü-zeef*	inclusief
key	*sler-terl*	sleutel
lift (elevator)	*lift*	lift
quiet	*stil*	stil
sheet	*laa-kern*	laken
shower	*doosh*	douche
swimming pool	*zwehm-baht*	zwembad
toilet	*way-say/twah-leht*	WC/toilet
toilet paper	*way-say/twah-leht pah-peer*	WC/toilet papier
towel	*hahn-dook*	handdoek
water	*waa-ter*	water
cold water	*kowt waa-ter*	koud water
hot water	*wahrm waa-ter*	warm water
window	*raam*	raam

DUTCH

DUTCH

Around Town

I'm looking for …
ik zook …   Ik zoek …

the city centre	*heht **sehn**-trerm*	het centrum
the … embassy	*der … ahm-baa-saa-der*	de … ambassade
the post office	*heht **post**-kahn-tor*	het postkantoor
a public toilet	*ern **oh**-pern-baa-rer way-**say**/**oh**-pern-baar twah-**leht***	een openbare WC/openbaar toilet
the telephone centre	*der tay-ler-**fohn**-sen-traa-ler*	de telefoon-centrale
the tourist information office	*der vay-vay-**vay**/heht too-**ris**-tern-bü-ro*	de VVV (in the Netherlands)/het toeristenbureau

What time does it open/close?
*hoo laat **oh**-pernt/slert heht?*   Hoe laat opent/sluit het?

At the Bank

What is the exchange rate?
*waht is der **wis**-serl-koors?*   Wat is de wisselkoers?
I want to exchange some
money/travellers' cheques.
*ik vil waht khehlt/**reys**-shehks (travellers' cheques) **wis**-ser-lern*   Ik wil wat geld/reischeques (travellers' cheques) wisselen.
How many guilders/francs per
dollar?
*hoo-vayl **kherl**-dern/**frahn**-kern pair **dol**-lahr?*   Hoeveel gulden/franken per dollar?

Can I have money transferred here from my bank?
*kahn ik khehlt vahn meyn bahnk **heer**-naar-too **laa**-tern oh-ver-maa-kern?*

Kan ik geld van mijn bank hiernaartoe laten overmaken?

How long will it take?
***hoo**-lahng doot heht ehr-oh-ver?*

Hoelang doet het erover?

Has my money arrived yet?
*is meyn khehlt ahl **aan**-kher-koh-mern?*

Is mijn geld al aangekomen?

banknotes	***bahnk**-bil-jeht-tern*	bankbiljetten
cashier	*kahs-**seer***	kassier
coins	***mern**-tern*	munten
credit card	*krer-**deet**-kaart*	creditcard
loose change	***wis**-serl-khehlt*	wisselgeld
signature	***hahnt**-tay-ker-ning*	handtekening

At the Post Office

I would like to send a/an…
*ik wil khraakh ern … ver-**stü**-rern*

Ik wil graag een … versturen.

aerogram	***lerkht**-post-blaht*	luchtpostblad
letter	*breef*	brief
postcard	***breef**-kaart*	briefkaart
parcel	*pah-**keht***	pakket
telegram	*tay-ler-**khrahm***	telegram

I'd like some stamps.
*ik wil khraakh waht **post**-zay-kherls*

Ik wil graag wat postzegels.

How much is the postage?
hoo-vayl is heht por-to?
Hoeveel is het porto?

How much does it cost to send this to …?
hoo-vayl kost heht om dit naar … ter stü-rern?
Hoeveel kost het om dit naar … te sturen?

airmail	**lerkht**-post	luchtpost
envelope	*ahn-ver-**lop***	envelop
mail box	**bree**-vern-bers	brievenbus
parcel	*pah-**keht***	pakket
registered mail	**aan**-kher-tay-kernt	aangetekend
surface mail	**zay**-post	zeepost

Telephone

I want to ring …
*ik vil … **beh**-lern*
Ik wil … bellen.

The number is …
*heht **ner**-mer is …*
Het nummer is …

I want to speak for three minutes.
*ik vil dree mee-**nü**-tern **spray**-kern*
Ik wil drie minuten spreken.

How much does a three-minute call cost?
*hoo-vayl kost ern kher-**sprehk** vahn dree mee-**nü**-tern?*
Hoeveel kost een gesprek van drie minuten?

How much does each extra minute cost?
*hoo-vayl kost ee-der-er mee-**nüt** ehk-**straa**?*
Hoeveel kost iedere minuut extra?

I'd like to speak to Mr Klep.
*ik vil khraakh mer-**near** klep **spray**-kern*
Ik wil graag meneer Klep spreken.

I want to make a reverse-charges phone call.
*ik vil ern ber-**taa**-ling ont-**vahng**-er kher-**sprehk***
Ik wil een betaling ontvanger gesprek.

It's engaged.
*heht is ber-**zeht***
Het is bezet.

I've been cut off.
*ik behn **ahf**-kher-bro-kern*
Ik ben afgebroken.

Sightseeing

What are the main attractions?
*waht zeyn der vor-**naam**-ster ber-zeens-**waar**-dikh-hay-dern?*
Wat zijn de voornaamste bezienswaardigheden?

How old is it?
hoo owt is heht?
Hoe oud is het?

Can I take photographs?
*kahn ik **foh**-tohs **nay**-mern?*
Kan ik foto's nemen?

What time does it open/close?
*hoo laat **oh**-pernt/slert heht?*
Hoe laat opent/sluit het?

ancient	*(zear) owt*	(zeer) oud
archaeological	*ahr-khay-oh-**loh**-khees*	archeologisch
beach	*strahnt*	strand
building	*kher-**bow***	gebouw
bulb(s)	*bol(-lern)*	bol(len)

DUTCH

castle	*kah-stayl, berkht*	kasteel, burcht
cathedral	*kah-tay-draal*	kathedraal
church	*kairk*	kerk
concert hall	*kon-sairt-kher-bow*	concertgebouw
flower(s)	*bloom(-ern)*	bloem(en)
library	*bee-blee-oh-tayk*	bibliotheek
main square	*pleyn/khrohter mahrkt*	plein/grote markt
market	*mahrkt*	markt
old city	*ow-der staht*	oude stad
palace	*pah-leys*	paleis
opera house	*oh-per-aa-kher-bow*	operagebouw
ruins	*rü-ee-ner*	ruïne
stadium	*staa-dee-on*	stadion
statues	*stahnt-bayl-dern*	standbeelden
tulip(s)	*terlp(-ern)*	tulp(en)
university	*ü-nee-vair-see-teyt*	universiteit
windmill	*moh-lern*	molen

Entertainment

What's there to do in the evenings?

waht vahlt air saa-vonts ter doon?

Wat valt er 's-avonds te doen?

Are there any nightclubs?

zeyn ehr dis-kohs?

Zijn er disco's?

Are there places where you can hear local music?

zeyn ehr plaat-sern waar jer mü-zeek vahn der strayk kernt hor-ern?

Zijn er plaatsen waar je muziek van de streek kunt horen?

How much is it to get in?		
hoo-vayl kost ahn-tray?		Hoeveel kost entree?

| cinema | bee-os-**kohp** | bioscoop |
| theatre | tay-**aa**-ter | theater |

In the Country
Weather

What's the weather like?		
hoo is heht wear?		Hoe is het weer?

It's … today.		
heht wear is vahn-daakh …		Het weer is vandaag …

cloudy	ber-**wolkt**	bewolkt
cold	kowt	koud
foggy	**mis**-terkh	mistig
hot	hayt	heet
raining	**ray**-kher-nern	regenen
snowing	**snay**-wern	sneeuwen
sunny	**zon**-nerkh	zonnig
windy	**win**-der-erkh	winderig

DUTCH

Camping

Are we allowed to camp here?		
moh-khern vey heer kahm-**pear**-ern?		Mogen wij hier kamperen?

Is there a campsite nearby?		
is air ern **kehm**-ping **dikht-bey?**		Is er een camping dichtbij?

backpack	**rerkh**-zahk	rugzak
can opener	**blik**-oh-per-ner	blikopener
compass	kom-**pahs**	kompas

firewood	**brahnt**-*howt*	brandhout
gas cartridge	**khahs**-*paa-trohn*	gaspatroon
hammock	**hahng**-*maht*	hangmat
mattress	*maa*-**trahs**	matras
penknife	**zahk**-*mehs*	zakmes
rope	*tow*	touw
tent	*tehnt*	tent
tent pegs	**haa**-*ring-ern*	haringen
torch (flashlight)	**zahk**-*lahmp*	zaklamp
sleeping bag	**slaap**-*zahk*	slaapzak
stove	**brahn**-*der*	brander
water bottle	**vehlt**-*flehs*	veldfles

Food

Dutch cuisine served in restaurants is not much to write home about, but at least you'll be well fed. Vegetarians are reasonably well catered for, also in regular restaurants. In the Netherlands you'll find Indonesian and Chinese restaurants (usually combined) even in the smallest town.

Flemish cuisine is always gratifying, offering French finesse in big servings. For a cheap, filling snack on the run, go for *frites* (French fries) with mayonnaise – Belgians are justifiably proud of their frites. A typical meal in a Belgian restaurant consists of a hearty soup followed by the main dish. A potential highlight is *mosselen*, mussels cooked in white wine, accompanied by frites and several goblets of *trappist*, beer.

breakfast	*ont*-**beyt**	ontbijt
lunch	**mid**-*dahg-ay-tern/* *lerntsh*	middageten/lunch
dinner	**aa**-*vont-ay-tern/* *dee-***nay**	avondeten/diner

Eating Out

Table for …, please.
taa-ferl vor …, ahls-tü-**bleeft**
Tafel voor …, alstublieft.

Can I see the menu, please?
*kahn ik heht mer-nü zeen, ahls-tü-**bleeft**?*
Kan ik het menu zien, alstublieft?

I'd like the set lunch, please.
*ik vil khraakh heht too-ris-tern-mer-nü, ahls-tü-**bleeft***
Ik wil graag het toeristen-menu, alstublieft.

What does it include?
waht is air-bey in-ber-khray-pern?
Wat is erbij inbegrepen?

Is service included?
is ber-dee-ning in-ber-khray-pern?
Is bediening inbegrepen?

Not too spicy please.
*neet ter hayt/skhehrp/pit-terkh ahls-tü-**bleeft***
Niet te heet/scherp/pittig alstublieft.

ashtray	*ahs-bahk*	asbak
the bill	*der ray-ker-ning*	de rekening
cup	*kop*	kop
drink	*drahnk-yer*	drankje
fork	*vork*	vork
glass	*khlahs*	glas
knife	*mehs*	mes
plate	*bort*	bord
spoon	*lay-perl*	lepel
teaspoon	*tay-lay-perl*	theelepel
toothpick	*tahn-dern-stoh-ker*	tandenstoker

DUTCH

Making Your Own Meal

For some key essentials for sandwich-making, etc, see page 73.

Vegetarian Meals

I am a vegetarian.
*ik behn vay-kher-**taa**-ree-yer*   Ik ben vegetariër.
I don't eat meat.
ik ayt khayn vlays   Ik eet geen vlees.
I don't eat chicken, fish or ham.
ik ayt khayn kip, vis off   Ik eet geen kip, vis of ham.
hahm

Breakfast & Lunch   Ontbijt & Middageten

Depending on the region, the main meal of the day is eaten either in the evening or at midday.

beschuit	Dutch crisp bread, eaten with cheese, *hagelslag* or *gestampte muisjes*.
hagelslag	Fine, vermicelli-like strands of chocolate or coloured aniseed sugar, a hit with kids.
havermoutpap	Oatmeal porridge.
koek, ontbijtkoek	Dutch honey cake.
leverworst	Liver sausage.
muisjes	Sugar-coated aniseed. *Gestampte muisjes* are ground muisjes.
roggebrood	Pumpernickel, rye bread, black bread, usually eaten with cheese.
rookvlees	Smoked beef, thinly sliced.
theeworst	Literally 'tea-sausage': spiced and smoked, light-pink liver-sausage.
uitsmijter	Sliced bread with cold meat (usually ham or thinly sliced roast beef), covered with fried eggs and garnish (pickles, etc).

bacon	*spek*
bread (brown, white, wholemeal)	*brood (bruin, wit, volkoren)*
croissants	*halve maantjes*
egg(s)	*ei(eren)*
boiled egg	*gekookt ei*
fried eggs	*gebakken eieren*
hard-boiled	*hardgekookt*
scrambled eggs	*roerei*
soft-boiled	*zachtgekookt*
honey	*honing*
sausage	*worst*

Dairy Products · Zuivelproducten

buttermilk	*karnemelk*
buttermilk residue – a favourite home dessert	*hangop*
cheese	*kaas*
cheese spread	*smeerkaas*
cream	*room*
custard	*vla*
matured, ripe	*belegen*
milk	*melk*
new	*jong*
newly matured	*jong belegen*

Snacks · Hapjes, Versnaperingen

bamibal	Egg roll with Chinese-noodle filling.
bitterballen	Small, round meat croquettes, usually served with mustard.
croque monsieur	See *tosti*.
frika(n)del	A roast sausage of minced meat.
frites met/zonder	French fries with/without mayonnaise.

DUTCH

kroket	Croquette with meat/fish/shrimp filling (*'vlees/vis/garnalen-kroket'*). Usually meat (beef) if filling not specified.
loempia	Egg roll.
nasibal	Egg roll with fried-rice filling.
russisch ei	Hard-boiled egg filled with mayonnaise and capers.
saucijzebroodje	Sausage roll.
tosti	Bread, usually with ham and cheese, grilled. (Flemish: *croque monsieur*)

Entrées	**Voorgerechten**
pastry (meat or fish)	*pastei*
soup	*soep*
oxtail	*ossestaart*
turtle	*schildpad*
vegetable	*groente*

Meat	**Vlees**
biefstuk tartaar	Raw minced beef with egg and spices.
blinde vink	Beef or veal wrapped in bacon, fried.
osseworst	Ox sausage, spiced and smoked.
pekelvlees	Salted meat.
rookworst	Smoked sausage (cooked, juicy).
slavink	Minced beef wrapped in bacon, fried.
sudderlap	Simmered meat (beef or pork).

bacon	*spek*
fillet of beef	*runderhaas*
fillet of beef, tenderloin	*ossehaas*
fillet of veal	*kalfsschijf*
goat	*geit*

DUTCH

lamb	*lam*
minced meat	*gehakt*
pork	*varken*
pork chop	*karbonade*
steak	*biefstuk*
(very) well-done	*(goed) gaar*
rare	*even aangebakken*
sweetbread	*zwezerik*
veal collop, escalope	*kalfsoester*

DUTCH

Seafood	**Visgerechten**
groene haring	Fresh, raw herring, untreated apart from being cleaned and kept on ice. Don't dismiss it until you've tried it.
haring	Herring, usually eaten raw with chopped onions at fish stalls.
lekkerbekje	Fried fish fillet.
meerval	Freshwater catfish.
nieuwe haring	'New' herring, fresh and mild-flavoured, in theory the first herring of the season, a favourite at fish stalls.
rolmops	Pickled herring wrapped around gherkin and/or onion.
zeewolf	Saltwater catfish.
zoute haring	Salted herring, kipper.

cod	*kabeljauw*
eel	*paling/aal*
fish	*vis*
freshwater ...	*zoetwater-*
haddock	*schelvis*

hake, stockfish	*stokvis*
lobster	*kreeft*
mussels	*mosselen*
octopus, squid	*inktvis*
pike	*snoek*
plaice	*schol*
salmon	*zalm*
shrimps, prawns	*garnalen*
trout	*forel*
tuna	*tonijn*
whiting	*wijting*

Poultry & Game

Gevogelte & Wild

chicken	*kip*
duck	*eend*
goose	*gans*
hare	*haas, haze-* (adj)
haunch of venison	*reebout*
pheasant	*fazant*
quail	*kwartel*
rabbit	*konijn*
turkey	*kalkoen*
wild pig/boar	*zwijn*

Vegetables

Groente

beans	*bonen, boontjes*
bean sprouts	*taugé*
beetroot	*bieten*
broad beans	*tuinbonen*
Brussels sprouts	*spruitjes*
butter-beans	*sperziebonen*

DUTCH

cabbage	*kool*
carrot	*peen*
carrots (small)	*wortel(tje)s*
cauliflower	*bloemkool*
chicory	*brussels lof*
corn on the cob	*maiskolf*
cucumber	*komkommer*
curly kale	*boerenkool*
endive	*andijvie*
garden-cress	*sterrekers*
green beans	*slabonen*
leek	*prei*
lentils	*linzen*
lettuce	*sla*
marrow peas (often served with bacon)	*kapucijners*
mushroom (big)	*paddestoel*
mushrooms (small & cultured)	*champignons*
onion	*ui* (Flemish: *ajuin*)
peas	*erwten*
potato(es)	*aardappel(en)*
new potatoes (small)	*jonge/nieuwe aardappelen*
mashed potatoes	*aardappelpuree*
French fries	*patat, patates frites*
podded peas, sugar peas	*peultjes*
pumpkin, squash	*pompoen*
purslane	*postelein*
red cabbage	*rode kool*
split peas	*spliterwten*
Swedish turnip	*koolraap*
turnip-tops	*raapstelen*

Fruit

apple	**Fruit, Vruchten**

Fruit

	Fruit, Vruchten
apple	*appel*
apricots	*abrikozen*
banana	*banaan*
berries (blue, bil, black)	*bessen (blauw, bos, braam)*
cherries	*kersen*
dried currants	*krenten*
grapes (white, black)	*druiven (witte, zwarte)*
lemon	*citroen*
mulberries	*moerbeien*
orange	*sinaasappel*
peach	*perzik*
pineapple	*ananas*
plum, prune	*pruim*
raisins, sultanas	*rozijnen*
raspberries	*frambozen*
strawberries	*aardbeien*

Indonesian Food   **Indonesisch Eten**

The ubiquitous Indonesian cuisine is a tasty legacy of Dutch colonial history. White rice (boiled or steamed) is the mandatory foundation of most dishes. Don't use chopsticks, or a knife and fork: those in the know eat their Indonesian food with a spoon, perhaps with the aid of a fork, from deep plates.

bami goreng	Fried thick noodles with onions, pork, shrimp and spices, often topped with a fried egg.
bami rames	Boiled thick noodles with various 'side dishes' on the same plate, not mixed in, often topped with a fried egg.
emping	Flattened melinjo nuts, deep-fried and salted, a slightly bitter accompaniment to meals.

gado-gado	Steamed vegetables (crispy) and hard-boiled eggs, served with peanut sauce.
ketjap	Soy sauce, either sweet, *manis*, or salty, *asin*. Usually sweet if not specified.
kroepoek	Shrimp crackers.
nasi goreng	Same as *bami goreng,* but with rice; sometimes shredded omelette instead of fried egg.
nasi rames	Same as *bami rames,* but with rice; in effect a one-plate *rijsttafel.*
rempejek	Fried, spiced wafers, usually with peanuts.
rendang	Meat (beef or mutton) curry – dry, very spicy.
rijsttafel	'Rice table', an Indonesian colonial dish consisting of white rice with heaps of side dishes. A great splurge.
sambal	Chilli paste. Varieties include *oelek* (red, very spicy) and *badjak* (dark, onion-based, mild).
saté, sateh	Indonesian kebab, marinaded in *ketjap*-based sauce.
sayor (sayur) lodeh	Vegetable soup in coconut-based broth, to be poured over white rice.
spekkoek	Multi-layered spice cake

DUTCH

banana	*pisang*
beef	*daging*
chicken	*ajam*
fish	*ikan*
goat (mutton)	*kambing*
pork	*babi*
shrimp, prawn	*udang*
shrimp paste	*trasi*
vegetable pickle	*atjar*
vegetables	*sayor (sayur)*

Dessert, Biscuits & Sweets   Dessert/Nagerecht/ Toetje, Koekjes & Snoep

aardbeien met slagroom	Strawberries with whipped cream.
appelbeignet	Apple fritter.
appelmoes	Apple sauce (chunky, if done properly).
bokkepoot	Literally 'billy-goat leg': a compound biscuit with filling and almond slivers, both ends dipped in chocolate.
boterletter, boterstaaf	Pastry with soft marzipan filling.
drop	Liquorice, often salty (the Dutch national 'sweet', hundreds of varieties and shapes).
flensjes	Thin pancakes, crêpes.
pannekoeken	Pancakes.
roomijs	Ice cream (cream-based, as opposed to water-based sherbet, or *'waterijs'*).
moorkop	Large cream-puff with chocolate icing.
oliebol	Dough fritter with currants, served with caster sugar. Popular New Year's treat.
poffertjes	A mound of tiny round pancakes, served with caster sugar.
speculaas	Brown biscuit, spiced (cinnamon, nutmeg, cloves), often with almond slivers.
stroopwafel	Two thin wafers glued together with treacle.
tompoes, tompouce	Thick custard between two layers of flaky pastry, topped with icing.
vlaai, Limburgse vlaai	Tangy fruit pie on bread-dough base.
wentelteefjes	Stale bread, soaked in egg, milk and cinnamon, fried and served with sugar.

Drinks – Nonalcoholic

chocolate milk	*Chocomel*
coffee	*koffie*
juice	*sap*
orange juice	*jus, jus d'orange*
freshly squeezed	*vers geperst*
tea	*thee*
with milk/lemon	*met melk/citroen*
water with ice	*water met ijs*

Drinks – Alcoholic

Beerenburg   A herbal 'genever' from Friesland.

genever, jenever   Dutch gin, based on juniper berries, drunk neat and chilled from small glasses, like schnapps. *Jonge* ('young') is smooth and relatively easy to drink, *oude* ('old') has a strong juniper flavour and can be an acquired taste.

lambic   Popular Belgian beer, spontaneously fermented. Many varieties: *gueuze* is sour(ish), *kriek* and *framboise* are sweet (cherry and raspberry flavoured, respectively).

sneeuwwitje   Literally 'Snow White': 50/50 lemonade and beer (shandy).

trappist   Dark and often very strong Belgian beer, drunk from goblets. Originally brewed by Trappist monks. Countless brands and varieties, graded by alcohol content (*dubbel, tripel*).

beer	*bier*	lager	*pils*
brandy	*vieux*		

wine	*wijn*		
dry	*droog*	red	*rood*
house wine	*huiswijn*	white	*wit*
sweet	*zoet*	bubbly, sparkling	*mousserend*

Shopping

bookshop	**book**-*wing-kerl*	boekwinkel
camera shop	*foh-toh-***wing***-kerl*	fotowinkel
general store, shop	**wing**-*kerl vor*	winkel voor
	ahl-ler-ley **waa**-*rern*	allerlei waren
laundry	*wahs-ser-***eht***-ter*	wasserette
newsagency	**teyt**-*skhrif-tern-*	tijdschrijftenwinkel
	wing-kerl	
stationer's	*kahn-***tor***-book-hahn-*	kantoorboekhandel
	derl	
pharmacy	*droh-***khist**	drogist
vegetable shop	**khroon**-*ter-wing-kerl*	groentewinkel
grocery shop	*krer-der-***neer**	kruidenier

How much is it …?
  hoo-*vayl kost heht …?*   Hoeveel kost het …?
I would like to buy …
  ik zow khraakh … vil-lern   Ik zou graag … willen
  koh-*pern*   kopen.
Do you have others?
  hayft ü **ahn**-*der-er?*   Heeft U andere?
I don't like it.
  *heht ber-***vahlt*** *mey neet* Het bevalt mij niet.
Can I look at it?
  *kahn ik heht ber-***key***-kern?* Kan ik het bekijken?
I'm just looking.
  *ik keyk ahl-***layn**   Ik kijk alleen.

DUTCH

Can you write down the price?
kernt ü der preys op-skhrey-vern?

Kunt U de prijs opschrijven?

Do you accept credit cards?
*ahk-sehp-teart ü krer-deet-kaar-tern/**kreh**-dit kahrts?*

Accepteert U kredietkaarten/credit cards?

You May Hear

Can I help you?
*kahn ik ü/yer **hehl**-pern?*

Kan ik U/je helpen?

Will that be all?
*is daht **ahl**-lers?*

Is dat alles?

Sorry, this is our only one.
*so-ree, dit is der ay-ni-kher (dee wer **hehb**-bern)*

Sorry, dit is de enige (die we hebben).

How many do you want?
***hoo**-vayl wilt ü?*

Hoeveel wilt U?

Essential Groceries

batteries	*bah-ter-**rey**-ern*	batterÿen
bread	*broht*	brood
butter	***boh**-ter*	noter
cheese	*kaas*	kaas
chocolate	*sjoh-koh-**laa**(-der)*	chocola/chocolade
coffee	***ko**-fee*	koffie
gas cartridge	***khahs**-paa-trohn*	gaspatroon
matches	*lü-see-fehrs*	lucifers
milk	*mehlk*	melk
mineral water	*mee-ner-**aal**-waa-ter/ spaa*	mineraalwater/ spa
fruit	*frert/**frerkh**-tern*	fruit, vruchten
soap	*zayp*	zeep

DUTCH

sugar	*ser*-ker	suiker
tea	*tay*	thee
toilet paper	*way*-**say**-pah-**peer**/	WC-papier/
	twah-**leht**-pah-**peer**	toiletpapier
toothpaste	*tahnt*-pahs-taa	tandpasta
washing powder	*wahs*-poo-der	waspoeder
yoghurt	*yo*-khert	yoghurt

Souvenirs

clogs	*klomp*-ern	klompen
diamonds	*dee-aa-mahn*-tern	diamanten
Delft blue	*dehlfts*-blow	Delfts blauw
earrings	*or*-behl-lern	oorbellen
handicraft	*hahnt*-wehrk	handwerk
necklace	*hahls*-snoor/*hahls*-	halssnoer/halsket-
	keht-ting	ting (cord/links)
pottery	*aar*-der-wehrk	aardewerk
rug	*klayt*	kleed

Clothing

clothing	*klay*-ding	kleding
coat	*yahs*	jas
jacket	*yahs*-yer	jasje
jumper (sweater)	*trer*	trui
shoes	*skhoo*-nern	schoenen
trousers	*brook*	broek

| It is too big/small. | *heht is ter* | Het is te |
| | *khroht/kleyn* | groot/klein. |

Toiletries

| condoms | *kon*-**dohms** | condooms |
| hairbrush | *bor*-sterl | borstel |

razor (blade)	*skhear-mehs*	scheermes
razor (electric)	*skhear-ahp-pah-raat*	scheerapparaat
sanitary napkins	*maant-ver-bahnd*	maandverband
shaving cream	*skhear-zayp*	scheerzeep
soap	*zayp*	zeep
sunblock cream	*zon-ner-brahnt-oh-lee*	zonnebrandolie
tampons	*tahm-pons*	tampons
tissues	*tis-yoos/pah-pee-rern zahk-dook-yers*	tissues/papieren zakdoekjes
toilet paper	*way-say-pah-peer/ twah-leht-pah-peer*	WC-papier/ toiletpapier
toothbrush	*tahn-dern-bor-sterl*	tandenborstel
toothpaste	*tahnt-pahs-taa*	tandpasta

Photography

How much is it to process this film?

hoo-vayl kost heht om day-zer film ter ont-wik-ker-lern?

Hoeveel kost het om deze film te ontwikkelen?

When will it be ready?

wahn-near is heht klaar?

Wanner is het klaar?

I'd like a film for this camera.

ik vil khraag film vor day-zer kaa-mer-aa

Ik wil graag film voor deze kamera.

B&W (film)	*zvahrt-vit*	zwart-wit
camera	*kaa-mer-aa*	kamera
colour (film)	*kler(-ern-film)*	kleur(enfilm)
flash	*flits*	flits
light meter	*likht-may-ter*	lichtmeter

Smoking

A packet of cigarettes, please.
*ern **pahk**-yer see-khaar-**eht**-tern, ahls-tü-**bleeft*** | Een pakje sigaretten, alstublieft.

Are these cigarettes strong/mild?
*zeyn day-zer see-khaar-**eht**-tern zwaar/likht?* | Zijn deze sigaretten zwaar/licht?

Do you have a light?
*hayft ü/hehp yer ern **vür**-tyer?* | Heeft U/heb je een vuurtje?

Do you mind if I smoke?
fint ü/yer heht ehrkh ahls ik rohk? | Vindt U/je het erg als ik rook?

Please don't smoke here.
*rohk heer ahls-tü-**bleeft** neet* | Rook hier alstublieft niet.

cigarettes	*see-khaar-**eht**-tern*	sigaretten
cigarette papers	*vlooee*	vloei
filtered	*meht **fil**-ter*	met filter
lighter	***aan**-stay-ker*	aansteker
matches	***lü**-see-fehrs*	lucifers
menthol	***men**-tol*	menthol
pipe	*peyp*	pijp

Health

Where is …?	*waar is …?*	Waar is …?
the doctor	*der **dok**-ter*	de dokter
the hospital	*het **zee**-kern-hers*	het ziekenhuis
the chemist	*der droh-**khist***	de drogist
the dentist	*der **tahnt**-ahrts*	de tandarts

I am sick.		
ik behn zeek		Ik ben ziek.
My friend is sick.		
meyn vreend/vreend-in is		Mijn vriend (m)/vriendin (f)
zeek		is ziek.
What's the matter?		
waht is ehr aan der hahnt?		Wat is er aan de hand?
My … hurts.		
meyn … doot peyn		Mijn … doet pijn.

DUTCH

Parts of the Body

back	*rerkh*	rug
chest	*borst*	borst
ear	*or*	oor
eye	*ohkh*	oog
foot	*voot*	voet
head	*hohft*	hoofd
leg	*bayn*	been
mouth	*mont*	mond
skin	*hert*	huid
stomach	*maakh*	maag
teeth	***tahn*-dern**	tanden

Ailments

I have …	*ik hehp …*	Ik heb …
anaemia	***bloot*-ahr-moo-der**	bloedarmoede
a burn	*ern ver-**brahn**-ding*	een verbranding
a cold	*ern ver-**kowd**-heyt*	een verkoudheid
constipation	*ver-**stop**-ping*	verstopping
a sore throat	*ern zear-er kayl*	een zere keel
diarrhoea	*dee-ah-**ray***	diarree
fever	*korts*	koorts

glandular fever	*zeek-ter vahn* **pfai**-*fer*	ziekte van Pfeiffer
a headache	**hohft**-*peyn*	hoofdpijn
indigestion	*in-dee-***khehs**-*tee*	indigestie
an infection	*ern ont-***stay**-*king*	een ontsteking
influenza	*khreep*	griep
itch	*yerk*	jeuk
low/high blood pressure	**hoh**-*kher/***laa**-*kher* **bloot**-*drerk*	hoge/lage bloeddruk
nausea	**mis**-*ser-lerk-heyt*	misselijkheid
a sprain	*ern ver-***ster**-*king*	een verstuiking
sunburn	**zon**-*ner-brahnt*	zonnebrand
a temperature	*korts*	koorts
a venereal disease	*ern ver-***near**-*ee-ser* **zeek**-*ter*	een venerische ziekte

Women's Health

Could I see a female doctor?
kahn ik ern **vrow**-*er-ler-ker ahrts zeen?*
Kan ik een vrouwelijke arts zien?

I'm pregnant.
ik behn **zwahng**-*er*
Ik ben zwanger.

I'm on the pill.
*ik kher-***brerk** *der pil*
Ik gebruik de pil.

I haven't had my period for … weeks.
*ik behn ahl … ***way**-*kern neet on-kher-***stehlt** *kher-wayst*
Ik ben al … weken niet ongesteld geweest.

| (unusual) bleeding | *(on-kher-woh-ner)* **bloo**-*ding* | (ongewone) bloeding |
| cramps | **krahm**-*pern* | krampen |

| cystitis | *blaas-ont-stay-king* | blaasontsteking |
| thrush | *sprüw* | spruw |

Specific Needs

I'm …	*ik behn …*	Ik ben …
asthmatic	*ahst-**maa**-tees*	astmatisch
diabetic	***ser**-ker-zeek*	suikerziek
epileptic	*ay-pee-**lehp**-tees*	epileptisch

I'm allergic to antibiotics/
penicillin.
   *ik behn ah-**lehr**-khees vor*   Ik ben allergisch voor
   ***ahn**-tee-bee-oh-tee-kaa/*   antibiotica/penicilline.
   pay-nee-see-lee-ner
I have been vaccinated.
   *ik behn **in**-kher-ehnt*   Ik ben ingéént.

Useful Words & Phrases

I feel better/worse.
   *ik vool mer **bay**-ter/*   Ik voel me beter/slechter.
   slehkh-ter

accident	*on-kher-lerk*	ongeluk
addiction	*ver-**slaa**-ving*	verslaving
antibiotics	***ahn**-tee-bee-oh-tee-kaa*	antibiotica
antiseptic	*ahn-tee-**sehp**-tee-kerm*	antisepticum
blood test	***bloot**-tehst*	bloedtest
contraceptive	*vor-ber-**hoots**-mid-derl*	voo...
		mid...

At the Chemist

I need medication for …
   *ik hehp may-dee-**sey**-nern*   Ik heb medic...
   noh-derkh vor …   voor …

DUTCH

I have a prescription.
*ik hehp ern rer-**sehpt***

Ik heb een recept.

At the Dentist
I have a toothache.
*ik hehp **kees**-peyn/**tahnt**-peyn*

Ik heb kiespijn (molars)/tandpijn (incisors).

I've lost a filling.
*ik behn ern **ver**-ling ver-**lor**-ern*

Ik ben een vulling verloren.

I've broken a tooth.
*ik hehp ern tahnt kher-**broh**-kern*

Ik heb een tand gebroken.

I don't want it extracted.
*ik vil neet daht heht kher-**trok**-kern wort*

Ik wil niet dat het getrokken wordt.

Please give me an anaesthetic.
*khayf mer ahls-tü-**bleeft** ern ver-**doh**-ving*

Geef me alstublieft een verdoving.

Time & Dates
What time is it?   *hoo laat is heht?*   Hoe laat is het?

It is … (o'clock)   *Het is … uur.*   heht is … ür
  in the morning   **smor**-*kherns*   's-morgens
  in the afternoon   **smid**-*dahkhs*   's-middags
  in the evening   **saa**-*vonts*   's-avonds

…at date is it today?
*…l-ker **daa**-term is heht*
  …aakh?

Welke datum is het vandaag?

DUTCH

Days of the Week

Monday	*maan-dahkh*	maandag
Tuesday	*dins-dahkh*	dinsdag
Wednesday	*voons-dahkh*	woensdag
Thursday	*don-der-dahkh*	donderdag
Friday	*vrey-dahkh*	vrijdag
Saturday	*zaa-ter-dahkh*	zaterdag
Sunday	*zon-dahkh*	zondag

Months

January	*jah-nü-aa-ree*	januari
February	*fay-brü-aa-ree*	februari
March	*maart*	maart
April	*ah-pril*	april
May	*mey*	mei
June	*yü-nee*	juni
July	*yü-lee*	juli
August	*ow-khers-ters*	augustus
September	*sehp-tehm-ber*	september
October	*ok-toh-ber*	oktober
November	*noh-vehm-ber*	november
December	*day-sehm-ber*	december

Seasons

summer	*zoh-mer*	zomer
autumn	*hehrfst, naa-yaar*	herfst, najaar
winter	*win-ter*	winter
spring	*lehn-ter, vor-yaar*	lente, voorjaar

Present

today	*vahn-daakh*	vandaag
this morning	*day-zer mor-khern*	deze morgen
tonight	*vahn-aa-vont*	vanavond

DUTCH

this week/year	*day-zer wayk/dit yaar*	deze week/dit jaar
now	*nü*	nu

Past

yesterday	***khis**-ter-ern*	gisteren
day before yesterday	*ear-**khis**-ter-ern*	eergisteren
yesterday morning	***khis**-ter-ern-**mor**-khern*	gisterenmorgen
last night	***khis**-ter-ern-**aa**-vont*	gisterenavond
last week/year	*vor-i-kher **wayk**/vor-ikh **yaar***	vorige week/vorig jaar

Future

tomorrow	***mor**-khern*	morgen
day after tomorrow	*oh-ver-**mor**-khern*	overmorgen
tomorrow morning	***mor**-khern-**okh**-ternt*	morgenochtend
tomorrow afternoon/evening	***mor**-khern-**mid**-dahkh/**mor**-khern-**aa**-vont*	morgenmiddag/ morgenavond
next week	***vol**-khern-der **wayk***	volgende week
next year	***vol**-khernd **yaar***	volgend jaar

During the Day

afternoon	***mid**-dahkh*	middag
dawn, very early	***daa**-khe-**raat**,*	dageraad,
morning	***smor**-kherns vrookh*	's-morgens vroeg
day	*dahkh*	dag
early	*vrookh*	vroeg
late	*laat*	laat
midnight	***mid**-der-**nahkht***	middernacht
morning	***okh**-ternt*	ochtend

night	*nahkht*	nacht
noon	*twaalf ür **smid**-dahkhs/*	12 uur 's-middags/
	mid-dakh-ür	middaguur
sundown	*zons-**on**-der-khahng*	zonsondergang
sunrise	*zons-**op**-khahng*	zonsopgang

Numbers & Amounts

0	*nerl*	nul
1	*ayn*	één
2	*tway*	twee
3	*dree*	drie
4	*veer*	vier
5	*veyf*	vijf
6	*zehs*	zes
7	*zay-vern*	zeven
8	*ahkht*	acht
9	*nay-khern*	negen
10	*teen*	tien
11	*elf*	elf
12	*twaalf*	twaalf
13	*dehr-teen*	dertien
14	*vear-teen*	veertien
15	*veyf-teen*	vijftien
16	*zehs-teen*	zestien
17	*zay-vern-teen*	zeventien
18	*ahkh-teen*	achttien
19	*nay-khern-teen*	negentien
20	*tvin-terkh*	twintig
30	*dehr-terkh*	dertig
40	*vear-terkh*	veertig
50	*veyf-terkh*	vijftig

DUTCH

60	*zehs*-terkh	zestig
70	*zay-vern*-terkh	zeventig
80	*tahkh*-terkh	tachtig
90	*nay-khern*-terkh	negentig
100	*hon*-dert	honderd
1000	*der*-zernt	duizend
one million	*ayn mil*-**yoon**	één miljoen

1st	*ear*-ster	eerste – 1e
2nd	*tway*-der	tweede – 2e
3rd	*dehr*-der	derde – 3e

¼	*ern* **kwahrt**	een kwart
⅓	*ern* **dehr**-der	een derde
½	*ern hahlf*	een half
¾	*dree*-kwahrt	driekwart

Amounts

small	*kleyn*	klein
big	*khroht*	groot
a little (amount)	*ern* **bay**-tyer	een beetje
double	*der*-berl	dubbel
a dozen	*ern doh*-**zeyn**	een dozijn
Enough!	*kher*-**nookh**!	Genoeg!
few	*wey*-nikh-er	weinige
less	*min*-der	minder
many	*vay*-ler	vele
more	*mear*	meer
much	*vayl*	veel
once	*ayns/ayn*-maal	eens/eenmaal
a pair	*ern paar*	een paar

DUTCH

percent	*pro-**sehnt***	procent
some	*som-mer-kher*	sommige
too much	*ter-**vayl***	teveel
twice	*tway-maal*	tweemaal

Abbreviations

ANWB	Dutch motoring federation
BTW	VAT (value-added tax)
BV	Pty, private company
fl or f	Dutch guilder
F or BF	Belgian franc
M/Mevr	Mr/Mrs, Ms
NV	Ltd, Inc
TCB	Belgian Motoring (automobile) Club
-str/-weg/-pl	St/Rd/Sq
v.Chr./n.Chr.	AD/BC
VVV	Dutch tourist information

DUTCH

Paperwork

name	naam
address	adres
date of birth	geboortedatum
place of birth	eboorteplaats
age	leeftijd
sex	geslacht
nationality	nationaliteit
religion	godsdienst
reason for visit	reden voor bezoek
profession	beroep
marital status	huwelijkse staat
passport	paspoort

passport number	paspoortnummer
visa	visum
tourist card	toeristenkaart
identification	legitimatie
birth certificate	geboortebewijs
driver's licence	rijbewijs
car owner's title	kentekenbewijs
car registration	kenteken
customs	douane
immigration	immigratie
border	grens

Emergencies

POLICE	*POLITIE*
POLICE STATION	*POLITIEBUREAU*

Help! — *help!* — Help!

Go away! — *khaa wehkh!* — Ga weg!

Thief! — *deef!* — Dief!

I'll call the police!
ik roop der poh-leet-see! — Ik roep de politie!

It's an emergency!
heht is ern noht-kher-vahl! — Het is een noodgeval!

There's been an accident!
ehr is ern orn-kher-lerk kher-bert! — Er is een ongeluk gebeurd!

Call a doctor!
haal ern dok-ter! — Haal een dokter!

Call an ambulance!
haal ern zee-kern-oh-toh! — Haal een ziekenauto!

Call the police!
haal der poh-leet-see!

Haal de politie!

Where is the police station?
waar is heht poh-leet-see-bü-roh?

Waar is het politiebureau?

I've been raped.
ik behn aan-kher-rahnd

Ik ben aangerand.

I've been robbed!
ik behn ber-rohft!

Ik ben beroofd!

I am ill.
ik behn zeek

Ik ben ziek.

I am lost.
ik behn der wehkh kweht

Ik ben de weg kwijt.

Where are the toilets?
waar zeyn de twah-leht-tern/way-says?

Waar zijn de toiletten/WC's?

Could you help me please?
kernt ü mey ahls-tü-bleeft/ kern yer mey ahls-yer-bleeft hehl-pern?

Kunt U mij alstublieft/ kun je mij alsjeblieft helpen?

Could I please use the telephone?
zow ik moh-khern behl-lern?

Zou ik mogen bellen?

I'm sorry. (I apologise)
heht speyt mer/so-ree

Het spijt me./Sorry.

I didn't realise I was doing anything wrong.
ik haht neet in der khaa-tern daht ik eets ver-kearts dayt

Ik had niet in de gaten dat ik iets verkeerds deed.

DUTCH

I didn't do it.
  ik hehp heht neet kher-daan   Ik heb het niet gedaan.

I wish to contact my
embassy/consulate.
  ik wil kon-tahkt op-nay-   Ik wil kontakt opnemen met
  mern meht meyn ahm-bah-   mijn ambassade/
  saa-der/kon-sü-laat   consulaat.

I speak English.
  ik sprayk ehng-erls   Ik spreek Engels.

I have medical insurance.
  ik behn may-dees ver-zay-   Ik ben medisch verzekerd.
  kert

My luggage is insured.
  meyn baa-khaa-zher is   Mijn bagage is verzekerd.
  ver-zay-kert

My … was stolen.
  meyn … is kher-stoh-lern!   Mijn … is gestolen!

I've lost my …
  ik behn meyn … ver-lor-ern   Ik ben mijn … verloren.

bags	*tahs-sern*	tassen
handbag	*hahnd-tahs*	handtas
money	*khehlt*	geld
travellers'	*reys-shehks/*	reischeques/
cheques	*travellers' cheques*	travellers' cheques
passport	*pahs-port*	paspoort

FRENCH

FRENCH

French

Introduction

French, like Italian, Spanish, Romanian and Portuguese, is one of the Romance languages – those descended from Latin. It began to emerge as a distinct language in the 9th century AD. The earliest surviving text in French is that of the *Strasbourg Oaths* (842 AD), an agreement uniting two of Charlemagne's grandsons against the third in a quarrel over the division of the empire. It was not until the 11th century, however, that a vernacular literature really established itself in France, with the development of verse epics called *chansons de gestes*.

During the 13th and 14th centuries, the emergence of France as a centralised state favoured the spread of the dialect of the Parisian region (Francien), to the detriment of regional dialects and the Provençal language in the south.

The edict of Villers-Cotterets, issued by François I in 1539, made the use of French compulsory for official documents. During the French Rennaissance, in the 16th century, efforts were made to enrich and dignify the national tongue, to make it a worthy vehicle for serious literature. This involved coining words from Greek and Latin roots, and the adoption of etymological spellings, which later reformers have not been able to rationalise. During the 17th century there was a reaction to this trend. The poet Malherbe and the grammarian Vaugelas, a founding member of the French Academy, *Académie française*, were influential in a movement to 'purify' the language and codify its usage, establishing norms which have, to a large extent, remained in force.

The Academy, established in 1635, has preserved its purist stand, opposing, in recent years, the introduction of English words such as 'look' or 'background'. The widespread use of such 'franglais', though it may pose a threat to the integrity of the French language, does not make communication significantly easier for the Anglophone in France.

There are about 90 million Francophones throughout the world, of whom about 54 million live in France. French is one of the official languages in Belgium, Switzerland and Luxembourg, which have around four million, 1.2 million and 300,000 Francophones respectively. French is also spoken by about 150,000 inhabitants of the Val d'Aosta in north-western Italy, and it has a million speakers in Monaco. Major areas outside Europe where you'll find French spoken are Africa, Indochina, the Pacific, Canada (Quebec), and the USA (especially Maine and Louisiana).

French grammar is similar to that of the other Romance languages. An important distinction is made between *tu* and *vous* (singular), which both correspond to 'you.' *Tu* is only used in addressing people you know well, children and animals. When addressing an adult, *vous* should be used unless the person invites you to use *tu (Tu peux me tutoyer)*. In general, younger people insist less on this distinction, and they may use *tu* right from the beginning of an acquaintance.

All nouns in French are either masculine or feminine, or both, and adjectives reflect the gender. The feminine form of both nouns and adjectives is indicated by a silent 'e' added to the masculine form: student, *étudiant* (m)/*étudiante* (f). As in the example here, throughout this chapter the feminine word or variant follows the masculine. The gender of a noun is often indicated by a preceding article 'the/a/some': *le/un/du* (m), *la/une/*

de la (f); or possessive adjective 'my/your/his/her': *mon/ton/son* (m), *ma/ta/sa* (f). The possessive adjectives agree in number and gender with the thing possessed: his/her mother, *sa mère*.

There are three ways of asking questions in French: you can invert the subject and the verb *(Avez-vous l'heure?)*; you can begin with *est-ce que* and keep the normal word order *(Est-ce que vous avez l'heure?)*; or you can rely on intonation to indicate a question *(Vous avez l'heure?)*. The first way of asking questions is formal. The other two ways are more common in spoken French, and are used for most of the questions in this section.

Pronunciation

Stress in French is much weaker than in English – all it really does is lengthen the final syllable of the word – so it is important for the Anglophone to make an effort to pronounce each syllable with approximately equal stress.

French has a number of sounds which are notoriously difficult to produce. The main causes of trouble are:

1) The distinction between *ü* (as in *tu*) and *oo* (as in *tout*). For both sounds, the lips are rounded and projected forward, but for *ü*, the tongue is towards the front of the mouth, its tip against the lower front teeth, while for *oo* the tongue is towards the back of the mouth, its tip behind the gums of the lower front teeth.

2) The nasal vowels. During the production of nasal vowels the breath escapes partly through the nose and partly through the mouth. There are no nasal vowels in English; in French there are three, indicated in the text as *õ, ē, ã*, as in *bon vin blanc*, 'good white wine'. These sounds occur where a syllable ends in a single *n* or *m*: the *n* or *m* in this case is not pronounced, but indicates the nasalisation of the preceding vowel.

ã   as for the 'ah' sound in 'father', but with a slightly smaller opening between the lips, and the breath escaping partly through the nose. The usual spellings are *an*, *am*, *en*, and *em*.

õ   as for the 'o' in 'pot', but with the lips closer and rounded, and the breath escaping partly through the nose. The usual spelling is *on*, *om*. It is important to distinguish this sound from *ã*.

ẽ   as for the 'eh' sound in 'bet', but with a slightly larger opening between the lips, and the breath escaping partly through the nose. The usual spellings are *in*, *im*, *yn*, *ym*, *ain*, *aim*, *ein*, *eim*, *en* preceded by *i* or *é*, *un* or *um*.

Remember that for *õ*, the jaws are closer together and the lips rounded. Practice distinguishing pairs of words such as *tonton*, *tõtõ*, 'uncle', and *tentant*, *tãtã*, 'tempting.'

3) *l* and *r*. The French *l* is always pronounced with the tip of the tongue touching the back of the upper incisors, and the surface of the tongue higher than for an English 'l'. Be especially careful to maintain this tongue position for *l*'s at the ends of words, as in il or elle. The standard r of Parisian French is produced by moving the bulk of the tongue backwards to constrict the air flow in the pharynx, while the tip of the tongue rests behind the lower front teeth. It is quite similar to the noise made by some people before spitting, but with much less friction. For those who know Spanish, it is also like the *jota* (*j*), except that it is 'softer' and voiced (involves vibration of the vocal cords).

Greetings & Civilities
Top Useful Phrases

Hello.	*bõ-zhoor*	Bonjour.
Goodbye.	*oh rer-vwahr*	Au revoir.
Yes/No.	*wee/nõ*	Oui/Non.
Excuse me.	*ehk-skü-zei mwah*	Excusez-moi.
Please.	*seel voo plei*	S'il vous plaît.
Thank you.	*mehr-see*	Merci.
Many thanks.	*mehr-see boh-koo*	Merci beaucoup.

May I? Do you mind?
voo pehr-meh-tei? sah ner voo fei ryẽ?
Vous permettez? Ça ne vous fait rien?

Sorry. (excuse me, forgive me)
pahr-dõ
Pardon.

That's fine. You're welcome.
trei byẽ. zher voo zã pree
Très bien. Je vous en prie.

Greetings

Good morning.	*bõ-zhoor*	Bonjour.
Good afternoon.	*bõ-zhoor*	Bonjour.
Good evening/night.	*bõ-swahr*	Bonsoir.
How are you?	*ko-mã tah-lei voo?*	Comment allez-vous?
Well, thanks.	*byẽ mehr-see!*	Bien, merci!

Forms of Address

Madam/Mrs	*mah-dahm*	Madame
Sir/Mr	*mer-syer*	Monsieur
Miss	*mahd-mwah-zehl*	Mademoiselle
companion, friend	*ah-mee*	ami (m)/amie (f)

FRENCH

Language Difficulties

Do you speak English?
  voo pahr-lei ã-glei?

Vous parlez anglais?

Does anyone speak English?
  *ehs-keel-yah kehl-kē kee
  pahrl ã-glei?*

Est-ce qu'il y a quelqu'un
qui parle anglais?

I speak a little French
  zher pahrl ē per der frã-sei

Je parle un peu de français.

I (don't) understand.
  zher (ner) kõ-prã (pah)

Je (ne) comprends (pas).

Could you speak more slowly?
  *eh-sker voo poo-ryei
  pahr-lei plü lã-tmã?*

Est-ce que vous pourriez
parler plus lentement?

Could you repeat that?
  *eh-sker voo poo-ryei
  rei-pei-tei?*

Est-ce que vous pourriez
répéter?

How do you say …?
  ko-mã tehs-kõ dee …?

Comment est-ce qu'on dit …?

What does … mean?
  ker ver deer ...?

Que veut dire …?

Small Talk
Meeting People

What is your name?
  ko-mã voo zah-plei voo?

Comment vous appelez-vous?

My name is …
  zher mah-pehl …

Je m'appelle …

I'd like to introduce you to …
  zhem-rei voo prei-zã-tei …

J'aimerais vous présenter …

Pleased to meet you.
  ã-shã-tei

Enchanté/-ée.

FRENCH

Nationalities

It may be a good idea to learn how the French say the name of your country, as the sounds and even words are often quite different from English. We've listed just a few here.

Where are you from?
voo ver-ne doo?   Vous venez d'où?

I am …
zher vyē …   Je viens …

from Australia	*do-strah-lee*	d'Australie
from England	*dã-gler-tehr*	d'Angleterre
from France	*der frãs*	de France
from India	*der lĩnd*	de l'Inde
from Japan	*dü **zhah**-pã*	du Japon
from Latin America	*dah-mei-**reek** **lah**-teen*	d'Amérique Latine
from the Middle East	*dü **mwai**-ē or-ree-ē*	du Moyen-Orient
from New Zealand	*der noo-vehl zei-lãd*	de Nouvelle-Zélande
from Scotland	*dei-kos*	d'Écosse
from South-East Asia	*der **lah**-zee dü sü-dest*	de l'Asie du Sud-Est
from Switzerland	*der swees*	de Suisse
from the USA	*dei **zei**-tah zü-nee*	des États-Unis
from Wales	*dü pei-ee der gahl*	du Pays de Galles

Age

How old are you?
voo zah-vei kehl ahzh?   Vouz avez quel âge?

I am … years old.
zhei … ã   J'ai … ans.

Occupations

What (work) do you do?

keh-sker voo feht dā lah vee?

Qu'est-ce que vous faites dans la vie?

I am (a/an) …
zher swee …

Je suis …

artist	*ahr-teest*	artiste
business person	*om/fahm dah-fehr*	homme (m)/femme (f) d'affaires
doctor	*mehd-sē*	médecin
engineer	*ē-zhen-yerr*	ingénieur
farmer	*ah-gree-kül-terr*	agriculteur
journalist	*zhoor-nah-leest*	journaliste
lawyer	*ah-vo-kah*	avocat
mechanic	*mei-kah-nee-syē*	mécanicien (m)
	mei-kah-nee-syehn	mécanicienne (m)
nurse	*ē-feer-myei*	infirmier (m)
	ē-feer-myehr	infirmière (f)
office worker	*ā-plwah-yei der bü-roh*	employé/-ée de bureau
scientist	*syā-tee-feek*	scientifique
student	*ei-tü-dyā*	étudiant (m)
	ei-tü-dyāt	étudiante (f)
teacher	*pro-feh-serr*	professeur
waiter	*sehr-verr*	serveur (m)
	sehr-verz	serveuse (f)
writer	*ei-kreev-ē*	écrivain

FRENCH

Religion

What is your religion?

kehl ei votr rer-lee-zhyō?

Quelle est votre religion?

I am not religious.
*zher ner swee pah
krwah-yã*

Je ne suis pas croyant.

I am …
zher swee …

Je suis …

Buddhist	*boo-deest*	bouddhiste
Catholic	*kah-to-leek*	catholique
Christian	*krei-tyē/kreit-yehn*	chrétien (m)
		chrétienne (f)
Hindu	*ē-doo*	hindou (m)
		hindoue (f)
Jewish	*zhweef/zhweev*	juif (m)/juive (f)
Muslim	*mü-zül-mã*	musulman (m)
	mü-zül-mahn	musulmane (f)

FRENCH

Family

Are you married?
voo zeht mah-ryei?

Vous êtes marié/-ée?

I am single.
zher swee sei-lee-bah-tehr

Je suis célibataire.

I am married.
zher swee mah-ryei

Je suis marié/-ée.

How many children do you
have?
voo zah-vei kõ-byē dā-fã?

Vous avez combien d'enfants?

I don't have any children.
zher nei pah dā-fã

Je n'ai pas d'enfants.

I have a daughter/a son.
zhei ün feey/ē fees

J'ai une fille/un fils.

Is your husband/wife here?
*eh-sker votr mahree/fahm
ei lah?*

Est-ce que votre mari/
femme est là?

Do you have a boyfriend/
girlfriend?

eh-sker voo zah-vei ē
per-tee tah-mee/ün per-teet
ah-mee?

Est-ce que vous avez un
petit ami/une petite amie?

brother	*ler frehr*	le frère
children	*lei zãfã*	les enfants
daughter	*lah feey*	la fille
family	*lah fah-meey*	la famille
father	*ler pehr*	le père
grandfather	*ler grã-pehr*	le grand-père
grandmother	*lah grã-mehr*	la grand-mère
husband	*ler mah-ree*	le mari
mother	*lah mehr*	la mère
sister	*lah serr*	la soeur
son	*ler fees*	le fils
wife	*lah fahm*	la femme

FRENCH

Useful Phrases

Sure.	*byē sür*	Bien sûr.
Just a minute.	*ah-tã-dei ün mee-nüt*	Attendez une minute.
It's important.	*sei tē-por-tã*	C'est important.
It's not important.	*ser nei pah zē-por-tã*	Ce n'est pas important.
It's possible.	*sei po-seebl*	C'est possible.
It's not possible.	*ser nei pah po-seebl*	Ce n'est pas possible.
Good luck!	*bon shãs!*	Bonne chance!
Wait!	*ah-tã-dei!*	Attendez!

Signs

EMERGENCY EXIT	*ISSUE DE SECOURS*
ENTRANCE	*ENTRÉE*
EXIT	*SORTIE*
FREE ADMISSION	*ENTRÉE GRATUITE*
HOT/COLD	*CHAUDE/FROIDE*
INFORMATION	*RENSEIGNEMENTS*
NO ENTRY	*ENTRÉE INTERDITE*
NO SMOKING	*DÉFENSE DE FUMER*
OPEN/CLOSED	*OUVERT/FERMÉ*
PROHIBITED	*INTERDIT*
RESERVED	*RÉSÉRVÉ*
TELEPHONE	*TÉLÉPHONE*
TOILETS	*TOILETTES*

FRENCH

Getting Around

What time does ... leave/arrive?	*... pahr/ahreev ah kehl err?*	... part/arrive à quelle heure?
the (air)plane	*lah-vyō*	l'avion
the boat	*ler bah-toh*	le bateau
the bus (city)	*l(o-to-)büs*	l'(auto)bus
the bus (intercity)	*l(o-to-)kahr*	l'(auto)car
the train	*ler trē*	le train
the tram	*ler trahm-wei*	le tramway

Finding Your Way

Do you have a guidebook/
local map?

*ehs-ker voo zah-ve ē geed
too-ree-steek/ün kahrt der
lah rei-zhyō?*

Est-ce que vous avez un
guide touristique/une carte
de la région?

Where is …?		
oo ei …?		Où est …?

How do I get to …?
   ko-mã fehr poor ah-lei   Comment faire pour
   ah …?   aller à…?

Is it far from/near here?
   sei lwē/pah lwē dee-see?   C'est loin/pas loin d'ici?

Can I walk there?
   zher per ee ah-lei ah pyei?   Je peux y aller à pied?

Can you show me (on the map)?
   eh-sker voo poo-vei mer   Est-ce que vous pouvez me
   ler mõ-trei (sür lah kahrt)?   le montrer (sur la carte)?

Are there other means of
getting there?
   ehs-keel-yah ē nohtr   Est-ce qu'il y a un autre
   mwah-yē dee ah-lei?   moyen d'y aller?

Directions

Go straight ahead.
   kō-teen-wei too drwah   Continuez tout droit.

It's two blocks down.
   sei der rü plü lwah   C'est deux rues plus loin.

Turn left …	*toor-nei ah gohsh …*	Tournez à gauche …
Turn right …	*toor-nei ah drwaht …*	Tournez à droite …
at the next corner	*oh pro-shē kwē*	au prochain
	der roo	coin de rue
at the traffic lights	*oh fer*	aux feux

behind	*deh-ryehr*	derrière
in front of	*der-vã*	devant
far	*lwē*	loin

| near | *prosh* | proche |
| opposite | *ā fahs der* | en face de |

Buying Tickets

TICKET OFFICE	*GUICHET*

Excuse me, where is the ticket office?
ehk-skü-zei mwah oo ei ler gee-shei?
Excusez-moi, où est le guichet?

Where can I buy a ticket?
oo ehs-ker zher per ahsh-tei ē bee-yei?
Où est-ce que je peux acheter un billet?

I want to go to …
zher ver ah-lei ah …
Je veux aller à …

Do I need to book?
ehs-keel foh rei-zehr-vei ün plahs/lei plahs?
Est-ce qu'il faut réserver une place/les places?

You need to book.
eel foh rei-zehr-vei ün plahs/lei plahs
Il faut réserver une place/les places.

I'd like to book a seat to …
zher voo-drei re-zehr-vei ün plahs poor …
Je voudrais réserver une place pour …

It is full.
sei kō-plei
C'est complet.

Is it completely full?
eel nyah vreh-mā pah der plahs?
Il n'y a vraiment pas de place?

FRENCH

Can I get a stand-by ticket?
ehs-ker zher per ahsh-tei
ẽ bee-yei sã gah-rã-tee?

Est-ce que je peux acheter un billet sans garantie?

I would like …
zher voo-drei …

Je voudrais …

a one-way ticket	*ẽ bee-yei ah-lei sẽpl*	un billet aller simple
a return ticket	*ẽ bee-yei ah-lei ei rertoor*	un billet aller et retour
two tickets	*der bee-yei*	deux billets
a student's fare	*ẽ bee-yei ah tah-reef rei-dwee (zher swee zei-tü-dyã/ zei-tü-dyãt)*	un billet à tarif réduit (je suis étudiant (m)/ étudiante (f)
a child's/ pensioner's fare	*ẽ bee-yei ah tah-reef rei-dwee (sei poor ẽ ã-fã/zher swee rer-treh-tei)*	un billet à tarif réduit (c'est pour un enfant/je suis retraité/-ée)
1st class	*prer-myehr klahs*	Première classe
2nd class	*ser-gõd/der-zyehm klahs*	Seconde/Deuxième classe

Air

CHECK-IN COUNTER	*ENREGISTREMENT*
CUSTOMS	*DOUANE*
LUGGAGE PICKUP	*LIVRAISON DE BAGAGES*

Is there a flight to …?
ehs-keel-yah ẽ vol poor …?

Est-ce qu'il y a un vol pour ...?

When is the next flight to …?
ah kehl err pahr ler pro-shẽ nah-vyõ poor …?

A quelle heure part le prochain avion pour …?

How long is the flight?
ler vol dür kõ-byē der tã?

Le vol dure combien de temps?

What is the flight number?
kehl ei ler nü-mer-oh dü vol?

Quel est le numéro du vol?

You must check in at …
voo der-ve voo prei-sã-tei ah lã-rei-zhee-strermã ah …

Vous devez vous présenter à l'enregistrement à …

airport tax	*tahks dah-ei-ro-por*	taxes d'aéroport
boarding pass	*kahrt dã-bahr-ker-mã*	carte d'embarquement

Bus & Tram

BUS STATION	GARE ROUTIÈRE
BUS/TRAM STOP	ARRÊT D'AUTOBUS/ DE TRAMWAY

Where is the bus/tram stop?
oo ei lah-rei do-to-büs/der trahm-wei?

Où est l'arrêt d'autobus/de tramway?

Which bus goes to …?
kehl büs vah ah …?

Quel bus va à …?

Does this bus go to …?
ehs-ker ser büs vah ah …?

Est-ce que ce bus va à …?

How often do buses pass by?
lei büs pahs ah kehl frei-kãs?

Les bus passent à quelle fréquence?

What time is the … bus?
ler büs … pahs ah kehl err?

Le bus … passe à quelle heure?

FRENCH

next	*pro-shē*	prochain (m)
	pro-shehn	prochaine (f)
first	*prer-myei*	premier (m)
	prer-myehr	première (f)
last	*dehr-nyei*	dernier (m)
	dehr-nyehr	dernière (f)

Could you let me know when
we get to …?
 ehs-ker voo poo-vei mer   Est-ce que vous pouvez me
 deer kã noo zah-ree-ver-ō   dire quand nous arriverons
 ah …?   à …?
I want to get off!
 zher ver dehs-ādr!   Je veux descendre!

Train

TRAIN STATION	*GARE*
TIMETABLE	*HORAIRE*
PLATFORM	*QUAI*

Is this the right platform
for …?
 sei byē ler kei poor …?   C'est bien le quai pour …?
The train leaves from
platform …
 ler trē pahr dü kei …   Le train part du quai …

Passengers must …	*lei vwah-yah-zherr*	Les voyageurs
	dwahv …	doivent …
change trains	*shã-zhei der trē*	changer de train
change platforms	*shã-zhei der kei*	changer de quai

dining car	*vah-gō rehs-toh-rã*	wagon-restaurant
express	*rah-peed*	rapide
sleeping car	*vah-gō lee*	wagon-lit

Metro

CHANGE (for coins)	*DISTRIBUTEUR DE MONNAIE*

Which line goes to …?
 kehl leeny/rahm vah ah …?   Quelle ligne/rame va à …?
What is the next station?
 kehl ei lah pro-shehn   Quelle est la prochaine
 stah-syō?   station?

Taxi

Can you take me to …?
 ehs-ker voo poo-vei mer   Est-ce que vous pouvez me
 kō-dweer ah ...?   conduire à …?
Please take me to …
 kō-dwee-ze mwah ah …,   Conduisez-moi à …, s'il
 seel voo plei   vous plaît.
How much does it cost to go to …?
 kehl ei ler pree der lah   Quel est le prix de la course
 koors zhüs-kah …?   jusqu'à …?

Instructions

Here is fine, thank you.
 ee-see sah vah, mehr-see   Ici ça va, merci.
The next corner, please.
 oh pro-shẽ kwẽ der rü,   Au prochain coin de rue,
 seel voo plei   s'il vous plaît.

The next street to the left/right.
lah pro-shehn rü ah gohsh/ drwaht

La prochaine rue à gauche/ droite.

Stop here!
ah-reh-tei voo ee-see!

Arrêtez-vous ici!

Please slow down.
roo-lei plü lãt-mã, seel voo plei

Roulez plus lentement, s'il vous plaît.

Please wait here.
ah-tã-de ee-see seel voo plei

Attendez ici, s'il vous plaît.

Useful Phrases

The train is delayed/cancelled.
ler trẽ ah dü rer-tahr/ah ei-tei ah-nü-lei

Le train a du retard/a été annulé.

How long will it be delayed?
eel yo-rah kõ-byẽ der tã der rer-tahr?

Il y aura combien de temps de retard?

There is a delay of … hours.
eel yo-rah ẽ rer-tahr der … err

Il y aura un retard de … heures.

Can I reserve a place?
ehs-ker zher per rei-zehr-vei ün plahs?

Est-ce que je peux réserver une place?

How long does the trip take?
ler trah-zhei dü-rer-rah kõ-byẽ der tã?

Le trajet durera combien de temps?

Is it a direct route?
sei tẽ trẽ dee-rehkt?

C'est un train direct?

Is that seat taken?
ehs-ker seht plahs ei to-kü-pei?

Est-ce que cette place est occupée?

FRENCH

I want to get off at …
zher ver dehs-ādr ah …   Je veux descendre à …
Excuse me.
ehk-skü-ze mwah   Excusez-moi.

Car & Bicycle

DETOUR	*DÉVIATION*
FREEWAY	*AUTOROUTE*
GARAGE	*GARAGE/STATION SERVICE*
GIVE WAY	*CÉDEZ LA PRIORITÉ*
MECHANIC	*MÉCANICIEN*
NO ENTRY	*ENTRÉE INTERDITE*
NO PARKING	*STATIONNEMENT INTERDIT*
ONE WAY	*SENS UNIQUE*
REPAIRS	*RÉPARATIONS*
SELF SERVICE	*LIBRE-SERVICE*
UNLEADED	*SANS PLOMB*

FRENCH

Where can I hire a car/bicycle?
oo ehs-ker zher per lwei ün   Où est-ce que je peux louer
vwah-tür/ē vei-loh?   une voiture/un vélo?
How much is it daily/weekly?
kehl ei ler tah-reet pahr   Quel est le tarif par jour/par
zhoor/pahr ser-mehn?   semaine?
Does that include insurance/
mileage?
ehs-ker lah-sü-rãs/ler kee-   Est-ce que l'assurance/le
lo-mei-trahzh ei kō-pree?   kilométrage est compris?

Where's the next petrol station?

oo ei lah pro-shehn stah-syō sehr-vees?

Où est la prochaine station-service?

Please fill the tank.

ler plē seel voo plei

Le plein, s'il vous plaît.

I want … litres of petrol (gas).

do-ne mwah … leetr dehs-ās seel voo plei

Donnez-moi … litres d'essence, s'il vous plaît.

Please check the oil and water.

kō-tro-lei lweel ei loh seel voo plei

Contrôlez l'huile et l'eau, s'il vous plaît.

How long can I park here?

poor kō-byē der tā ehs-ker zher peux stah-syō-nei ee-see?

Pour combien de temps est-ce que je peux stationner ici?

Does this road lead to?

ehs-ker seht root mehn ah …?

Est-ce que cette route mène à …?

air (for tyres)	*ler kō-prehs-err* *(poor gō-flei le pner)*	le compresseur (pour gonfler les pneus)
battery	*lah bah-tree*	la batterie
brakes	*le frē*	les freins
clutch	*lā-bre-yahzh*	l'embrayage
driving licence	*ler pehr-mee der kō-dweer*	le permis de conduire
engine	*ler mo-terr*	le moteur
lights	*le fahr*	les phares
oil	*lweel*	l'huile
puncture	*lah krer-ve-zō*	la crevaison

FRENCH

radiator	*ler rah-dyah-ter*	le radiateur
road map	*lah kahrt roo-tyehr*	la carte routière
tyres	*le pner*	les pneus
windscreen	*ler pahr breez*	le pare-brise

Car Problems

I need a mechanic.
zhei ber-zwē dē mei-kah-nee-syē   J'ai besoin d'un mécanicien.

What make is it?
kehl ei lah mahrk?   Quelle est la marque?

The battery is flat.
lah bah-tree ei tah plah   La batterie est à plat.

The radiator is leaking.
ler rah-dyah-terr fwee   Le radiateur fuit.

I have a flat tyre.
ler pner sei dei-gō-flei   Le pneu s'est dégonflé.

It's overheating.
ler mo-terr shohf   Le moteur chauffe.

It's not working.
sa ner mahrsh pah   Ça ne marche pas.

Accommodation

CAMPING GROUND	CAMPING
GUEST HOUSE	PENSION DE FAMILLE
HOTEL	HÔTEL
MOTEL	MOTEL
YOUTH HOSTEL	AUBERGE DE JEUNESSE

Finding Accommodation

I'm looking for …	*zher shehrsh …*	Je cherche …
Where is …?	*oo ei …?*	Où est …?
a cheap hotel	*ē-noh-tehl bō mahr-shei*	un hôtel bon marché
a good hotel	*ē-bō-noh-tehl*	un bon hôtel
a nearby hotel	*ē-noh-tehl pah lwē dee-see*	un hôtel pas loin d'ici
a clean hotel	*ē-noh-tehl propr*	un hôtel propre

What is the address?
kehl ei lah-drehs? — Quelle est l'adresse?

Could you write the address, please?
ehs-ker voo poo-vei ei-kreer lah-drehs seel voo plei? — Est-ce vous pouvez écrire l'adresse, s'il vous plaît?

Booking a Room

Do you have any rooms available?
ehs-ker voo zah-vei de shābr leebr? — Est-ce que vous avez des chambres libres?

I'd like to book a room.
zher voo-drei rei-zair-vei ün chābr — Je voudrais réserver une chambre.

for one night/four nights
poor ün/kahtr nü-ee — pour une/quatre nuit(s)

from tonight/Tuesday
der ser swahr/mahr-dee — de ce soir/mardi

I'm staying for …	*zher rehs-ter-rei …*	Je resterai …
one day	*ē zhoor*	un jour
two days	*der zhoor*	deux jours
one week	*ün ser-mehn*	une semaine

I would like …	*zher voo-drei …*	Je voudrais …
a single room	*ün shãbr ah ē lee*	une chambre à un lit
a double room	*ün shãbr doobl*	une chambre double
a room with a bathroom	*ün shãbr ah-vehk ün sahl der bē*	une chambre avec une salle de bain
to share a dorm	*koo-shei dã zē dor-twahr*	coucher dans un dortoir
a bed	*ē lee*	un lit

At the Hotel

How much is it per night/
per person?
*kehl ei ler pree pahr
nwee/pahr pehr-son?*

Quel est le prix par nuit/
par personne?

Can I see it?
zher per lah vwahr?

Je peux la voir?

Are there any others?
eel yã-nah dohtr?

Il y en a d'autres?

Are there any cheaper rooms?
*voo nah-vei ryē der
shãbr mei-yerr mahr-shei?*

Vous n'avez rien de
chambres meilleur marché?

Can I see the bathroom?
*zher per vwahr lah sahl
der bē?*

Je peux voir la salle de bain?

Is there a reduction for
students/children?
*ehs-ker voo zah-vei ē
tah-reef rei-dwee poor lei
zei-tü-dyã/le zã-fã?*

Est-ce que vous avez un
tarif réduit pour les
étudiants/les enfants?

Does it include breakfast?
*ehs-ker ler per-tee
dei-zher-nei ei kõ-pree?*

Est-ce que le petit déjeuner
est compris?

It's fine, I'll take it.
  sei byē zher lah prã

C'est bien, je la prends.

I'm not sure how long I'm staying.
  zher ner sei pah ehg-zahk-ter-mã kõ-byē der tã zher rehs-ter-rei

Je ne sais pas exactement combien de temps je resterai.

Is there a lift (elevator)?
  ehs-keel-yah ē nah-sã-serr?

Est-ce qu'il y a un ascenseur?

Where is the bathroom?
  oo ei lah sahl der bē?

Où est la salle de bain?

Is there hot water all day?
  ehs-keel-yah der loh shohd pã-dã toot lah zhoor-nei?

Est-ce qu'il y a de l'eau chaude pendant toute la journée?

You May Hear

Sorry, we're full.
  dei-zo-lei me sei kõ-plei

Désolé, mais c'est complet.

Do you have identification?
  ehs-ker voo zha-vei ün pyehs dee-dã-tee-tei?

Est-ce que vous avez une pièce d'identité?

Your membership card, please.
  votr kahrt dah-dei-rã seel voo plei

Votre carte d'adhérent, s'il vous plaît.

How long will you be staying?
  voo rehs-ter-re kõ-byē der tã?

Vous resterez combien de temps?

It's … per day/per person.
  ler pree ei … pahr zhoor/ pahr pehr-son

Le prix est … par jour/par personne.

Requests & Complaints

Is there somewhere to wash clothes?

ehs-keel-yah ē ā-drwah oo õ per fehr lah lehs-eev?

Est-ce qu'il y a un endroit où on peut faire la lessive?

Can I use the kitchen?

ehs-ker zher per mer sehr-veer der lah kwee-zeen?

Est-ce que je peux me servir de la cuisine?

Can I use the telephone?

ehs-ker zher per ü-tee-lee-zei ler tei-lei-fon?

Est-ce que je peux utiliser le téléphone?

Do you have a safe where I can leave my valuables?

ehs-ker voo zah-vei ē kofr for poor dei-poh-zei mei zob-zhei der vah-lerr?

Est-ce que vous avez un coffre-fort pour déposer mes objets de valeur?

Please wake me up at …

rei-vei-yei mwah ah …, seel voo plei

Réveillez-moi à …, s'il vous plaît.

The room needs to be cleaned.

eel foh neh-twah-yei lah shābr

Il faut nettoyer la chambre.

The window is stuck.

lah fer-nehtr ei blo-kei

La fenêtre est bloquée.

I've locked myself out of my room.

ma port ei fair-mei ei zher swee dei-or

Ma porte est fermée et je suis dehors.

The toilet won't flush.

lah shahs doh ner mahrsh pah

La chasse d'eau ne marche pas.

I don't like this room.
seht shãbr ner mer plei pah Cette chambre ne me plaît pas.

It's too small.	*ehl ei troh per-teet*	Elle est trop petite.
It's noisy.	*ehl ei brü-yãt*	Elle est bruyante.
It's too dark.	*ehl ei troh sõbr*	Elle est trop sombre.
It's expensive.	*sei shehr*	C'est cher.

Checking Out

I am/We are leaving now.
zher pahr/noo pahr-tõ mē-tnã Je pars/Nous partons maintenant.

I'd like to pay the bill.
zher voo-dre rei-glei (lah not) Je voudrais régler (la note).

address	*lah-drehs*	l'adresse
name	*prei-nõ*	prénom
surname	*nõ*	nom
room number	*nü-mei-roh der shãbr*	numéro de chambre

Useful Words

air-con	*klee-mah-tee-zei*	climatisé
bathroom	*lah sahl der bẽ*	la salle de bain
bed	*ler lee*	le lit
clean	*propr*	propre
dark	*sõbr*	sombre
dirty	*sahl*	sale
double bed	*ler lee doobl*	le lit double
electricity	*lei-lehk-tree-see-tei*	l'électricité
excluded	*pah kõ-pree*	pas compris

FRENCH

fan	*ler vā-tee-lah-terr*	le ventilateur
included	*kõ-pree*	compris
key	*lah klei*	la clé
quiet	*ler kahlm*	le calme
sheet	*ler drah*	le drap
shower	*lah doosh*	la douche
swimming pool	*lah pee-seen*	la piscine
toilet	*lah kü-veht*	la cuvette
toilet paper	*ler pah-pyei*	le papier
	ee-zhyei-neek	hygiénique
towel	*ün sehr-vyeht der*	une serviette de
	bĕ	bain
water	*loh*	l'eau
cold water	*loh frwahd*	l'eau froide
hot water	*loh shohd*	l'eau chaude
window	*lah fer-nehtr*	la fenêtre

Around Town

I'm looking for …
  zher shehrsh …   Je cherche …

a bank	*ün bāk*	une banque
the city centre	*ler sãtr veel*	le centre-ville
the … embassy	*lā-bah-sahd der …*	l'ambassade de …
the market	*ler mahr-shei*	le marché
the post office	*ler bü-roh der post*	le bureau de poste
a public toilet	*dei twah-leht*	des toilettes
the telephone	*lei kah-been tei-lei-*	les cabines
exchange	*fo-neek*	téléphoniques
the tourist	*lo-fees der too-reesm/*	l'office de
information office	*ler sĕ-dee-kah*	tourisme/le
	dee-nee-syah-teev	syndicat d'initiative

What time does it open?
kehl ei lerr der
loo-vehr-tür?

Quelle est l'heure
d'ouverture?

What time does it close?
kehl ei lerr der
fehr-mer-tür?

Quelle est l'heure de
fermeture?

What street/suburb is this?
sei kehl rü/kehl kahr-tye?

C'est quelle rue/quel quartier?

At the Bank

What is the exchange rate?
kehl ei ler koor dü dolahr?

Quel est le cours du dollar?

How many francs per dollar?
kõ-byē der frã ler dolahr?

Combien de francs le dollar?

I want to exchange some
money/travellers' cheques.
zher ver shã-zhei der
lahr-zhã/dei shehk der
vwah-yahzh

Je veux changer de l'argent/
des chèques de voyage.

Can I have money transferred
here from my bank?
ehs-ker zher per fehr ee-see
ē veer-mã der mõ kõt ã bāk?

Est-ce que je peux faire ici
un virement de mon compte
en banque?

How long will it take to arrive?
kõ-byē der tã ehs-keel
foh-drah ah-tãdr?

Combien de temps est-ce
qu'il faudra attendre?

Has my money arrived yet?
ehs-ker mõ nahr-zhã ei
tah-ree-vei?

Est-ce que mon argent est
arrivé?

FRENCH

FRENCH

bank notes	*dei bee-yei der bāk*	des billets de banque
cashier	*ler kehs-yei*	le caissier (m)
	lah kehs-yehr	la caissière (f)
coins	*der lah mone/dei pyehs*	de la monnaie/des pièces
credit card	*ün kahrt der krei-dee*	une carte de crédit
exchange	*ler shāzh*	le change
loose change	*der lah per-teet mone*	de la petite monnaie
signature	*lah seen-yah-tür*	la signature

At the Post Office

I'd like to send …

zher voo-drei ā-vwah-yei …   Je voudrais envoyer …

an aerogram	*ē-nah-ei-ro-grahm*	un aérogramme
a letter	*ün lehtr*	une lettre
a postcard	*ün kahrt pos-tahl*	une carte postale
a parcel	*ē ko-lee*	un colis

I would like some stamps.

zher voo-drei dei tēbr   Je voudrais des timbres.

How much does it cost to send this to …?

sei kō-byē poor ē-vwah-yei sei-see ah…?   C'est combien pour envoyer ceci à …?

airmail	*pahr ah-vyō*	par avion
envelope	*ün āv-lop*	une enveloppe
mail box	*ün bwaht oh lehtr*	une boîte aux lettres
post office	*lah pohst*	la poste
registered mail	*ā rer-ko-mā-dei*	en recommandé
surface mail	*pahr vwah tehr-es-trei/pahr vwah mah-ree-teem*	par voie terrestre/par voie maritime

Telephone

I want to ring …
    zher voo-drei ah-plei …
Je voudrais appeler …

The number is …
    ler nü-mei-roh ei …
Le numéro est …

It's engaged.
    la leeny ei to-kü-pei
La ligne est occupée.

I've been cut off.
    noo zah-võ ei-tei koo-pei
Nous avons été coupés.

Hello?
    ah-loh
Allo!

I'd like to speak to Mr Clouseau.
    zher voo-drei pahr-lei ah-vehk mer-syer kloo-soh
Je voudrais parler à Monsieur Clouseau.

I want to speak for three minutes.
    zher ver pahr-lei trwah mee-nüt
Je veux parler trois minutes.

How much does a three-minute call cost?
    kehl ei ler pree dün ko-mü-nee-kah-syõ der trwah mee-nüt?
Quel est le prix d'une communication de trois minutes?

How much is each extra minute?
    kehl ei ler pree der shahk mee-nüt sü-plei-mā-tehr?
Quel est le prix de chaque minute supplémentaire?

I want to make a reverse-charges (collect) call.
    zher ver tei-lei-fo-nei ā pei-sei-vei
Je veux téléphoner en PCV.

FRENCH

Sightseeing

What are the main attractions?
*kehl sō le zā-drwah le plü
zē-tei-rehs-ā?*

Quels sont les endroits les
plus intéressants?

How old is it?
de kō daht-eel?

De quand date-t-il?

Can I take photographs?
*ehs-ker zher per prādr
dei fo-toh?*

Est-ce que je peux prendre
des photos?

What time does it open/close?
*kehl ei lerr doo-vehr-tür/
der fehr-mer-tür?*

Quelle est l'heure
d'ouverture/de fermeture?

ancient	*ā-teek*	antique
archaeological	*ahr-kei-o-lo-zheek*	archéologique
beach	*lah plahzh*	la plage
building	*ler bah-tee-mā*	le bâtiment
castle	*ler shah-toh*	le château
cathedral	*lah kah-tei-drahl*	la cathédrale
church	*lei-gleez*	l'église
concert hall	*lah sahl der kō-sehr*	la salle de concert
library	*lah bee-blyo-tehk*	la bibliothèque
main square	*lah plahs sā-trahl*	la place centrale
monastery	*ler mo-nah-stehr*	le monastère
monument	*ler mo-nü-mā*	le monument
old city	*lah vyehy veel*	la vieille ville
palace	*lei pah-lei*	le palais
opera house	*(ler tei-ahtr der) lo-pei-rah*	(le théâtre de) l'opéra
ruins	*lei rü-ween*	les ruines
stadium	*ler stahd*	le stade
university	*lü-nee-vehr-see-tei*	l'université

Entertainment

What is there to do in the
evenings?

kehs-kõ per fehr ler swahr?   Qu'est-ce qu'on peut faire
                                le soir?

cinema	*ler see-nei-mah*	le cinéma
concert	*ler kõ-sehr*	le concert
theatre	*ler tei-ahtr*	le théâtre

Are there places where you
can hear local music?

ehs-keel-yah dei zẽ-drwah   Est-ce qu'il y a des endroits
oo õ per ei-koo-tei der lah   où on peut écouter de la
mü-seek lo-kahl?   musique locale?

How much is it to get in?

kehl ei ler pree der lã-trei?   Quel est le prix d'entrée?

In the Country
Weather

What's the weather like?

kehl tã feh-teel?   Quel temps fait-il?

The weather is ... today.

eel fei ... oh-zhoor-dwee   Il fait ... aujourd'hui.

Will it be ... tomorrow?

ehs-keel fer-ra ... der-mẽ?   Est-ce qu'il fera ... demain?

It is ...	*eel fei ...*	Il fait ...
cold	*frwah*	froid
foggy	*dü broo-yahr*	du brouillard
hot	*shoh*	chaud
sunny	*boh*	beau
windy	*dü vã*	du vent

FRENCH

It's cloudy.	ler tä ei koo-vehr	Le temps est couvert.
It's frosty.	eel zhehl	Il gèle.
It's raining.	eel pler	Il pleut.
It's snowing.	eel nehzh	Il neige.

Camping

Am I allowed to camp here?
| ehs-ker zher per kä-pei ee-see? | Est-ce que je peux camper ici? |

Is there a campsite nearby?
| ehs-keel-yah ē kä-peeng preh dee-see | Est-ce qu'il y a un camping près d'ici? |

backpack	ler sah-kah-doh	le sac-à-dos
can opener	loovr bwaht	l'ouvre-boîtes
compass	lah boo-sol	la boussole
crampons	lei krä-pō	les crampons
firewood	ler bwah ah brü-lei	le bois à brûler
gas cartridge	lah kahr-toosh ah gahz	la cartouche à gaz
hammock	ler ah-mahk	le hamac
ice axe	ler pyo-lei	le piolet
mattress	ler maht-lah	le matelas
penknife	ler kah-neef	le canif
rope	lah kord	la corde
tent	lah tät	la tente
tent pegs	lei pee-kei der tät	les piquets de tente
torch (flashlight)	lah läp der posh	la lampe de poche
sleeping bag	ler sahk der koo-shahzh	le sac de couchage
stove	ler rei-shoh	le réchaud
water bottle	lah goord	la gourde

Food

breakfast	*ler per-tee dei-zher-nei*	le petit déjeuner
lunch	*ler dei-zher-nei*	le déjeuner
dinner	*ler dee-nei*	le dîner

Eating Out

Table for ..., please.
ün tahbl poor ... pehr-son, seel voo plei

Une table pour ... personnes, s'il vous plaît.

Can I see the menu please?
ehs-ker zher per vwahr lah kahrt?

Est-ce que je peux voir la carte?

I'd like the set lunch, please.
zher prã ler mer-nü

Je prends le menu.

What does it include?
kehs-ker sah kõ-prã?

Qu'est-ce que ça comprend?

Is service included in the bill?
ehs-ker ler sehr-vees ei kõ-pree?

Est-ce que le service est compris?

an ashtray	*ẽ sã-drye*	un cendrier
the bill	*lah-dee-syõ*	l'addition
a cup	*ün tahs*	une tasse
dessert	*ler de-sehr*	le dessert
a drink	*ün bwah-sõ*	une boisson
a fork	*ün foor-sheht*	une fourchette
a glass	*ẽ vehr*	un verre
a knife	*ẽ koo-toh*	un couteau
a plate	*ẽ plah*	un plat
a spoon	*ün kwee-yehr*	une cuillère
toothpick	*ẽ kür dã*	un cure-dent

FRENCH

Making Your Own Meal

For some key essentials for sandwich-making, etc, see page 134.

Vegetarian Meals

I am a vegetarian.
zher swee vei-zhei-tahr-yē/
vei-zhei-tahr-yehn
Je suis végétarien (m)/
végétarienne (f).

I don't eat meat.
zher ner māzh pah der vyād
Je ne mange pas de viande.

I don't eat chicken, fish or ham.
zher ner māzh pah der
poo-lei, der pwah-sõ oo der
zhã-bõ
Je ne mange pas de poulet,
de poisson ou de jambon.

Breakfast

breakfast cereal
a hard-boiled egg
bread, butter, jam

Petit Dejeuner

des céréales
un oeuf dur
du pain, du beurre, de la
confiture

Snacks

Casse-croûtes

un cornet de frites
A paper cone of chips.

une crêpe au sucre/au citron/au miel/à la confiture
Thin pancake with sugar/with lemon/with honey/with jam.

un croque-madame
Grilled cheese-and-ham sandwich with a fried egg.

un croque-monsieur
Grilled cheese-and-ham sandwich.

marrons chauds
Roast chestnuts.

un sandwich au fromage/jambon
A cheese/ham sandwich.

FRENCH

In the Delicatessen

bean salad
cheese
gherkins
ham
mayonnaise
liver/rabbit/farmhouse pâté

potted meat (pork or goose)
Russian salad
a carton
a portion
a slice

Á la Charcuterie

des haricots en salade
du fromage
des cornichons
du jambon
de la mayonnaise
du pâté de foie/de lapin/de campagne
des rillettes
de la salade russe
une barquette
une part
une tranche

Starters

anchovies
artichoke hearts
clear soup
hard-boiled egg with mayonnaise
hearts of palm
Marseillais fish soup
mussels with shallots in white-wine sauce
oysters
raw vegetables with dressings
scallops
shellfish soup
snails
thick soup, usually vegetable

Hors d'Œuvres/ Entrées

anchois
coeurs d'artichaut
consommé

oeuf mayonnaise
coeurs de palmier
bouillabaisse
moules marinières

huîtres
crudités
coquilles Saint-Jacques
bisque
escargots
potage

FRENCH

Meat & Poultry

chicken	*poulet*
duck	*canard*
mutton	*mouton*
rabbit	*lapin*
ribsteak	*entrecôte*
sausage made of intestines	*andouille*
sirloin roast	*contrefilet*
sirloin steak	*faux filet*
spicy red sausage	*merguez*
thick slices of fillet	*tournedos*
tripe	*tripes*
turkey	*dinde, dindon, dindonneau*
veal	*veau*

Viandes et Volailles

Seafood

bream	*brème*
clams	*palourdes*
eels	*anguilles*
fresh cod	*cabillaud*
herring	*hareng*
John Dory	*Saint-Pierre*
king prawns	*gambas*
lobster	*homard*
mackerel	*maquereau*
octopus	*poulpe*
prawns	*crevettes roses*
salmon	*saumon*
salt cod	*morue*
sea bream	*daurade*
shrimps	*crevettes grises*

Fruits de Mer

FRENCH

squid	*calmar*
spiny lobster	*langouste*
trout	*truite*
tuna	*thon*

Vegetables

Légumes

asparagus	*asperges*
avocado	*avocat*
broad beans	*fèves*
cabbage	*chou*
cauliflower	*chou-fleur*
chickpeas	*pois chiches*
corn	*maïs*
cucumber	*concombre*
dwarf kidney beans	*flageolets*
french or string beans	*haricots verts*
garlic	*ail*
gherkin	*cornichon*
leek	*poireau*
lettuce	*laitue*
mushrooms	*champignons*
onion	*oignon*
peas	*petits pois*
potato	*pomme de terre*
pumpkin	*citrouille*
radish	*radis*
rice	*riz*
spinach	*épinards*
sweet pepper or capsicum	*poivron*
truffles	*truffes*

FRENCH

Fruit & Nuts

almonds	*amandes*
apple	*pomme*
cherries	*cerises*
chestnuts	*marrons*
grapefruit	*pamplemousse*
grapes	*raisins*
greengages (kind of plum)	*mirabelles*
hazelnuts	*noisettes*
peach	*pêche*
peanuts	*cacahouètes*
pear	*poire*
plum	*prune*
raspberries	*framboises*
strawberries	*fraises*
walnuts	*noix*
watermelon	*pastèque*

Typical Dishes   Plats Typiques

boeuf bourgignon	Beef stew with burgundy, onions and mushrooms.
cassoulet	Casserole of beans and meat (often goose).
choucroute	Pickled cabbage with sausages, bacon and salami.
coq au vin	Chicken cooked with wine, onions and mushrooms.
poulet roti	Roast chicken.
ratatouille	Eggplant, zucchini, tomato and garlic dish.
steak au poivre	Steak with pepper sauce.
steak frites	Steak with chips.
steak tartare	Raw chopped beef, raw onion and egg yolk.

FRENCH

Sample Menu One

An average menu from Toulouse: *Une entrée, une viande, une boisson* – an entrée, a meat dish, and a drink.

Entrées

confit de canard
  Conserve of duck.
terrine de poisson
  Fish pâté.
salade multicolore au basilic
  Salad with peppers, tomatoes, radishes, cucumber, egg, corn and basil.
salade au bleu
  Salad with blue cheese and walnuts.
salade crudité
  Raw vegetable salad.

Main Dishes

andouillette sauce au poivre
  Tripe sausage with pepper sauce.
brochette de coeurs
  Heart kebab.
entrecôte grillée, sauce au bleu ou au poivre
  Grilled rib steak with blue cheese or pepper sauce.
cotriade
  Fillet of fish with seafood and a saffron sauce.
brochette de volailles au citron
  Poultry kebab with lemon.
tagliatelles Bolognaise ou au bleu
  Tagliatelli with bolognese or blue cheese sauce.
¼ *de vin compris*
  A quarter of a litre of wine included.

FRENCH

Sample Menu Two

A typical budget Parisian menu:

un kir	Blackcurrant juice and white wine.
hors d'oeuvres à volonté	A choice of entrées.
plat au choix	A choice of the following main courses:
pavé grillé	A thick steak, grilled.
côte d'agneau	Lamb cutlet.
truite aux amandes	Trout with almonds.
brochettes mixtes	Kebabs.
fromage ou dessert	Cheese or dessert.
vin compris	(Table) wine included.

Sample Menu Three

A more expensive Parisian menu:

Entrées

concombre à la crème – ciboulette
  Cucumber with cream and chives.
salade de tomates – basilic, huile vierge
  Tomato salad with basil and virgin olive oil.
suchi de poisson cru – sur lit de soja croquant
  Raw fish sushi on a bed of crunchy soya bean sprouts.
fromage blanc battu aux fines herbes
  Cream cheese blended with sweet herbs.
méli-mélo de légumes vapeur
  Mixed steamed vegetables.
boudin antillais – feuille de chêne, des pommes de terre en robe des champs
  West-Indian sausage with lettuce and hot potatoes in their jackets.

Main Courses

filets de rascasse grillés aux tagliatelles safranées
  Grilled fillets of scorpion fish with tagliatelli seasoned with saffron.

emincé de haddock fumé, pommes mousselines
  Slivers of smoked haddock with mashed potatoes.

moelleux de porc au curry, riz sauvage
  Tender pork curry with wild rice.

demi canette rôtie, pommes château
  Half a roast duckling with quartered potatoes sautéed in butter.

emincé de poulet mariné, aux grains de coriandre en salade
  Slivers of marinated chicken with coriander seeds and salad.

Desserts

charlotte	Custard and fruit in lining of almond fingers.
clafoutis	Fruit tart, usually with berries.
fromage blanc	Cream cheese.
glace	Ice cream.
île flottante, crème vanille	Soft meringues floating on custard with vanilla cream.
mousse au chocolat, crème anglaise	Chocolate mousse with custard.
parfait	Frozen mousse.
poires Belle Hélène	Pears and ice-cream in a chocolate sauce.
sorbet aux choix	A choice of sorbets.
tarte aux pommes fines	Apple tart.

FRENCH

Drinks – Nonalcoholic

a short black coffee	*un café*
a large/small milk coffee	*un grand/petit crème*
a grapefruit juice	*un jus de pamplemousee*
an orange juice	*un jus d'orange*
a cup of tea	*un thé*
lemon/white tea	*thé au citron/au lait*

Drinks – Alcoholic
Pre-dinner Drinks — *Apéritifs*

blackcurrant juice and white wine	*kir*
blackcurrant juice and champagne	*kir royal*
aniseed liqueur, served with water	*pastis*
beer mixed with a sweet liqueur	*picon bière*
cognac and grape juice	*pineau*
fermented gentian	*suze*

Wines — *Vins*

dry	*sec*
mature and sparkling	*méthode champenoise*
red	*rouge*
sparkling	*mousseux*
sweet	*demi-sec*
table wine	*vin de table/vin ordinaire*
very dry	*brut*
very sweet	*doux*
white	*blanc*

Shopping

bookshop	*ün lee-breh-ree*	une librairie
camera shop	*ē mah-gah-zē der fo-to*	un magasin de photo
delicatessen	*ün shahr-kü-tree*	une charcuterie
general store, shop	*ē mah-gah-zē dah-lee-mā-tah-syō zhei-nei-rahl*	un magasin d'alimentation générale
laundry	*ün blā-shees-ree*	une blanchisserie
market	*ē mahr-shei*	un marché
newsagency/ stationers	*ün pah-pei-tree*	une papeterie
supermarket	*ē sü-pehr-mahr-shei*	un supermarché
vegetable shop	*ē mahr-shā der lei-güm*	un marchand de légumes

How much is it?
sei kō-byē?
C'est combien ?

I would like to buy …
zher voo-drei …
Je voudrais …

Do you have others?
ehs-ker voo zā nah-vei dohtr?
Est-ce que vous en avez d'autres?

I don't like it.
sah ner mer plei pah
Ca ne me plaît pas.

Can I look at it?
ehs-ker zher per ler/lah vwahr?
Est-ce que je peux le/la voir?

I'm just looking.
zher ner fei ker rer-gahr-dei
Je ne fais que regarder.

FRENCH

Can you write down the price?
ehs-ker voo poo-vei
ei-kreer ler pree?

Est-ce que vous pouvez
écrire le prix?

Do you accept credit cards?
ehs-ker zher per peh-yei
ah-vehk mah kahrt der
krei-dee?

Est-ce je peux payer avec
ma carte de crédit?

Could you lower the price?
voo ner poo-vei pah bei-sei
ler pree?

Vous ne pouvez pas baisser
le prix?

You May Hear

Can I help you?
zher per voo zei-dei?

Je peux vouz aider?

Will that be all?
ohtr shohz?

Autre chose?

Sorry, this is the only one.
dei-zo-lei eel-nyah ker
ser-lwee see/sehl see

Désolé/-ée, il n'y a que
celui-ci (m)/celle-ci (f).

How many do you want?
voo zã dei-zee-rei kõ-byẽ?

Vous en désirez combien?

Essential Groceries

batteries	*dei bah-tair-ee*	des batteries
bread	*dü pã*	du pain
butter	*dü ber*	du beurre
cereal	*der lah sei-rei-ahl*	de la céréale
cheese	*dü froh-mahzh*	du fromage
chocolate	*dü shok-oh-lah*	du chocolat
coffee	*dü kah-fei*	du café
gas cylinder	*lah kahr-toosh*	la cartouche à gaz
	ah gahz	

FRENCH

matches	*deiz ah-lü-met*	des allumettes
milk	*dü lei*	du lai
mineral water	*der loh mee-nei-rahl*	de l'eau minérale
fruit	*dei frü-ee*	des fruits
shampoo	*dü shāp-wē*	du shampooing
soap	*dü sah-vō*	du savon
sugar	*dü sükr*	du sucre
tea	*dü tei*	du thé
toilet paper	*dü pah-pyei*	du papier
	ee-zhyei-neek	hygiénique
toothpaste	*dü dā-tee-frees*	du dentifrice
washing powder	*lah les-eev*	la lessive
yoghurt	*yah-oot*	yaourt

Souvenirs

earrings	*dei bookl do-rehy*	des boucles
		d'oreilles
handicraft	*dei zob-zhei*	des objets
	ahr-teez-ah-noh	artisanaux
jewellery	*der lah bee-zhoo-tree*	de la bijouterie
lace	*der lah dā-tehl*	de la dentelle
miniature statue	*ün stah-tweht*	une statuette
necklace	*ē ko-lyei*	un collier
poster	*ē pos-tehr*	un poster
pottery	*dei po-tree*	des poteries
ring	*ün bahg*	une bague
rug	*ē per-tee tah-pee/ün*	un petit tapis/une
	kahr-peht	carpette

Clothing — **Vêtements**

| coat | *ē mā-toh* | un manteau |
| jacket | *ün vehst* | une veste |

jumper (sweater)	*ē pü-lo-verr*	un pullover
shoes	*de shoh-sür*	des chaussures
trousers	*ē pā-tah-lō*	un pantalon

It is too ...	*sei troh ...*	C'est trop ...
big	*grā/grād*	grand(e)
small	*per-tee/per-teet*	petit(e)

Toiletries

condoms	*dei prei-zehr-vah-teef*	des préservatifs
deodorant	*ē dei-o-do-rā*	un déodorant
hairbrush	*ün bros ah sher-ver*	une brosse à cheveux
razor	*ē rahz-wahr*	un rasoir
sanitary napkins	*dei sehr-vyeht ee-zhyei-neek*	des serviettes hygiéniques
shampoo	*dü shāp-wē*	du shampooing
shaving cream	*der lah moos ah rah-zei*	de la mousse à raser
soap	*dü sah-vō*	du savon
sunblock cream	*der la krehm oht pro-tehk-syō*	de la crème haute protection
tampons	*dei tāpō ee-zhyei-neek*	des tampons hygiéniques
tissues	*dei moo-shwahr ā pah-pyei*	des mouchoirs en papier
toilet paper	*dü pah-pyei ee-zhyei-neek*	du papier hygiénique
toothbrush	*ün bros ah dā*	une brosse à dents
toothpaste	*dü dā-tee-frees*	du dentifrice

Photography

How much is it to process this film?

kō-byē koo-trah ler deiv-lop-mā der ser feelm?

Combien coûtera le développement de ce film?

When will it be ready?

kā teh-sker ser-lah ser-rah preh?

Quand est-ce que cela sera prêt?

I'd like a film for this camera.

zher voo-drei ē feelm poor seht ah-pah-rehy der fo-toh

Je voudrais un film pour cet appareil de photo.

B&W (film)	*nwahr ei blā*	noir et blanc
camera	*ē nah-pah-rehy der fo-toh*	un appareil de photo
colour (film)	*koo-lerr*	couleurs
film	*ē feelm*	un film
flash	*ē flahsh*	un flash
lens	*ē nob-zhehk-teef*	un objectif
light meter	*ē pohz-mehtr*	un posemètre

FRENCH

Smoking

A packet of cigarettes, please.

ē pah-ket der see-gah-reht seel voo plei

Un paquet de cigarettes, s'il vous plaît.

Are these cigarettes strong/mild?

ehs-ker sei see-gah-reht sō fort/lei-zehr?

Est-ce que ces cigarettes sont fortes/légères?

Do you have a light?

voo zah-ve dü fer?

Vous avez du feu?

Do you mind if I smoke?
sah voo dei-rāzh see zher füm? — Ça vous dérange si je fume.

Please don't smoke.
voi-ei der ner pah fümei — Veuillez de ne pas fumer.

cigarettes	*dei see-gah-reht*	des cigarettes
cigarette papers	*dei pah-pyei ah see-gah-reht*	des papiers à cigarettes
filtered	*a-vehk feeltr*	avec filtre
lighter	*ē bree-kei*	un briquet
matches	*dei zah-lü-meht*	des allumettes
menthol	*mā-to-lei*	mentholées
pipe	*ün peep*	une pipe
tobacco (pipe)	*dü tah-bah (poor lah peep)*	du tabac (pour la pipe)

Health

Where is …? *oo ei …?* — Où est …?

the doctor	*ler meid-sē*	le médecin
the hospital	*lo-pee-tahl*	l'hôpital
the chemist	*ler fahr-mah-syē*	le pharmacien
the dentist	*ler dā-teest*	le dentiste

I am sick.
zher swee mah-lahd — Je suis malade.

My friend is ill.
mō nah-mee ei mah-lahd — Mon ami/-e est malade.

What's the matter?
kehs-keel-ya/kehs-kee ner vah pah? — Qu'est-ce qu'il y a/Qu'est-ce qui ne va pas?

FRENCH

My ... hurts.
   mō/mah ... mer fei mahl   Mon (m)/Ma (f) ... me fait mal.

Parts of the Body

arm	*brah*	bras
back	*doh*	dos
ear	*o-rehy*	oreille
eye	*er-y*	oeil
foot	*pyei*	pied
hand	*mē*	main
head	*teht*	tête
heart	*kerr*	coeur
leg	*zhāb*	jambe
nose	*nei*	nez
skin	*poh*	peau
stomach	*ehs-to-mah*	estomac
teeth	*dā*	dents

Ailments

I have ...	*zhei ...*	J'ai ...
an allergy	*ün ah-lehr-zhee*	une allergie
a burn	*ün brü-lür*	une brûlure
a cough	*ün too*	une toux
diarrhoea	*lah dyah-rei*	la diarrhée
fever	*der lah fyehvr*	de la fièvre
glandular fever	*la mo-no-nü-klei-ohz ē-fehk-syerz*	la mononucléose infectieuse
a headache	*mahl ah lah teht*	mal à la tête
hepatitis	*lei-pah-teet*	l'hépatite
indigestion	*ün ē-dee-zhehs-tyō*	une indigestion
an infection	*ün ē-fehk-syō*	une infection

FRENCH

influenza	*lah greep*	la grippe
nausea	*lah noh-zei*	la nausée
a pain	*ün doo-lerr*	une douleur
sore throat	*mahl ah lah gorzh*	mal à la gorge
a stomachache	*mahl oh vãtr*	mal au ventre
a venereal disease	*ün mah-lah-dee vei-nei-ryehn*	une maladie vénérienne

I have a cold.
zher swee ã-rü-mei　　Je suis enrhumé/-ée.

I have constipation.
zher swee kõ-stee-pei　　Je suis constipé/-ée.

I have a sprain.
zher mer swee fei ün ã-tors　　Je me suis fait une entorse.

I have sunburn.
zhei pree ē koo der so-lehy　　J'ai pris un coup de soleil.

Women's Health

Could I see a female doctor?
ehs-ker zher per vwahr ün fahm meid-sē/ün dok-tor-es?　　Est-ce que je peux voir une femme médecin/une doctoresse?

I'm pregnant.
zher swee ã-sēt　　Je suis enceinte.

I'm on the pill.
zher prã lah pee-lül　　Je prends la pilule.

I haven't had my period for … weeks.
zher nei pah ü mei rehgl der-pwee … ser-mehn　　Je n'ai pas eu mes règles depuis … semaines.

FRENCH

(unusual) bleeding
sen-nyer-mã ã der-or dü seekl
saignements (en dehors du cycle)

cramps	*krãm*	crampes
cystitis	*sees-teet*	cystite
thrush	*mü-gü-ei*	muguet

Specific Needs

I'm …	*zher swee …*	Je suis …
anaemic	*ah-nei-meek*	anémique
asthmatic	*ah-smah-teek*	ashtmatique
diabetic	*dyah-bei-teek*	diabétique
epileptic	*ei-pee-lehp-teek*	épileptique

I have low/high blood pressure.
zher fei der lee-pehr-tã-syõ/ lee-poh-tã-syõ
Je fais de l'hypertension/ l'hypotension.

I'm allergic to antibiotics/ penicillin
zher swee ah-lehr-zheek oh zã-tee-byo-teek/ah lah pei-nee-see-leen
Je suis allergique aux anti-biotiques/à la pénicilline

I have been vaccinated.
zher mer swee fei vahk-see-nei
Je me suis fait vacciné/-ée.

I have my own syringe.
zhei mah propr serrẽg
J'ai ma propre seringue.

Useful Words & Phrases

I feel better/worse.
zher mer sã myer/plü mahl
Je me sens mieux/plus mal.

accident	*ē nahk-see-dā*	un accident
addiction	*lah dei-pā-dās/lah tok-see-ko-mah-nee*	la dépendance/la toxicomanie
antibiotics	*dei zā-tee-byo-teek*	des antibiotiques
antiseptic	*der lā-tee-sehp-teek*	de l'antiseptique
bite	*ün mor-sür*	une morsure
blood test	*ü-nah-nah-leez der sā*	une analyse de sang
contraceptive	*ē kõ-trah-sehp-teef*	un contraceptif
injection	*ün nē-zhehk-syõ/ün pee-kür*	une injection/une piqûre
vitamins	*dei vee-tah-meen*	des vitamines

At the Chemist

I need medication for …
  zhei ber-zwē dē mei-dee-kah-mã poor …
J'ai besoin d'un médicament pour …

I have a prescription.
  zhei ün or-do-nãs
J'ai une ordonnance.

At the Dentist

I have a toothache.
  zhei mahl oh dã
J'ai mal aux dents.

I've lost a filling.
  zhei pehr-dü ē plõ-bahzh
J'ai perdu un plombage.

I've broken a tooth.
  zher mer swee kah-sei ün dã
Je me suis cassé une dent.

I don't want it extracted.
  zher ner ver pah ker voo lah-rah-shye
Je ne veux pas que vous l'arrachiez.

Please give me an anaesthetic.
  ah-vehk ah-nehs-tei-zee seel voo plei
Avec anesthésie, s'il vous plaît.

Time & Dates

Note that the French normally use the 24-hour clock.

What time is it?	*kehl err ei teel?*	Quelle heure est-il?

It is ...	*eel ei ... err*	Il est ... heures.
in the morning	*dü mah-tē*	du matin
in the afternoon	*der lah-preh mee-dee*	de l'après midi
in the evening	*dü swahr*	du soir

What date is it today?	Nous sommes quel jour
noo som kehl zhoor	aujourd'hui?
oh-zhoor-dwee?	

Days of the Week

Monday	*lē-dee*	lundi
Tuesday	*mahr-dee*	mardi
Wednesday	*mehr-krer-dee*	mercredi
Thursday	*zher-dee*	jeudi
Friday	*vā-drer-dee*	vendredi
Saturday	*sahm-dee*	samedi
Sunday	*dee-māsh*	dimanche

FRENCH

Months

January	*zhā-vye*	janvier
February	*feiv-rye*	février
March	*mahrs*	mars
April	*ah-vreel*	avril
May	*meh*	mai
June	*zhwē*	juin
July	*zhwee-yeh*	juillet

August	*oo(t)*	août
September	*sehp-tābr*	septembre
October	*ok-tobr*	octobre
November	*no-vābr*	novembre
December	*dei-sābr*	décembre

Seasons

summer	*lei-tei*	l'été
autumn	*lo-ton*	l'automne
winter	*lee-vehr*	l'hiver
spring	*ler prē-tã*	le printemps

Present

today	*oh-zhoor-dwee*	aujourd'hui
this morning	*ser mah-tē*	ce matin
tonight	*ser swahr*	ce soir
this week/year	*seht ser-mehn/ah-nei*	cette semaine/année
now	*mēt-nã*	maintenant

Past

yesterday	*yehr*	hier
day before yesterday	*ah-vã tyehr*	avant-hier
yesterday morning	*yehr mah-tē*	hier matin
last night	*yehr swahr*	hier soir
last week/year	*lah-nei/lah ser-mehn dehr-nyehr*	l'année/la semaine dernière

Future

| tomorrow | *der-mē* | demain |
| day after tomorrow | *ah-preh der-mē* | après-demain |

FRENCH

tomorrow morning	*der-mē mah-tē*	demain matin
tomorrow after-noon/evening	*der-mē ah-preh mee-dee/swahr*	demain après midi/soir
next week	*lah ser-mehn proshehn*	la semaine prochaine
next year	*lah-nei pro-shehn*	l'année prochaine

During the Day

afternoon	*lah-preh mee-dee*	l'après-midi
dawn, very early morning	*lohb*	l'aube
day	*ler zhoor*	le jour
early	*toh*	tôt
midnight	*meen-wee*	minuit
morning	*ler mah-tē*	le matin
night	*lah nwee*	la nuit
noon	*mee-dee*	midi
sundown	*ler koo-shei dü so-lehy*	le coucher du soleil
sunrise	*ler ler-vei dü so-lehy*	le lever du soleil

FRENCH

Numbers & Amounts

0	*zeiroh*	zéro
1	*ē*	un
2	*der*	deux
3	*trwah*	trois
4	*kahtr*	quatre
5	*sēk*	cinq
6	*sees*	six
7	*seht*	sept

8	*weet*	huit
9	*nerf*	neuf
10	*dees*	dix
11	*õz*	onze
12	*dooz*	douze
13	*trehz*	treize
14	*kah-torz*	quatorze
15	*kēz*	quinze
16	*sehz*	seize
17	*dee-seht*	dix-sept
18	*dee-zweet*	dix-huit
19	*deez-nerf*	dix-neuf
20	*vē*	vingt
21	*vē tei ē*	vingt et un
22	*vē der*	vingt-deux
30	*trāt*	trente
40	*kah-rāt*	quarante
50	*sē-kāt*	cinquante
60	*swah-sāt*	soixante
70	*swah-sāt dees*	soixante-dix
80	*kahtr vē*	quatre-vingts
90	*kahtr vē dees*	quatre-vingt-dix
100	*sā*	cent
1000	*meel*	mille
one million	*ē mee-lyō*	un million

1st	*prer-myei*	premier (m) (1er)
	prer-myehr	première (f) (1ère)
2nd	*ser-gō/ser-gōd*	second/-e (2e)
	der-zyehm	deuxième
3rd	*trwah-zyehm*	troisième (3e)

¼	*ē kahr*	un quart
⅓	*ē tyehr*	un tiers
½	*ē der-mee*	un demi
¾	*trwah kahr*	trois quarts

Amounts

small	*per-tee/per-teet*	petit/-e
big	*grā/grād*	grand/-e
a little (amount)	*ē per*	un peu
double	*doobl*	double
a dozen	*ün doo-zehn*	une douzaine
Enough!	*ah-se!*	Assez!
few	*per der/kehl-ker*	peu de/quelques
less	*mwē*	moins
many	*boh-koo der*	beaucoup de
too much/many	*troh*	trop
more	*plü*	plus
once	*ün fwah*	une fois
a pair	*ün pehr*	une paire
percent	*poor sā*	pour cent
some	*dü/der lah/de*	du/de la/des
too much	*troh*	trop
twice	*der fwah*	deux fois

Abbreviations

ap. J.-C./av. J.-C.	AD/BC
la CGT	association of French trade unions
HLM	public housing flats
M/Mme/Mlle	Mr/Mrs/Ms
le PC	the Communist Party
le PS	the Socialist Party

PTT	on post boxes and post offices
RER	system of trains serving the outer suburbs of Paris
Rte/Av	Rd/Av
le SIDA	AIDS
TTC	all inclusive

Paperwork

name	nom et prénom
address	adresse
date of birth	date de naissance
place of birth	lieu de naissance
age	âge
sex	sexe
nationality	nationalité
religion	confession
reason for travel	raison du voyage
profession	métier
marital status	situation de famille
passport	passeport
passport number	numéro de passeport
visa	visa
identification	pièce d'identité
birth certificate	extrait de naissance
driver's licence	permis de conduire
car owner's title	titre de propriété d'une voiture
car registration	carte grise
customs	douane
immigration	immigration
border	frontière

FRENCH

Emergencies

POLICE STATION	*(COMMISSARIAT DE) POLICE*

Help!   *oh ser-coor!*   Au secours!
Go away!   *lei-sei mwah trã-keel!*   Laissez-moi tranquille!
Thief!   *oh vo-lerr!*   Au voleur!

There's been an accident!
    eel-yah ü ē nak-see-dā!   Il y a eu un accident!
Call an ambulance/doctor!
    ah-plei ün ã-bü-lãs/ē
    meid-sē!   Appelez une ambulance/un
    médecin!
I've been raped.
    zhei ei-tei vyo-lei   J'ai été violée.
Call the police!
    ah-plei lah po-lees!   Appelez la police!
Where is the police station?
    oo ei ler ko-mee-sahr-yah
    der po-lees?   Où est le commissariat de
    police?
I've been robbed!
    zhei ei-tei volei!   J'ai été volé/-ée!
I am ill.
    zher swee mah-lahd   Je suis malade.
I am lost.
    zher mer swee ei-gah-rei   Je me suis égaré/-ée.
Where are the toilets?
    oo sõ lei twah-leht?   Où sont les toilettes?
Could you help me please?
    eh-sker voo poo-ryei
    mei-dei seel voo plei?   Est-ce que vous pourriez
    m'aider, s'il vous plaît?

FRENCH

Could I please use the telephone?
eh-sker zher poo-rei
ü-tee-lee-zei ler tei-lei-fon?
Est-ce que je pourrais
utiliser le téléphone?

I'm sorry. I apologise.
zher swee dei-zo-lei
zher mehk-süz
Je suis désolé/-ée.
Je m'excuse.

I didn't realise I was doing
anything wrong.
zher nei sah-vei pah ker
zhah-vei tor der ler fehr
Je ne savais pas que j'avais
tort de le faire.

I didn't do it.
ser nei pah mwah kee lay fei
Ce n'est pas moi qui l'ai fait.

I wish to contact my embassy/
consulate.
zher ver ah-pe-lay
lā-bah-sahd/ler kõ-sü-lah
Je veux apeler
l'Ambassade/le Consulat.

I speak English.
zher pahrl ã-glei
Je parle anglais.

I have medical insurance.
zhei der lah-sü-rãs
mah-lah-dee
J'ai une assurance maladie.

My possessions are insured.
mei byẽ sõ tah-sü-rei
Mes biens sont assurés.

I've lost ...	*zhei pehrdü ...*	J'ai perdu ...
my bags	*mei bah-gahzh*	mes bagages
my handbag	*mõ sahk ah mẽ*	mon sac à main
my money	*mõ nahr-zhã*	mon argent
my travellers' cheques	*mei shehk der vwah-yahzh*	mes cheques de voyage
my passport	*mõ pahs-por*	mon passeport

GERMAN

GERMAN

German

Introduction

It might be a surprise to know that German is, in fact, a close relative of English. English, German and Dutch are all known as West Germanic languages. It means that you know lots of German words already – *Arm*, *Finger*, *Gold* – and you'll be able to figure out many others – *Mutter* (mother), *trinken* (drink), *gut* (good). A primary reason why English and German have grown apart is that the Normans, on invading England in 1066, brought with them a large number of non-Germanic words. This has meant that English has lots of synonyms, with the more basic word being Germanic, and the more literary or specialised one coming from French; for instance, 'start' and 'green' as opposed to 'commence' and 'verdant'.

German grammar is often described as difficult – it is often cited that there are many different ways to say 'the', and that words have 'lots of endings'. However, most of these concepts that seem so alien actually have remnants in English. German also has the advantage of being comparatively easy to pronounce. It is beyond the scope of this book to outline how to put your own sentences together from scratch, but there are many examples of model sentences where you can choose the key word you want: for instance 'It is too … (big/small/ short/long)'.

German is spoken throughout Germany and Austria, and in most of Switzerland. It is also extremely useful in Eastern Europe, especially with older people. Although you may hear different dialects, there is a strong tradition of a prescribed official language, used in this book, which will always be understood. In some tourist centres English is so widely spoken that you may not have a chance to use German, even if you want to! However, as soon as you try to meet ordinary people or move out of the big cities, especially in what was East Germany, the situation is totally different. Your efforts to speak the local language will be very much appreciated and will make your trip much more enjoyable and fulfilling.

One distinctive feature of German is that all nouns are written with a capital letter. The language has a fairly complicated grammar involving gender, whereby words are given masculine, feminine or neuter forms. In this chapter, the feminine form is given first, the masculine second.

Pronunciation

German is a relatively 'phonetic' language; that is, its spelling isn't as weird as English! You can almost always tell how a word is pronounced by the way it's spelt. Some letters can be pronounced several ways, but you can normally tell which way to use from the context.

Unlike English or French, German does not have silent letters: you pronounce the **k** at the start of the word *Knie*, 'knee', the **p** at the start of *Psychologie*, 'psychology', and the **e** at the end of *ich habe*, 'I have'.

Vowels

As in English, vowels can be pronounced long (like the 'o' in 'pope') or short (like the 'o' in 'pop'). As a rule, German vowels are long before one consonant and short before two consonants: the **o** is long in the word *Dom*, 'cathedral', but short in the word *doch*, 'after all'.

Letter/s	Pronunciation Guide	Sounds
a	*ah*	short, as the 'u' sound in 'cut'
	aa	long, as in 'father'
au	*ow*	as in 'vow'
ä	*a*	short, as in 'act'
	air	long, as in 'hair'
äu	*oy*	as in 'boy'
e	*eh*	short, as the 'e' in 'bet'
	eh	short, as in 'bet'
	ay	long, as in 'day'
ei	*ai*	as the 'ai' in 'aisle'
	oy	as in 'boy'
eu	*oy*	as in 'boy'
i	*ee*	long, as in 'see'
i	*i*	short, as in 'in'
ie	*ee*	as in 'see'
o	*oh*	long, as in 'note'
	o	short, as in 'pot'
ö	*er*	halfway between 'er' in 'fern' and 'o' in 'hope'
u	*u*	as the 'u' in 'pull'
ü	*ü*	like the 'u' in 'pull' but with stretched lips

Consonants

Most German consonants sound similar to their English counterparts. One important difference is that **b, d** and **g** sound like 'p', 't' and 'k', respectively, at the end of a word.

GERMAN

Letter/s	Pronunciation Guide	Sounds
b	*b/p*	normally the English 'b', but 'p' at end of a word
ch	*kh*	as *ch* in the Scottish *loch*
d	*d/t*	normally as the English 'd', but 't' at end of a word
g	*gh/k/ch*	normally as the hard English 'g', but 'k' at the end of a word and *ch*, like Scottish *loch,* at the end of a word and after **i**
j	*y*	as the 'y' in 'yet'
qu	*kv*	'k' plus 'v'
r	*r*	as the English 'r', but rolled at the back of the mouth
s	*s/z*	normally as the 's' in 'sun'; as the 'z' in 'zoo' when followed by a vowel
sch	*sh*	as the 'sh' in 'ship'
sp, st	*shp/sht*	at the start of a word like 'sh' in 'ship'
tion	*tsiohn*	the **t** sounds like the 'ts' in 'hits'
ß	*s*	as in 'sun' (in some books, written as **ss**)
v	*f*	as the 'f' in 'fan'
w	*v*	as the 'v' in 'van'
z	*ts*	as the 'ts' in 'hits'

GERMAN

Stress

Stressed syllables are highlighted in bold in the pronunciation guide. However, stress in German is very straightforward; the overwhelming majority of German words are stressed on the first syllable. Some prefixes are not stressed (such as *besetzt* is stressed on the *setzt*); and certain foreign words, especially from French, are stressed on the last syllable (*Organisation, Appetit*).

Greetings & Civilities
Top Useful Phrases

Hello. (Good day)	*ghu-tehn taak*	Guten Tag.
Goodbye.	*owf vee-dehr-zayn*	Auf Wiedersehen.
Yes/No.	*yaa/nain*	Ja/Nein.
Excuse me.	*ehnt-**shul**-di-ghung*	Entschuldigung.
Please.	*bi-teh*	Bitte.
Thank you.	*dahng-keh*	Danke.
Many thanks.	*fee-lehn dahngk*	Vielen Dank.
That's fine/ You're welcome.	*bi-teh zayr*	Bitte sehr.

May I? Do you mind?		
dahrf ikh?/makht ehs ee-nehn eht-vahs ows?		Darf ich? Macht es Ihnen etwas aus?
Sorry. (excuse me, forgive me)		
*ehnt-**shul**-di-ghung*		Entschuldigung.

Greetings

Good morning.	*ghu-tehn **mor**-ghehn*	Guten Morgen.
Good afternoon.	*ghu-tehn taak*	Guten Tag.
Good evening.	*ghu-tehn **aa**-behnt*	Guten Abend.
Goodnight.	*ghu-teh nahkht*	Gute Nacht.
How are you?	*vee ghayt ehs ee-nehn?*	Wie geht es Ihnen?
Well, thanks.	*dahng-keh, ghut*	Danke, gut.

Forms of Address

| Madam/Mrs | *ghnair-di-gheh frow/frow* | Gnädige Frau/ Frau |
| Sir/Mr | *main hehr/hehr* | Mein Herr/Herr |

GERMAN

Miss	*froy-lain*	Fräulein
companion, friend	*froyn-din*	Freundin (f)
	froynt	Freund (m)

As yet there is no equivalent of Ms. *Frau* is regarded as a respectful address for older women whether they are married or not.

Language Difficulties

Do you speak English?
  shpreh-*khehn zee* **ehng**-*lish?* Sprechen Sie Englisch?
Does anyone here speak English?
  shprikht heer **yay**-*mahnt* **ehng**-*lish?* Spricht hier jemand Englisch?
I speak a little German.
  ikh **shpreh**-*kheh ain* **bis**-*khehn doych* Ich spreche ein bißchen Deutsch.
I don't speak …
  ikh **shpreh**-*kheh kain* … Ich spreche kein …
I (don't) understand.
  *ikh fehr-***shtay**-*eh (nikht)* Ich verstehe (nicht).
Could you speak more slowly please?
  kern-*tehn zee* **bi**-*teh* **lahng**-*zahm-ehr* **shpreh**-*khehn?* Könnten Sie bitte langsamer sprechen?
Sorry? (I didn't hear.)
  bi-*teh?* Bitte?
Could you repeat that?
  kern-*tehn zee dahs vee-dehr-***hoh**-*lehn?* Könnten Sie das wiederholen?

GERMAN

How do you say …?
vahs haist … owf doych?   Was heißt … auf deutsch?
What does … mean?
vahs beh-doy-teht …?   Was bedeutet …?

Small Talk
Meeting People
What is your name?
*vee **hai**-sehn zee?*   Wie heißen Sie?
My name is …
*ikh **hai**-seh …*   Ich heiße …
I'd like to introduce you to …
*kahn ikh **ee**-nehn …*
*for-**shteh**-lehn?*   Kann ich Ihnen …
    vorstellen?
I'm pleased to meet you.
***ahn**-gheh-naym*   Angenehm.

Nationalities
As with some other languages in this book, the German pronunciation of many placenames is often close enough for you to be
understood if you just say it in English. We've included a few
here which differ a little more, and those where German is spoken.

Where are you from?
*voh-**hayr** ko-mehn zee?*   Woher kommen Sie?

I am from …	*ikh **ko**-meh ows …*	Ich komme aus …
Australia	*ow-**straa**-li-yehn*	Australien
Austria	*er-ste-raikh*	Österreich
France	*frahnk-raikh*	Frankreich
Germany	***doych**-lahnt*	Deutschland
the Middle East	*dayr nahr ost-en*	der Naher Osten

GERMAN

New Zealand	*noy-zay-lahnt*	Neuseeland
Switzerland	*dayr shvaits*	der Schweiz
the USA	*dayn fay-rai-nikh-*	den Vereinigten
	tehn shtaa-tehn	Staaten

Age

How old are you?
   vee ahlt zint zee?   Wie alt sind Sie?

I am … years old.
   ikh bin … yaa-reh ahlt   Ich bin … Jahre alt.

Occupations

What (work) do you do?
   vahs mah-kehn zee für   Was machen Sie für beruf?
   beroof?

I am a/an …
   ikh bin …   Ich bin …

artist	*künst-lehr-in*	Künstlerin (f)
	künst-lehr	Künstler (m)
business person	*geh-shafts-frow*	Geschäftsfrau (f)
	geh-shafts-mahn	Geschäftsmann (m)
doctor	*arts-tin/ahrtst*	Ärztin (f)/Arzt (m)
engineer	*in-zheh-ni-yer-in*	Ingenieuerin (f)
	in-zhe-ni-yer	Ingenieur (m)
factory worker	*fah-breek-ahr-bai-tehr-in/fah-breek-ahr-bai-tehr*	Fabrikarbeiterin (f) Fabrikarbeiter (m)
farmer	*boy-yehr-in*	Bäuerin (f)
	bow-ehr	Bauer (m)
journalist	*zhur-nah-list-in*	Journalistin (f)
	zhur-nah-list	Journalist (m)

lawyer	*reh***khts**-*ahn-vahlt-in*	Rechtsanwältin (f)
	*reh***khts**-*ahn-vahlt*	Rechtsanwalt (m)
mechanic	*meh-***khah**-*ni-kehr-in*	Mechanikerin (f)
	*meh-***khah**-*ni-kehr*	Mechaniker (m)
nurse	***krahng**-kehn-shveh-stehr*	Kranken-schwester (f)
	***krahng**-kehn-pflay-ghehr*	Kranken-pfleger (m)
office worker	*bü-**roh**-ahn-gheh-shtehl-teh*	Büroangestellte (f)
	*bü-**roh**-ahn-gheh-shtehl-tehr*	Büroange-stellter (m)
scientist	*vi-sehn-***shahft**-lehr-in*	Wissenschaft-lerin (f)
	*vi-sehn-***shahft**-lehr*	Wissenschaftler (m)
student	*shtu-**dehnt**-in*	Studentin (f)
	*shtu-**dehnt***	Student (m)
teacher	*lay-rehr-in*	Lehrerin (f)
	lay-rehr	Lehrer (m)
waiter	***kehl**-nehr-in*	Kellnerin (f)
	***kehl**-nehr*	Kellner (m)
writer	***shrift**-shtehl-ehr-in*	Schriftstellerin (f)
	***shrift**-shtehl-ehr*	Schriftsteller (m)

Religion

What is your religion?
   *vahs ist **i**-reh reh-li-ghi-**ohn**?*   Was ist Ihre Religion?

I am not religious.
   *ikh bin nikht reh-li-gi-**ers***   Ich bin nicht religiös.

GERMAN

I am …	*ikh bin …*	Ich bin …
Buddhist	*bu-**dist**-in*	Buddhistin (f)
	*bu-**dist***	Buddhist (m)
Catholic	*kah-to-**leek**-in*	Katholikin (f)
	*kah-to-**leek***	Katholik (m)
Christian	***khrist**-in*	Christin (f)
	khrist	Christ (m)
Hindu	***hin**-du*	Hindu
Jewish	*yü-din*	Jüdin (f)
	yü-deh	Jude (m)
Muslim	***mos**-lehm*	Moslem

Family

Are you married?
*zint zee fehr-**hai**-rah-teht?*   Sind Sie verheiratet?

I am single.
*ikh bin un-fehr-**hai**-rah-teht*   Ich bin unverheiratet.

I am married.
*ikh bin fehr-**hai**-rah-teht*   Ich bin verheiratet.

How many children do you
have?
*vee-**fee**-leh **kin**-dehr*   Wieviele Kinder haben Sie?
***haa**-behn zee?*

I don't have any children.
*ikh **haa**-beh kai-neh*   Ich habe keine Kinder.
***kin**-dehr*

I have a daughter/a son.
*ikh **haa**-beh ai-neh*   Ich habe eine Tochter/einen
***tokh**-tehr/ai-nehn zohn*   Sohn.

Do you have any brothers or sisters?
> *haa-behn zee nokh gheh-shvi-stehr?*

Haben Sie noch Geschwister?

Is your husband/wife here?
> *ist ihr mahn/ih-reh frow heer?*

Ist Ihr Mann/Ihre Frau hier?

Do you have a boyfriend/girlfriend?
> *haa-behn zee ai-nehn froynt/ai-neh froynd-in?*

Haben Sie einen Freund/eine Freundin?

brother	*bru-dehr*	Bruder
children	*kin-dehr*	Kinder
daughter	*tokh-tehr*	Tochter
family	*fah-mi-li-eh*	Familie
father	*faa-tehr*	Vater
grandfather	*ghrohs-vaa-tehr*	Großvater
grandmother	*ghrohs-mu-tehr*	Großmutter
husband	*mahn*	Mann
mother	*mu-tehr*	Mutter
sister	*shveh-stehr*	Schwester
son	*zohn*	Sohn
wife	*frow*	Frau

Useful Phrases

Sure.
> *klahr!*

Klar!

Just a minute.
> *ain moh-mehnt!*

Ein Moment!

GERMAN

It's (not) important.
ehs ist (nikht) **vikh**-*tikh* Es ist (nicht) wichtig.

It's (not) possible.
ehs ist (nikht) **mergh**-*likh* Es ist (nicht) möglich.

Wait!
vahr-*tehn zee maal!* Warten Sie mal!

Good luck!
feel ghlük! Viel Glück!

Signs

EMERGENCY EXIT	*NOTAUSGANG*
ENTRANCE	*EINGANG*
EXIT	*AUSGANG*
FREE ADMISSION	*EINTRITT FREI*
HOT/COLD	*HEIß/KALT*
INFORMATION	*AUSKUNFT*
NO ENTRY	*KEIN ZUTRITT*
NO SMOKING	*RAUCHEN VERBOTEN*
OPEN/CLOSED	*OFFEN/GESCHLOSSEN*
PROHIBITED	*VERBOTEN*
RESERVED	*RESERVIERT*
TELEPHONE	*TELEFON*
TOILETS	*TOILETTEN (WC)*

Getting Around

What time does ... arrive?
vahn komt ... ahn? Wann kommt ... an?

the (air)plane	*dahs* **fluk**-*tsoyk*	das Flugzeug
the boat	*dahs bowt*	das Boot

GERMAN

the bus (city)	*dayr bus*	der Bus
the bus (intercity)	*dayr (ü-behr-lahnt-) bus*	der (Überland-)bus
the train	*dayr tsuk*	der Zug
the tram	*dee **shtrah**-sehn-baan*	die Straßenbahn

What time does ... leave?
vahn fairt ... ahp?   Wann fährt ... ab?

Finding Your Way

| map | ***kahr**-teh* | karte |

Do you have a guidebook/
street map?
***haa**-behn zee **ai**-nehn rai-zeh-fü-rehr/**shtaht**-plahn?*   Haben Sie einen Reiseführer/Stadtplan?

Where is ...?
voh ist ...?   Wo ist ...?

How do I get to ...?
*vee **ko**-meh ikh nahkh ...?*   Wie komme ich nach ...?

Is it far from/near here?
*ist ehs vait/in dayr **na**-yeh?*   Ist es weit/in der Nähe?

Can I walk there?
*kahn ikh tsu fus **ghay**-ehn?*   Kann ich zu Fuß gehen?

Can you show me (on the map)?
***ker**-nehn zee mir (owf dayr **kahr**-teh) **tsai**-ghehn?*   Können Sie mir (auf der Karte) zeigen?

Are there other means of
getting there?
*ghipt ehs **ahn**-deh-reh **mer**-ghlikh-kai-tehn, dort-**hin** tsu **faa**-rehn?*   Gibt es andere Möglichkeiten, dorthin zu fahren?

I'm looking for …
*ikh **zu**-kheh* …   Ich suche …

What's the name of …?
vee haist …?   Wie heißt …?
this street   ***dee**-zeh **shtrah**-seh*   diese Straße
this suburb   ***dee**-zehr **for**-ort*   dieser Vorort

Directions

Go straight ahead.
***ghay**-ehn zee gheh-**raa**-*
deh-ows   Gehen Sie geradeaus.
It's two streets down.
*ehs ist tsvai **shtrah**-sehn*
vai-tehr   Es ist zwei Straßen weiter.

Turn left …
***bee**-ghehn zee … lingks ahp*   Biegen Sie … links ab.
Turn right …
***bee**-ghehn zee … rehkhts*
ahp   Biegen Sie … rechts ab.
at the next corner
*bai dayr **nakh**-stehn **eh**-keh*   bei der nächsten Ecke
at the traffic lights
*bai dayr **ahm**-pehl*   bei der Ampel

behind   ***hin**-tehr*   hinter
in front of   *for*   vor
far   *vait*   weit
near   ***naa**-eh*   nahe
opposite   *ghay-ghehn-**ü**-behr*   gegenüber

Buying Tickets

TICKET OFFICE	*FAHRKARTENSCHALTER*

Excuse me, where is the ticket office?
> *ehnt-**shul**-di-ghung, voh ist dayr **faar**-kahr-tehn-shahl-tehr?*

Entschuldigung, wo ist der Fahrkartenschalter?

I want to go to …
> *ikh **merkh**-teh nahkh … **fah**-rehn*

Ich möchte nach … fahren.

Do I need to book?
> *mus mahn **ai**-nehn plahts reh-zehr-**vee**-rehn **lah**-sehn?*

Muß man einen Platz reservieren lassen?

You need to book.
> *mahn mus **ai**-nehn plahts reh-zehr-vee-rehn **lah**-sehn*

Man muß einen Platz reservieren lassen.

I'd like to book a seat to …
> *ikh **merkh**-teh **ai**-nehn plahts nahkh … reh-zehr-**vee**-rehn **lah**-sehn*

Ich möchte einen Platz nach … reservieren lassen.

I would like …
> *ikh **merkh**-teh …*

Ich möchte …

a one-way ticket	*ai-neh **ain**-tsehl-kahr-teh*	eine Einzelkarte
a return ticket	*ai-neh **rük**-fahr-kahr-teh*	eine Rückfahrkarte
two tickets	*tsvai **fahr**-kahr-tehn*	zwei Fahrkarten

student's concession	*mit fahr-prais-ehr-mas-i-ghung für shtu-dehn-tehn*	mit Fahrpreiser-mäßigung für Studenten
with child/pensioner concession	*mit fahr-prais-ehr-mas-i-ghung für kindehr/rehnt-nehr*	mit Fahrpreiser-mäßigung für Kinder/Rentner
1st class	*ehr-steh klah-seh*	erste Klasse
2nd class	*tsvai-teh klah-seh*	zweite Klasse

It is full.
ehr ist ows-gheh-bukht   Er ist ausgebucht.

Is it completely full?
ist ehr ghahnts ows-gheh-bukht?   Ist er ganz ausgebucht?

Can I get a stand-by ticket?
*kahn ikh ain **stand**-bai ti-keht **kow**-fehn?*   Kann ich ein Standby-Ticket kaufen?

Air

ARRIVALS	*ANKUNFT*
DEPARTURES	*ABFAHRT*
CHECKING IN	*ABFERTIGUNG*
CUSTOMS	*ZOLL*
LUGGAGE PICKUP	*GEPÄCKAUSGABE*

GERMAN

Is there a flight to …?
*ghipt ehs **ai**-nehn fluk nahkh …?*   Gibt es einen Flug nach …?

When is the next flight to …?
*vahn ist dayr **nakh**-steh fluk nahkh …?*   Wann ist der nächste Flug nach …?

How long does the flight take?
*vee **lahng**-eh **dow**-ehrt dayr fluk?*

Wie lange dauert der Flug?

What is the flight number?
***vehl**-kher **flug**-nu-mehr ist ehs?*

Welcher Flugnummer ist es?

You must check in at ...
*zee **mü**-sehn um ... **ain**-cheh-kehn*

Sie müssen um ... einchecken.

airport tax	***fluk**-hah-fehn-gheh-bür*	Flughafengebühr
boarding pass	***bort**-kahr-teh*	Bordkarte
customs	*tsol*	Zoll

Bus & Tram

BUS STOP	*BUSHALTESTELLE*
TRAM STOP	*STRAßENBAHNHALTE-STELLE*

Where is the bus/tram stop?
*voh ist dee **bus**-hahl-teh-shteh-leh/**shtrah**-sehn-bahn-hahl-teh-shteh-leh?*

Wo ist die Bushaltestelle/Straßenbahnhaltestelle?

Which bus goes to ...?
***vehl**-khehr bus fairt nahkh ...?*

Welcher Bus fährt nach ...?

Does this bus go to ...?
*fairt **dee**-zayr bus nahkh ...?*

Fährt dieser Bus nach ...?

How often do buses pass by?
*vee oft **faa**-rehn **bu**-seh for-**bai**?*

Wie oft fahren Busse vorbei?

Could you let me know when
we get to ...?
> *kern*-tehn zee mir *bi*-teh
> *zaa*-*ghehn, vehn vir in ...*
> *ahn*-ko-mehn?

Könnten Sie mir bitte
sagen, wenn wir in ...
ankommen?

I want to get off!
> ikh *merkh*-teh *ows-shtai-*
> *ghehn!*

Ich möchte aussteigen!

What time is the ... bus?
> *vahn fairt dayr ... bus?*

Wann fährt der ... Bus?

next	*nakh*-steh bus	nächste
first	*ehr*-steh	erste
last	*lehts*-teh	letzte

Train

TIMETABLE	*FAHRPLAN*
TRAIN STATION	*BAHNHOF (Bhf/Bf)*
PLATFORM NO	*BAHNSTEIG*

The train leaves from
platform ...
> *dayr tsuk fairt owf*
> *baan*-shtaik ... ahp

Der Zug fährt auf Bahsteig
... ab.

Passengers must ...
> *pah-sah-zhee-reh*
> *mü-sehn ...*

Passagiere müssen ...

change trains	*um*-shtai-ghehn	umsteigen
change platforms	*owf ai-nehn ahn-*	auf einen anderen
	deh-rehn baan-	Bahnsteig gehen
	shtaik *ghay-ehn*	

Is this the right platform
for …?
fairt dayr tsuk nahkh … owf
dee-*zehm baan*-*shtaik ahp?*   Fährt der Zug nach … auf
diesem Bahnsteig ab?

dining car	**shpai**-*zeh-vaa-ghehn*	Speisewagen
express	**shnehl**-*tsuk*	Schnellzug
local	**naa**-*vehr-kehrs-tsuk*	Nahverkehrszug
sleeping car	**shlaaf**-*vah-ghehn*	Schlafwagen

Metro

METRO/UNDERGROUND	*U-BAHN*
CHANGE (for coins)	*WECHSELGELD*
THIS WAY TO	*AUSGANG ZU*

Which line takes me to …?
vel-*kheh* **li**-*ni-yeh fairt*
nahkh …?   Welche Linie fährt nach …?
What is the next station?
vee haist dayr **nakh**-*steh*
baan-*hof?*   Wie heißt der nächste
Bahnhof?

Taxi

Can you take me to …?
kern-*ehn zee mir tsu …*
bring-*ehn?*   Können Sie mich zu …
bringen?
Please take me to …
bring-*ehn zee mikh* **bi**-*teh*
tsu …   Bringen Sie mich bitte zu …
How much is it to go to …?
vahs **ko**-*steht ehs bis …?*   Was kostet es bis …?

Instructions

Here is fine, thank you.
hahl-tehn zee *bi*-teh heer

Halten Sie bitte hier.

The next corner, please.
ahn dayr **nakh**-stehn
eh-keh, **bi**-teh

An der nächsten Ecke, bitte.

Continue!
vai-tehr!

Weiter!

The next street to the left/right.
bee-ghehn zee ahn dayr
nakh-stehn **eh**-keh lingks/
rehkhts ahp

Biegen Sie an der nächsten Ecke links/rechts ab.

Please slow down.
faa-rehn zee **bi**-teh
lahng-sahm-ehr

Fahren Sie bitte langsamer.

Please wait here.
bi-teh **vahr**-tehn zee heer

Bitte warten Sie hier.

Useful Phrases

The train is delayed/cancelled.
dayr tsuk haht fehr-**shpair**-
tung/**falt** ows

Der Zug hat Verspätung/
fällt aus.

How long will it be delayed?
vee-**feel** fehr-**shpair**-tung
virt ehr **haa**-behn?

Wieviel Verspätung wird er haben?

There is a delay of … hours.
ehr haht … **shtun**-dehn
fehr-**shpair**-tung

Er hat … Stunden Verspätung.

Can I reserve a place?
kahn ikh **ai**-nehn plahts
reh-zehr-vee-rehn **lah**-sehn?

Kann ich einen Platz reservieren lassen?

How long does the trip take?	
*vee **lahng**-eh **dow**-ehrt dee **rai**-zeh?*	Wie lange dauert die Reise?
Is it a direct route?	
*ist ehs ai-neh dí-**rehk**-teh **fehr-bin**-dung?*	Ist es eine direkte Verbindung?
Is that seat taken?	
*ist **dee**-zayr plahts beh-**zehtst**?*	Ist dieser Platz besetzt?
I want to get off at …	
*ikh **merkh**-teh in … **ows**-shtai-ghehn*	Ich möchte in … aussteigen.
Excuse me.	
*ehnt-**shul**-di-ghung*	Entschuldigung.

Car & Bicycle

DETOUR	*UMLEITUNG*
FREEWAY	*AUTOBAHN*
GARAGE	*TANKSTELLE*
GIVE WAY	*VORFAHRT GEWÄHREN*
MECHANIC	*MECHANIKER*
NO ENTRY	*KEIN EINGANG*
NO PARKING	*PARKEN VERBOTEN*
ONE WAY	*EINBAHNSTRAßE*
REPAIRS	*REPARATUREN*
SELF SERVICE	*SELBSTBEDIENUNG*
STOP	*HALT*
SUPER	*SUPER*

GERMAN

Where can I hire a car?
*voh kahn ikh ain ow-toh
mee-tehn?*

Wo kann ich ein Auto
mieten?

Where can I hire a bicycle?
*voh kahn ikh ain faar-raht
mee-tehn?*

Wo kann ich ein Fahrrad
mieten?

How much is it daily/weekly?
*vee-feel ko-steht ehs proh
taak/proh voh-kheh?*

Wieviel kostet es pro
Tag/pro Woche?

Does that include insurance/
mileage?
*ist dee fehr-zi-khehr-ung/
dahs ki-lo-may-tehr-ghehlt
in-beh-ghri-fehn?*

Ist die Versicherung/das
Kilometergeld inbegriffen?

Where's the next petrol station?
*voh ist dee nakh-steh
tahngk-shteh-leh?*

Wo ist die nächste
Tankstelle?

Please fill the tank.
fol-tahng-kehn, bi-teh

Volltanken, bitte.

I want … litres of petrol (gas).
*ghay-behn zee mir …
li-tehr behn-tsin*

Geben Sie mir … Liter
Benzin.

Please check the oil and water.
*bi-teh zay-ehn zee nahkh
erl unt vah-sehr*

Bitte sehen Sie nach Öl und
Wasser.

How long can I park here?
*vee lahg-eh kahn ikh heer
pahr-kehn?*

Wie lange kann ich hier
parken?

Does this road lead to?
*fürt dee-zeh shtrah-seh
nahkh …?*

Führt diese Straße nach …?

air (for tyres)	*luft*	Luft
battery	***bah-teh-ree***	Batterie
brakes	***brehm***-*zehn*	Bremsen
clutch	***kup***-*lung*	Kupplung
driving licence	***fü-rehr-shain***	Führerschein
engine	***moh***-*tor*	Motor
lights	***shain***-*vehr-fehr*	Scheinwerfer
oil	*erl*	Öl
puncture	***rai***-*fehn-pah-neh*	Reifenpanne
radiator	***kü***-*lehr*	Kühler
road map	***shtraa***-*sehn-kahr-teh*	Straßenkarte
tyres	***rai***-*fehn*	Reifen
windscreen	***vint***-*shuts-shai-beh*	Windschutzscheibe

Car Problems

I need a mechanic.
*ikh **brow**-kheh ai-nehn*   Ich brauche einen
*meh-**khah**-ni-kehr*   Mechaniker.

What make is it?
***vehl**-kheh **mar**-keh ist ehs?*   Welche Marke ist es?

The battery is flat.
*dee bah-**teh-ree** ist layr*   Die Batterie ist leer.

The radiator is leaking.
*dayr **kü**-lehr ist **un**-dikht*   Der Kühler ist undicht.

I have a flat tyre.
*ikh **hah**-beh ai-neh **pah**-neh*   Ich habe eine Panne.

It's overheating.
ehs loyft hais   Es läuft heiß.

It's not working.
*ehs fungk-tsi-o-**neert** nikht*   Es funktioniert nicht.

Accommodation

CAMPING GROUND	*CAMPINGPLATZ*
GUESTHOUSE	*PENSION or GASTHAUS*
HOTEL	*HOTEL*
MOTEL	*MOTEL*
YOUTH HOSTEL	*JUGENDHERBERGE*

Finding Accommodation

I am looking for …
  *ikh **zu**-kheh* …   Ich suche …
Where is …?
  voh ist …?   Wo ist …?

a cheap hotel	*ain **bi**-li-ghehs hoh-**tehl***	ein billiges Hotel
a good hotel	*ain **ghu**-tehs hoh-**tehl***	ein gutes Hotel
a nearby hotel	*ain hoh-**tehl** in dayr **na**-yeh*	ein Hotel in der Nähe
a clean hotel	*ain **zow**-beh-rehs hoh-**tehl***	ein sauberes Hotel

What is the address?
  *vahs ist dee ah-**dreh**-seh?*   Was ist die Adresse?
Could you write the address, please?
  ***kern**-tehn zee **bi**-teh dee ah-**dreh**-seh owf-**shrai**-behn?*   Könnten Sie bitte die Adresse aufschreiben?

Booking a Room

Do you have any rooms available?
  *haa-behn zee nokh **frai**-yeh tsi-mehr?*   Haben Sie noch freie Zimmer?

GERMAN

I'd like to book a room.
*ikh **merkh**-teh ain tsi-mehr boo-kehn*
Ich möchte eine Zimmer buchen.

for one night/four nights
*für aine nakht/veer **nakh**-teh*
für eine nacht/vier nachte

from (Tuesday)
*bis (**deen**-stahg)*
bis (dienstag)

I would like …
*ikh **merkh**-teh …*
Ich möchte …

a single room
*ain **ain**-tsehl-tsi-mehr*
ein Einzelzimmer

a double room
*ain **do**-pehl-tsi-mehr*
ein Doppelzimmer

a room with a bathroom
*ain **tsi**-mehr mit baat*
ein Zimmer mit Bad

to share a dorm
*ai-nehn **shlaaf**-zaal tai-lehn*
einen Schlafsaal teilen

At the Hotel

How much per night/per person?
*vee-**feel kos**-teht ehs proh nahkht/proh pehr-**zohn**?*
Wieviel kostet es pro Nacht/pro Person?

Can I see it?
*kahn ikh ehs **zay**-ehn?*
Kann ich es sehen?

Are there any others?
*haa-behn zee nokh **ahn**-deh-reh?*
Haben Sie noch andere?

Is there anything cheaper?
*ghipt ehs **eht**-vahs **bi**-li-ghehr-ehs?*
Gibt es etwas Billigeres?

Does it include breakfast?
*ist **frü**-shtük **in**-beh-ghri-fehn?*
Ist Frühstück inbegriffen?

Is there a reduction for
students/children?
*ghipt ehs ehr-**ma**-si-ghung
für shtu-**dehn**-tehn/**kin**-
dehr?* — Gibt es Ermäßigung für
Studenten/Kinder?

It's fine, I'll take it.
*ehs ist ghut, ikh **nay**-meh ehs* — Es ist gut, ich nehme es.

I'm going to stay for …
*ikh **blai**-beh …* — Ich bleibe …

one day	*ai-neh nahkht*	eine Nacht
two days	*tsvai **nakh**-teh*	zwei Nächte
one week	*ai-neh vo-kheh*	eine Woche

I'm not sure how long I'm
staying.
*ikh vais nikht, vee **lahng**-eh
ikh **blai**-beh* — Ich weiß nicht, wie lange
ich bleibe.

Is there a lift?
*ghipt ehs **ai**-nehn owf-zoog?* — Gibt es einen Aufzug?

Where is the bathroom?
voh ist dahs baat? — Wo ist das Bad?

Is there hot water all day?
*ghipt ehs dayn **ghahn**-tsehn
taak **vahrm**-ehs vah-sehr?* — Gibt es den ganzen Tag
warmes Wasser?

You May Hear

Do you have identification?
*ker-nehn zee zikh
ows-vai-zehn?* — Können Sie sich ausweisen?

GERMAN

Your membership card, please.
  mit-ghleets-ows-vais, bi-teh   Mitgliedsausweis, bitte.
Sorry, we're full.
  ehnt-shul-di-ghung, vir haa-behn kai-neh tsi-mehr frai   Entschuldigung, wir haben keine Zimmer frei.
How long will you be staying?
  vee lahng-eh blai-behn zee?   Wie lange bleiben Sie?
It's … per day/per person.
  ehs kos-teht … proh nahkht/proh pehr-zohn   Es kostet … pro Nacht/pro Person.

Requests & Complaints

Can I use the kitchen?
  kahn ikh dee kü-kheh beh-nu-tsehn?   Kann ich die Küche benutzen?
Can I use the telephone?
  kahn ikh dahs teh-leh-fohn beh-nu-tsehn?   Kann ich das Telefon benutzen?
Do you have a safe where I can leave my valuables?
  haa-behn zee ai-nehn sayf, in daym ikh mai-neh vehrt-zah-khehn lah-sehn kahn?   Haben Sie einen Safe, in dem ich meine Wertsachen lassen kann?
Is there somewhere to wash clothes?
  kahn mahn ir-ghehnt-voh va-sheh vah-shehn?   Kann man irgendwo Wäsche waschen?
Please wake me up at …
  bi-teh veh-kehn zee mikh um …   Bitte wecken Sie mich um …

Please change the sheets.
  *vekh-zehln zee bi-teh dee
  beht-va-sheh*

Wechseln Sie bitte die
Bettwäsche.

I can't open/close the window.
  *ikh kahn dahs fehn-stehr
  nikht owf-mah-khehn/tsu-
  mah-khehn*

Ich kann das Fenster nicht
aufmachen/zumachen.

I've locked myself out of my
room.
  *ikh haa-beh mikh ows
  mai-nehm tsi-mehr
  ows-gheh-shpehrt*

Ich habe mich aus meinem
Zimmer ausgesperrt.

The toilet won't flush.
  *dee shpü-lung in dayr
  to-ah-leh-teh fungk-tsi-o-
  neert nikht*

Die Spülung in der Toilette
funktioniert nicht.

I don't like this room.
  *dahs tsi-mehr gheh-falt mir
  nikht*

Das Zimmer gefällt mir
nicht.

It's too …	*ehs ist tsu …*	Es ist zu …
small	*klain*	klein
noisy	*lowt*	laut
dark	*dung-kehl*	dunkel
expensive	*toy-ehr*	teuer

Checking Out

I am/We are leaving now.
  *ikh rai-zeh/vir rai-zehn
  yehtst*

Ich reise/Wir reisen jetzt.

I would like to pay the bill.
  *kahn ikh bi-teh dee
  rehkh-nung haa-behn?*

Kann ich bitte die
Rechnung haben?

name	*naa*-meh	Name
surname	*nahkh-naa*-meh	Nachname
address	*ah-dreh*-seh	Adresse
room number	*tsi-mehr-nu-mehr*	Zimmernummer

Useful Words

air-con	*mit kli-mah-ahn-laa-gheh*	mit Klimaanlage
bath	*baat*	Bad
bed	*beht*	Bett
clean	*zow-behr*	sauber
dirty	*shmut-tsikh*	schmutzig
double bed	*do-pehl-beht*	Doppelbett
electricity	*eh-lehk-trits-i-**tairt***	Elektrizität
excluding ...	*ow-sehr/ows-gheh-no-mehn ...*	außer/ausgenom-men ...
fan	*vehn-ti-laa-tor*	Ventilator
... included	*... in-beh-ghri-fehn*	... inbegriffen
key	*shlü-sehl*	Schlüssel
quiet	*ru-ikh*	ruhig
sheet	*beht-laa-kehn*	Bettlaken
shower	*du-sheh*	Dusche
swimming pool	*shvim-baat*	Schwimmbad
toilet	*to-ah-leh-teh*	Toilette
toilet paper	*to-ah-leh-tehn-pah-peer*	Toilettenpapier
towel	*hahnt-tukh*	Handtuch
view	*ows-zikht*	Aussicht
water	*vah-sehr*	Wasser
cold water	*kahl-tehs vah-sehr*	kaltes Wasser
hot water	*vahrm-ehs vah-sehr*	warmes Wasser
window	*fehn-stehr*	Fenster

Around Town

I'm looking for …	*ikh zu-kheh …*	Ich suche …
a bank	*ai-neh bahngk*	eine Bank
the city centre	*dee i-nehn-shtaht*	die Innenstadt
the … embassy	*dee … boht-shahft*	die … Botschaft
my hotel	*main hoh-tehl*	mein Hotel
the market	*dayn mahrkt*	den Markt
the post office	*dahs post-ahmt*	das Postamt
a public toilet	*ai-neh er-fehnt-likh-eh to-ah-leh-teh*	eine öffentliche Toilette
the telephone centre	*dee teh-leh-fohn-tsehn-trah-leh*	die Telefonzentrale
the tourist information office	*dahs frehm-dehn-fehr-kehrz-bü-roh*	das Fremdenverkehrsbüro

What time does it open?
um vee-feel ur mahkht ehs owf?
Um wieviel Uhr macht es auf?

What time does it close?
um vee-feel ur mahkht ehs tsu?
Um wieviel Uhr macht es zu?

What's the name of …?
vee haist …?
Wie heißt …?

this street	*dee-zeh shtrah-seh*	diese Straße
this suburb	*dee-zehr for-ort*	dieser Vorort

At the Bank

I want to exchange some money.
ikh merkh-teh ghehlt um-tow-shehn
Ich möchte Geld umtauschen.

I want to change some travellers' cheques.
*ikh **merkh**-teh rai-zeh-sheks **ain**-ler-zehn*

Ich möchte Reiseschecks einlösen.

What is the exchange rate?
*vee ist dayr **vehkh**-sehl-kurs?*

Wie ist der Wechselkurs?

How many marks per dollar?
*vee-**fee**-leh mahrk für **ai**-nehn **do**-lahr?*

Wieviele Mark für einen Dollar?

Can I have money transferred here from my bank?
*kahn ikh ghehlt ows **mai**-nehr bahngk ü-behr-**vai**-zehn **lah**-sehn?*

Kann ich Geld aus meiner Bank überweisen lassen?

When will it arrive?
*vahn virt ehs **ahn**-koh-mehn?*

Wann wird es ankommen?

Has my money arrived yet?
*ist main ghehlt shon **ahn**-ghe-ko-mehn?*

Ist mein Geld schon angekommen?

bank notes	**bahngk**-noh-tehn	Banknoten
cashier	kah-**seer**-ehr-in	Kassiererin (f)
	kah-**seer**-ehr	Kassierer (m)
coins	**mün**-tsehn	Münzen
commission	gheh-**bür**	Gebühr
credit card	kreh-**deet**-kahr-teh	Kreditkarte
exchange office	**vehkh**-sehl-shtu-beh	Wechselstube
loose change	**klain**-ghehlt	Kleingeld
signature	**un**-tehr-shrift	Unterschrift

At the Post Office

I'd like to send …
   *ikh **merkh**-teh … **zehn**-dehn* Ich möchte … senden.

an aerogram	*ai-nehn **luft**-post-laikht-breef*	einen Luftpost-leichtbrief
a letter	*ai-nehn breef*	einen Brief
a postcard	*ai-neh **pohst**-kahr-teh*	eine Postkarte
a parcel	*ain pah-**kayt***	ein Paket
a telegram	*ain teh-leh-**grahm***	ein Telegramm

I would like some stamps.
   *ikh **merkh**-teh breef-mahr-kehn **kow**-fehn* Ich möchte Briefmarken kaufen.

How much is the postage?
   *vee-**feel** kos-teht dahs **por**-to?* Wieviel kostet das Porto?

How much does it cost to send this to …?
   *vee-**feel** kos-teht ehs, dahs nahkh … tsu **zehn**-dehn?* Wieviel kostet es, das nach … zu senden?

airmail	*pehr **luft**-post*	per Luftpost
envelope	*um-shlaak*	Umschlag
mailbox	***breef**-kahs-tehn*	Briefkasten
parcel	*pah-**kayt***	Paket
registered mail	*payr ain-shrai-behn*	per Einschreiben
surface mail	*gheh-**vern**-likh-eh pohst*	gewöhnliche Post

Telephone

Hello?
   yah/ello Ja/Hello?

I want to make a long-distance call to …
> *bi-teh ain **fehrn**-gheh-shprakh nahkh …*

Bitte ein Ferngespräch nach …

The number is …
> *dee **nu**-mehr ist …*

Die Nummer ist …

I want to speak for three minutes.
> *ikh **merkh**-teh drai mi-**nu**-tehn lahng **shpreh**-khen*

Ich möchte drei Minuten lang sprechen.

How much does a three-minute call cost?
> *vee-**feel kos**-teht ain drai mi-**nu**-tehn gheh-**shprakh**?*

Wieviel kostet ein drei Minuten Gespräch?

How much does each extra minute cost?
> *vee-**feel kos**-stet **yay**-deh tsu-**zats**-likh-eh mi-**nu**-teh?*

Wieviel kostet jede zusätzliche Minute?

I want to make a reverse-charges (collect) call.
> *ikh **merkh**-teh ain **air**-gheh-shprakh*

Ich möchte ein R-Gespräch.

It's engaged.
> *ehs ist beh-**zetst***

Es ist besetzt.

I've been cut off.
> *ikh bin un-tehr-**bro**-khen **vor**-dehn*

Ich bin unterbrochen worden.

I'd like to speak to Mrs Schmidt.
> *ikh **merkh**-teh frow shmit **shpreh**-khen*

Ich möchte Frau Schmidt sprechen.

Sightseeing

What are the main attractions?
*vahs zint dee **howpt**-zay-ehns-vür-dikh-kai-tehn?*
Was sind die Hauptsehenswürdigkeiten?

How old is it?
vee ahlt ist dahs?
Wie alt ist das?

Can I take photographs?
*dahrf ikh foh-to-grah-**fee**-rehn?*
Darf ich fotografieren?

What time does it open/close?
vahn mahkht ehs owf/tsu?
Wann macht es auf/zu?

ancient	*ahlt*	alt
archaeological	*ahr-kha-o-**loh**-ghish*	archäologisch
beach	*shtrahnt*	Strand
building	*gheh-**boy**-deh*	Gebäude
castle	*shlos*	Schloß
cathedral	*dohm*	Dom
church	*kir-kheh*	Kirche
concert hall	*kon-tsehrt-ha-leh*	Konzerthalle
library	*bi-bli-oh-**tehk***	Bibliothek
main square	*howpt-plahts*	Hauptplatz
monastery	*klo-stehr*	Kloster
monument	*dehngk-mahl*	Denkmal
old city	*ahlt-shtaht*	Altstadt
opera house	*oh-pehrn-hows*	Opernhaus
palace	*pah-lahst*	Palast
ruins	*ru-ee-nehn*	Ruinen
stadium	*shtaa-di-on*	Stadion
statues	*shtaa-tu-ehn*	Statuen
university	*u-ni-vehr-si-tairt*	Universität

GERMAN

Entertainment

What's there to do in the evenings?
   vahs kahn mahn aa-behnts un-tehr-nay-mehn?

Was kann man abends unternehmen?

Are there any nightclubs?
   ghipt ehs heer nahkht-klub-en?

Gibt es hier Nachtkluben?

Are there places where you can hear local music?
   kahn mahn heer ir-ghehnt-voh ert-li-kheh mu-zeek her-rehn?

Kann man hier irgendwo örtliche musik hören?

How much is it to get in?
   vee-feel ko-steht dayr ain-trit?

Wieviel kostet der Eintritt?

cinema	*kee-noh*	Kino
concert	*kon-tsehrt*	Konzert
theatre	*tay-aa-tehr*	Theater

In the Country
Weather

What's the weather like?
   vee ist dahs veh-tehr?

Wie ist das Wetter?

Will it rain?
   virt ehs raygh-nehn?

Wird es regnen?

Will it snow?
   virt ehs shnai-yehn?

Wird es schneien?

The weather is … today.
   dahs veh-tehr ist hoy-teh …

Das Wetter ist heute …

Will it be … tomorrow?

*virt ehs **mor**-ghehn … zain?*   Wird es morgen … sein?

cloudy	*vol-kikh*	wolkig
cold	*kahlt*	kalt
fine	*shern*	schön
foggy	*nay-blikh*	neblig
frosty	***fro**-stikh*	frostig
hot	*hais*	heiß
windy	*vin-dikh*	windig

Camping

Am I allowed to camp here?

*kahn ikh heer **tsehl**-tehn?*   Kann ich hier zelten?

Is there a campsite nearby?

*ghipt ehs in dayr **nay**-yeh*   Gibt es in der Nähe einen
***ai**-nehn **kehm**-ping-plahts?*   Campingplatz?

backpack	*ruk-zahk*	Rucksack
can opener	*doh-zehn-erf-nehr*	Dosenöffner
compass	*kom-pahs*	Kompaß
crampons	*shtaig-ai-zehn*	Steigeisen
firewood	*brehn-holts*	Brennholz
gas cartridge	*ghaas-flah-sheh*	Gasflasche
hammock	*hang-eh-mah-teh*	Hängematte
ice axe	*ais-pi-kehl*	Eispickel
mattress	*mah-trah-tseh*	Matratze
penknife	*tah-shehn-meh-sehr*	Taschenmesser
rope	*zail*	Seil
tent	*tsehlt*	Zelt
tent pegs	*tsehlt-hay-ring-eh*	Zelteringe

torch (flashlight)	*tah-shehn-lahm-peh*	Taschenlampe
sleeping bag	*shlaaf-zahk*	Schlafsack
stove	*hayrt*	Herd
water bottle	*fehlt-flah-sheh*	Feldflasche

Food

Germans love a big breakfast. Wherever you stay in all German-speaking areas, breakfast will almost always be included as part of the price. Even at cheap hotels you may get ham, sausage, herrings, boiled eggs, bread rolls, and fresh fruit, as well as coffee, milk and fruit juice. Some Germans have a 'second breakfast' *(zweites Frühstück)* mid-morning, which can be like a smaller version of the earlier breakfast, only sometimes with beer; or it may be just a morning tea with cakes and coffee.

Traditionally lunch is the biggest meal of all, with dinner often being like a small breakfast – some eating places, in fact, have a main menu for lunch and a smaller one for the evening. However, at most restaurants (called a *Restaurant* or *Gaststätte*) you can get a large dinner if you want.

Ethnic German food tends to be filling – lots of meat, especially pork and chicken. Offal is quite common. Pickles (like sauerkraut-pickled cabbage), rather than fresh vegetables, are very popular. And of course sausage – you'll see lots of snack bars (called an *Imbiß* or *Schnellimbiß*) basically just selling a range of sausages. Now there are also all sorts of Asian and Turkish restaurants and takeaways; and, of course, the international fast-food chains.

Some areas, especially southern Germany and Austria, are renowned for their cakes and pastries – you are probably already familiar with apple strudel *(Apfelstrudel)* and Black Forest cake *(Schwarzwälder Kirschtorte)*. Vienna has been called the café capital of the world, with an unbelievable array of elegant establishments to visit for coffee and cake.

Pubs (*Bierstube*) are popular and similar to those in England or Australia. They generally sell snacks and light food.

Restaurants normally have a menu displayed outside, so you can figure out what it all means first! Many offer a good-value set menu (a *Gedeck* or *Tagesmenü*). You do not usually wait to be seated when you enter, and it is common in less expensive restaurants for other people to sit at your table. The bill at the end of a meal always includes tax and service charge; however, you can leave a small tip – about 5% – if the service has been really good.

breakfast	*frü-shtük*	Frühstück
lunch	*mi-tahg-eh-sehn*	Mittagessen
dinner	*aa-behnt-eh-sehn*	Abendessen

Eating Out

Table for ..., please.
  ai-nehn tish für ..., bi-teh   Einen Tisch für ..., bitte.

Can I see the menu please?
  kahn ikh bi-teh dee shpai-   Kann ich bitte die
  zeh-kahr-teh haa-behn?   Speisekarte haben?

I'd like the set lunch, please.
  ikh ha-teh ghehrn dahs   Ich hätte gern das
  taa-ghehs-meh-nü bi-teh   Tagesmenü bitte.

What does it include?
  vahs ehnt-halt dahs?   Was enthält das?

Is service included in the bill?
  ist dee beh-dee-nung   Ist die Bedienung
  in-beh-ghri-fehn?   inbegriffen?

GERMAN

Not too spicy please.

bi-teh nikht zayr **vür**-tsikh		Bitte nicht sehr würzig.

an ashtray	ain **ah**-shehn-beh-khehr	ein Aschenbecher
the bill	dee **rehkh**-nung	die Rechnung
a cup	ai-neh **tah**-seh	eine Tasse
dessert	**nahkh**-shpai-zeh	Nachspeise
a drink	ain gheh-**trangk**	ein Getränk
a fork	ai-neh **ghaa**-behl	eine Gabel
fresh	frish	frisch
a knife	ain **meh**-sehr	ein Messer
a plate	ain **teh**-lehr	ein Teller
spicy	**vür**-tsikh	würzig
a spoon	ain **ler**-fehl	ein Löffel
stale	ahlt	alt
sweet	züs	süß
teaspoon	**tay**-ler-fehl	Teelöffel
toothpick	**tsaan**-shto̧-khehr	Zahnstocher

Making Your Own Meal

For some key essentials for sandwich-making, etc, see page 197.

Vegetarian Meals

I am a vegetarian.

ikh bin veh-gheh-**taa**-ri-ehr-in	Ich bin Vegetarierin. (f)
ikh bin veh-gheh-**taa**-ri-ehr	Ich bin Vegetarier. (m)

I don't eat meat.

ikh **eh**-seh kain flaish	Ich esse kein Fleisch.

I don't eat chicken, fish or ham.

ikh **eh**-seh kain **hün**-khehn, **kai**-nehn fish, unt **kai**-nehn **shing**-kehn	Ich esse kein Hühnchen, keinen Fisch, und keinen Schinken.

Breakfast

fried egg	*Spiegelei*
ham	*Schinken*
honey	*Honig*
jam	*Marmelade*
sausage	*Wurst*
scrambled eggs	*Rührei*

Staples & Condiments

bread	*Brot*
butter	*Butter*
cheese	*Käse*
mustard	*Senf*
noodles	*Nudeln*
pepper	*Pfeffer*
rice	*Reis*
rolls	*Brötchen*
salt	*Salz*
tomato sauce	*Tomatensause*

Snacks — Vorspeisen

Belegtes Brot	open sandwich
Kleine/Kalte Gerichte	small/cold dishes
Pfannkuchen	pancake
Pilze	mushrooms
Rollmops	pickled herrings
Russische Eier	eggs with mayonnaise
Schnitten	selection of cold meats and vegetables
Wurst	sausage
Blutwurst	blood sausage
Bockwurst	pork sausage

GERMAN

Bratwurst	fried pork sausage
Leberwurst	liver sausage
Weißwurst	veal sausage
Zwiebelwurst	liver-and-onion sausage

Soups

Bauernsuppe	'farmer's soup', cabbage and sausage
Erbsensuppe	pea soup
Fleischbrühe	consommé
Gemüsesuppe	vegetable soup
Graupensuppe	barley soup
Hühnersuppe	chicken soup
Tomatensuppe	tomato soup

Meat & Seafood

Fischgerichte	fish dishes
Fleischgerichte	meat dishes
Hauptgerichte	main courses
Beefsteak	hamburger
Frikadellen	meatballs
Hackbraten	meatloaf
Hasenpfeffer	hare stew with mushrooms and onions
Kohlroulade	cabbage leaves stuffed with minced meat
Königsberger Klops	meatballs in a sour-cream-and-caper sauce
Kotelette	chops
Labskaus	thick meat-and-potato stew
Ragout	stew
Schlachtplatte	selection of pork and sausage
Schmorbraten	beef pot roast

GERMAN

beef	*Rindfleisch*
chicken	*Hähnchen*
fried chicken	*Backhähnchen*
roast chicken	*Brathuhn*
fish	*Fisch*
lamb	*Lamm(fleisch)*
liver	*Leber*
pork	*Schweinefleisch*
roast pork	*Schweinebraten*
tongue	*Zunge*
tripe	*Kutteln*
veal	*Kalbfleisch*
crumbed veal	*Wiener Schnitzel*

Vegetables — Gemüse

beans	*Bohnen*
beetroot	*rote Beete*
cabbage	*Kohl*
carrots	*Karotten*
cauliflower	*Blumenkohl*
chips (French fries)	*Pommes frites*
cucumber, gherkins	*Gurken*
lettuce	*Salat*
onions	*Zwiebeln*
peas	*Erbsen*
potato salad	*Kartoffelsalat*
potatoes	*Kartoffeln*
mashed potatoes	*Kartoffelbrei*
fried potatoes	*Bratkartoffeln*
pumpkin	*Kürbis*
red cabbage	*Rotkohl*
salad	*grüner Salat*

GERMAN

Dessert & Pastries Nachspeisen und Kuchen

Apfelstrudel	apple strudel
Berliner Pfannkuchen	jam doughnut
Eis	ice cream
Königstorte	rum-flavoured fruit cake
Schwarzwälder Kirschtorte	Black Forest cake (chocolate layer cake filled with cream and cherries)
Spekulatius	almond biscuits
Torte	layer cake

Drinks – Nonalcoholic

apple juice	*Apfelsaft*
coffee	*Kaffee*
Vienna coffee (black, topped with whipped cream)	*Einspänner*
white coffee	*Milchkaffee*
fruit juice	*Fruchtsaft*
milkshake	*Milchshake*
mineral water (without bubbles)	*Mineralwasser (ohne Kohlensäure)*
peppermint tea	*Pfefferminztee*
tea	*Tee*
water	*Wasser*
with/without	*mit/ohne*
cream	*Sahne*
milk	*Milch*
sugar	*Zucker*

Drinks – Alcoholic

apple brandy	*Apfelschnaps*
apple cider	*Apfelwein*

beer		*Bier*
bitter		*Altbier*
malt beer, similar to stout		*Malzbier*
dark/strong		*Bock/Starkbier*
type of lager		*Pilsener*
made with wheat		*Weizenbier*
brandy		*Weinbrand*
champagne		*Sekt*
cherry brandy		*Kirschwasser*
spirit made from grain, often		*Schnaps*
drunk after a meal		
wine		*Wein*
chilled		*gekühlt*
dry		*trocken*
late harvest		*Spätlese*
mulled wine		*Glühwein*
red wine		*Rotwein*
sweet		*süß*
white wine		*Weißwein*
with ice		*mit Eis*

Shopping

bookshop	**bukh**-hahnt-lung	Buchhandlung
camera shop	**foh**-to-gheh-shaft	Fotogeschäft
chemist/pharmacy	ah-po-**tay**-keh	Apotheke
delicatessen	deh-li-kah-**teh**-sehn-gheh-shaft	Delikatessen-geschäft
department store	**vaa**-rehn-hows	Warenhaus
laundry	**va**-sheh-rai	Wäscherei
market	**mahrkt**	Markt

GERMAN

| newsagency/ stationer's | *tsai*-tungs-hant-lehr/ *shraip*-vah-rehn-gheh-shaft | Zeitungshändler/ Schreibwaren-geschäft |
| vegetable shop | gheh-*mü*-zeh-hahnt-lung | Gemüsehandlung |

How much is it?
   vee-feel ko-steht ehs?   Wieviel kostet es?

I would like to buy …
   ikh *merkh*-teh … *kow-fehn*   Ich möchte … kaufen.

Do you have others?
   haa-behn zee nokh
   ahn-deh-reh?   Haben Sie noch andere?

I don't like it.
   ehs gheh-*falt* mir nikht   Es gefällt mir nicht.

Can I look at it?
   ker-nehn zee ehs mir
   tsai-ghehn?   Können Sie es mir zeigen?

I'm just looking.
   ikh *show*-eh mikh nur um Ich schaue mich nur um.

Can you write down the price?
   ker-nehn zee dayn prais   Können Sie den Preis
   owf-shrai-behn?   aufschreiben?

Do you accept credit cards?
   nay-mehn zee kreh-*deet*-
   kahr-tehn?   Nehmen Sie Kreditkarten?

You May Hear

Can I help you?
   kahn ikh *ee*-nehn *hehl*-fehn? Kann ich Ihnen helfen?

How much/many do you want?
   vee-feel/vee-fee-leh   Wieviel/Wieviele möchten
   merkh-tehn zee?   Sie?

GERMAN

Anything else?
 *zonst nokh **eht**-vahs?*

Sonst noch etwas?

Sorry, this is the only one.
 *ehnt-**shul**-di-ghung, dahs ist dahs **ain**-tsi-gheh*

Entschuldigung, das ist das einzige.

Essential Groceries

batteries	*bah-tair-**ee**-en*	Baterien
bread	*broht*	Brot
butter	*boo-ter*	Butter
cereal	*froo-shtook/ sair-ray-**ahl***	Fruhstuck/Cereale
cheese	*kay-zeh*	Käse
chocolate	*sho-ko-**lah**-deh*	Chokolade
coffee	*kah-feh*	Kaffee
gas cylinder	*aird-gahz*	erdgas
ham	*shin-ken*	Schinken
matches	*zoon-den shtook*	Zunden Stück
milk	*milkh*	Milch
mineral water (without bubbles)	*meen-air-ahl vah-ser*	Mineralwasser (ohne Kohlensäure)
fruit	*frükht*	Frücht
shampoo	*shahm-pu*	Shampoo
soap	*zai-feh*	Seife
sugar	*tsoo-ker*	Zucker
tea	*tay*	Tee
toilet paper	*to-ah-**leh**-tehn-pah-peer*	Toilettenpapier
toothpaste	*tsahn-pah-stah*	Zahnpasta
washing powder	*vah-shen pool-ver*	Wachen pulver
yoghurt	*joo-goort*	Jougurt

GERMAN

Souvenirs

beer stein	*beer-kruk*	Bierkrug
cuckoo clock	*ku-kuks-ur*	Kuckucksuhr
earrings	*ohr-ring-eh*	Ohrringe
embroidery	*shti-keh-rai*	Stickerei
handicraft	*kunst-hahnt-vehrk*	Kunsthandwerk
necklace	*hahls-keh-teh*	Halskette
porcelain	*por-tseh-laan*	Porzellan
ring	*ring*	Ring

Clothing

coat	*mahn-tehl*	Mantel
jumper (sweater)	*pul-oh-vehr*	Pullover
shirt	*hehmt*	Hemd
shoes	*shu-eh*	Schuhe
trousers	*hoh-zeh*	Hose

It is too big/small
ehs ist tsu ghrohs/klain   Es ist zu groß/klein

Toiletries

condoms	*kon-doh-meh*	Kondome
deodorant	*day-oh-do-rahnt*	Deodorant
hairbrush	*haar-bür-steh*	Haarbürste
razor	*rah-zeer-meh-sehr*	Rasiermesser
sanitary napkins	*daa-mehn-bin-dehn*	Damenbinden
shampoo	*shahm-pu*	Shampoo
shaving cream	*rah-zeer-kray-meh*	Rasiercreme
soap	*zai-feh*	Seife
sunblock cream	*sahn-blok-kray-meh*	Sunblockcreme
tampons	*tahm-pons*	Tampons
tissues	*pah-peer-tü-khehr*	Papiertücher

GERMAN

toilet paper	*to-ah-leh-tehn-pah-peer*	Toilettenpapier
toothbrush	***tsahn-bür-steh***	Zahnbürste
toothpaste	***tsahn-pah-stah***	Zahnpasta

Photography

When will the photos be ready?

| *vahn **wehr**-dehn dee foh-tohs **fehr**-tikh zain?* | Wann werden die Fotos fertig sein? |

I'd like a film for this camera.

| *ikh **merkh**-teh ai-nehn film für **dee**-zeh **kah**-meh-rah* | Ich möchte einen Film für diese Kamera. |

B&W (film)	***shvahrts**-vais*	schwarzweiß
camera	***kah**-meh-rah*	Kamera
colour (film)	***fahrp**-film*	Farbfilm
film	*film*	Film
flash	*blits*	Blitz
lens	***lin**-zeh*	Linse
light meter	*beh-**likh**-tungs-meh-seh*	Belichtungsmesse

Smoking

A packet of cigarettes, please.

| ***ai**-neh **shahkh**-tehl tsi-ghah-**reh**-tehn **bi**-teh* | Eine Schachtel Zigaretten bitte. |

Are these cigarettes strong/ mild?

| *zint **dee**-zeh tsi-ghah-**reh**-tehn **shtahrk**/milt?* | Sind diese Zigaretten stark/mild? |

Do you have a light?

| ***haa**-behn zee **foy**-ehr?* | Haben Sie Feuer? |

GERMAN

May I smoke here?		
*dahrf ikh heer **row**-khen?*		Darf ich heir rachen?
Please don't smoke here.		
***kern**-en zee beet-teh nikht **row**-khen?*		Können Sie bitte nicht rachen?

cigarettes	*tsi-ghah-**reh**-tehn*	Zigaretten
cigarette papers	*tsi-ghah-**reh**-tehn-pah-pee-reh*	Zigarettenpapiere
filtered	*mit **fil**-tehr*	mit Filter
lighter	*foy-ehr-tsoyk*	Feuerzeug
matches	***shtraikh**-herl-tsehr*	Streichhölzer
menthol	***mehn**-tol*	Menthol
pipe	***pfai**-feh*	Pfeife
tobacco (pipe)	***taa**-bahk (**pfai**-fehn-taa-bahk)*	Tabak (Pfeifen-tabak)

Health

Where is …?	*voh ist …?*	Wo ist …?
the doctor	*dayr ahrtst*	der Arzt
the hospital	*dahs **krahng**-kehn-hows*	das Krankenhaus
the chemist	*dee ah-po-**tay**-keh*	die Apotheke
the dentist	*dayr **tsaan**-ahrtst*	der Zahnarzt

I am ill.		
ikh bin krahngk		Ich bin krank.
My friend is ill.		
***mai**-neh froynd-in/ froynt ist krahngk*		Meine Freundin (f)/Mein Freund (m) ist krank.
What's the matter?		
voh faylt ehs?		Wo fehlt es?

Where does it hurt?
voh **haa**-*behn zee*
shmehr-*tsehn?*　　　　　Wo haben Sie Schmerzen?

My … hurts.
mir tut … vay　　　　　　Mir tut … weh.

Parts of the Body

arm	*dayr ahrm*	der Arm
back	*dayr* **rü**-*kehn*	der Rücken
ear	*dahs korp*	das Ohr
eye	*dahs* **ow**-*gheh*	das Auge
foot	*dayr fus*	der Fuß
hand	*dee hahnt*	die Hand
head	*dayr kopf*	der Kopf
heart	*dahs hehrts*	das Herz
leg	*dahs bain*	das Bein
skin	*dee howt*	die Haut
teeth	*dee* **tsair**-*neh*	die Zähne

Ailments

I have …
ikh **haa**-*beh* …　　　　　Ich habe …

an allergy	**ai**-*neh ah*-**lehr**-*ghee*	eine Allergie
anaemia	*ah-na-***mee**	Anämie
a cold	**ai**-*neh ehr*-**kal**-*tung*	eine Erkältung
constipation	*fehr-***shtop**-*fung*	Verstopfung
a cough	**hu**-*stehn*	Husten
diarrhoea	**durkh**-*fahl*	Durchfall
fever	**fee**-*behr*	Fieber
a headache	**kopf**-*shmehr-tsehn*	Kopfschmerzen
indigestion	**ai**-*neh* **maa**-*ghehn-fehr-shti-mung*	eine Magenver-stimmung

GERMAN

an infection	*ai-neh in-fek-tsi-ohn*	eine Infektion
influenza	*dee ghri-peh*	die Grippe
low/high blood pressure	*nee-dri-ghehn/how-ehn blut-druk*	niedrigen/hohen Blutdruck
a pain	*shmehr-tsehn*	Schmerzen
sore throat	*hahls-shmehr-tsehn*	Halsschmerzen
sunburn	*zo-nehn-brahnt*	Sonnenbrand
a venereal disease	*ai-neh gheh-shlehkhts-krahngk-hait*	eine Geschlechts-krankheit

Women's Health

Could I see a female doctor?
   *kahn ikh **ai**-neh **arts**-tin*
   ***shpreh**-khehn?*
   Kann ich eine Ärztin sprechen?

I'm pregnant.
   *ikh bin **shvahng**-ehr*
   Ich bin schwanger.

I'm on the pill.
   *ikh **nay**-meh dee **pi**-leh*
   Ich nehme die Pille.

I haven't had my period for ... weeks.
   *ikh **haa**-beh zait ... **vo**-khen*
   ***mai**-neh peh-ri-oh-deh*
   *nikht gheh-**hahbt***
   Ich habe zeit ... wöchen meine Periode nicht gehabt.

(unusual) bleeding	*zvish-ehn-**bloo**-toong*	(Zwischen)bluting
cramps	***krahmp**-feh*	Krampfe
cystitis	***blah**-zen-ehn-**tsün**-doong*	Blasenentzündung
thrush	*pilts-**krow**-kite*	Pilzkraukheit

GERMAN

Specific Needs

I'm …	*ikh bin …*	Ich bin …
asthmatic	*ahst-**maa**-ti-keh-rin*	Asthmatikerin (f)
	*ahst-**maa**-ti-kehr*	Asthmatiker (m)
diabetic	*di-ah-**bay**-ti-kehr-in*	Diabetikerin (f)
	*di-ah-**bay**-tik*	Diabetiker (m)
epileptic	*eh-pi-**lehp**-ti-keh-rin*	Epileptikerin (f)
	*eh-pi-**lehp**-ti-kehr*	Epileptiker (m)

I'm allergic to antibiotics/
penicillin.
> *ikh bin **ghay**-ghehn ahn-ti-*
> *bi-**oh**-ti-kah/peh-ni-**tsi**-lin*
> *ah-**lehr**-ghish*

Ich bin gegen Antibiotika/
Penizillin allergisch.

I have been vaccinated.
> *ikh bin gheh-**impft***

Ich bin geimpft.

I feel better/worse.
> *ikh **fü**-leh mikh beh-sehr/*
> ***shli**-mehr*

Ich fühle mich besser/
schlimmer.

accident	*un-fahl*	Unfall
addiction	*zukht*	Sucht
antiseptic	*ahn-ti-**sehp**-ti-kum*	Antiseptikum
blood test	*blut-proh-beh*	Blutprobe
nausea	*ü-behl-kait*	Übelkeit
vitamins	*vi-tah-**mee**-neh*	Vitamine

At the Chemist

I need medication for …
> *ikh **brow**-kheh **eht**-vahs*
> ***ghay**-ghehn …*

Ich brauche etwas gegen …

I have a prescription.
*ikh **haa**-beh ain reh-**tsehpt***   Ich habe ein Rezept.

| antibiotics | *ahn-ti-bi-**oh**-ti-kah* | Antibiotika |
| medicine | *meh-di-**tseen*** | Medizin |

At the Dentist

I have a toothache.
*ikh **haa**-beh **tsaan**-shmehr-tsehn*   Ich habe Zahnschmerzen.

I've lost a filling.
*ikh **haa**-beh **ai**-ne **fü**-lung fehr-**lo**-rehn*   Ich habe eine Füllung verloren.

I've broken a tooth.
*mir ist ain tsaan **ahp**-gheh-bro-khehn*   Mir ist ein Zahn abgebrochen.

I don't want it extracted.
*ikh vil een nikht **tsee**-yehn **lah**-sehn*   Ich will ihn nicht ziehen lassen.

Please give me an anaesthetic.
***ghay**-behn zee mir **bi**-teh **ai**-neh **shpri**-tseh*   Geben Sie mir bitte eine Spritze.

Time & Dates

What time is it?   *vee shpayt ist ehs?*   Wie spät ist es?

It is … o'clock.	*ehs ist … ur*	Es ist … Uhr.
in the morning	***mor**-ghehns*	morgens
in the afternoon	***nahkh**-mi-tahks*	nachmittags
in the evening	***aa**-behnts*	abends

GERMAN

What date is it today?
dayr vee-feel-teh ist hoy-teh?   Der wievielte ist heute?

Days of the Week

Monday	*mohn-taak*	Montag
Tuesday	*deens-taak*	Dienstag
Wednesday	*mit-vokh*	Mittwoch
Thursday	*do-nehrs-taak*	Donnerstag
Friday	*frai-taak*	Freitag
Saturday	*zahms-taak*	Samstag
Sunday	*zon-taak*	Sonntag

Months

January	*yah-nu-aar*	Januar
February	*feh-bru-aar*	Februar
March	*marts*	März
April	*ah-pril*	April
May	*mai*	Mai
June	*yu-ni*	Juni
July	*yu-li*	Juli
August	*ow-ghust*	August
September	*zehp-tehm-behr*	September
October	*ok-toh-behr*	Oktober
November	*noh-vehm-behr*	November
December	*day-tsehm-behr*	Dezember

Seasons

summer	*zo-mehr*	Sommer
autumn	*hehrpst*	Herbst
winter	*vin-tehr*	Winter
spring	*frü-ling*	Frühling

GERMAN

Present

today	**hoy**-teh	heute
this morning	**hoy**-teh **mor**-ghehn	heute morgen
tonight	**hoy**-teh **aa**-behnt	heute abend
this week	**dee**-zeh vo-kheh	diese Woche
year	**dee**-zehs yaar	dieses Jahr
now	**yehtst**	jetzt

Past

yesterday	**gheh**-stehrn	gestern
day before yesterday	**for**-gheh-stehrn	vorgestern
yesterday morning	**gheh**-stehrn **mor**-ghehn	gestern morgen
last night	**leht**-steh nahkht	letzte Nacht
last week	**leht**-steh vo-kheh	letzte Woche
last year	**leht**-stehs yaar	letztes Jahr

Future

tomorrow	**mor**-ghehn	morgen
day after tomorrow	**ü**-behr-**mor**-ghehn	übermorgen
tomorrow morning	**mor**-ghehn frü	morgen früh
tomorrow after-noon/evening	**mor**-ghehn **nahkh**-mi-tahk/**aa**-behnt	morgen nachmittag/abend
next week	**nakh**-steh vo-kheh	nächste Woche
next year	**nakh**-stehs yaar	nächstes Jahr

During the Day

afternoon	**nahkh**-mi-tahk	Nachmittag
day	taak	Tag
early	frü	früh

GERMAN

midnight	*mi-tehr-nahkht*	Mitternacht
morning	*mor-ghehn*	Morgen
night	*nahkht*	Nacht
noon	*mi-tahk*	Mittag
sundown	*zo-nehn-un-tehr-ghahng*	Sonnenuntergang
sunrise	*zo-nehn-owf-ghahng*	Sonnenaufgang

Numbers & Amounts

0	*nul*	null
1	*ains*	eins
2	*tsvai (tsvoh)*	zwei (zwo on the telephone)
3	*drai*	drei
4	*feer*	vier
5	*fünf*	fünf
6	*zehkhs*	sechs
7	*zee-behn*	sieben
8	*ahkht*	acht
9	*noyn*	neun
10	*tsayn*	zehn
11	*ehlf*	elf
12	*tsverlf*	zwölf
13	*drai-tsayn*	dreizehn
14	*feer-tsayn*	vierzehn
15	*fünf-tsayn*	fünfzehn
16	*zehkh-tsayn*	sechzehn
17	*zeep-tsayn*	siebzehn
18	*ahkht-tsayn*	achtzehn
19	*noyn-tsayn*	neunzehn
20	*tsvahn-tsikh*	zwanzig

GERMAN

30	*drai*-sikh	dreißig
40	*feer*-tsikh	vierzig
50	*fünf*-tsikh	fünfzig
60	*zehkh*-tsikh	sechzig
70	*zeep*-tsikh	siebzig
80	*ahkht*-tsikh	achtzig
90	*noyn*-tsikh	neunzig
100	*hun*-dehrt	hundert
1000	*tow*-zehnt	tausend
one million	*ai*-neh mi-li-*ohn*	eine Million
1st	*ehr*-steh	erste
2nd	*tsvai*-teh	zweite
3rd	*dri*-teh	dritte
¼	ain *feer*-tehl	ein Viertel
⅓	ain *dri*-tehl	ein Drittel
½	*ai*-neh *half*-teh	eine Hälfte
¾	drai *feer*-tehl	drei Viertel

Amounts

small	*klain*	klein
big	*ghrohs*	groß
a little (amount)	ain *bis*-khehn	ein bißchen
double	nokh *ain*-mahl zoh	noch einmal so
(literally: 'the same again')		
a dozen	ain *du*-tsehnt	ein Dutzend
Enough!	*gheh*-**nuk**!	Genug!
a few	ain *paar*	ein paar
less	*vay*-ni-ghehr	weniger
not as much/not as	nikht zoh feel/nikht	nicht so viel/nicht
many	zoh *fee*-leh	so viele
a lot, much	*feel*	viel

many	*fee-leh*	viele
more	*mayr*	mehr
once	*ain-mahl*	einmal
a pair	*ain paar*	ein Paar
percent	*proh-tsehnt*	Prozent
some	*ai-ni-gheh*	einige
too much	*tsu feel*	zu viel
twice	*tsvai-mahl*	zweimal

Abbreviations

Ausw.	ID
Bhf	Station
DB	German Federal Railways
DJH	Youth Hostel (name of association)
DM	German Mark
HPA or HA	GPO (Main Post Office)
n. Chr./v. Chr.	AD/BC
Str.	St/Rd/etc
U	Underground (Railway)
vorm./nachm.	am/pm

Paperwork

name	Name
address	Adresse
date of birth	Geburtsdatum
place of birth	Geburtsort
age	Alter
sex	Geschlecht
nationality	Nationalität
religion	Religion
profession	Beruf
marital status	Familienstand

GERMAN

passport	(Reise)paß
passport number	Paßnummer
visa	Visum
identification	Ausweispapiere
birth certificate	Geburtsurkunde
driver's licence	Führerschein
car owner's title/ registration	(Kraft)fahrzeug-brief
customs	Zoll
immigration	Einwanderung
border	Grenze

Emergencies

POLICE	POLIZEI
POLICE STATION	POLIZEIWACHE

Help!	**hil**-*feh!*	Hilfe!
Thief!	*deep!*	Dieb!
Go away!	*ghay-ehn zee vehk!*	Gehen Sie weg!

It's an emergency!
*ehs ist ain **noht**-fahl!*   Es ist ein Notfall!
There's been an accident!
*ehs haht **ai**-nehn **un**-fahl*   Es hat einen Unfall gegeben!
*gheh-**ghay**-behn!*
Call a doctor!
hoh-*lehn zee **ai**-nehn ahrtst!*   Holen Sie einen Arzt!
Call an ambulance!
ru-*fehn zee **ai**-nehn*   Rufen Sie einen
krahng-*kehn-vaa-ghehn!*   Krankenwagen!

GERMAN

I've been raped.
*ikh bin fehr-**vahl**-tikht*
***vor**-dehn*

Ich bin verwaltigt worden.

I've been robbed!
*ikh bin beh-**shtoh**-lehn*
***vor**-dehn!*

Ich bin bestohlen worden!

Call the police!
***ru**-fehn zee dee po-li-**tsai**!*

Rufen Sie die Polizei!

I am ill.
ikh bin krahngk

Ich bin krank.

I am lost.
*ikh **haa**-beh mikh fehr-**irt***

Ich habe mich verirrt.

I've lost …
*ikh **haa**-beh … vehr-**loh**-rehn*

Ich habe … verloren.

my bags	*mai-neh **rai**-zeh-tah-shehn*	meine Reisetaschen
my handbag	*mai-neh **hahnt**-tah-sheh*	meine Handtasche
my money	*main ghehlt*	mein Geld
my travellers' cheques	*mai-neh **rai**-zeh-shehks*	meine Reiseschecks
my passport	***main**(-ehn) pahs*	mein(en) Paß (Use -en in Ich habe meinen Paß verloren)

My possessions are insured.
*mai-neh **zah**-khehn zint*
*fehr-**zi**-khehrt*

Meine Sachen sind versichert.

Where are the toilets?
*voh ist dee toh-ah-**leh**-teh?*

Wo ist die Toilette?

Could you help me please?
*ker-nehn zee mir **bi**-teh **hehl**-fehn?*

Könnten Sie mir bitte helfen?

Could I please use the telephone?
*kern-teh ikh **bi**-teh dahs teh-leh-**fohn** beh-**nu**-tsehn?*

Könnte ich bitte das Telefon benutzen?

I'm sorry. I apologise.
*ehs tut mir lait ehnt-**shul**-di-ghehn zee **bi**-teh*

Es tut mir leid.
Entschuldigen Sie bitte.

I didn't do it.
*dahs **haa**-beh ikh nikht gheh-**tahn***

Das habe ich nicht getan.

I didn't realise I was doing anything wrong.
*ikh vahr mir nikht beh-**vust**, **eht**-vahs **un**-rehkht-ehs gheh-**tahn** tsu **haa**-behn*

Ich war mir nicht bewußt, etwas Unrechtes getan zu haben.

I wish to contact my embassy/consulate.
*ikh **merkh**-teh mikh mit **mai**-nehr **boht**-shahft/ **mai**-nehm kon-zu-**laat** in fehr-**bin**-dung **zeht**-tsehn*

Ich möchte mich mit meiner Botschaft/meinem Konsulat in Verbindung setzen.

I speak English.
*ikh **shpreh**-kheh **ehng**-lish*

Ich spreche Englisch.

I have medical insurance.
*ikh bin in **ai**-nehr **krahng**-kehn-kah-seh*

Ich bin in einer Krankenkasse.

GREEK

GREEK

Greek

Introduction

Modern Greek is the language of about 9.5 million people in Greece and the Greek islands and about half a million in Cyprus. It is also spoken in isolated villages in Turkey and southern Italy, and wherever Greeks have migrated, notably Australia and North America.

Greek has had a huge influence on the history and culture of Europe; the international languages of science and philosophy, in particular, have borrowed heavily from it. The Greek language, which can be traced back as far as 1500 BC, is a member of the Indo-European family of languages; a huge language group which includes Germanic, Romance and Slavic languages. From the 4th century BC, after a thousand years of Greek dialects, a standard variety of Greek known as Koine became the common language. Modern Greek derives directly from Koine.

Greek, unlike Latin, never spawned a generation of new languages, so no language can be used as a convenient springboard to learn Greek in the way that, say, Italian can be used to learn Portuguese or Romanian. It is this fact, coupled with a theoretically difficult alphabet, that has given rise to such expressions as 'It's all Greek to me…'. Nonetheless, Greek is no more difficult than most Indo-European languages. Its pronunciation rules are more logical than those of English, and the grammar is no harder than German.

Accent differs from region to region and some accents may be more difficult to understand than others, but overall there is a general homogeneity in the everyday language. As a visitor to

Greece, your efforts to speak Greek will be richly rewarded, particularly as a lot of tourists don't make the effort.

Pronunciation

Greek is not difficult to pronounce, despite the formidable-looking initial barrier of the alphabet.

The Alphabet

The following alphabet shows the Greek letters in both capitals and lower case letters, the letter in English that it corresponds to and which we have used throughout the chapter as a guide, and an explanation of the sound, (these can only ever be approximate).

Letters	Pronunciation Guide	Sounds
A α	*a*	as in standard British 'but'
B β	*v*	as in 'van'
Γ γ	*gh, y*	somewhere between a hard 'g' as in 'got' and 'y'(before'a' and 'o' ou') then like 'y' (before'e', 'i'). Takes a bit of practice.
Δ δ	*dh*	as in 'then'
E ε	*e*	as in 'then'
Z ζ	*z*	as in 'zoo'
H η	*i*	as in 'pin'
Θ θ	*th*	as in 'thick'
I ι	*i*	as in 'pin'
K κ	*k*	as in 'king'
Λ λ	*l*	as in 'lamp'
M μ	*m*	as in 'mad'
N ν	*n*	as in 'not'
Ξ ξ	*x*	as in 'axe'

Ο ο	o	as in the British 'hot'
Π π	p	as in 'pin'
Ρ ϱ	r	as in 'run', but slightly trilled
Σ σ	s	as in 'sand'
ς	s	as in 'games', found only at the end of a word
Τ τ	t	as in 'ten'
Υ υ	i	as the 'y' in 'many'
Φ φ	f	as in 'food'
Χ χ	h, ch	'ch' as in Scottish 'loch', but more aspirated (before a', 'o' and 'ou'). Before 'i' and 'e' it is pronounced like the 'h' in 'hee-hee'). Another tricky one!
Ψ ψ	ps	as in 'lapse'.
Ω ω	o	as in the British 'hot'

Vowels

There are only five basic vowel sounds, and they correspond to 'a', 'e', 'i', 'o' and 'u' as as in 'but', 'bet', 'beet', 'bot', 'boot'.

Diphthongs

Greek has some interesting diphthong combinations, but the basic pronunciation pattern of vowel sounds never changes. Consider the following Greek diphthongs and their pronunciations.

αι	e	as in 'then'
οι	i	as in 'pin'
ει	i	as in 'pin'
υι	i	as in 'pin'
ου	u	as in 'mood'
αυ	av, af	as in 'average' or 'after'
ευ	ev, ef	as in 'seven' or 'left'

GREEK

In the preceding cases, the pronunciation depends on whether the following sound is 'voiced' (ie pronounced with a sound from the larynx, like 'b' or 'd'), or unvoiced, like 'p' or 't'. In most cases, if you pronounce the words naturally, you will get the correct sound.

Consonants

There are two main areas of difficulty with Greek: these are the letters 'γ' and 'χ'. The difficulty is not in the pronunciation, but in the fact that there are no real equivalents in standard English. The best strategy, once you arrive in Greece or Cyprus, is to listen out for these sounds and practise them a few times.

The letter 'γ', when before the 'a', 'i' and 'ou', sounds like an English 'g' with the back of the throat open. Try it and see what happens when you don't close the back of the throat with your tongue. Before 'e' and 'i' it naturally sounds like the 'y' in 'yes'.

Similarly, the Greek letter 'χ' when pronounced before 'a', 'o' and 'ou' is pronounced like the 'ch' in the Scottish word 'loch'. With 'e' and 'i' the passage to the throat becomes naturally narrowed and the 'ch' sound becomes more like a hissing sound.

Some other consonant clusters that you need to be aware of are as follows:

μπ	*b, mb*	as in '**b**ed' at the beginning of a word; '**mb**' in the middle of a word
ντ	*d, nd*	as in '**d**og' at the beginning of a word; '**nd**' in the middle of a word
γκ	*g*	as in '**g**o'
γγ	*ng*	as in 'si**ng**er'
γχ	*nch*	as in 'bro**nch**ial'
τσ	*ts*	as in 'ha**ts**'
τζ	*dz*	as in 'a**dz**e'

Double consonant clusters such as σσ, λλ, μμ, or ϱϱ are normally pronounced the same as the one consonant. Some regional differences will accentuate the pronunciation of the cluster.

Greetings & Civilities
Top Useful Phrases

Hello.	*ya sas*	Γεια σας
Goodbye.	*andio*	Αντίο.
Yes.	*ne*	Ναι.
No.	*ohi*	Όχι.
Please.	*parakalo*	Παρακαλώ.
Thank you.	*efharisto*	Ευχαριστώ.
Excuse me/sorry!	*me sinhorite/ sighnomi!*	Με συγχωρείτε/ συγγνώμη!
It doesn't matter/ that's all right.	*dhen pirazi*	Δεν πειράζει.

Greetings & Goodbyes

Good morning.	*kalimera*	Καλημέρα.
Good evening.	*kalispera*	Καλησπέρα.
Good afternoon.	*he-rete*	Χαίρετε.
Pleased to meet you.	*hero poli*	Χαίρω πολύ.
How are you?	*ti kanete?*	Τι κάνετε;
	ti kanis?	Τι κάνεις; (inf)
Well, thanks.	*ka-la efhari-sto*	καλά ευχαριστώ
Goodbye.		
andio		Αντίο.
Goodbye. (same as 'hello')		
ya sas/ya sou		Γεια σας/γεια σου. (inf)

See you!
  sto kalo!
  Στο καλό!
Good night.
  kalinihta
  Καληνύχτα.

Forms of Address

The main point to watch out for here is the use of the polite and informal forms of address. In this chapter we have used the polite form throughout. You can usually start using the informal form when someone uses it with you, or when talking to children or animals.

When addressing someone directly, use the following terms:

Mr ...	*kirie ...*	Κύριε ...
Mrs ...	*kiria ...*	Κυρία ...
Miss ...	*dhespinis ...*	Δεσποινίς ...

The Greeks have not devised a term for Ms yet. Often, when addressing someone of status, or with a professional position, you will use that person's title.

Doctor ...	*yatre ...*	Ιατρέ ...
Professor ...	*kirie kathiyita ...*	Κύριε Καθηγητά ...
Director ...	*kirie dhiefthinda ...*	Κύριε Διευθυντά ...
Minister ...	*kirie ipourghe ...*	Κύριε Υπουργέ ...

Language Difficulties

Do you speak English?
  mi-la-te angli-ka?
  Μιλάτε Αγγλικά;
Does anyone speak English?
  mi-la-i ka-nis angli-ka?
  Μιλάει κανείς Αγγλικά;

I understand.
  kataleveno   Καταλαβαίνω.
I see.
  katalava   Κατάλαβα.
I don't understand.
  den kataleveno   Δεν καταλαβαίνω.

Could you please speak more
slowly?
  sas parakalo, borite na   Σας παρακαλώ, μπορείτε να
  milisete pio argha?   μιλήσετε πιο αργά;
Sorry, what did you say?
  signomi, ti ipate?   Συγγνώμη, τι είπατε;
Could you please write that
down?
  sas parakalo, borite na   Σας παρακαλώ μπορείτε να
  mou to grapsete?   μου το γράψετε;

What does that mean?
  ti simeni afto?   Τι σημαίνει αυτό;
Just a minute! (eg while you
look something up)
  mya stighmi!   Μια στιγμή!

Small Talk
Meeting People
What is your name?
  pos sas lene/pos legeste?   Πώς σας λένε/πώς λέγεστε;
My name is …
  me lene …   Με λένε …

Nationalities

Where are you from?

apo pou iste? Από πού είστε;

I am from …	*ime apo …*	Είμαι από …
Australia	*tin afstralia*	την Αυστραλία
America	*tin ameriki*	την Αμερική
England	*tin anglia*	την Αγγλία
France	*ti gallia*	τη Γαλλία
Germany	*ti yermania*	τη Γερμανία
Ireland	*tin irlandhia*	την Ιρλανδία
Japan	*ti yaponia*	τη Ιαπωνία
the Middle East	*ti mesi anatoli*	τη Μέση Ανατολή
New Zealand	*ti nea zilandhia*	τη Νέα Ζηλανδία
Scotland	*ti skotia*	τη Σκωτία
South Africa	*ti notia afriki*	τη Νότια Αφρική
Spain	*tin ispania*	την Ισπανία
Switzerland	*tin elvetia*	την Ελβετία
Wales	*tin uallia*	την Ουαλλία

Unfortunately we can't list all countries here. You may have to find out from a local how to pronounce your country name, or find a good dictionary that has transliteration for Greek sounds.

Age

How old are you?

poson hronon iste? Πόσων χρονών είστε;

How old is your child?

poson hronon ine to pedhi sas? Πόσων χρονών είναι το παιδί σας;

I am 24.

ime ikosi tesaron hronon Είμαι είκοσι τεσσάρων χρονών.

Refer to page 279 for a full list of numbers.

GREEK

Occupations

What (work) do you do?
ti dhoulya kanete?		Τι δουλειά κάνετε;

I'm a/an ...	*ime ...*	Είμαι ...
accountant	*loghistis* (m)	λογιστής
	loghistria (f)	λογίστρια
actor	*ithopiyos*	ηθοποιός
artist (painter)	*zoghrafos*	ζωγράφος
businessman/	*epihirimatias*	επιχειρηματίας
businesswoman		
carpenter	*marangos*	μαραγγός
chef	*mayiras* (m)	μάγειρας
	mayirisa (f)	μαγείρισσα
doctor	*yatros*	ιατρός
driver	*odhighos*	οδηγός
engineer	*mihanikos*	μηχανικός
farmer	*aghrotis* (m)	αγρότης
	aghrotisa (f)	αγρότισσα
fisherman/	*psaras*	ψαράς
fisherwoman		
homemaker	*nikokiris* (m)	νοικοκύρης
	nikokira (f)	νοικοκυρά
journalist	*dhimosioghrafos*	δημοσιογράφος
labourer	*erghatis* (m)	εργάτης
	erghatria (f)	εργάτρια
musician	*mousikos*	μουσικός
nurse	*nosokomos* (m)	νοσοκόμος
	nosokoma (f)	νοσοκόμα
office worker	*ipallilos ghrafiou*	υπάλληλος γραφείου
pastor/priest	*papas*	παπάς

salesman	*politis*	πωλητής
saleswoman	*politria*	πωλήτρια
scientist	*epistimonas*	επιστήμονας
soldier	*stratiotis*	στρατιώτης
student	*fititis* (m)	φοιτητής/
	fititria (f)	φοιτήτρια
teacher	*dhaskalos* (m)	δάσκαλος
	dhaskala (f)	δασκάλα
waiter	*servitoros* (m)	σερβιτόρος
	servitora (f)	σερβιτόρα
writer	*singhrafeas*	συγγραφέας

Religion

What is your religion?
ti thriskevma iste?   Τι θρήσκευμα είστε;
I am not religious.
dhen ime thriskos/a   Δεν είμαι θρήσκος/α.

I am (a/an) ...	*ime ...*	Είμαι ...
Buddhist	*voudhistis*	Βουδιστής
Catholic	*katholikos/i*	καθολικός/ή
Christian	*hristianos/i*	χριστιανός/ή
Hindu	*indhouistis*	ινδουϊστής
Jewish	*evreos/evrea*	εβραίος/εβραία
Muslim	*mousoulmanos/a*	μουσουλμάνος/α
Protestant	*dhiamartiromenos/i*	διαμαρτυρόμενος/η

Family

Are you married?
iste pantremenos/
pantremeni?   Είστε παντρεμένος/
    παντρεμένη;

I am single.
  ime anipandros   Είμαι ανύπαντρος.
I am married.
  ime pandremenos/i   Είμαι παντρεμένος/η.
Do you have any children?
  ehete pedhya?   Έχετε παιδιά;
We have one (child).
  ehoume ena pedhi   Έχουμε ένα παιδί.
We don't have any
(children).
  dhen ehoume pedhya   Δεν έχουμε παιδιά.

husband	*andras*	άντρας
wife	*yineka*	γυναίκα
boyfriend	*filos*	φίλος
girlfriend	*fili*	φίλη
son	*yios*	γιος
daughter	*gori*	κόρη
father	*bateras*	πατέρας
mother	*mitera*	μητέρα

Some Icebreakers

I'm here on business.
  ime edho ya dhoulyes.   Είμαι εδώ για δουλειές.
I'm on holiday.
  ime se dhiakopes.   Είμαι σε διακοπές.
Nice weather, isn't it?
  poli oreos keros!   Πολύ ωραίος καιρός!
Are you waiting too?
  perimenete ki esis?   Περιμένετε κι εσείς;
Do you live near here?
  menete edho konda?   Μένετε εδώ κοντά;

We like it here.
mas aresi edho

Μας αρέσει εδώ.

This is my address.
afti ine i dhiefthinsi mou.

Αυτή είναι η διεύθυνσή μου.

May I have your address?
mou dhinete ti dhiefthinsi sas?

Μου δίνετε τη διεύθυνσή σας;

It's (not) important.
(dhen) axizi

(Δεν) αξίζει.

Really!
alithya!

Αλήθεια!

Signs

CASH DESK (in banks & shops)	ΤΑΜΕΙΟ
CUSTOMS	ΤΕΛΩΝΕΙΟΝ
DOCTOR'S SURGERY	ΙΑΤΡΕΙΟ
ENTRY	ΕΙΣΟΔΟΣ
EXIT	ΕΞΟΔΟΣ
FROM ...	ΑΠΟ ...
HOSPITAL	ΝΟΣΟΚΟΜΕΙΟ
INFORMATION	ΠΛΗΡΟΦΟΡΙΕΣ
MEN (toilets)	ΑΝΔΡΩΝ
NO SMOKING	ΑΠΑΓΟΡΕΥΕΤΑΙ ΤΟ ΚΑΠΝΙΣΜΑ
POLICE	ΑΣΤΥΝΟΜΙΑ
PROHIBITED	ΑΠΑΓΟΡΕΥΕΤΑΙ
PULL	ΕΛΞΑΤΕ
PUSH	ΩΘΗΣΑΤΕ
TO ...	ΠΡΟΣ ...
WOMEN (toilets)	ΓΥΝΑΙΚΩΝ

GREEK

Getting Around

What time does the ... leave/
arrive?

ti ora fevyi/ftani to ... ?		Τι ώρα φεύγει/φτάνει το ... ;

boat	*karavi*	καράβι
bus	*leofo-ri-o*	λεωφορείο
train	*treno*	τραίνο

Finding Your Way

How do I get to ...?	*pos tha pao sto ...?*	Πώς θα πάω στο ...;
Where is ...?	*pou ine ...?*	Πού είναι ...;

the bus station	*o stathmos leoforion*	ο σταθμός λεωφορείων
the train station	*o sidhirodhromikos stathmos*	ο σιδηροδρομικός σταθμός
the airport	*to aerodhromio*	το αεροδρόμιο
the subway station	*o stathmos tou ilektriku*	ο σταθμός του Ηλεκτρικού
the taxi stand	*i stasi ton taxi*	η στάση των ταξί
the port	*to limani*	το λιμάνι
the ticket office	*to ekdhotirio isitirion*	το εκδοτήριο εισιτηρίων

Is it nearby?

ine konda?	Είναι κοντά;

Is it far?

ine makria?	Είναι μακριά;

Can I walk there?

boro na pao eki me ta podhya?	Μπορώ να πάω εκεί με τα πόδια;

Can you show me on the
map?
>   *borite na mou to dhixete*   Μπορείτε να μου το δείξετε
>   *sto harti?*   στο χάρτη;

Directions

Be prepared when asking directions in Greece. People are a bit
more laid back when it comes to direction giving. That 'five minutes' may be 25 minutes; 'near' the post office may mean on the
opposite side of town from the post office.

Go straight ahead.
>   *piyenete katefthian*   Πηγαίνετε κατ'ευθείαν.

Turn left …	*stripste aristera* …	Στρίψτε αριστερά …
Turn right …	*stripste dexia* …	Στρίψτε δεξιά …
at the corner	*sti gonia*	στη γωνία
at the traffic lights	*sta fanaria*	στα φανάρια
at the square	*stim blatia*	στην πλατεία

back	*piso*	Πίσω
behind	*pi-so*	Πίσω
in front of	*mpro-sta a-po*	Μπροστά από
far	*makri-a*	Μακρυά
near	*ko-nda*	Κοντά
opposite	*a-pe-nandi*	Απέναντι

up	*pano*	Πάνω
down	*kato*	Κάτω
near	*konda*	Κοντά
far	*makria*	Μακριά

GREEK

What … is this?	*pyos/pya/pyo … ine?*	Ποιος/ποια/ποιο… είναι;
street	*dhromos*	δρόμος
square	*platia*	πλατεία
suburb	*proastio*	προάστειο

Buying Tickets

TICKET OFFICE	*ΕΚΔΟΤΗΡΙΑ ΕΙΣΙΤΗΡΙΩΝ*
TICKETS	*ΕΙΣΙΤΗΡΙΑ*

Excuse me, where is the ticket office?
me singyho-ri-te pu i-ne to gra-fi-o isiti-ri-on?
Με συγχωρείτε πού είναι το γραφείο εισιτηρίων;

Where can I buy a ticket?
pu bo-ro nagho-ra-so e-na isi-ti-rio?
Πού μπορώ ν' αγοράσω ένα εισιτήριο;

I want to go to ...
the-lo na pa-o sto/sti ...
Θέλω να πάω στο/στη . . .

Do I need to book?
hri-a-zete na kli-so the-si
Χρειάζεται να κλείσω θέση;

You need to book.
hri-a-zete na kli-sis the-si
Χρειάζεται να κλείσεις θέση.

I'd like to book a seat to ...
tha i-thela na kli-so .
the-si ya to ..
Θα ήθελα να κλείσω θέση για το . . .

How much is …?		
poso kani …?		Πόσο κάνει …;

I'd like …	*tha ithela …*	Θα ήθελα …
one ticket to Mykonos	*ena isitirio ya ti Mikono*	ένα εισιτήριο για τη Μύκονο
two tickets to Mykonos	*dhio isitiria ya ti Mikono*	δυο εισιτίρια για τη Μύκονο
a reservation	*na kliso mya thesi*	να κλείσω μια θέση
single (ticket)	*ablo (isitirio)*	απλό (εισιτήριο)
return (ticket)	*(isitirio) me epistrofi*	(εισιτήριο) με επιστροφή
economy	*touristiki thesi*	τουριστική θέση
business class (air)	*dhiakekrimeni thesi*	διακεχριμένη θέση
first class	*proti thesi*	πρώτη θέση
2nd class	*dhef-teri the-si*	δεύτερη θέση

It is full.
  dhen i-pa-rhi the-si   Δεν υπάρχει θέση
Is it completely full?
  i-ne ende-los ghe-ma-to?   Είναι εντελώς γεμάτο;
Can I get a stand-by ticket?
  *mi-pos bo-ro na pa-ro
  isi-ti-rio anamo-nis?*   Μήπως μπορώ να πάρω
          εισιτήριο αναμονής;

Air

ARRIVALS	*ΑΦΙΞΕΙΣ*
BAGGAGE CLAIM	*ΠΑΡΑΛΑΒΗ ΑΠΟΣΚΕΥΩΝ*
DEPARTURE	*ΑΝΑΧΩΡΗΣΕΙΣ*

GREEK

DUTY FREE SHOP	ΚΑΤΑΣΤΗΜΑ ΑΦΟΡΟΛΟΓΗΤΩΝ
LOST PROPERTY	ΓΡΑΦΕΙΟ ΑΠΩΛΕΣΘΕΝΤΩΝ
MONEY EXCHANGE	ΣΥΝΑΛΛΑΓΜΑ
PASSPORT CONTROL	ΕΛΕΓΧΟΣ ΔΙΑΒΑΤΗΡΙΩΝ
TELEPHONE OFFICE	ΟΤΕ (ΟΡΓΑΝΙΣΜΟΣ ΤΗΛΕΠΙΚΟΙΝΩΝΙΩΝ ΕΛΛΑΔΟΣ)
TOURIST POLICE	ΤΟΥΡΙΣΤΙΚΗ ΑΣΤΥΝΟΜΙΑ

Is there a flight to (Chania)?
iparhi mya ptisi ya ta (Hania)?
Υπάρχει μια πτήση για τα (Χανιά);

When is the next flight to (Santorini)?
pote ine i epomeni ptisi ya ti (Sandorini)?
Πότε είναι η επόμενη πτήση για τη (Σαντορίνη);

What is the flight number?
pyos ine o arithmos tis ptisis?
Ποιος είναι ο αριθμός της πτήσης;

Where do we check in?
pou ghinete o elenchos ton isitirion?
Πού γίνεται ο έλεγχος των εισιτηρίων;

When do we have to check in?
pote prepi na elenchthoun ta isitiria?
Πότε πρέπει να ελεγχθούν τα εισιτήρια;

One hour/two hours before
departure.
mya ora/dhio ores prin
apo tin anahorisi

Μια ώρα/δυο ώρες πριν
από την αναχώρηση.

Where do you pick up
luggage?
pou prepi na paralavoume
tis aposkeves?

Πού πρέπει να παραλάβουμε
τις αποσκευές;

Bus & Trolleybus

STOP (Bus/Trolleybus)	ΣΤΑΣΗ

Where is the nearest bus/
trolley stop?
pou ine i plisiesteri stasi
tou leoforiou/tou trolley?

Πού είναι η πλησιέστερη στάση
του λεωφορείου/του τρόλλεϋ;

Which bus goes to Syntagma
Square?
pyo leoforio pai stim
blatia sindagmatos?

Ποιο λεωφορείο πάει στην
Πλατεία Συντάγματος;

Where can I buy a bus ticket?
pou boro naghoraso isitirio
gia to leoforio?

Πού μπορώ ν'αγοράσω
εισιτήριο για το λεωφορείο;

Does this bus go to ... ?
pi-ghe-ni a-fto to
leofo-ri-o sto/sti ...?

Πηγαίνει αυτό το
λεωφορείο στο/στη ... ;

Please let me know when it is
my stop.
borite na mou pite otan
tha ftasoume sti stasi mou

Μπορείτε να μου πείτε όταν
θα φτάσουμε στη στάση μου;

How long does it take to get
to the airport?

posi ora kani ya to aerodhromio?	Πόση ώρα κάνει για το αεροδρόμιο;

Excuse me, I'd like to get off!

me sinhorite, thelo na katevo!	Με συγχωρείτε, θέλω να κατεβώ!

Can you tell me where we are?

borite na mou pite pou imaste?	Μπορείτε να μου πείτε πού είμαστε;

Please tell the driver to stop.

parakalo, peste ston odhigo na stamatisi	Παρακαλώ, πέστε στον οδηγό να σταματήσει.

Train

express train	*treno expres*	Τραίνο Εξπρές
international train	*dhiethnes treno*	Διεθνές Τραίνο
intercity train	*treno Inter City*	Τραίνο Ιντερ Σίτυ
kiosk	*periptero*	Περίπτερο
left luggage	*horos aposkevon*	Χώρος αποσκευών
local train	*topiko treno*	Τοπικό Τραίνο
railway station	*sidhirodromikos stathmos*	Σιδηροδρομικός Σταθμός
timetable	*dhromologhio*	Δρομολόγιο
train	*treno*	Τραίνο
platform	*apovathra*	Αποβάθρα
waiting room	*ethousa anamonis*	Αίθουσα Αναμονής

I'd like a ticket to
(Thessaloniki).

thelo ena isitirio ya (ti Thessaloniki)	Θέλω ένα εισιτήριο για (τη Θεσσαλονίκη).

I'd like a sleeper.
   thelo mya kouketta   Θέλω μια κουκέτα.
Can I make a reservation?
   boro na kliso mya thesi?   Μπορώ να κλείσω μια θέση;
I'd like a smoking seat.
   tha ithela mya thesi stous   Θα ήθελα μια θέση στους
   kapnizondes.   καπνίζοντες.
I'd like a non-smoking seat.
   tha ithela mya thesi stous   Θα ήθελα μια θέση στους
   mi kapnizondes.   μη καπνίζοντες.
Do I need to change trains?
   prepi na allakso trena?   Πρέπει να αλλάξω τραίνα;
What time does the train
leave/arrive?
   ti ora fevyi/ftani to treno?   Τι ώρα φεύγει/φτάνει το
                            τραίνο;

Metro

Where is the nearest metro
station?
   pou ine o plisiesteros   Πού είναι ο πλησιέστερος
   stathmos tou ilektrikou?   σταθμός του Ηλεκτρικού;
Where do I purchase a ticket?
   pou prepi naghoraso   Πού πρέπει ν'αγοράσω
   isitirio?   εισιτήριο;
Please give me a book of
tickets.
   sas parakalo, dhoste mou   Σας παρακαλώ, δώστε μου
   mya dhezmi isitirion   μια δέσμη εισιτηρίων.
Which station is this?
   pyos stathmos ine aftos?   Ποιος σταθμός είναι αυτός;

Taxi

| Taxi | *taxi* | Ταξί |

I want to go (to the airport).
thelo na pao (sto aerodhromio)   Θέλω να πάω (στο αεροδρόμιο).

Could you take me …?   *borite na me pate …?*   Μπορείτε να με πάτε …;

How much is it to (the city centre)?
poso kani mehri to (kendro tis polis)?   Πόσο κάνει μέχρι το (κέντρο της πόλης);

Car

| NO PARKING | ΑΠΑΓΟΡΕΥΕΤΑΙ Η ΣΤΑΘΜΕΥΣΗ |

Where can I hire a car?
pou boro na nikiaso ena aftokinito?   Πού μπορώ να νοικιάσω ένα αυτοκίνητο;

How much does it cost per day?
poso kani tin imera?   Πόσο κάνει την ημέρα;

How much does it cost per week?
poso kani tin evdhomadha?   Πόσο κάνει την εβδομάδα;

Is insurance included?
ine asfalismeno?   Είναι ασφαλισμένο;

Give me … litres of petrol (gasoline).
dhoste mou, parakalo … litra venzinis
Δώστε μου, παρακαλώ, … λίτρα βενζίνης.

Fill it up.
yemiste to
Γεμίστε το.

Unleaded petrol (gasoline).
amolivdhi (venzini)
Αμόλυβδη (βενζίνη).

Can you tell me the way to (Patra)?
borite na mou dhixete to dhromo ya tin Batra?
Μπορείτε να μου δείξετε το δρόμο για (την Πάτρα);

Are we on the right road to (Ioannina)?
piyenoume kala ya ta Yannina?
Πηγαίνουμε καλά για (τα Ιωάννινα);

How far is it to (Kavala)?
poso makria ine mehri tin Gavala?
Πόσο μακριά είναι μέχρι (την Καβάλα);

How far is the next service station?
poso makria ine mehri to epomeno venzinadhiko?
Πόσο μακριά είναι μέχρι το επόμενο βενζινάδικο;

Is it OK to park here?
boro na parkaro edho?
Μπορώ να παρκάρω εδώ;

air (for tyres)	*a-e-ras (ya la-stiha)*	αέρας (για λάστιχα)
battery	*bata-ri-a*	μπαταρία
brakes	*fre-na*	φρένα
clutch	*sim-ble-htis*	συμπλέκτης

driver's licence	a-thia othi-yi-sis	άδεια οδήγησης
engine	mi-han	μηχανή
lights	fo-ta	φώτα
oil	la-dhi	λάδι
puncture	tri-pio la-stiho	τρύπιο λάστιχο
radiator	psi-yi-o	ψυγείο
road map	odhi-kos har-tis	οδικός χάρτης
tyres	la-stiha	λάστιχα
windscreen	bam-briz	παρμπρίζ

Car Problems

My car has broken down.
   to aftokinito mou halase   Το αυτοκίνητό μου χάλασε.
Can you help me?
   borite na me voithisete?   Μπορείτε να με βοηθήσετε;
I need a mechanic.
   hri-a-zome e-na mihani-ko   Χρειάζομαι ένα μηχανικό.
What make is it?
   ti mo-nde-lo i-ne?   Τι μοντέλο είναι;

The battery is flat.
   i bata-ri-a e-hi a-THia-si   Η μπαταρία έχει αδειάσει.
The radiator is leaking.
   to psi-yi-o sta-zi   Το ψυγείο στάζει .
I have a flat tyre.
   me-hi pia-si la-stiho   Μ' έχει πιάσει λάστιχο .
It's overheating.
   e-hi a-na-psi   Έχει ανάψει .
It's not working.
   The thu-le-vi   Δε δουλεύει .

I've lost my way.
eho hasi to dhromo   Έχω χάσει το δρόμο.

Boat

When is the next boat to (Ios)?
pote fevyi to epomeno   Πότε φεύγει το επόμενο
karavi ya tin Io?   καράβι για την `Ιο;

Can I have a cabin?
mou dhinete mya kambina?   Μου δίνετε μια καμπίνα;

How much is the cheapest ticket?
poso kani to ftinotero   Πόσο κάνει το φτηνότερο
isitirio?   εισιτήριο;

How many hours is it to (Folegandros)?
posez ores ine mehri   Πόσες ώρες είναι μέχρι
ti Foleghandro?   (τη Φολέγανδρο);

Does the boat stop at (Milos)?
stamatai to karavi   Σταματάει το καράβι
sti Milo?   (στη Μήλο);

What time does the boat depart/arrive?
ti ora fevyi/ftani   Τι ώρα φεύγει/φτάνει
to karavi?   το καράβι;

Where does the boat leave from?
apo pou fevyi to karavi?   Από πού φεύγει το καράβι;

Can I book a ticket today?
boro na kopso isitirio   Μπορώ να κόψω εισιτήριο
simera?   σήμερα;

Is there a restaurant on board?
to karavi ehi estiatorio?   Το καράβι έχει εστιατόριο;
Do you accept Eurailpass?
dheheste Eurailpass?   Δέχεστε EURAILPASS;
Do you have student discounts?
dhinete fititikez ekptosis?   Δίνετε φοιτητικές εκπτώσεις;

Accommodation
Finding Accommodation

Can you tell me	*borite na mou pite*	Μπορείτε να μου πείτε
where there's ...?	*pou iparhi ...?*	πού υπάρχει ... ;
a good hotel	*ena kalo xenodhohio*	ένα καλό ξενοδοχείο
a cheap hotel	*ena ftino xenodhohio*	ένα φτηνό ξενοδοχείο
a room for the night	*ena dhomatio ya apopse*	ένα δωμάτιο για απόψε
a youth hostel	*enas xenonas neotitos*	ένας ξενώνας νεότητος
an information bureau	*ena ghrafio pliroforion*	ένα γραφείο πληροφοριών
a camping site	*ena kamping*	ένα κάμπιγκ

Booking a Room

Do you have any rooms available?
e-hete dhia-the-sima dho-ma-tia?   Έχετε διαθέσιμα δωμάτια;
I'd like to book a room.
thelo na kliso dhomatio   Θέλω να κλείσω δωμάτιο

for one night/four nights
ya ena vradhi — για ένα βράδυ/τέσσερα βράδια

from tonight/Tuesday
apo apopse/ Triti — από απόψε/Τρίτη

I'd like a …	*thelo ena …*	Θέλω ένα …
single room	*mono dhomatio*	μονό δωμάτιο
double room	*dhiplo dhomatio*	διπλό δωμάτιο
room for …?	*dhomatio ya …*	δωμάτιο για …
people	*atoma*	άτομα
room with a	*dhomatio me dous*	δωμάτιο με ντους
shower and toilet	*ke toualetta*	και τουαλέττα

At the Hotel

How much is the room …?	*poso kani to dhomatio …*	Πόσο κάνει το δωμάτιο …
per night	*ti vradhya*	τη βραδυά
for … nights	*ya … vradhyes*	για … βραδυές
per week	*tin evdhomadha*	την εβδομάδα

Is breakfast included?
simberilamvani ke proïno? — Συμπεριλαμβάνεται και πρωϊνό;

What time do I have to check out?
ti ora prepi na figho apo to dhomatio? — Τι ώρα πρέπει να φύγω από το δωμάτιο;

Can I see the room?
boro na dho to dhomatio? — Μπορώ να δω το δωμάτιο;

Can you show me another room?
borite na mou dhixete allo dhomatio? — Μπορείτε να μου δείξετε άλλο δωμάτιο;

GREEK

Thanks, but it's not suitable.
  sas efharisto, alla dhe   Σας ευχαριστώ, αλλά δε
  mou kani   μου κάνει.
Can I see the bathroom?
  bo-ro-na dho to ba-njo?   Μπορώ να δω το μπάνιο;
Is there a reduction for
students/children?
  i-pa-rhi e-kptosi ya ma   Υπάρχει έκπτωση για
  thi-tes/pe-dhia?   μαθητές/παιδιά;

It's fine, I'll take it.
  i-ne e-nda-ksi tha to pa-ro   Είναι εντάξει θα το πάρω.
Can I have my passport
please?
  mou dhinete, parakalo,   Μου δίνετε, παρακαλώ
  to dhiavatirio mou?   το διαβατήριό μου;

You May Hear
Do you have identification?
  e-hete ta-fto-tita?   Έχετε ταυτότητα;
Your membership card, please.
  tin ka-rta sindhro-mis sas   Την κάρτα συνδρομής σας
  paraka-lo   παρακαλώ.
Sorry, we're full
  si-ghno-mi a-la i-maste   Συγγνώμη αλλά είμαστε
  yje-ma-ti   γεμάτοι.
How long will you be staying?
  po-so tha ka-thi-sete?   Πόσο θα καθήσετε;

How many nights?
po-sa vra-dhia? Πόσα βράδια;...

It's ... per day/per person.
*i-ne ... ya ka-the me-ra/
ka-the a-tomo* Είναι για κάθε μέρα/
κάθε άτομο.

Requests & Complaints

I'll take the room.
tha to paro to dhomatio Θα το πάρω το δωμάτιο.

The room is too small.
to dhomatio ine mikro Το δωμάτιο είναι μικρό.

Can I have some more blankets?
mou dhinete ki allez kouvertez Μου δίνετε κι άλλες κουβέρτες;

Is there hot water available?
ehi zesto nero? Έχει ζεστό νερό;

The shower doesn't work.
to dous dhe dhoulevi Το ντους δε δουλεύει.

There is no hot water.
dhen ehi zesto nero Δεν έχει ζεστό νερό.

I can't open the window.
dhem boro nanikso to parathiro Δε μπορώ να ανοίξω το παράθυρο.

Can I leave my valuables here?
boro nafiso ta andikimena axias mazi sas? Μπορώ ν'αφήσω τα αντικείμενα αξίας μαζί σας;

Checking Out

I am/We are leaving now.
fev-gho/fev-ghume to-ra Φεύγω/φεύγουμε τώρα.

GREEK

I'd like to pay the bill.
> *the-lo na pli-ro-so*   Θέλω να πληρώσω
> *ton logharia-smo*   το λογαριασμό.

Can I leave my luggage here?
> *mporo nafiso tis*   Μπορώ ν'αφήσω τις
> *aposkevez mou edho*   αποσκευές μου εδώ;

Can you call me a taxi?
> *borite na tilefonisete*   Μπορείτε να τηλεφωνήσετε
> *ya ena taxi?*   για ένα ταξί;

name	*o-noma*	όνομα
surname	*e-pi-theto*	επίθετο
room number	*ari-thmos*	αριθμός
	dhomatiou	δωματίου

Useful Words

air-con	*klimatizmos*	κλιματισμός
bed	*krevati*	κρεββάτι
cupboard	*doulapi*	ντουλάπι
door	*porta*	πόρτα
fan	*anemistiras*	ανεμιστήρας
heating	*thermansi*	θέρμανση
light	*fos*	φως
lock	*klidharia*	κλειδαριά
sheets	*sendonia*	σεντόνια
toilet	*toualetta*	τουαλέττα
toilet paper	*harti iyias*	χαρτί υγείας
towel	*petseta*	πετσέτα
wash basin	*niptiras*	νιπτήρας
window	*parathiro*	παράθυρο

Around Town

I'm looking for ...
psa-hno ...   Ψάχνω ...

the art gallery	*tin pinako-thi-ki*	την πινακοθήκη
a bank	*tin tra-peza*	την τράπεζα
the church	*tin ekli-si-a*	την εκκλησία
the city centre	*to ke-ndro*	το κέντρο της
	tis po-lis	της πόλης
the ... embassy	*tin ... pre-svi-a*	την ... πρεσβεία
my hotel	*to ksenodho-hi-o mu*	το ξενοδοχείο μου
the market	*tin agho-ra*	την αγορά
the museum	*to mu-si-o*	το μουσείο
the police	*tin astino-mi-a*	την αστυνομία
the post office	*to tahidhro-mi-o*	το ταχυδρομείο
a public toilet	*dhimo-ti-kes*	δημοτικές
	tua-le-tes	τουαλέτες
the telephone centre	*tilefoni-ko ke-ntro*	τηλεφωνικό κέντρο
the tourist information office	*ghra-fi-o turisti-kon plirofori-on*	γραφείο τουριστι-κών πληροφοριών

What time does it open?
ti o-ra a-ni-yi?   Τι ώρα ανοίγει;
What time does it close?
ti o-ra kli-ni?   Τι ώρα κλείνει;

At the Bank

BANK	*ΤΡΑΠΕΖΑ*
CURRENCY EXCHANGE	*ΣΥΝΑΛΛΑΓΜΑ*
CASHIER	*ΤΑΜΕΙΟ*
AUTOMATIC CASH MACHINE	*ΑΥΤΟΜΑΤΗ ΧΡΗΜΑΤΟΘΥΡΙΔΑ*
MANAGER	*ΔΙΕΥΘΥΝΤΗΣ*

Do you change travellers' cheques?
  exaryironete taxidhiotikes epitayes? Εξαργυρώνετε ταξιδιωτικές επιταγές;

I'd like to change this money into drachmas.
  tha ithela na kano afta ta lefta se dhrahmes Θα ήθελα να κάνω αυτά τα λεφτά σε δραχμές.

How many drachmas will that be?
  poses dhrahmes tha ine? Πόσες δραχμές θα είναι;

Do you take a commission?
  pernete promithya? Παίρνετε προμήθεια;

Could you please write that down?
  borite na mou to grapsete? Μπορείτε να μου το γράψετε;

What is the exchange rate?
  poso pai to sinallaghma? Πόσο πάει το συνάλλαγμα;

Can I have some money transferred to here?
  boro na metafero hrimata edho? Μπορώ να μεταφέρω χρήματα εδώ;

GREEK

How long will it take?
   poson gero tha pari?   Πόσον καιρό θα πάρει;
Have you received my money
yet?
   ehete lavi ta hrimata mou?   Έχετε λάβει τα χρήματά μου;

At the Post Office

Where is the post office?
   pou ine to tahidhromio?   Πού είναι το ταχυδρομείο;
What time does the post
office open?
   ti ora anighi to   Τι ώρα ανοίγει το
   tahidhromio?   ταχυδρομείο;
Where is the nearest
letterbox?
   pou ine to plisiestero   Πού είναι το πλησιέστερο
   ghrammatokivotio?   γραμματοκιβώτιο;
I'd like to send this letter to
(Australia).
   tha ithela na stilo afto to   Θα ήθελα να στείλω αυτό το
   ghramma stin (Afstralia)   γράμμα στην (Αυστραλία).

envelope	*fakelos*	φάκελος
padded bag	*enischimenos fakelos*	ενισχυμένος φάκελος
postal order	*tahidhromiki epitayi*	ταχυδρομική επιταγή
receipt	*apodhiksi*	απόδειξη
stamp	*ghrammatosimo*	γραμματόσημο
airmail	*aeropori-kos*	αεροπορικώς
parcel	*the-ma*	δέμα
registered mail	*sisti-me-ni*	συστημένη
	aliloghra-fi-a	αλληλογραφία
surface mail	*dhi-a tha-la-sis*	διά θαλάσσης

GREEK

Telephone

TELEPHONE	ΤΗΛΕΦΩΝΟ
TELECARD	ΤΗΛΕΚΑΡΤΑ
GREEK	ΟΡΓΑΝΙΣΜΟΣ
TELECOMMUNICATIONS	ΤΗΛΕΠΙΚΟΙΝΩΝΙΩΝ
ORGANISATION (OTE)	ΕΛΛΑΔΟΣ (OTE)
CASHIER	ΤΑΜΕΙΟ

I'd like to make a call to
(Ireland).
   thelo na tilefoniso stin   Θέλω να τηλεφωνήσω στην
   (Irlandhia)   (Ιρλανδία).

How much does it cost per
minute?
   poso kani to lepto?   Πόσο κάνει το λεπτό;

How much do I owe you?
   posa sas hrostao?   Πόσα σας χρωστάω;

I got the wrong number!
   pira lathos arithmo!   Πήρα λάθος αριθμό.

We were cut off.
   mas dhiekopsan.   Μας διέκοψαν.

Can I make a reverse call to
(Scotland)?
   mporo na hreoso to   Μπορώ να χρεώσω το
   tilefonima sti (skotia)?   τηλεφώνημα στη (Σκωτία);

The number is engaged.
   milai   Μιλάει.

Do you have a telephone
directory?
   ehete tilefoniko katalogho? Έχετε τηλεφωνικό κατάλογο;

Every country has its own way of answering phone calls. When you call a Greek phone number you will commonly hear the following responses …

Εμπρός!	embros!	Hello!
Λέγετε …	leyete …	(lit) 'You may speak …'
Ναι …	ne	Yes …

This is Mr/Ms …
  milai o kirios/i kiria … Μιλάει ο κύριος/η κυρία …

I'd like to speak to Mr/Ms …
  tha ithela na miliso
  ston kirio/stin kiria … Θα ήθελα να μιλήσω
  στον κύριο/στην κυρία …

Could I speak with someone who speaks English?
  boro na miliso me kapyon
  pou xeri anglika? Μπορώ να μιλήσω με κάποιον
  που ξέρει Αγγλικά;

Could I have extension number … ?
  mou dhinete ton esoteriko
  arithmo …? Μου δίνετε τον εσωτερικό
  αριθμό …;

Could you speak more loudly?
  milate pyo dhinata,
  parakalo? Μιλάτε πιο δυνατά
  παρακαλώ;

I'm sorry, I can't hear you.
  sighnomi, dhe sas akouo Συγγνώμη, δε σας ακούω.

I'll call again.
  tha sas xanaparo Θα σας ξαναπάρω.

Sightseeing

How much is the entry fee?
poso kani i isodhos?   Πόσο κάνει η είσοδος;

Do you have a student discount?
echete fititiki ekptosi?   Έχετε φοιτητική έκπτωση;

Is there an English-speaking guide?
iparhi anglofonos xenaghos?   Υπάρχει αγγλόφωνος ξεναγός;

May I take photographs?
boro na vghalo fotoghrafies?   Μπορώ να βγάλω φωτογραφίες;

What are the opening hours?
pyes ores anighi?   Ποιες ώρες ανοίγει;

What time does it close?
ti ora klini?   Τι ώρα κλείνει;

ancient	*ar-he-o*	αρχαίο
archaeological	*arheoloyi-ko*	αρχαιολογικό
beach	*para-li-a*	παραλία
castle	*ka-stro*	κάστρο
cathedral	*kathedhri-kos na-os*	καθεδρικός ναός
church	*ekli-si-a*	εκκλησία
concert hall	*e-thusa sinavli-on*	αίθουσα συναυλιών
library	*vivlio-thi-ki*	βιβλιοθήκη
main square	*kentri-ki pla-ti-a*	κεντρική πλατεία
market	*agho-ra*	αγορά
monastery	*mona-sti-ri*	μοναστήρι
monument	*mni-mi-o*	μνημείο
mosque	*dza-mi*	τζαμί

old city	*pa-lia po-li*	παλιά πόλη
palace	*pa-la-ti*	παλάτι
ruins	*e-ri-pia*	ερείπια
stadium	*sta-dhio*	στάδιο
statues	*a-ghal-mata*	αγάλματα
temple	*na-os*	ναός
university	*panepi-sti-mio*	πανεπιστήμιο

Entertainment

I'd like to go …	*tha ithela na pao …*	Θα ήθελα να πάω…
to the 'bouzoukia'	*sta bouzoukia*	στα μπουζούκια
to a traditional restaurant	*sena paradhosiako estiatorio*	σ' ένα παραδοσιακό εστιατόριο
to a movie	*sto sinema*	στο σινεμά
to a night club	*sena night club*	σ' ένα νάιτ κλαμπ
to a Greek play	*sena elliniko theatriko ergho*	σ' ένα ελληνικό θεατρικό έργο
to a quiet bar	*sena isiho bar*	σ' ένα ήσυχο μπαρ
to a soccer match	*sena podhosferiko aghona*	σ' ένα ποδοσφαιρικό αγώνα
to a concert	*se mya sinavlia*	σε μια συναυλία
to an (Italian) restaurant	*sena (italiko) estiatorio*	σ' ένα (Ιταλικό) εστιατόριο
to the beach	*sti thalassa*	στη θάλασσα

Do you have a table free?
ehete kanena elefthero trapezi?   Έχετε κανένα ελεύθερο τραπέζι;

GREEK

Is there live music?
   ehi zondani mousiki?   Έχει ζωντανή μουσική;
Is the movie in English?
   to ergho ine sta anglika?   Το έργο είναι στα Αγγλικά;
Could I have two tickets?
   mou dhinete dhio isitiria?   Μου δίνετε δύο εισιτήρια;
Is there an entrance fee?
   ehi timi isodhou?   Έχει τιμή εισόδου;
How much is it?
   poso kani?   Πόσο κάνει;

In the Country
Weather

What will the weather be like
today?
   ti kero tha kani simera?   Τι καιρό θα κάνει σήμερα;
What is the temperature?
   ti thermokrasia ehoume?   Τι θερμοκρασία έχουμε;

It's hot.	*kani zesti*	Κάνει ζέστη.
It's humid.	*ehi ighrasia*	Έχει υγρασία.
It's cold.	*kani krio*	Κάνει κρύο.
It's chilly.	*kani psihra*	Κάνει ψύχρα.
It's windy.	*fisaee*	Φυσάει.
It's snowing.	*hionizi*	Χιονίζει.
It's raining.	*vrehi*	Βρέχει.
It's sunny.	*ehi ilio*	Έχει ήλιο.

Camping

Greece is well endowed with attractive and well-equipped camping sites, so you should never have trouble finding somewhere to

pitch your tent. Should you find it necessary to 'bush camp', respect nature and others nearby. Leave your site as you found it.

Where is the camping ground?
pou ine to camping?   Πού είναι το κάμπιγκ;
Can I camp here?
boro na kataskinoso edho?   Μπορώ να κατασκηνώσω εδώ
How much is it per night?
poso kani ti vradhya?   Πόσο κάνει τη βραδιά;
Where is the office?
pou ine to grafio?   Πού είναι το γραφείο;
Where are the toilets?
pou ine i toualettez?   Πού είναι οι τουαλέττες;
Can we light a fire?
boroume nanapsoume   Μπορούμε ν'ανάψουμε
fotia?   φωτιά;
Where can I get water?
pou boro na paro nero?   Πού μπορώ να πάρω νερό;

Food
Eating Out
Many Greek restaurants tend to be informal affairs and you can usually go along to the kitchen to see what is on display. Otherwise, the menus tend to be in Greek and, usually, English. Bread and water are always placed on the table. Service charge is normally included, though it is common courtesy to leave a small tip.

Do you have a table for two?
ehete trapezi ya dhio   Έχετε τραπέζι για δυο
atoma?   άτομα;

GREEK

Can I see the menu please?
   boro na dho to menou?   Μπορώ να δω το μενού;
Do you have a menu in
English?
   ehete menou sta anglika?   Έχετε μενού στα Αγγλικά;
Can I look in the kitchen?
   boro na kitaxo stin   Μπορώ να κοιτάξω στην
   kouzina?   κουζίνα;

What do you recommend?
   ti sinistate?   Τι συνιστάτε;
What is this/that?
   ti ine afto/ekino?   Τι είναι αυτό/εκείνο;
I would like …
   tha ithela …   Θα ήθελα …
I want the same as his/hers.
   thelo to idhio me to dhiko   Θέλω το ίδιο με το δικό
   tou/tis   του/της.
Can I try that?
   boro na dhokimaso ekino?   Μπορώ να δοκιμάσω εκείνο;

I just want a Greek salad.
   thelo mya horiatiki salata   Θέλω μια χωριάτικη σαλάτα
   mono   μόνο.
Could we have some house
wine?
   mas fernete krasi tou   Μας φέρνετε κρασί του
   maghaziou?   μαγαζιού;
I am (very) hungry.
   pinao (poli)   Πεινάω (πολύ).
I am (very) thirsty.
   dhipsao (poli)   Διψάω (πολύ).

Could we try your speciality?

boroume na dhokimasoume ti spesialite sas?   Μπορούμε να δοκιμάσουμε τη σπεσιαλιτέ σας;

Could you bring us a good local wine?

mas fernete ena kalo topiko krasi?   Μας φέρνετε ένα καλό τοπικό κρασί;

We need some more bread.

hriazomaste ligo akoma psomi.   Χρειαζόμαστε λίγο ακόμα ψωμί.

Do you have a chair for the baby?

ehete kareklaki ya to moro?   Έχετε καρεκλάκι για το μωρό;

Where are the toilets?

pou ine i toualetes?   Πού είναι οι τουαλέτες;

Can we put two tables together?

boroume na valoume dhio trapezia mazi?   Μπορούμε να βάλουμε δύο τραπέζια μαζί;

The meal was delicious.

to fayito itan nostimotato   Το φαγητό ήταν νοστιμότατο.

Could we have the bill?

mas fernete to loghariazmo?   Μας φέρνετε το λογαριασμό;

ashtray	*stahto dho-hi-o*	σταχτοδοχείο
the bill	*o logharia-smos*	ο λογαριασμός
a cup	*ena fli-ntza-ni*	ένα φλυντζάνι
dessert	*epidhorpio*	επιδόρπιο
a drink	*ena po-to*	ένα ποτό
a fork	*ena pi-ru-ni*	ένα πηρούνι
fresh	*fre-sko*	φρέσκο
a glass	*ena po-ti-ri*	ένα ποτήρι

a knife	*ena ma-he-ri*	ένα μαχαίρι
a plate	*ena pia-to*	ένα πιάτο
spicy	*pipe-ra-to*	πιπεράτο
a spoon	*ena ku-ta-li*	ένα κουτάλι
stale	*ba-yja-tiko*	μπαγιάτικο
sweet	*ghli-ko*	γλυκό
teaspoon	*kuta-la-ki tsa-yu*	κουταλάκι τσαγιού
toothpick	*odhondoghli-fi-tha*	οδοντογλυφίδα

Making Your Own Meal

For some key essentials for sandwich-making, etc, see page 266.

Vegetarian Meals

Greeks are not normally 'declared' vegetarians but some eat 'vegetarian' food as a fact of life. While Greeks tend to be big meat eaters, many rural dishes are based on vegetables and pulses only and provide some of the tastiest meals that you will find.

I am a vegetarian.
　ime hortofaghos.　　　　　Είμαι χορτοφάγος.
Do you serve vegetarian food?
　servirete fayito ya　　　　Σερβίρετε φαγητό για
　hortofaghous?　　　　　　χορτοφάγους;

Breakfast

Breakfast is generally not a big affair in Greece. Most Greeks make do with a Greek coffee and maybe a piece of bread and cheese. As a visitor, you will normally be able to find what you are used to. A popular one is a simple coffee and *voutiro-meli*, βούτυρο-μέλι – bread, butter and honey.

I'd like some breakfast please.

tha ithela proïno,   Θα ήθελα πρωινό,
parakalo   παρακαλώ.

Could I have some bread,
butter and honey?

mou fernete ligho psomi,   Μου φέρνετε λίγο ψωμί,
voutiro ke meli?   βούτυρο και μέλι;

Do you have … ?	*mipos ehete …?*	Μήπως έχετε … ;
boiled eggs	*avgha vrasta*	αυγά βραστά
cereals	*dhimitriaka*	δημητριακά
cold milk	*krio ghala*	κρύο γάλα
croissants	*krouassan*	κρουασσάν
fried eggs	*avgha tighanita*	αυγά τηγανητά
a Greek coffee	*ena elliniko kafe*	ένα ελληνικό καφέ
marmalade/jam	*marmeladha*	μαρμελάδα
a Nescafé (instant)	*ena neskafe*	ένα νεσκαφέ
an omelette	*mya omeleta*	μια ομελέττα
tea	*tsaee*	τσάι

Lunch

Lunch tends to be the major meal of the day and is eaten after work any time after, say, 1 pm. People in a hurry may eat at a *mayirio*, μαγειρείο – a restaurant with homemade food and an emphasis on informality, or at any number of fast food outlets *fastfoudadhika,* φαστφουντάδικα. Home cooking is the usual option.

Do you know a good
restaurant?

mipos xerete ena kalo   Μήπως ξέρετε ένα καλό
estiatorio?   εστιατόριο;

I'd like something light.
  thelo kati elafri   Θέλω κάτι ελαφρύ.
I'd like some seafood.
  thelo thalassina   Θέλω θαλασσινά.
I prefer traditional Greek
food.
  protimo tin paradhosiaki   Προτιμώ την παραδοσιακή
  elliniki kouzina   ελληνική κουζίνα.

Here are some common menu terms that you'll find on most
menus.

Σούπες	*soupes*	soups
Ορεκτικά	*orektika*	starters/appetisers
Στιφάδο	*stifadho*	stew
Ψαρικά	*psarika*	fish dishes
Ζυμαρικά	*zimarika*	pasta dishes
Κρέατα	*kreata*	meat dishes
Μεζέδες	*mezedhes*	snacks
Χόρτα	*horta*	greens
Πιλάφι	*pilafi*	rice
Τηγανητ–ός/ή/ό	*tighanit–os/i/o*	fried
Βραστ–ός/ή/ό	*vrast–os/i/o*	boiled
Ψητ–ός/ή/ό	*psit–os/i/o*	roast
Γεμιστ–ός/ή/ό	*yemist–os/i/o*	stuffed
Της ώρας	*tis oras*	to order
Της σχάρας	*tis scharas*	grilled

Dinner

Dinner tends to be a more elaborate affair, if taken at all. However many Greeks make do with a light snack in the evening, if
they are not eating out. If they do eat out, it will commonly be at

a family *taverna,* ταβέρνα, a *psistarya,* ψησταριά specialising in meats, or perhaps at a *pizzeria,* πιτσαρία which are very popular options. Meals eaten out often start late – after 10 pm – and end late. Other than in smarter big city restaurants, it is not usually necessary to book.

| Της ώρας | *tis oras* | to order |
| Της σχάρας | *tis scharas* | grilled |

Staples

beans	*fasolia*	φασόλια
bread	*psomi*	ψωμί
cheese	*tiri*	τυρί
flour	*alevri*	αλεύρι
lentils	*fakez*	φακές
olive oil	*eleoladho*	ελαιόλαδο
olives	*elyez*	ελιές
pasta	*zimarika*	ζυμαρικά
rice	*rizi*	ρύζι
salt	*alati*	αλάτι

Breads

bread	*psomi/artos*	ψωμί – άρτος
croissant	*krouassan*	κρουασσάν
dark (brown) bread	*mavro psomi*	μαύρο ψωμί
dry biscuit	*paximadhi*	παξιμάδι
loaf	*frandzola*	φραντζόλα
roll	*psomaki*	ψωμάκι
rusk	*frighanya*	φρυγανιά
rye bread	*psomi sikaleos*	ψωμί σικάλεως
wheat bread	*sitarenio psomi*	σιταρένιο ψωμί

GREEK

Bread is bought by weight, so ...

A kilo of brown (dark) bread.
  ena kilo mavro psomi   Ένα κιλό μαύρο ψωμί.
Half a kilo of rye (bread).
  miso kilo sikaleos   Μισό κιλό σικάλεως.

Dairy Produce

Although there is plenty of milk to be had in Greece, milk is no
as popular in the average Greek's diet as it is in, say, northern
Europe. Many Greek children have been brought up on sweet-
ened condensed milk instead of 'real' milk, though things are
changing. Feta cheese is a mainstay of most Greeks' diets and is
usually found in a traditional 'Greek' salad.

butter	*voutiro*	βούτυρο
cheese	*tiri*	τυρί
ricotta cheese	*mizithra*	μυζήθρα
cream	*krema*	κρέμα
feta (sheep's milk cheese)	*feta*	φέτα
Gruyère	*ghraviera*	γραβιέρα
hard cheese like parmesan	*kefalotiri*	κεφαλοτύρι
margarine	*margharini*	μαργαρίνη
milk	*ghala*	γάλα
whipped cream	*sandiyi*	σαντιγύ
yellowish sheep's milk cheese	*kaseri*	κασέρι

Appetisers

aubergine dip	*melidzanosalata*	μελιτζανοσαλάτα
cheese pie	*tiropita*	τυρόπιττα

fish roe dip	*taramosalata*	ταραμοσαλάτα
fried feta cheese	*saghanaki*	σαγανάκι
meat balls	*keftedhakya*	κεφτεδάκια
octopus	*htapodhi*	χταπόδι
potato & garlic dip	*skordhalya*	σκορδαλιά
sausages	*loukanika*	λουκάνικα
shrimps	*gharidhes*	γαρίδες
spicy yoghurt dip	*dzadziki*	τζατζίκι
spinach pie	*spanakopita*	σπανακόπιττα
squid	*kalamaria*	καλαμάρια
stuffed vine leaves	*dolmadhez*	ντολμάδες

Soup

bean soup	*fasoladha*	φασολάδα
chicken soup	*kotosoupa*	κοτόσουπα
(Easter) entrail soup	*mayiritsa*	μαγειρίτσα
egg & lemon soup	*avgholemono*	αυγολέμονο
fish soup	*psarosoupa*	ψαρόσουπα
lentil soup	*faki soupa*	φακή σούπα
tripe soup	*patsas*	πατσάς
vegetable soup	*hortosoupa*	χορτόσουπα

Meat

beef	*vodhino*	βοδινό
chicken	*kotopoulo*	κοτόπουλο
chops	*brizolez*	μπριζόλες
entrails	*endosthia*	εντόσθια
hare	*laghos*	λαγός
kidney	*nefra*	νεφρά
lamb	*arni*	αρνί
liver	*sikoti*	σηκώτι
mince	*kimas*	κιμάς

GREEK

mixed entrails on the spit	kokoretsi	κοκορέτσι
pork	hirino	χοιρινό
sausage	loukaniko	λουκάνικο
souvlaki (meat cubes on skewers)	souvlaki	σουβλάκι
spare ribs	paeedhakya	παϊδάκια
veal	moschari	μοσχάρι
yiros (combined meats on skewers)	yiros	γύρος

Seafood

cod	bakalyaros	μπακαλιάρος
cuttlefish	soupya	σουπιά
lobster	astakos	αστακός
red mullet	barbouni	μπαρμπούνι
mussels	midhya	μύδια
oysters	stridhya	στρείδια
prawns	garidhes	γαρίδες
salmon	solomos	σολωμός
sole	ghlosa	γλώσσα
sea pike	zarghana	ζαργάνα
swordfish	xifias	ξιφίας
trout	pestrofa	πέστροφα
whitebait	maridha	μαρίδα

Salads

cabbage salad	lahanosalata	λαχανοσαλάτα
lettuce salad	maroulosalata	μαρουλοσαλάτα
potato salad	patatasalata	πατατοσαλάτα
Russian salad	rossiki salata	ρώσσικη σαλάτα

GREEK

tomato & cucumber salad	*angourodomato- salata*	αγγουροντοματο- σαλάτα
village (Greek) salad	*horiatiki salata*	χωριάτικη σαλάτα
wild greens salad	*horta*	χόρτα

Vegetables

artichokes	*anginares*	αγγινάρες
aubergines (eggplants)	*melidzanes*	μελιτζάνες
beetroot	*pandzari*	παντζάρι
cabbage	*lahano*	λάχανο
cauliflower	*kounoupidhi*	κουνουπίδι
courgettes (zucchini)	*kolokithakya*	κολοκυθάκια
green beans	*fasolakya*	φασολάκια
leeks	*prasa*	πράσσα
lettuce	*marouli*	μαρούλι
okra (ladies fingers)	*bamies*	μπάμιες
onions	*kremidhya*	κρεμμύδια
peas	*arakas*	αρακάς
peppers (capsicums)	*piperyes*	πιπεριές
potatoes	*patates*	πατάτες
spinach	*spanaki*	σπανάκι
tomatoes	*domates*	ντομάτες

Greek Dishes

Here are some common dishes you will encounter as you travel across Greece and Cyprus.

μουσακάς
  mousakas – mousakas (shepherd's pie). Layers of potatoes and aubergines, mincemeat sauce topped with béchamel sauce.

GREEK

παστίτσιο
    pastitsio – macaroni pie. Similar to mousakas, but with macaroni instead of potatoes and aubergines.
στιφάδο
    stifadho – stew. Usually done in red-wine sauce and very tasty.
φασολάδα
    fasoladha – bean soup
γιουβαρλάκια
    youvarlakya – mincemeat balls in rice, egg and lemon soup
κεφτέδες
    keftedhes – fried mincemeat balls

aubergines 'imam'	*melitzanez imam*	μελιτζάνες ιμάμ
hamburgers	*biftekia*	μπιφτέκια
kebab	*tas kebab*	τας κεμπάμπ
lamb on the spit	*arni souvlas*	αρνί σούβλας
ragoût potatoes	*patatez yahni*	πατάτες γιαχνί
rissoles	*soudzoukakya*	σουτζουκάκια
spaghetti with meat sauce	*makaronia me kima*	μακαρόνια με κιμά
spinach with rice	*spanakorizo*	σπανακόρυζο
stuffed aubergines	*papoutsakia*	παπουτσάκια
stuffed (peppers or tomatoes)	*yemista*	γεμιστά
veal casserole	*moschari stifadho*	μοσχάρι στιφάδο

Condiments

basil	*vasilikos*	βασιλικός
mint	*dhiozmos*	δυόσμος
oregano	*righani*	ρίγανη
parsley	*maeedanos*	μαϊντανός

| pepper | *piperi* | πιπέρι |
| salt | *alati* | αλάτι |

Fruit

apples	*mila*	μήλα
apricots	*verikoka*	βερίκοκα
bananas	*bananes*	μπανάνες
cantaloupe (melon)	*peponi*	πεπόνι
cherries	*kerasia*	κεράσια
figs	*sika*	σύκα
grapes	*stafilia*	σταφύλια
oranges	*portokalia*	πορτοκάλια
peaches	*rodhakina*	ροδάκινα
watermelon	*karpouzi*	καρπούζι

Desserts & Sweets

While desserts tend to be mainly fresh fruit, sweets are in another league again. If you have a sweet tooth, you can indulge in your passion at any time of the day with the following sweets.

μπακλαβάς
    baklavas – baklava. Sections of flaky pastry filled with honey and nuts.
μπουγάτσα
    boughatsa – bougatsa. Custard cream.
Φρούτα της εποχής
    frouta tis epohis – fruit in season. Whatever is going at the time.
χαλβάς
    halvas – halva. In Greece this is a kind of semolina cake.
καταΐφι
    kataifi – kataïfi. A syrupy sweet made of shredded filo pastry, honey and almonds.

custard pie	*ghalaktoboureko*	γαλακτομπούρεκο
honey macaroons	*melomakarona*	μελομακάρονα
honey puffs	*loukoumadhes*	λουκουμάδες
rice pudding	*rizoghalo*	ρυζόγαλο
shortbread biscuits	*kourabiedhes*	κουραμπιέδες
Turkish delight	*loukoumi*	λουκούμι
turnovers	*dhiples*	δίπλες

Drinks – Nonalcoholic

capuccino	*capoutsino*	καπουτσίνο
espresso	*espresso*	εσπρέσσο
Greek coffee	*ellinikos kafes*	ελληνικός καφές
iced coffee	*frappé*	φραππέ
milk	*ghala*	γάλα
mineral water	*metalliko nero*	μεταλλικό νερό
mountain tea	*tsaï tou vounou*	τσάι του βουνού
Nescafé (instant)	*nescafé*	νεσκαφέ
soft drink	*anapsiktiko*	αναψυκτικό
tea	*tsaï*	τσάι

Drinks – Alcoholic

ούζο
   ouzo – ouzo. Popular local drink with a strong aniseed
   flavour.

ρετσίνα
   retsina – retsina. Resinated white wine.

ρακί
   raki – raki. A strong spirit distilled from grain.

beer	*bira*	μπύρα
bottled ...	... *se boukali*	... σε μπουκάλι
draught ...	... *hima*	... χύμα

cognac	*konyak*	κονιάκ
whisky	*whisky*	ουίσκυ
wine	*krasi*	κρασί
dry wine	*xiro krasi*	ξηρό κρασί
house wine	*krasi hima*	κρασί χύμα
red wine	*kokkino krasi*	κόκκινο κρασί
sweet wine	*ghliko krasi*	γλυκό κρασί
white wine	*aspro krasi*	άσπρο κρασί

Shopping

bookshop	*vivliopo-li-o*	βιβλιοπωλείο
camera shop	*magha-zi foto-ghrafi-kon i-thon*	μαγαζί φωτο-γραφικών ειδών
clothing store	*i-thi ruhi-smu*	είδη ρουχισμού
delicatessen	*ba-ka-liko*	μπακάλικο
general store, shop	*pantopo-li-o*	παντοπωλείο
laundry	*plin-ti-rio*	πλυντήριο
market	*agho-ra*	αγορά
newsagency/ stationer's	*efimeridhopolio/ hartopolio*	εφημεριδοπωλείο/ χαρτοπωλείο
pharmacy	*farma-ki-o*	φαρμακείο
shoeshop	*ipothimatopo-li-o*	υποδηματοπωλείο
souvenir shop	*ka-ta-stima suvenir*	κατάστημα σουβενίρ
supermarket	*iperagho-ra*	υπεραγορά
vegetable shop	*oporopo-li-o*	οπωροπωλείο

How much is it?		
poso kani?		Πόσο κάνει;

| I'd like to buy ... | *tha ithela naghoraso ...* | Θα ήθελα ν'αγοράσω ... |

That's too expensive.
   ine poli akrivo   Είναι πολύ ακριβό.
Can you make me a better price?
   mou kanete mya kaliteri timi?   Μου κάνετε μια καλύτερη τιμή;
I am just looking.
   aplos kitazo   Απλώς κοιτάζω.
How much all together?
   posa kanoun ola mazi?   Πόσα κάνουν όλα μαζί;
Do you take credit cards?
   pernete pistotikez kartez? Παίρνετε πιστωτικές κάρτες;
That's all, thanks.
   tipote allo, efharisto   Τίποτε άλλο, ευχαριστώ.
OK, I'll take it.
   endaxi, tha to paro   Εν τάξει, θα το πάρω.

You May Hear

Can I help you?
   bo-ro na sas voi-thi-so?   Μπορώ να σας βοηθήσω;
Will that be all?
   the-lete ti-pota a-lo?   Θέλετε τίποτα άλλο;
Sorry, this is the only one.
   si-ghno-mi a-fto i-ne to mo-no   Συγγνώμη αυτό είναι το μόνο.
How much/many do you want?
   po-sa the-lis?   Πόσα θέλεις;

Essential Groceries

batteries	*mbataries*	μπαταρίες
bread	*psomi/artos*	ψωμί – άρτος

butter	*voutiro*	βούτυρο
cereal	*sitira*	σιτηρά
	proyevmatos	προγεύματος
cheese	*tiri*	τυρί
chocolate	*sokolata*	σοκολάτα
coffee	*kafe*	καφέ
gas cylinder	*kilindhro*	κύλινδρος
	iyraeriou	υγραερίου
matches	*spirta*	σπίρτα
milk	*ghala*	γάλα
mineral water	*metalliko nero*	μεταλλικό νερό
shampoo	*ena sambouan*	ένα σαμπουάν
soap	*ena sapouni*	ένα σαπούνι
sugar	*zahari*	ζάχαρι
tea	*tsaï*	τσάι
toilet paper	*hartis iyias*	χάρτης υγείας
toothbrush	*mya odhondovourtsa*	μια οδοντόβουρτσα
tube of toothpaste	*mya odhondokrema*	μια οδοντόκρεμα
washing powder	*skoni plisimatos*	σκόνη πλυσίματος
yoghurt	*yiaurti*	γιαούρτι

Souvenirs

bag/handbag	*tsanda*	τσάντα
embroidery	*kendimata*	κεντήματα
hat	*kapello*	καπέλλο
key ring	*brelok*	μπρελόκ
postcard	*karta*	κάρτα
pottery	*keramika*	κεραμικά
purse/wallet	*portofoli*	πορτοφόλι
statue	*aghalma*	άγαλμα

Clothing

jacket	*sakkaki*	σακκάκι
overcoat	*palto*	παλτό
raincoat	*adhiavroho*	αδιάβροχο
shirt	*poukamiso*	πουκάμισο
shoes	*papoutsia*	παπούτσια
jumper (sweater)	*pullover/blouza*	πουλόβερ/μπλούζα
swimwear	*mayo*	μαγιό
trousers	*pandeloni*	παντελόνι
underwear	*esorouha*	εσώρουχα

It doesn't fit.
then me horai   Δεν με χωράει

It's too ...	*ine poli ...*	Είναι πολύ...
big	*me-gha-lo*	μεγάλο
small	*mi-kro*	μικρό

Toiletries

Can I have ...?	*mou dhinete ...?*	Μου δίνετε ... ;
a syringe	*mya siringa*	μια σύριγγα
some cotton wool	*vamvaki*	βαμβάκι
some Band-aids	*merika lefkoplast*	μερικά λευκοπλάστ
a packet of condoms	*ena paketo profilaktika*	ένα πακέτο προφυλακτικά
some sanitary towels	*ena paketo serviettes*	ένα πακέτο σερβιέττες
some disinfectant	*apolimandiko*	απολυμαντικό
some cough drops	*pastilyes ya viha*	παστίλιες για βήχα

Do I need a prescription?
   mipoz hriazome sindayi?   Μήπως χρειάζομαι συνταγή;

deodorant	*ena aposmitiko*	ένα αποσμητικό
insect repellant	*apothitiko*	απωθητικό
	endomon	εντόμων
razor	*ena xirafi*	ένα ξυράφι
soap	*ena sapouni*	ένα σαπούνι
shampoo	*ena sambouan*	ένα σαμπουάν
shaving cream	*krema xirizmatos*	κρέμα ξυρίσματος
sunblock	*krema iliou*	κρέμα ηλίου
talcum powder	*poudhra*	πούδρα
packet of tissues	*ena paketo*	ένα πακέτο
	hartomandila	χαρτομάντηλα
toilet paper	*harti iyias*	χάρτη υγείας
toothbrush	*mya odhondovourtsa*	μια οδοντόβουρτσα
tube of toothpaste	*mya odhondokrema*	μια οδοντόκρεμα

Photography

Do you sell film?
   mipos poulate film?   Μήπως πουλάτε φιλμ;

I'd like film for …	*mou dhinete ena*	Μου δίνετε ένα
	film ya …	φιλμ για …
colour prints	*enhromes*	έγχρωμες
	fotoghrafies	φωτογραφίες
colour slides	*enhromes*	έγχρωμες
	dhiafanies	διαφάνειες
B&W photos	*aspromavres*	ασπρόμαυρες
	fotoghrafies	φωτογραφίες

Can you develop this film?
borite na emfanisete   Μπορείτε να εμφανίσετε
afto to film?   αυτό το φιλμ;
When will the photos be ready?
pote tha ine etimez i   Πότε θα είναι έτοιμες οι
fotoghrafies?   φωτογραφίες;
Can you develop slides?
borite na emfanisete   Μπορείτε να εμφανίσετε
dhiafanies?   διαφάνειες;
Can I have two of each?
mou dhinete apo dhio?   Μου δίνετε από δύο;

B&W (film)	*ma-vro-aspro*	μαυρόασπρο
camera	*fotoghrafi-ki*	φωτογραφική
	miha-ni	μηχανή
colour (film)	*e-hromo film*	έγχρωμο
film	*film*	φιλμ
filter	*filtro*	φίλτρο
flash	*flas*	φλας
light meter	*fotometro*	φωτόμετρο
telephoto lens	*tilefakos*	τηλεφακός
tripod	*tripodhas*	τρίποδας
wide-angle lens	*evrighonios fakos*	ευρυγώνιος φακός

Smoking

NO SMOKING	*ΑΠΑΓΟΡΕΥΕΤΑΙ ΤΟ ΚΑΠΝΙΣΜΑ*

A packet of …
  ena paketo …   Ένα πακέτο …
Do you sell tobacco?
  poulate kapno?   Πουλάτε καπνό;
A box of matches please.
  ena kouti spirta, parakalo   Ένα κουτί σπίρτα
                                    παρακαλώ.

Do you have a light?
  e-his fo-tja?   Έχετε φωτιά;
Do you mind if I smoke?
  sas pirazi an kapniso?   ας πειράζει αν καπνίσω;
Please don't smoke here.
  parakalo mi kapnizete   Παρακαλώ μη καπνίζετε
  etho   εδώ.

cigarette papers	*zha-rtia tsi-gha-ru*	χαρτιά τσιγάρου
cigarettes	*tsi-gha-ra*	τσιγάρα
lighter	*ana-pti-ras*	αναπτήρας
matches	*spi-rta*	σπίρτα
menthol	*me-ntas*	μέντας
pipe	*pi-pa*	πίπα
tobacco (pipe)	*ka-pno (pipas)*	καπνό πίπας
filter cigarettes	*tsighara me filtra*	τσιγάρα με φίλτρα
non-filter cigarettes	*tsighara horis*	τσιγάρα χωρίς
	filtra	φίλτρα

Health

I need a doctor.
  hriazome yatro   Χρειάζομαι γιατρό.
It is an emergency!
  ine epighon!   Είναι επείγον!

I've injured myself.
htipisa	Χτύπησα.

I am feeling sick.
esthanome arostos	Αισθάνομαι άρρωστος.

Can you take me to a
hospital?
borite na me pate sto nosokomio?	Μπορείτε να με πάτε στο νοσοκομείο;

You May Hear

What's the matter?
ti simveni?	Τι συμβαίνει;

Where does it hurt?
pu po-na-te?	Πού πονάτε;

Parts of the Body

arm	*heri/bratso*	χέρι/μπράτσο
ear	*afti*	αυτί
eye	*mati*	μάτι
foot	*podhi*	πόδι
hand	*heri*	χέρι
head	*kefali*	κεφάλι
heart	*kardhya*	καρδιά
kidney	*nefro*	νεφρό
leg	*podhi*	πόδι
muscle	*mis*	μυς
nose	*miti*	μύτη
stomach	*stomahi*	στομάχι

Ailments

I'm suffering   *pascho apo ...*   Πάσχω από ...
from …

an earache	*pono sto afti*	πόνο στο αυτί
food poisoning	*trofiki dhilitiriasi*	τροφική δηλητηρίαση
a headache	*ponokefalo*	πονοκέφαλο
a sore throat	*ponolemo*	πονόλαιμο
a stomachache	*pono sto stomahi*	πόνο στο στομάχι
sunburn	*iliako engavma*	ηλιακό έγκαυμα

I have sprained my ankle.
  eho stramboulixi ton   Έχω στραμπουλήξει τον
  astraghalo   αστράγαλο.
I have burned myself.
  kaeeka   Κάηκα.
I have a pain here.
  ponao edho   Πονάω εδώ.

allergy	*alerghia*	αλλεργία
appendicitis	*skolikoeedhitidha*	σκωληκοειδίτιδα
cold	*kriologhima*	κρυολόγημα
constipation	*dhiskiliotita*	δυσκοιλιότητα
cough	*vihas*	βήχας
cramps	*kramba*	κράμπα
diarrhoea	*dhiaria*	διάρροια
a fever	*piretos*	πυρετός
hepatitis	*ipatitidha*	ηπατίτιδα
high blood pressure	*psili artiriaki piesi*	ψηλή αρτηριακή πίεση
indigestion	*dhispepsia*	δυσπεψία
an infection	*molinsi*	μόλυνση

influenza	*ghripi*	γρίππη
low blood pressure	*hamili artiriaki piesi*	χαμηλή αρτηριακή πίεση
venereal disease	*afrodhisio nosima*	αφροδίσιο νόσημα

Women's Health

Could I see a female doctor?
   tha bo-ru-sa na dho
   yji-ne-ka ya-tro?
Θα μπορούσα να δω
γυναίκα γιατρό;

I'm on the pill.
   pe-rno andisilipti-ka
Παίρνω αντισυλληπτικά.

I haven't had my period for ... weeks.
   dhen i-rthe i pe-ri-odhos
   mu yja ... evdhomathes
Δεν ήρθε η περίοδός
μου για ... εβδομάδες.

(unusual) bleeding	*emoraghia*	αιμορραγία
cramps	*kramba*	κράμπα
pregnant	*engios*	έγκυος
thrush	*mikitodhi*	μυκητώδη
	kolpitidha	κολπίτιδα

Specific Needs

I'm ...	*i-me ...*	Είμαι ...
diabetic	*dhiaviti-kos* (m)	διαβητικός
	dhiaviti-ki (f)	διαβητική
epileptic	*epili-pti-kos* (m)	επιληπτικός
	epile-pti-ki (f)	επιληπτική
asthmatic	*asthmati-kos* (m)	ασθματικός
	asthmati-ki (f)	ασθματική

I'm allergic to ...	*i-me aleryji-kos* (m)/ *aleryji-ki* (f)*sta ...*	Είμαι αλλεργικός/ αλλεργική στα . . .
antibiotics	*andivioti-ka*	αντιβιοτικά
penicillin	*peniki-li-ni*	πενικιλλίνη

I have been vaccinated.
  e-ho ka-ni e-mvo-lio Έχω κάνει εμβόλιο.
I have my own syringe.
  e-ho dhi-kia mu si-riga Έχω δικιά μου σύριγγα.

At the Chemist

Do you have something
for ...?
  mipoz ehete kati ya ...? Μήπως έχετε κάτι για ... ;
Can you make up this
prescription?
  borite na mou ftiaxete Μπορείτε να μου φτιάξετε
  afti ti sindaghi? αυτή τη συνταγή;
When will it be ready?
  pote tha ine etimo? Πότε θα είναι έτοιμο;
How many times a day?
  poses fores tin imera? Πόσες φορές την ημέρα;

antibiotics	*andiviotika*	αντιβιοτικά
antiseptic	*andisiptiko*	αντισηπτικό
medication	*farmako*	φάρμακο
ointment	*alifi*	αλοιφή
pills	*hapia*	χάπια
prescription	*sinday̆i*	συνταγή

GREEK

At the Dentist

I have a toothache.
   mou ponaee to dhondi   Μου πονάει το δόντι.

I think I need a filling.
   nomizo pos hriazome   Νομίζω πως χρειάζομαι
   sfraghizma   σφράγισμα.

Please don't take my tooth out!
   sas parakalo, mi mou   Σας παρακαλώ, μη μου
   vghalete to dhondi!   βγάλετε το δόντι!

Can you give me a local
anaesthetic?
   borite na mou kanete   Μπορείτε να μου κάνετε
   topiki anesthisia?   τοπική αναισθησία;

Could I have a receipt?
   mou dhinete, parakalo   Μου δίνετε, παρακαλώ,
   mya ghrapti apodhixi? μια γραπτή απόδειξη;

Time

Telling the Time

What time is it, please?
   ti ora ine, parakalo?   Τι ώρα είναι, παρακαλώ;

It is …	*ine …*	Είναι …
1 o'clock	*mia i ora*	μια η ώρα
2 o'clock	*dhio i ora*	δύο η ώρα
6 o'clock	*exi i ora*	έξη η ώρα

… :15	*… ke tetarto*	… και τέταρτο
… :30	*… ke misi*	… και μισή
… :45	*… para tetarto*	… πάρα τέταρτο

in the morning	*to proi*	το πρωί
in the afternoon	*to mesimeri*	το μεσημέρι
in the evening	*to vradhi*	το βράδυ
at night	*ti nihta*	τη νύχτα

Days of the Week

Sunday	*kiriaki*	Κυριακή
Monday	*deftera*	Δευτέρα
Tuesday	*triti*	Τρίτη
Wednesday	*tetarti*	Τετάρτη
Thursday	*pempti*	Πέμπτη
Friday	*paraskevi*	Παρασκευή
Saturday	*savato*	Σάββατο

Months

January	*yanouarios*	Ιανουάριος
February	*fevrouarios*	Φεβρουάριος
March	*martios*	Μάρτιος
April	*aprilios*	Απρίλιος
May	*mayios*	Μάϊος
June	*younios*	Ιούνιος
July	*youlios*	Ιούλιος
August	*avghoustos*	Αύγουστος
September	*septemvrios*	Σεπτέμβριος
October	*octovrios*	Οκτώβριος
November	*noemvrios*	Νοέμβριος
December	*dekemvrios*	Δεκέμβριος

Seasons

| summer | *kalokeri* | Καλοκαίρι |
| autumn/fall | *fthinoporo* | Φθινόπωρο |

GREEK

| winter | *himonas* | Χειμώνας |
| spring | *aniksi* | Ανοιξη |

Present

today	*simera*	σήμερα
now	*tora*	τώρα
this morning	*to proi*	το πρωί
this afternoon	*to apoyevma*	το απόγευμα
this evening	*apopse*	απόψε
this week	*afti tin evdhomadha*	αυτή την εβδομάδα
this month	*afto to mina*	αυτό το μήνα
this year	*fetos*	Φέτος

Past

yesterday	*hthes*	χθες
then	*tote*	τότε
the day before yesterday	*prohthes*	προχθές
last Saturday	*to perazmeno savato*	το περασμένο Σάββατο
last week	*tim berazmeni evdhomadha*	την περασμένη εβδομάδα
last month	*tom berazmeno mina*	τον περασμένο μήνα
last year	*perisi*	πέρυσι

Future

tomorrow	*avrio*	αύριο
the day after tomorrow	*methavrio*	μεθαύριο
tomorrow morning	*avrio to proi*	αύριο το πρωί

next Sunday	*tin alli kiriaki*	την άλλη Κυριακή
next week	*tin alli evdhomadha*	την άλλη εβδομάδα
next month	*ton allo mina*	τον άλλο μήνα
next year	*tou hronou*	του χρόνου

During the Day

afternoon	*a-po-yevma*	απόγευμα
dawn	*ha-rama/po-li pro-i*	χάραμα/ πολύ πρωί
day	*me-ra*	μέρα
early	*no-ris*	νωρίς
midnight	*me-sa-nihta*	μεσάνυχτα
morning	*proi*	πρωί
night	*ni-hta*	νύχτα
noon	*mesi-me-ri*	μεσημέρι
sundown	*iliova-si-lema*	ηλιοβασίλεμα
sunrise	*anato-li*	ανατολή

Numbers & Amounts

1	*enas/mia/ena*	ένας/μία/ένα (m/f/n)
2	*dhio*	δύο
3	*tris*	τρεις (m & f)
	tria	τρία (n)
4	*teseris*	τέσσερεις (m & f)
	tesera	τέσσερα (n)
5	*pende*	πέντε
6	*exi*	έξη
7	*efta*	εφτά
8	*ohto*	οχτώ
9	*enea*	εννέα
10	*dheka*	δέκα
11	*endheka*	ένδεκα

GREEK

12	*dhodheka*	δώδεκα	
13	*dheka-tris*	δεκατρείς (m & f)	
	dheka-tria	δεκατρία (n)	
14	*dheka-teseris*	δεκατέσσερεις (m & f)	
	dheka-tesera	δεκατέσσερα (n)	
15	*dheka-pende*	δεκαπέντε	
16	*dheka-exi*	δεκαέξη	
17	*dheka-efta*	δεκαεφτά	
18	*dheka-ohto*	δεκαοχτώ	
19	*dheka-enea*	δεκαεννέα	
20	*ikosi*	είκοσι	
21	*ikosi-ena*	εικοσιένα (m & n)	
	ikosi-mia	εικοσιμία (f)	
30	*trianda*	τριάντα	
40	*saranda*	σαράντα	
50	*peninda*	πενήντα	
60	*exinda*	εξήντα	
70	*evdhominda*	εβδομήντα	
80	*oghdhonda*	ογδόντα	
90	*eneninda*	ενενήντα	
100	*ekato(n)*	εκατό	
200	*dhiakosi-i/es/a*	διακόσι-οι/ες/α	
1000	*hili-i/es/a*	χίλι-οι/ες/α	
one million	*ena ekatomirio*	ένα εκατομμύριο	
1st	*prot-os/i/o*	πρώτ-ος/η/ο	
2nd	*defter-os/i/o*	δεύτερ-ος/η/ο	
3rd	*tritos/i/o*	τρίτ-ος/η/ο	
¼	*tetarto*	τέταρτο	
⅓	*trito*	τρίτο	
½	*miso*	μισό	
¾	*tria tetarta*	τρία τέταρτα	

Amounts

small	*mi-**kro***	μικρό
big	*me-**gha**-lo*	μεγάλο
heavy	*va-**ri***	βαρύ
light	*ela-**fri***	ελαφρύ
more	*peri-so-**tero***	περισσότερο
less	*li-**gho**-tero*	λιγότερο
too much/many	***pa**-ra po-la/po-li*	πάρα πολλά/πολύ
many	*po-**la***	πολλά
enough	*arke-**ta***	αρκετά
also	*e-**pi**-sis*	επίσης
a little bit	*li-**gho***	λίγο
a little (amount)	*e-na mi-**kro** (po-so)*	ένα μικρό ποσό
double	*dhi-**plo***	διπλό
Enough!	*arke-**ta***	αρκετά
few	*li-**ghi**/es/a*	λίγοι/ ες/ α
less	*liyotera*	λιγότερα
many	*po-**la***	πολλά
more	*peri-so-**tera***	περισσότερα
once	***mi**-a fo-**ra***	μια φορά
a pair	*ze-**vgha**-ri*	ζευγάρι
percent	*tis eka-**ton***	τοις εκατόν
some	*li-**gha**/merika*	λίγα/ μερικά
too much	***pa**-ra po-**la***	πάρα πολλά
twice	***dhi**-o fo-**res***	δύο φορές

Abbreviations

Π.Χ./ Μ.Χ.	AD/BC
π.μ./ μ.μ.	am/pm
εκ./μ./χλμ.	cm/m/km
γραμ./κιλό	gm/kg

ΤΑΧΥΔΡΟΜΕΙΟ	GPO
Βόρεια/ Νότια	Nth/Sth
Οδός/ Δρόμος	St/Rd

Paperwork

Greeks are great bureaucrats and you may be asked to fill in a form at some stage of your visit to Greece. Usually someone will be on hand to help you, but it helps to know what it is you are filling in. The following terms are some of the more common ones that you will come across.

Name	Όνομα
Surname	Επώνυμο
Father's name	Όνομα πατρός
Address	Διεύθυνση
Date of birth	Ημερομηνία γεννήσεως
Place of birth	Τόπος γεννήσεως
Age	Ηλικία
Sex	Φύλο
Religion	Θρήσκευμα
Profession	Επάγγελμα
Passport Number	Αριθμός Διαβατηρίου
Identity Card	Ταυτότητα
Residence Permit	Αδεια Παραμονής
Birth Certificate	Πιστοποιητικό Γεννήσεως
Driver's Licence	Αδεια Οδηγήσεως
Car registration certificate	Αδεια Κυκλοφορίας Αυτοκινήτου

| Car registration number | | Αριθμός Κυκλοφορίας Αυτοκινήτου |
| Duty Stamp (always required on official documents) | | Χαρτόσημο |

Emergencies

Help!	*voithya!*	Βοήθεια!
Watch out!	*prosohi!*	Προσοχή!
Go away!	*fighe!*	Φύγε!
Get lost!	*hasou!*	Χάσου!
Stop it!	*stamata!*	Σταμάτα!
Police!	*astinomia!*	Αστυνομία!
Thief!	*kleftis!*	Κλέφτης!

Call a doctor!
  fonaxte ena yatro!   Φωνάξτε ένα γιατρό.
There's been an accident.
  eyine atihima   Έγινε ατύχημα.
Call an ambulance.
  tilefoniste ya asthenoforo   Τηλεφωνήστε για
ασθενοφόρο.

I am ill.
  ime arostos   Είμαι άρρωστος.
I am lost.
  eho hathi   Έχω χαθεί.
I've been raped.
  me viase kapyos   Με βίασε κάποιος.

I've been robbed.
  meklepse kapyos   Μ'έκλεψε κάποιος.

GREEK

I've lost …	*eho hasi …*	Εχω χάσει …
my bag	*tin dzanda mou*	την τσάντα μου
my money	*ta lefta mou*	τα λεφτά μου
my passport	*to dhiavatirio mou*	το διαβατήριό μου
my travellers'	*tis taxidhiotikez*	τις ταξιδιωτικές
cheques	*mou epitayez*	μου επιταγές

Could I use the telephone?
boro na hrisimopüso
to tilefono?

Μπορώ να χρησιμοποιήσω
το τηλέφωνο;

I have medical insurance.
eho yatriki asfalya

Εχω ιατρική ασφάλεια.

Irish

Introduction

Irish (the correct legal and linguistic term) is the national and first official language of Ireland, and the ancestral language of the 70-million-strong Irish diaspora, and of most Scots, throughout the world. It belongs, together with Scottish Gaelic, Manx, Welsh, Breton and Cornish, to the Celtic branch of the Indo-European language family, once spoken across Europe from Ireland to Anatolia (modern Turkey). Irish and Scottish Gaelic shared a common literary language from the 6th to the late 18th centuries. Indeed the Latin word *Scotus* meant simply an Irish speaker, whether from Ireland or Scotland.

Irish largely inspired the movement that brought about Ireland's national independence in the early 20th century. It has thus been an obligatory subject at all first and second level schools since independence in 1922, and the number of Irish-medium schools has been rapidly growing in recent years. Since 1913 it has been essential for matriculation at the National University of Ireland. The 1991 census showed a total of 1.14 million Irish speakers in the Irish state, and 140,000 Irish speakers in Northern Ireland. Irish is now the everyday language in *Gaeltacht*, or traditional Irish-speaking areas, and is increasingly heard in urban areas, particularly in Dublin and Belfast. Its literature is flourishing. Irish has been included in the European Community LINGUA program, an ambitious project to promote the teaching of European languages throughout the Member States, and is one of the languages on the common EU passport.

The usual word order in Irish is verb–subject–object. The initial consonant of feminine nouns changes after the definite article, for example, 'woman: the woman', *bean: an bhean*, (pronounced *ban: on van)*. The verb is inflected for tense:

kiss	*pohg*	póg
she kissed	*fohg shee*	phóg sí
she kisses	*pohg-an shee*	pógann sí
she will kiss	*pohg-hee shee*	pógfaidh sí
she would kiss	*fohg-hokh shee*	phógfadh sí
she used to kiss	*fohg-okh shee*	phógadh sí
kissing	*eh pohg-a*	ag pógadh
kissed	*pohg-ha*	pógtha

Irish Words in English

Some well-known English words have been borrowed from Irish:

whiskey	*ish-keh ba-ha*	uisce beatha – 'water of life'
slogan	*sloo-a gorr-im*	slua-ghairm – 'crowd call'
glen	*glyan*	gleann – 'a valley'
colleen	*col-yeen*	cailín – 'a girl'
cairn	*corr-an*	carn – 'a pile of stones'
clan	*klon*	clann – 'people with common ancestor'
shamrock	*sham-rohg*	seamróg
tory	*tohr-ee*	tóraí – 'a pursuer, an outlaw'

Pronunciation

There are a number of Irish sounds not found in English, and an
approximation to these will be given. Stress is normally on the
first syllable. Long vowels are marked by an acute accent: 'a
poem', *dán* (pronounced *daan*).

bh, mh	'v'
ch	before **i** and **e**, like the 'h' in Hugh, or the German *ich*
ch	before **a, o**, and **u**, like the Scottish *loch*
dh, gh	a 'y' sound before **i** and **e**
dh, gh	a 'g' sound before **a, o** and **u** (approximately)
fh	silent
ph	'f'
sh, th	'h'
r	trilled
mb	'm'
gc	'g'
nd	'n'
bhf	'v'
ng	'ng' as in 'sing', occurs initially, as in Japanese
bp	'b'
ts	't'

The four diphthong sounds are written and pronounced as follows:

'ay'	*sice*	saghas – 'a kind'
	ay-rk	adharc – 'a horn'
'ow'	*ow-in*	abhainn – 'a river'
	down	domhan – 'world'
	bour	bodhar – 'deaf'
	row	rogha – 'choice'
'oo-a'	*foo-ar*	fuar – 'cold'
'ee-a'	*shee-ad*	siad – 'they'

Greetings & Civilities

Greetings

Hi/Good morning/ Good afternoon.	*dee-a gwit*	Dia duit. (lit. 'God to you')
Good night.	*ee-ha vo*	Oíche mhaith.
How are you?	*kunas taa too?*	Conas tá tú?
Well.	*go mo*	Go maith.
Very well, thanks.	*go hon vo, go-ra mo ogot*	Go han-mhaith, gura maith agat.
What's new?	*kayn shkay-al?*	Cén scéal?

Goodbyes

Goodbye.	*slaan*	Slán.
See you later.	*slaan go foh-il*	Slán go fóill.
Take care.	*toor ara*	Tabhair aire.

Civilities

Please.
  lyeh do hull — Le do thoil.

Thank you.
  go-ra mo ogot — Gura maith agat.

Thank you very much.
  go-ra myee-la mo ogot — Gura míle maith agat.

You're welcome.
  taa faa-il-tyeh roht — Tá fáilte romhat.

Excuse me.
  gov mo lyeh-shkay-al — Gabh mo leithscéal.

I'd like to present you to ...
  sho ... — Seo ...

I'm pleased to meet you.
  taa aa-hass o-rom boo-la lyat — Tá áthas orm bualadh leat.

Forms of Address

| Sir/Mr ...! | *a gwin-a oo-as-il!* | A dhuine uasail! |
| Madame/Mrs ...! | *a van oo-as-al!* | A bhean uasal! |

Language Difficulties

Do you speak Irish?
  will Gwayl-gye ogot?   An bhfuil Gaeilge agat?
No/Yes a little.
  nyee/taa, byug-aan   Níl/Tá, beagán.
How do you say that in Irish?
  kunas a dyair-faa shin oss   Conas a déarfá sin as
  gwayl-gyeh?   Gaeilge?
I understand/don't understand
you.
  tig-im/nyee hig-im hoo.   Tuigim/Ní thuigim thú.
Say it again, please.
  obb-ir a-reesh ay, lyeh do   Abair arís é, le do thoil.
  hull
Write it down, please.
  shkreev sheess ay, lyeh do   Scríobh síos é, le do thoil.
  hull

Small Talk

What's your name?
  kod iss an-im dit?   Cad is ainm duit?
I'm ...
  iss mish-a ...   Is mise ...
Who is that?
  kyay hay shin?   Cé hé sin?
I don't know.
  nyeel iss ogom   Níl a fhios agam.

Where are you from?
   kod oss dit?   Cad as duit?

I'm from …   *oss …*   As …

Australia	*on os-traa-il*	an Astráil
Canada	*kyan-ada*	Ceanada
England	*soss-ana*	Sasana
Ireland	*ay-rin*	Éirinn
New Zealand	*on noo-a hay-lin*	an Nua-Shéalainn
Scotland	*ol-bwin*	Albain
Wales	*an mrat-in vyug*	an mBreatain Bheag
the USA	*mer-ik-aa … dum*	Meiriceá … dom

NB Listed above are some countries where English-speaking travellers may come from. Unfortunately we can't list all countries here, so this could be a good time for you to enter conversation with a local and find out from them how to pronounce your country.

Are you married?
   will too pohs-ta   An bhfuil tú pósta?
Do you have children?
   will paash-tyee ogot   An bhfuil páistí agat?
Where do you live?
   kaa will kohn-ee ort?   Cá bhfuil cónaí ort?
Where are you working?
   kaa will too egg obb-ir   Cá bhfuil tú ag obair?

Useful Phrases
Where's the toilet, please?
   kaa will on lyeh-aras, lyeh   Cá bhfuil an leithreas, le do
   do hull?   thoil?

Where's the toilet, please?
kaa will on lyeh-aras, lyeh do hull? — Cá bhfuil an leithreas, le do thoil?

On the left. *ehr klay* — Ar clé.
On the right. *ehr yesh* — Ar dheis.
Straight on. *dyee-rokh ehr ay* — Díreach ar aghaidh.

I like ...
iss mo lyum... — Is maith liom ...
Yes, I'd like to/Certainly!
bo vryaa lyum ay/kyin-tyeh — Ba bhreá liom é/Cinnte!
Great, good idea!
har borr, on-smweenev — Thar barr, an-smaoineamh
Agreed. You're right.
ayn-teem. taa on kyart ogot. — Aontaím. Tá an ceart agat.
Me too/Neither do I.
mish-a lyesh/naa mish-a — Mise leis/ná mise.
I'm sorry, I can't.
brohno-rom, nyee fyay-dyir lyum. — Brón orm, ní féidir liom.
Amazing!
do-khred-tye! — Dochreidte!
How strange!
noch at ay! — nach ait é!
That's terrible!
guy hoo-ah-faass-och! — Go huafásach
Impossible!
nyee fyay-dyir ay. — Ní féidir é!

Have a good journey!
   *guh nyigh-ree on boh-har
   lyat!*   Go n-éirí an bóthar leat!
Happy Christmas!
   nol-ig ho-na!   Nollaig shona!
Happy Easter!
   kaashk ho-na!   Cáisc shona!

Food

Waiter!
   a rass-tal-ee!   A fhreastalaí!
Are you hungry/thirsty?
   will ok-ras/tort ort?   An bhfuil ocras/tart ort?
What will you drink/eat?
   kod a ohl-hee/ees-hee too?   Cad a ólfaidh/íosfaidh tú?
I'd like ...
   bo vo lyum ...   Ba mhaith liom ...
A little bread, please.
   *byug-aan a-raan, lyeh do
   hull*   Beagán aráin, le do thoil.

a beer	*byohr*	beoir
a drop of ...	*breen*	braon
apple juice	*soo ool*	sú úll
dessert	*myil-shohg*	milseog
fish	*ee-ask*	iasc
meat	*fyoh-il*	feoil
mineral water	*ish-keh myee-an-ree*	uisce mianraí
orange juice	*soo or-aash-teh*	sú oráiste
potatoes	*praa-tee*	prátaí

salmon and brown bread	*brad-aan og-as a-raan don*	bradán agus arán donn
soup	*on-ra*	anraith
vegetables	*gloss-ree*	glasraí
water	*ish-keh*	uisce
wine	*fee-on*	fíon
whiskey	*ish-keh ba-ha*	uisce beatha

Signs & Irish Words Commonly Heard

NO SMOKING	*NÁ CAITEAR TOBAC*
CITY CENTRE (on buses)	*AN LÁR*

A hundred thousand welcomes.	Céad míle fáilte.
Lower House of Parliament	Dáil Éireann
Prime Minister	An Taoiseach
Presidential Residence	Áras an Uachtaráin

ITALIAN

ITALIAN

Italian

Introduction

Italian is a Romance language, related to French, Spanish, Portuguese and Romanian. The Romance languages belong to the larger Indo-European group of languages, which include English. Indeed, as English and Italian share common roots in Latin, you'll find many Italian words which you will recognise.

Modern literary Italian began to be developed in the 13th and 14th centuries, predominantly through the works of Dante, Petrarch and Boccaccio, who wrote chiefly in the Florentine dialect. The language drew on its Latin heritage, and the many dialects of Italy, to develop into the standard Italian of today. While many and varied dialects are spoken in everyday conversation, standard Italian is the national language of schools, media and literature, and is understood throughout the country.

There are 57 million speakers of Italian in Italy, half a million in Switzerland, where Italian is one of the four official languages, and 1.5 million speakers in France and the former Yugoslavia. As a result of migration, Italian is also widely spoken in the USA, Argentina, Brazil and Australia.

Opera, film and literature, from the great Renaissance works to modern writers such as Umberto Eco and Alberto Moravia, have all contributed to portraying Italian as the vibrant, melodic and rich language that it is. It is not, however, a difficult language for English-speakers to learn and Italians will welcome your attempts to communicate with them.

Italian words are expressed in either feminine or masculine forms. In this chapter, the feminine form is given first, the masculine second. Informal forms of words are given within brackets after the formal word, or indicated with (inf).

Pronunciation

Italian is not difficult to pronounce. Although some of the more clipped vowels, and stress on double letters, require careful practice for English speakers, it is easy enough to make yourself understood.

Vowels

Vowels are generally more clipped than in English.

a	as the second 'a' in 'camera'
e	as the 'ay' in 'day', although without the 'i' sound
i	as in 'see'
o	as in 'dot'
u	as in 'too'

Consonants

The pronunciation of many consonants is similar to English. The following sounds depend on certain rules:

c	like 'k' before **a**, **o** and **u**
	like the 'ch' in 'choose' before **e** and **i**
ch	a hard 'k' sound
g	a hard 'g' as in 'get' before **a**, **o** and **u**
	before **e** and **i**, like the 'j' in 'job'
gh	a hard 'g' as in 'get'
gli	as the 'lli' in 'million'
gn	as the 'ny' in 'canyon'
h	always silent
r	a rolled 'rrr' sound

ITALIAN

sc before before **e** and **i**, like the 'sh' in 'sheep'

before **h**, **a**, **o** and **u**, a hard sound as in 'school'

z as in 'zoo', as the 'ts' in 'lights' or as the 'ds'in 'beds'

Stress

Double consonants are pronounced as a longer, often more forceful sound than a single consonant.

Stress often falls on the next to last syllable, as in *spa-**ghet**-ti.* When a word has an accent, the stress is on that syllable, as in *cit-**tà**,* 'city'.

Greetings & Civilities
Top Useful Phrases

Hello.	*chahw*	Ciao.
Goodbye.	*ah-rree-ve-**dair**-chee/chahw*	Arrivederci/Ciao.
Yes./No.	*see/no*	Sì./No.
Excuse me.	*mee **skoo**-zee*	Mi scusi.

May I? Do you mind?
pos-so? vee dis-pee-ah-chei? Posso? Vi dispiace?

Sorry. (excuse me, forgive me)
*mee **skoo**-zee/mee per-**do**-nee* Mi scusi. Mi perdoni.

Please.
*per fah-**vor**-rei/per pee-ah-**chair**-rei* Per favore./Per piacere.

Thank you.
ghrah-tsee-e Grazie.

Many thanks.
*ghrah-tsee-e mee-lei/ghrah-tsee-e **tahn**-to* Grazie mille. Grazie tanto.

That's fine. You're welcome.
prei-gho   Prego.

Greetings
Good morning.
bwon-jor-no   Buongiorno.
Good evening/night.
bwo-na-sair-rah/not-tei   Buonasera/notte.
How are you?
ko-mei stah?   Come sta?
ko-mei stah-ee?   Come stai? (inf)
Well, thanks.
be-ne, ghrah-tsee-e   Bene, grazie.

Forms of Address
Madam/Mrs/Ms	*see-nyor-ra*	Signora
Sir/Mr	*see-nyor-rei*	Signore
companion, friend	*ah-mee-kah/o*	amica/o

Language Difficulties
Do you speak English?
pahr-lah (pahr-lee)   Parla (Parli) inglese?
eng-ghlei-zei?
Does anyone speak English?
chei kwahl-koo-no kei   C'è qualcuno che parla
pahr-lah eeng-ghlei-zei?   inglese?
I speak a little Italian.
pahr-lo un po   Parlo un po' d'italiano.
dee-tah-lee-ah-no
I don't speak …
non pahr-lo …   Non parlo …

ITALIAN

I (don't) understand.
(non) kah-pees-ko

(Non) Capisco.

Could you speak more slowly please?
pwo pahr-lah-rei pee-oo len-tah-men-tei, pair fah-vor-rei?

Può parlare (più) lentamente, per favore?

Could you repeat that?
pwo ree-pe-tair-lo, pair fah-vor-rei?

Può ripeterlo, per favore?

How do you say …?
ko-mei see dee-chei …?

Come si dice …?

What does … mean?
kei (ko-zah) see-nyee-fee-kah/vwol dee-rei…?

Che (cosa) significa/vuole dire …?

Small Talk
Meeting People

What is your name?
koh-mei see kee-ah-mah?
koh-mei tee kee-ah-mee?

Come si chiama?
Come ti chiami? (inf)

My name is …
mee kee-ah-mo …

Mi chiamo …

I'd like to introduce you to …
vo-rrei pre-sen-tar-lah (pre-sen-tar-tee) ah …

Vorrei presentarla (presentarti) a …

I'm pleased to meet you.
pee-ah-chair-rei/lee-e-to dee ko-nosh-air-lah (ko-nosh-air-tee)

Piacere. Lieto di conoscerla (conoscerti).

Nationalities

Where are you from?
 dee doh-vei sei?   Di dove sei?

I am from …
 vehng-gho dah …   Vengo da …

England	*(l') eeng-ghil-tair-rrah*	(l') Inghilterra
Ireland	*(l') eer-lahn-dah*	(l') Irlanda
Japan	*jahp-po-nei*	Giappone
Middle East	*meh-dee-oh o-ree-en-tei*	Medio Oriente
New Zealand	*(lah) nwo-vah ze-lahn-dah*	(la) Nuova Zelanda
Scotland	*(lah) sko-tzee-ah*	(la) Scozia
the USA	*lyee stah-tee o-nee-tee*	gli Stati Uniti
Wales	*(eel) ghahl-les*	(il) Galles

Unfortunately we can't list all countries here, but try saying the name of your country in your language, as many country names have a similar pronunciation in Italian.

Age

How old are you?
 kwahn-tee ahn-nee ah (ah-ee)?   Quanti anni ha (hai)?

I am … years old.
 o … ahn-nee   Ho … anni.

Occupations

What (work) do you do?
 kei lah-vor-ro fah (fah-ee)?   Che lavoro fa (fai)?

ITALIAN

I am a/an …	so-no oo-nah/oon …	Sono una/un …
artist	ahr-tee-stah	artista
business person	don-nah/wo-mo dee ahf-fah-ree	donna (f)/uomo (m) di affari
doctor	do-tor-es-sa	dottoressa (f)
	do-tor-rei	dottore (m)
	me-dee-ko	medico
engineer	een-jen-yair-rei	ingegnere
farmer	ah-ghree-kol-tor-rei	agricoltore
journalist	jor-nah-lees-tah	giornalista
labourer	mah-no-vah-lei	manovale
lawyer	ahv-vo-kah-tess-ah	avvocatessa (f)
	ahv-vo-kah-to	avvocato (m)
mechanic	me-kah-nee-kah/ko	meccanica/o
nurse	een-feer-mee-air-rei	infermiera/e
office worker	eem-pee-e-ghah-tah/o	impiegata/o
scientist	shee-en-tzee-ah-tah/o	scienziata/o
student	stoo-den-tes-sah	studentessa (f)
	stoo-den-tei	studente (m)
teacher	een-seh-nyahn-tei	insegnante
waiter	kah-mair-ree-air-rah/ei	cameriera/e
writer	skreet-tor-rei	scrittore

Religion

What is your religion?

   dee kei rei-lee-jo-nei sei?   Di che religione sei?

I am not religious.

   non so-no re-lee-jo-sah/o   Non sono religiosa/o.

I am …	*so-no* …	Sono …
Buddhist	*boo-dee-stah*	buddista
Catholic	*kaht-to-lee-kah/o*	cattolica/o
Christian	*kree-stee-ah-nah/o*	cristiana/o
Hindu	*een-doo*	indù
Jewish	*e-brei-ah/o*	ebrea/o
Muslim	*mu-sul-mah-nah/o*	mussulmana/o

Family

Are you married?
  ei spo-sah-tah/o lei?   È sposata/o lei?

I am (not) married.
  (non) so-no spo-sah-tah/o   (Non) Sono sposata/o.

Is your wife/husband here?
  soo-ah moh-lyee-e/soo-o   Sua moglie/Suo marito è
  mah-ree-to ei kwee kon lei?   qui con lei?

How many children do you
have?
  kwahn-tee fee-lyee ah (ahee)?   Quanti figli ha (hai)?

I don't have any children.
  non oh fee-lyee   Non ho figli.

I have a daughter/a son.
  oh oo-nah fee-lyah/oon   Ho una figlia/un figlio.
  fee-lyo

How many sisters/brothers do
you have?
  kwahn-tei so-rehl-lei/   Quante sorelle/Quanti
  kwahn-tee frah-tehl-leeah   fratelli ha (hai)?
  (ahee)?

Are you alone?
  ei (sei) so-lah/o?   È (Sei) sola/o?

ITALIAN

Do you have a girlfriend/
boyfriend?

> *ah (ahee) oo-nah rah-ghah-*   Ha (Hai) una ragazza/un
> *tsah/oon rah-ghah-tso?*   ragazzo?

brother	*frah-tehl-lo*	fratello
children	*fee-lyee/bahm-bee-nee*	figli/bambini
daughter	*fee-lyah*	figlia
family	*fah-mee-lyah*	famiglia
father	*pah-drei*	padre
grandfather	*non-no*	nonno
grandmother	*non-nah*	nonna
husband	*mah-ree-to*	marito
mother	*mah-drei*	madre
sister	*sor-rrel-lah*	sorella
son	*fee-lyo*	figlio
uncle	*dzee-o*	zio
wife	*mo-lyei*	moglie

Useful Phrases

Sure.	*chair-to*	Certo.
Just a minute.	*oon mee-noo-to*	Un minuto.
It's (not) important.	*(non) eem-por-tah*	(Non) importa.
It's (not) possible.	*(non) eh pos-see-bee-lei*	(Non) È possibile.
Wait!	*ah-spet-tee!*	Aspetti!
	(ah-spet-ta!)	(Aspetta! – inf)
Good luck!	*bwo-nah for-too-na!*	Buona fortuna!

ITALIAN

Signs

BAGGAGE COUNTER	*DEPOSITO BAGAGLI*
CUSTOMS	*DOGANA*
EMERGENCY EXIT	*USCITA DI SICUREZZA*
ENTRANCE	*INGRESSO/ENTRATA*
EXIT	*USCITA*
FREE ADMISSION	*INGRESSO GRATUITO*
HOT/COLD	*CALDO/FREDDO*
NO ENTRY	*VIETATO ENTRARE*
INFORMATION	*INFORMAZIONI*
NO SMOKING	*VIETATO FUMARE*
OPEN/CLOSED	*APERTO/CHIUSO*
PROHIBITED	*PROIBITO/VIETATO*
RESERVED	*PRENOTATO/IN RISERVA*
TELEPHONE	*TELEFONO*
TOILETS	*GABINETTI*
POLICE	*POLIZIA/CARABINIERI*
POLICE STATION	*QUESTURA/CASERMA*

Getting Around

What time does … leave/
arrive?

　　*ah kei **or**-rah pahr-tei/ah-*　　A che ora parte/arriva …?
　　***ree**-vah …?*

the (air)plane	*lah-**air**-re-o*	l'aereo
the boat	*lah **bahr**-kah*	la barca
the ferry	*eel trah-**ghet**-to*	il traghetto
the bus	***lahw**-to-boos*	l'autobus
the train	*eel **trei**-no*	il treno

ITALIAN

Finding Your Way

Do you have a guidebook/
local map?

*ah oo-nah **ghwee**-dah too-
rees-tee-kah/pee-**ahn**-tahlo-
kah-lei?*

Ha una guida turistica/
pianta locale?

Where is …?

*do-**vei** …?*

Dov'è …?

How do I get to …?

*mee pwo **dee**-rei lah
strah-dah pair …?*

Mi può dire la strada per …?

Is it far from/near here?

*ei lon-**tah**-no/vee-**chee**-no?*

È lontano/vicino?

Can I walk there?

*chee pos-so ahn-**dah**-rei ah
pee-e-dee?*

Ci posso andare a piedi?

Can you show me (on the map)?

*mee **mo**-stree (sool-lah
kahr-tah/pee-ahn-**tee**-nah)*

Mi mostri (sulla carta/
piantina).

Are there other means of
getting there?

*chee so-no ahl-tree mo-dee
pair ahr-ree-**vahr**-chee?*

Ci sono altri modi per
arrivarci?

Directions

Go straight ahead.

*see vah (vah-ee) **sem**-prei
dee-**reet**-to*

Si va sempre diritto.

Turn left …

*jee-rah ah see-**nee**-strah …*

Gira a sinistra …

Turn right …

*jee-rah ah **de**-strah …*

Gira a destra …

ITALIAN

at the next corner
   *ahl **pros**-see-mo*
   ahng-gho-lo   al prossimo angolo
at the traffic lights
   *ah-ee se-**mah**-for-ree*   ai semafori

behind	*dee-e-tro*	dietro
in front of	*dah-**vahn**-tee*	davanti
far	*lon-**tah**-no*	lontano
near	*vee-**chee**-no*	vicino
opposite	*dee **fron**-te ah*	di fronte a

Buying Tickets

TICKET OFFICE	*BIGLIETTERIA*

Excuse me, where is the ticket
office?
   *skoo-zee, **do**-vei lah*
   *bee-lyet-**ter**-ree-ah?*   Scusi, dov'è la biglietteria?
Where can I buy a ticket?
   ***do**-vei **pos**-so/see pwo kom-*
   ***prah**-rei oon bee-**lyet**-to?*   Dove posso/si può
   comprare un biglietto?
I want to go to …
   ***vor**-rei ahn-**dah**-rei ah …*   Vorrei andare a …
Do I need to book?
   *see de-vei/bee-**zo**-nyah prei-*
   *no-**tah**-rei (oon po-sto)?*   Si deve/Bisogna prenotare
   (un posto)?
You need to book.
   *see, de-vei prei-no-**tah**-rei/*
   fah-rei oo-nah prei-no-ta-
   tsee-o-nei   Sì, deve prenotare/fare una
   prenotazione.

I'd like to book a seat to …
*vo-**rrei** prei-no-**tah**-rei oon* **po**-sto pair …

Vorrei prenotare un posto per …

I'd like …
*vo-**rrei** …*

Vorrei …

a one-way ticket
*(oon bee-**lyet**-to dee) so-lo ahn-**dah**-tah*

(Un biglietto di) Solo andata.

a return ticket
*(oon bee-**lyet**-to dee) ahn-**dah**-tah ei ree-**tor**-no*

(Un biglietto di) Andata e ritorno.

two tickets
*doo-ei bee-**lyet**-tee*

due biglietti

a student's/child's fare
*oo-nah tah-**reef**-ah/oo-no* **skon**-to pair stoo-**den**-tee/bahm-**bee**-nee

una tariffa/uno sconto per studenti/bambini

1st class
*pree-mah **klahs**-sei*

prima classe

2nd class
*se-**kon**-dah **klahs**-sei*

seconda classe

It is full.
ei pee-e-no

È pieno/tutto occupato.

Is it completely full?
*ei kom-ple-tah-**men**-tei pee-e-no?*

È completamente pieno?

Can I get on the waiting (stand-by) list?
*pos-so **met**-tair-mee nel-lah* **lee**-stah dah-**tei**-zah?

Posso mettermi nella lista d'attesa?

Air

ARRIVALS	*ARRIVI*
DEPARTURES	*PARTENZE*

Is there a flight to …?
chei oon vo-lo pair …?   C'è un volo per …?

When is the next flight to …?
ah kei or-rah pahr-tei eel   A che ora parte il prossimo
***pross**-ee-mo vo-lo pair...?*   volo per ...?

How long does the flight take?
***kwahn**-to tem-po **door**-rah*   Quanto tempo dura il volo?
*eel **vo**-lo?*

What is the flight number?
*kwahl ei eel **noo**-mair-ro*   Qual'è il numero di volo?
dee vo-lo?

| boarding pass | ***kahr**-tah deem-**bahr**-ko* | carta d'imbarco |
| customs | *do-**ghah**-nah* | dogana |

Bus & Tram

BUS STOP	*FERMATA DELL'AUTOBUS*
TRAM STOP	*FERMATA DEL TRAM*

Where is the bus/tram stop?
*doh-**vei** lah fair-**mah**-tah*   Dov'è la fermata
*del-**ahw**-to-bus/del trahm?*   dell'autobus/del tram?

Which bus goes to …?
***kwah**-lei **ahw**-to-bus vah*   Quale autobus va a …?
ah …?

Does this bus go to …?
*kwest **ahw**-to-bus vah a …?*   Quest'autobus va a …?

How often do buses pass by?
*o-nyee **kwahn**-to tem-po
pahss-ah-no lyee ahw-to-bus?*
Ogni quanto tempo passano gli autobus?

What time is the … bus?
*ah kei **or**-rah **pahs**-sah …
ahw-to-bus?*
A che ora passa … autobus?

next	*eel **pross**-ee-mo*	il prossimo
first	*eel **pree**-mo*	il primo
last	***lool**-tee-mo*	l'ultimo

Could you let me know when we get to …?
*mee pwo **deer**-rei **kwahn**-
do see ah-**ree**-vah …?*
Mi può dire quando si arriva a …?

I want to get off!
*deh-vo **shen**-dair-rei!*
Devo scendere!

Train

TIMETABLE	*ORARIO*
TRAIN STATION	*STAZIONE F.S.(FERROVIA DELLO STATO)*
PLATFORM NO	*BINARIO No.*
LEFT-LUGGAGE OFFICE	*DEPOSITO BAGAGLI*

Is this the right platform for …?
*ei **kwes**-do eel bee-**nah**-
ree-o pair …?*
È questo il binario per …?

The train leaves from platform …
*eel **trei**-no **pahr**-tei dahl
bee-**nah**-ree-o…*
Il treno parte dal binario …

ITALIAN

Passengers must …
*ee pahs-sej-**jair**-ree **deh**-vo-no …/bee-**zo**-nyah…*

I passeggeri devono …/
Bisogna …

change trains	*kam-bee-**ahr**-rei **trei**-nee*	cambiare treni
change platforms	*kam-bee-**ahr**-rei bee-**nah**-ree*	cambiare binari
dining car	*vah-**gho**-nei rees-tor-**rahn**-tei*	vagone ristorante
express	***rah**-pee-do*	rapido
local	*lo-**kah**-lei*	locale
sleeping car	*vah-**gho**-nei **let**-to*	vagone letto

Metro

CHANGE (for coins)	*SPICCIOLI*

Which line takes me to …?
*kwah-**lei** lah **lee**-nei-ah pair ahn-**dah**-rei ah …?*

Qual'è la linea per andare …?

What is the next station?
*kwah-**lei** lah **pros**-see-mah **stah**-tsee-o-nei?*

Qual'è la prossima stazione?

Taxi

Please take me to …
*mee **por**-tee ah …, pair pee-ah-**chair**-rei*

Mi porti a …, per piacere.

How much is it to go to …?
*kwahn-to kos-dah ahn-**dah**-rei ah …?*

Quanto costa andare a …?

ITALIAN

Instructions

Here is fine, thank you.
*kwee vah be-**nees**-see-mo, **ghrah**-tsee-e*

Qui va benissimo, grazie.

The next corner, please.
*ahl **pros**-see-mo **ahn**-gho-lo, pair fah-**vor**-rei*

Al prossimo angolo, per favore.

The next street to the left/right.
*ei lah **pros**-see-mah **strah**-dah ah see-**nee**-strah/**des**-tra*

È la prossima strada a sinistra/destra.

Stop here!
*see **fair**-mee kwah!*

Si fermi qua!

Please slow down.
*pwo rahl-len-**tahr**-rei, pair fah-**vor**-rei*

Può rallentare, per favore.

Please wait here.
*mee ahs-**spet**-tee kwee*

Mi aspetti qui.

Useful Phrases

The train is delayed/cancelled.
*eel **trei**-no ei een ree-**tahr**-do/kahn-chel-**lah**-to*

Il treno è in ritardo/cancellato.

There is a delay of ... hours.
*chee sah-**rah** oon ree-**tahr**-do dee ... or-rei*

Ci sarà un ritardo di ... ore.

Can I reserve a place?
*pos-so pre-no-**tah**-rei oon pos-do?*

Posso prenotare un posto?

I want to get off at ...
***vo**-lyo **shen**-dair-rei ah ...*

Voglio scendere a ...

How long does the trip take?
*kwahn-to doo-rah eel
vee-ahj-jo?*
Quanto dura il viaggio?

Is it a direct route?
*ei oon ee-tee-nair-rah-
ree-o dee-ret-to?*
È un itinerario diretto?

Is that seat taken?
*ei ok-koo-pah-to kwel
pos-do?*
È occupato quel posto?

Excuse me. (to get off)
pair-mes-so
Permesso.

Car & Bicycle

DETOUR	*DEVIAZIONE*
FREEWAY	*AUTOSTRADA*
PETROL STATION	*STAZIONE DI SERVIZIO*
GIVE WAY	*DARE LA PRECEDENZA*
MECHANIC	*MECCANICO*
NO ENTRY	*DIVIETO DI TRANSITO*
NO PARKING	*DIVIETO DI SOSTA*
NORMAL	*NORMALE*
ONE WAY	*SENSO UNICO*
REPAIRS	*RIPARAZIONI*

Where can I hire a car/bicycle?
*do-vei pos-so no-lej-jahr-
rei oo-nah mah-kee-nah/
bee-chee-klet-tah?*
Dove posso noleggiare una
macchina/bicicletta?

How much is it daily/weekly?
*kwahn-to kos-dah ahl jor-no/
ahl-lah set-tee-mah-nah?*
Quanto costa al giorno/alla
settimana?

ITALIAN

Does that include insurance/mileage?

*ei kom-**prei**-zo lahs-**see**-koor-ra-tsee-o-nei/eel kos-do pair kee-**lo**-me-tro?*

È compreso l'assicurazione/il costo per kilometro?

Where's the next petrol station?

*doh-vei lah **pros**-see-mah stah-tsee-o-nei dee sair-**vee**-tsee-o?*

Dov'è la prossima stazione di servizio?

Please fill the tank.

*pee-e-no, pair fah-**vor**-rei*

Pieno, per favore.

I want … litres of petrol (gas).

*vo-lyo … **lee**-tree (dee behn-**zee**-nah)*

Voglio … litri (di benzina).

Please check the oil and water.

*pwo kon-trol-**lahr**-rei lo-lyo ei **lah**-kwah, pair fah-**vor**-rei?*

Può controllare l'olio e l'aqua, per favore?

How long can I park here?

*pair **kwahn**-to **tem**-po pos-so pahr-kej-**jahr**-rei kwee?*

Per quanto tempo posso parcheggiare qui?

Does this road lead to?

*kwes-dah **strah**-dah chee por-tair-**rah** ah …?*

Questa strada ci porterà …?

air (for tyres)	**ah**-ree-ah	aria
battery	bah-tair-**ree**-ah	batteria
brakes	**frei**-nee	freni
clutch	free-tsee-o-nei	frizione

driver's licence	*pah-**tehn**-tei (dee ghwee-dah)*	patente (di guida)
engine	*mo-**tor**-rei*	motore
high beam lights	*ah-bah-lyee-**ahn**-tee*	abbaglianti
headlights	***ahn**-ah-bah-lyee-ahn-tee*	anabbaglianti
tail lights	*fah-nah-**lee**-nee dee **ko**-dah*	fanalini di coda
oil	*o-lyo*	olio
puncture	*for-rah-**too**-rah*	foratura
radiator	*rah-dee-ah-**tor**-rei*	radiatore
road map	*kar-tah strah-**dah**-lei*	carta stradale
tyres	***ghohm**-mei*	gomme
windscreen	*pah-rah-**bre**-tsah*	parabrezza

Car Problems

I need a mechanic.
*oh bee-**zo**-nyo dee oon me-**kah**-nee-ko*   Ho bisogno di un meccanico.

What make is it?
*kei **tee**-po dee **mah**-kee-nah ei?*   Che tipo di macchina è?

The battery is flat.
*lah ba-tair-**ree**-ah ei skah-**ree**-kah*   La batteria è scarica.

The radiator is leaking.
*eel rah-dee-ah-**tor**-rei pair-dei ah-kwah*   Il radiatore perde acqua.

It has a flat tyre.
*ah lah **ghom**-mah boo-**kah**-tah*   Ha la gomma bucata.

ITALIAN

It's overheating.
see stah soo-rree-skahl-
dahn-do   Si sta surriscaldando.
It's not working.
non foon-tsee-o-nah   Non funziona.

Accommodation

CAMPING GROUND	*CAMPING/CAMPEGGIO*
GUESTHOUSE	*PENSIONE*
HOTEL	*ALBERGO*
YOUTH HOSTEL	*OSTELLO DELLA*
	GIOVENTÙ

Finding Accommodation
I am looking for …
sto chair-kahn-do …   Sto cercando …
Where is a … hotel?
do-vei un ahl-bair-gho …?   Dov'è un albergo …?

cheap	*kei kos-dah po-ko*	che costa poco
good	***bwo**-no*	buono
nearby	*vee-**chee**-no*	vicino
clean	*pu-**lee**-to*	pulito

What is the address?
*kwah-**lei** leen-dee-**reets**-o?*   Qual'è l'indirizzo?
Could you write the address,
please?
mee pwo skree-vair-rei   Mi può scrivere l'indirizzo,
*leen-dee-**reets**-o, pair*   per favore?
*fah-**vor**-rei?*

Booking a Room

Do you have any rooms available?
*ah **del**-lei **kah**-mair-rei lee-**bair**-rei?*
Ha delle camere libere?

I'd like to book a room.
*vo-**rrei** ree-zair-**vahr**-ei oo-nah **kah**-mair-rah*
Vorrei riservare una camera.

for one night/four nights
*pair oo-nah **not**-tei/**kwaht**-tro **not**-tei*
per una notte/quattro notte

from tonight/Tuesday
*dee stah-**sair**-ah/dee mahr-te-**dee***
di stasera/di martedì

I'd like …	*vo-**rrei** …*	Vorrei …
a single room	*oo-nah **kah**-mair-rah **seeng**-gho-lah*	una camera singola
a double room	*oo-nah **kah**-mair-rah **dop**-pee-ah/pair **doo**-ei*	una camera doppia/per due
a room with a bathroom	*oo-nah **kah**-mair-rah kon **bah**-nyo*	una camera con bagno
to share a room	*dee-vee-**dair**-rei o-nah **stahn**-tsa*	dividere una stanza
a bed	*un **let**-to*	un letto

I'm staying for …	***res**-do pair …*	Resto per…
one day	*oon **jor**-no*	un giorno
two days	*doo-ei **jor**-nee*	due giorni
one week	*oo-nah set-tee-**mah**-nah*	una settimana

At the Hotel

How much is it per night/
per person?

*kwahn-to kos-dah ... pair
oo-nah **not**-tei/pair
chahs-**koo**-nah/o*

Quanto costa ... per una
notte/per ciascuna/o?

Can I see it?

*pos-so ve-**dair**-lah?*

Posso vederla?

Are there any others?

*chei nei so-no **ahl**-trei?*

Ce ne sono altre?

Are there any cheaper rooms?

*chee so-no **ahl**-trei
kah-mair-rei kei kos-dah-no
dee **me**-no?*

Ci sono altre camere che
costano di meno?

Can I see the bathroom?

*pos-so ve-**dair**-rei eel
bah-nyo?*

Posso vedere il bagno?

Is there a reduction for
students/children?

*chei oo-no **scon**-to pair
stoo-**den**-tee/bahm-**bee**-nee?*

C'è uno sconto per
studenti/bambini?

Does it include breakfast?

*lah ko-**lats**-ee-o-nei ei
kom-**prei**-zah (nel pre-tso)?*

La colazione è compresa
(nel prezzo)?

It's fine, I'll take it.

*vah be-nei, lah **pren**-do*

Va bene, la prendo.

I'm not sure how long I'm
staying.

*non **so**-no see-**koo**-rah/o
kwahn-to **tem**-po chee
res-tair-**ro***

Non sono sicura/o quanto
tempo ci resterà.

Is there a lift?
chei oon ah-chen-sor-rei?

C'è un ascensore?

Where is the bathroom?
do-vei eel bah-nyo?

Dov'è il bagno?

Is there hot water all day?
chei lah-kwah kahl-dah toot-to eel jor-no?

C'è l'aqua calda tutto il giorno?

You May Hear

Do you have identification?
ah oo-nah kar-tah dee-den-tee-tah?

Ha una carta d'identità?

Your membership card, please.
lah soo-ah tes-sair-ah, pair fah-vor-rei

La sua tessera, per favore.

Sorry, we're full.
mee dees-pee-ah-chei, ei pee-e-no/non chei pos-do

Mi dispiace, è pieno/non c'è posto.

How long will you be staying?
kwahn-to tem-po vwo-lei res-dahr-rei?

Quanto tempo vuole restare?

It's … per day/per person.
kos-dah … ahl jor-no/pair pair-so-nah

Costa … al giorno/per persona.

Requests & Complaints

Can I use the kitchen/telephone?
pos-so oo-zar-rei lah koo-chee-nah/te-le-fo-no?

Posso usare la cucina/telefono?

Please wake me up at …
mee sve-lyee ah …

Mi svegli a …

Is there somewhere to wash clothes?

*chei kwal-kei **pos**-do pair lah-**vahr**-rei ee ves-**tee**-tee?*

C'è qualque posto per lavare i vestiti?

Do you have a safe where I can leave my things?

*chei oo-nah kahs-**set**-tah dee see-koo-**re**-tsah pair lah ro-bah dee va-**lor**-rei?*

C'è una cassetta di sicurezza per la roba di valore?

I don't like this room.

*kwes-dah kah-**mair**-rah non mee pee-**ah**-chei*

Questa camera non mi piace.

It's too small.

*ei **trop**-po **pee**-ko-lah*

È troppo piccola.

It's noisy.

*chei **trop**-po roo-**mor**-rei*

C'è troppo rumore.

It's too dark.

*ei **trop**-po skoo-rah*

È troppo scura.

It's expensive.

*ei **trop**-po **kah**-rah*

È troppo cara.

The room needs to be cleaned.

*lah **kah**-mair-rah dev-**ess**-sair-rei poo-**lee**-tah*

La camera dev'essere pulita.

Please change the sheets.

*kahm-bee lei len-**zwo**-lah, pair pee-ah-**chair**-rei*

Cambi le lenzuola, per piacere.

The toilet won't flush.

*eel ghah-bee-**net**-to non fun-**tsee**-o-nah*

Il gabinetto non funziona.

I can't open/close the window.

*non **pos**-so ah-**pree**-rei/*
***kyoo**-dair-rei lah*
*fee-**nes**-strah*

Non posso aprire/chiudere
la finestra.

I've locked myself out of
my room.

*mee so-no **kyoo**-zah/o*
fwor-ree dahl-lah mee-ah
***kah**-mair-rah*

Mi sono chiusa/o fuori dalla
mia camera.

Checking Out

I am/We are leaving now.

***pahr**-to/pahr-tee-**ah**-mo*
*ah-**des**-so*

Parto/Partiamo adesso.

I would like to pay the bill.

*vo-**rrei** pah-**ghah**-rei eel*
kon-to

Vorrei pagare il conto.

address	*een-dee-**reets**-o*	indirizzo
name	*no-mei*	nome
surname	*ko-nyo-mei*	cognome
room number	*noo-**mair**-ro del-lah*	numero della
	***kah**-mair-rah*	camera

Useful Words

air-con	***ahr**-ree-ah kon-dee-* *tsee-o-**nah**-tah*	aria condizionata
bathroom	***bah**-nyo*	bagno
bed	***let**-to*	letto
clean	*pu-**lee**-tah/to*	pulita/o
dirty	***spor**-kah/o*	sporca/o
double bed	***let**-to mah-tree-mo-* *nee-**ahl**-lei*	letto matrimoniale

ITALIAN

excluded	es-**kloo**-zah/o	esclusa/o
fan	ven-tee-lah-**tor**-rei	ventilatore
included	een-**kloo**-zah/o	inclusa/o
key	kee-**ah**-vei	chiave
lock (n)	ser-rah-**too**-rah	serratura
quiet	trahn-**kweel**-lah/o	tranquilla/o
room (in hotel)	**kah**-mair-rah	camera
sheet	len-**zwo**-lo	lenzuolo
shower	**doch**-ah	doccia
swimming pool	pee-**shee**-nah	piscina
toilet	ghah-bee-**net**-to	gabinetto
toilet paper	kahr-tah ee-**jen**-ee-kah	carta igienica
towel	ah-shu-ghah-**mah**-no	asciugamano
water	**ah**-kwah	acqua
cold water	ah-kwah **fred**-dah	acqua fredda
hot water	ah-kwah **kahl**-dah	acqua calda
window	fee-**nes**-trah	finestra

Around Town

I'm looking for …
   *sto chair-**kahn**-do* …   Sto cercando …

a bank	lah **bahn**-kah	la banca
the city centre	eel **chen**-tro chee-**tah**)	il centro (città)
the … embassy	lahm-bah-**shah**-tah …	l'ambasciata …
my hotel	eel **mee**-o ahl-**bair**-gho	il mio albergo
the market	eel mair-**kah**-to	il mercato
the police	lah po-lee-**tzee**-ah	la polizia
the post office	lah **pos**-dah/oo-**fee**-chee-o pos-**dah**-lei	la posta/ufficio postale

a public toilet/ restrooms	*un ghah-bee-**net**-to/ **bah**-nyo pu-blee-ko/ sair-**vee**-tsee ee-je-nee-chee*	un gabinetto/ bagno pubblico/ servizi igienici
the telephone centre	*chen-tro te-lei-fo-nee-ko*	centro telefonico
the tourist information office	*len-tei del too-**reez**-mo/oo-**feech**-o deen-for-**mah**-tsee-o-nei*	l'Ente del Turismo/ ufficio d'informazione

What time does it open?
   *ah kei or-rah (see) **ah**-prei?* A che ora (si) apre?

What time does it close?
   ah kei or-rah (see) kee-oo-dei? A che ora (si) chiude?

What … is this?
   kei … ei kwes-dah/o? Che … è questa/o?
street ***strah**-dah* strada
suburb *kwar-tee-**air**-rei* quartiere

For directions, see the Getting Around section, page 306.

At the Bank

I want to exchange some
money/travellers' cheques.
   *vo-**rrei** kahm-bee-**ah**-rei del de-**nah**-ro/dei 'travellers' cheques'* Vorrei cambiare del denaro/ dei travellers' cheques.

What is the exchange rate?
   *kwahn-**tei** eel **kahm**-bee-o?* Quant'è il cambio?

ITALIAN

How many lire per dollar?
> *kwan-tei lee-rei ahl do-lah-ro?*

Quante lire al dollaro?

Can I have money transferred here from my bank?
> *po-sso trahs-fair-ree-rei del de-nah-ro dahl-lah mee-ah bahn-kah ah kwes-dah?*

Posso trasferire del denaro dalla mia banca a questa?

How long will it take to arrive?
> *kwahn-to tem-po chee vo-rrah pair trahs-fair-reer-lo?*

Quanto tempo ci vorrà per trasferirlo?

Has my money arrived yet?
> *ei ahr-ree-vah-to eel mee-o de-nah-ro?*

È arrivato il mio denaro?

cashier	*lah kahs-sah*	la cassa
coins	*spee-cho-lee*	spiccioli
credit card	*kahr-tah dee kre-dee-to*	carta di credito
exchange	*kahm-bee-o*	cambio
signature	*feer-mah*	firma

At the Post Office

I'd like to send …	*vo-rrei man-dah-rei …*	Vorrei mandare …
a letter	*oo-nah let-tair-rah*	una lettera
a postcard	*oo-nah kar-to-lee-nah*	una cartolina
a parcel	*un pah-ket-to*	un pacchetto
a telegram	*un te-lei-ghrahm-mah*	un telegramma

I would like some stamps.
> *vo-rrei`dei frahn-ko-bol-lee*

Vorrei dei francobolli.

How much does it cost to
send this to …?
  *kwahn-**tei** lahf-frahn-kah-**too**-rah pair **kwes**-do, pair …?*

Quant'è l'affrancatura per questo, per …?

airmail	*vee-ah ah-**air**-ree-ah*	via aerea
envelope	***boo**-sdah*	busta
mailbox	*kahs-**set**-tah pos-**dah**-lei*	cassetta postale
registered mail	*(**pos**-dah) rah-ko-mahn-**dah**-tah*	(posta) raccoman-data
surface mail	***pos**-dah **non**-ah-air-ree-ah/or-dee-**nah**-ree-ah*	posta non-aerea/ordinaria

Telephone

I want to ring …
  *vo-rrei te-lei-fo-**nah**-rei*

Vorrei telefonare …

The number is …
  *eel **noo**-mair-ro ei …*

Il numero è …

Hello?
  pron-to

Pronto.

I'd like to speak to Mr Costanza.
  *vo-rrei pahr-**lah**-rei kon el see-nyor kos-**tahn**-tsah*

Vorrei parlare con il signor Costanza.

I've been cut off.
  *ei kah-**doo**-tah lah lee-nei-ah*

È caduta la linea.

It's engaged.
  *lah **lee**-ne-ah ei ok-koo-**pah**-tah*

La linea è occupata.

I want to speak for three
minutes.
*vo-lyo pahr-lah-re pair trei
mee-noo-tee*

Voglio parlare per tre minuti.

How much does a three-
minute call cost?
*kwahn-to kos-dah oo-nah
te-lei-fo-nah-tah dee trei
mee-noo-tee?*

Quanto costa una telefonata
di tre minuti?

How much does each extra
minute cost?
*kwahn-to kos-da o-nyee
mee-noo-to een pyoo?*

Quanto costa ogni minuto
in più?

I want to make a reverse-
charges phone call.
*vo-lyo fah-rei oo-nah kee-
ah-mah-tah ah kah-ree-ko
del de-stee-nah-tah-ree-o*

Voglio fare una chiamata a
carico del destinatario.

Sightseeing

What are the main attractions?
*kwah-lei so-no lei ah-trah-
tsee-o-nee pee-oo sah-lee-
en-ti?*

Quali sono le attrazioni più
salienti?

How old is it?
*kwahn-tee ahn-nee ah? dee
ke e-po-kah ei?*

Quanti anni ha? Di che
epoca è?

Can I take photographs?
*pos-so fah-rei fo-to-ghrah-
fee-ei?*

Posso fare fotografie?

What time does it open/close?
 ah **kei** or-rah *(see)*
 ah-prei/kee-**oo**-dei?

A che ora (si) apre/chiude?

ancient	**ahn**-tee-kah/ko	antica/o
archaeological	ahr-kee-o-**lo**-jee-kah/ko	archeologica/o
beach	spee-**ahj**-jah	spiaggia
building	e-dee-**fee**-cho	edificio
castle	kah-**stel**-lo	castello
cathedral	kah-tei-**drah**-lei/**dwo**-mo	cattedrale/duomo
church	kee-**ei**-zah	chiesa
concert hall	sah-lah pair kon-**chair**-tee/tei-**ah**-tro ko-moo-**nah**-lei	sala per concerti/teatro comunale
library	beeb-lee-o-**te**-kah	biblioteca
main square	pee-**ah**-tsah preen-chee-**pah**-lei	piazza principale
monastery	mon-ahs-**dair**-o	monastero
monument	mon-oo-**men**-to	monumento
old city	cheet-tah-**del**-lah	cittadella
palace	pah-**lah**-tso	palazzo
opera house	tei-**ah**-tro del **oh**-pair-ah	teatro dell'opera
ruins	ro-**vee**-nei	rovine
stadium	**stah**-dee-o	stadio
statues	**stah**-too-ei	statue
temple	**tem**-pee-o	tempio
university	oo-nee-vair-see-**tah**	università

Entertainment

What's there to do in the evenings?
*ko-zah chei dah **fah**-rei ahl-lah **sair**-rah?*
Cosa c'è da fare alla sera?

Are there any dance clubs?
chee so-no del-lei dees-ko-te-kei kwah?
Ci sono delle discoteche qua?

How much is it to get in?
*len-**trah**-tah, kwahn-to kos-dah?*
Quanto costa l'entrata?

cinema	**chee**-nei-mah	cinema
concert	kon-**chair**-to	concerto
theatre	tei-**ah**-tro	teatro

In the Country
Weather

What's the weather like?
*ko-**mei** eel tem-po?*
Com' è il tempo?

The weather is ... today.
oj-jee e ...
Oggi è ...

Will it be ... tomorrow?
*sah-**rah** ... do-**mah**-nee?*
Sarà ...domani?

cloudy	noo-vo-**lo**-so	nuvoloso
cold	**fred**-do	freddo
foggy	neb-bee-o-so	nebbioso
frosty	je-lee-do	gelido
hot	**kahl**-do	caldo
It's raining.	pee-o-**vei**	Piove.

It's snowing.	*ne-vee-kah*	Nevica.
It's good weather.	*fah bel tem-po*	Fa bel tempo.
It's windy.	*tee-rah ven-to*	Tira vento.

Camping

Am I allowed to camp here?
   *see pwo pee-ahn-**tah**-rei*   Si può piantare la tenda qui?
   lah ten-dah kwee?

Is there a campsite nearby?
   *chei oon kahm-**pej**-jo kwee*   C'è un campeggio qui vicino?
   vee-**chee**-no?*

backpack	*dzah-**ee**-no*	zaino
can opener	*ah-pree-**skah**-to-lei*	apriscatole
compass	***boos**-so-lah*	bussola
crampons	*rahm-**po**-nee*	ramponi
firewood	*le-nyah pair eel **fwo**-ko/dah **ahr**-dair-rei*	legna per il fuoco/da ardere
gas cartridge	***bom**-bo-lah del ghahs*	bombola del gas
hammock	*ah-**mah**-kah*	amaca
mattress	*mah-tair-**rahs**-so*	materasso
penknife	*tem-pair-**ee**-no*	temperino
rope	***kor**-dah*	corda
tent	***ten**-dah*	tenda
tent pegs	*pee-**ket**-tee (pair lah **ten**-dah)*	picchetti (per la tenda)
torch (flashlight)	*lah **tor**-chah*	la torcia
sleeping bag	*sah-ko ah **pe**-lo*	sacco a pelo
stove (portable)	***stoo**-fah (ah **ghahs**)*	stufa (a ghas)
water bottle/flask	*lah bor-**rah**-cha*	la borraccia

ITALIAN

Food

breakfast	*(pree-mah) ko-la-tsee-o-nei*	(prima) colazione
lunch	***prahn**-zo/ko-la-tsee-o-nei*	pranzo/colazione
dinner	*che-nah*	cena

Eating Out

Table for ..., please.
*oon tah-vo-lo pair ..., pair fah-**vor**-rei*
Un tavolo per ..., per favore.

Can I see the menu?
*pos-so ve-**dair**-rei eel me-**noo**?*
Posso vedere il menù?

I would like the set lunch, please.
*vo-**rrei** eel me-**noo** too-ree-stee-ko, pair fah-**vor**-rei*
Vorrei il menù turistico, per favore.

What does it include?
*ko-zah kom-**pren**-dei?*
Cosa comprende?

Is service included in the bill?
*eel sair-**vee**-tsee-o ei om-**prei**-zo nel kon-to?*
Il servizio è compreso nel conto?

Not too spicy please.
*non **trop**-po pee-**kahn**-tei, pair fah-**vor**-rei*
Non troppo piccante, per favore.

ashtray	*por-tah-**che**-nair-rei*	portacenere
bill	***kon**-to*	conto
cup	*tah-tsah*	tazza
fork	*for-**ket**-tah*	forchetta

fresh	*fre-skah/o*	fresca/o
glass	*bee-kee-air-rei*	bicchiere
knife	*col-tel-lo*	coltello
plate	*pee-aht-to*	piatto
a spoon	*koo-kee-ah-ee-o*	cucchiaio
stale	*ve-kee-o*	vecchio
sweet	*dol-chei*	dolce
toothpick	*stoo-tsee-kah-den-tei*	stuzzicadente

Places to Eat

Pizzerie and *ristoranti* speak for themselves, but you may like to try eating at some of these:

tavola calda – cheap self-service with a selection of hot dishes
taverna – small restaurant of a rustic nature, though not always cheap
trattoria, (h)osteria – offering simple local dishes, they generally cater for locals rather than tourists
rosticceria – grilled meat, often takeaway only

Making Your Own Meal

For some key essentials for sandwich-making, etc, see page 341.

Vegetarian Meals

I am a vegetarian.
   so-no ve-je-tah-ree-ah-nah/o   Sono vegetariana/o.
I don't eat meat.
   non mahn-jo kar-nei   Non mangio carne.
I don't eat chicken, or fish, or pork.
   non mahn-jo nei pol-lo, nei pe-shei, nei mah-ee-ah-lei   Non mangio nè pollo, nè pesce, nè maiale.

ITALIAN

Staples

bread	*pane*
butter	*burro*
eggs	*uova*
garlic	*aglio*
oil	*olio*
pepper	*pepe*
salt	*sale*

Appetisers / Antipasti

antipasto misto	Assortment of cold appetisers.
caponata (alla siciliana)	Eggplant dish from Sicily, with capers, olives, onion and anchovies.
ceci con oregano	Marinated chickpeas with oregano.
condimento al pepe	Pepper relish.
melone con prosciutto	Melon with cured ham.
sottaceti	Pickled vegetables.

Soup / Zuppa/Brodo

capelletti	A form of ravioli, with various stuffings, in broth.
minestrone	Vegetable soup, often with beef stock and pork.
stracciatella	Chicken and vegetable soup.
zuppa pavese	Pavian soup: bread, butter, chicken broth and eggs.
paparot	Spinach soup. (Istria)

Pasta & Rice   Pastasciutta e Riso

Pastasciutta is the collective name for over 500 varieties of products made from flour, water and sometimes eggs. If you want your pasta to be cooked to perfection, ask for it to be *ahl den-tei*, 'al dente'. Note that pasta dishes are generally larger than the 'main' course, so this is the course to fill up on if you're very hungry.

agnolotti	Small pasta pockets stuffed with meat sauce. (Turin/Piedmont)
bomba di riso	Rice with pigeon. (Parma)
cannelloni	Wide strips of pasta rolled around meat or spinach-and-cheese.
gnocchi	Flour and potato dumplings.
lasagne	Sheets of pasta, layered alternately with mincedmeat, tomato sauce, and cheese or béchamel sauce.
polenta	Cornmeal, often sliced and deep-fried.
ravioli	Square pockets of pasta, filled with meat paste.
risi e bisi	Risotto with green peas. (Venice/Veneto)
risotto in capro roman	Risotto with mutton. (Venice)
sartù	Savoury rice dish. (Naples)
spaghetti	Needs no introduction.
supplì	Deep-fried balls of rice with mozzarella cheese and tomato sauce inside.
tagliatelle & fettucine	Ribbon pasta.
tortellini	Small envelopes of pasta wrapped around meat.
tuoni e lampo	Varieties of pasta, with chick peas and tomato sauce.(Capri)

ITALIAN

Sauces

Italian sauces are delicious, and it is quite acceptable to use the unsalted bread provided to mop up your sauce.

aglio e olio	Garlic and olive oil.
alfredo	Butter, cream, parmesan cheese and parsley.
alla checca	Cold summer sauce of ripe tomatoes, olives, basil, capers and oregano. (Rome)
bolognese/al ragù	Minced beef, tomatoes, onions and herbs.
carbonara	Cured bacon *(pancetta)*, cream, paprika, egg and parmesan cheese.
matriciana	Spicy tomato and bacon.
misto di mare	Mixed seafood, often in cream and wine.
pescatore/ marinara	Mixed seafood, often in tomato sauce.
pesto	Basil, pine nuts and garlic.
puttanesca	Spicy tomato sauce with anchovies, olives and basil.
siciliana	Eggplant, anchovies, olives, capers, tomato and garlic.
tonno e funghi	Tuna and mushrooms in tomato and cream sauce.

Meat	Carne
beef	*manzo*
pork	*maiale*
hare	*lepre*
kid	*capretto*
lamb	*agnello*
liver	*fegato*
mutton	*montone*
tripe	*trippa*
veal	*vitello*

Seafood

Frutti di Mare

anelletti gratinati Crumbed fried cuttlefish rings. (Sicily)
baccalà Purée of salt cod, served with polenta.
   montecato (Venice/Veneto)
bottarga Fish roe. (Sicily)
burrida/ciuppa/ Fish stews. (Genoa/Liguria)
   zimmo
cuscucu Fish soup. (Sicily)
sfogie in saòr Sole with herbs and garlic. (Venice/Veneto)

anchovies	*acciughe*
cockles	*vongole*
cod	*baccalà/merluzzo/*
	stoccafisso
crayfish	*gambero*
fish	*pesce*
lobster	*aragosta*
mussels	*cozze*
oysters	*ostriche*
prawns	*gamberoni*
red mullet	*triglia*
shrimp	*scampi*
spider crabs	*granevole/graneole*

Poultry & Wildfowl

Pollame & Selvaggina

chicken	*pollo*
duck	*anitra*
partridges	*pernici*
pigeons	*piccioni*
quail	*quaglia*
turkey	*tacchino*

Vegetables   Verdure

You usually need to order vegetables or salad as extras. *Insalata* is simply lettuce. *Insalata mista* is a tossed salad.

artichokes	*carciofi*
beans	*fagioli(ni)*
cabbage	*cavoli*
chickpeas	*ceci*
eggplant (aubergine)	*melanzane*
mushrooms	*funghi*
onion	*cipolla*
peas	*piselli*
tomatoes	*pomodori*
capsicum	*peperoni*

Specific Dishes   Piatti Speciali

abbacchio	Young lamb. (Rome/Lazio)
bistecca alla fiorentina	Huge grilled T-bone steak. Often priced *all'etto*, 'per hundred weight', so ask how much an average steak would be: *Di solito, quanto costa una bistecca fiorentina?* (Florence)
bollito	Various meats boiled together in one pot and served with vegetables. (Turin/iedmont)
bruschetta	Crisp baked bread slices in oil, often with tomato brushed on top. (Florence/Tuscany)
busella	Tripe dish. (Milan/Lombardy)
calzone	Folded pizza. (Naples)
capon magro	Salad of vegetables and fish. (Genoa/Liguria)
cima	Cold veal, stuffed with pork, sweetbreads, nuts, peas and eggs. (Genoa)

cotechino	Sausage, stuffed with raw spiced pork. (Emiglia-Romagna)
fasœil al fùrn	Oven-baked beans. (Piedmont)
finocchiona	Spicy salami, with fennel seeds. (Florence/Tuscany)
grissini	Slender bread sticks. (Turin/Piedmont)
involtini	Stuffed veal rolls. (Bologna/Emiglia-Romagna)
mostarda	Candied fruits in mustard. (Cremona)
polenta e osei	Small roasted birds, served with polenta. (Milan/Lombardy)
rane dorate	Fried frogs legs. (North)
saltimbocca	Veal rolled with ham and sage, cooked in wine or Marsala. (Rome)
tacchino con sugo di melagrana	Turkey with pomegranate sauce. (Venice/Veneto)
testarelle di abbacchio	Lamb's heads. (Rome/Lazio)
tortino	Flat omelette with vegetables. (Florence/Tuscany)
zampone	Pig's foot, stuffed with raw spiced sausage. (Modena)

Fruit	**Frutta**
apple	*mela*
apricot	*albicocca*
cherries	*ciliegie*
grapes	*uva*
orange	*arancia*
plum	*prugna/susina*
raspberries	*lamponi*
strawberries	*fragole*

ITALIAN

Desserts — Dolci

bignè alla cioccolata	Puff pastry filled with cream and covered with chocolate.
cassata	Pudding of sponge, cream, fruit and chocolate. Also an ice-cream flavour. (Sicily)
crema inglese	Custard.
granita di limone	Lemon-water ice.
macedonia	Fruit salad.
panettone	Large, dry yeast cake.
zabaglione/ zabaione	Egg yolks whipped with sugar and Marsala.
zuccotto	Almond and hazelnut cake with brandy and liqueur.
zuppa inglese	Trifle.

Cheese — Formaggio

fontina	Creamy kind of Gruyère. (Piedmont)
gorgonzola	Soft, rich, blue-veined cheese.
mozzarella	Traditionally made from buffalo's milk.
parmigiano	Parmesan – often simply called *grana*.
pecorino	Hard cheese, usually made from ewe's milk, popular at the end of a meal.
ricotta	Soft ewe's-milk cheese.

Drinks – Nonalcoholic — Bevande

milk	*latte*
tea	*tè*
mineral water	*acqua minerale*
orange juice	*succo d'arancia*
soft drink	*gassosa/gazzosa*

caffè latte	Coffee with milk.
caffè macchiato	Strong coffee with a little milk.
cappuccino	Named after the Capuchin monks who wore robes of chocolate and cream colours, cappuccino is considered a morning drink by Italians.
espresso	Very strong black coffee served in small cups and taken at any time of the day.
latte macchiato	Hot milk with a little coffee.

Drinks – Alcoholic

beer	*birra*
brandy	*acquavite*
wine	*vino*
bitter or very dry	*amaro*
dry	*secco/asciutto*
red	*rosso*
semi-sparkling	*frizzante*
slightly sweet	*abboccato*
sparkling	*spumante*
sweet	*amabile*
white	*bianco*

Shopping

How much is it?

kwahn-to kos-dah?   Quanto costa?

bookshop	*lee-brair-**ree**-ah*	libreria
camera shop	*fo-**to**-ghrah-fo*	fotografo
greengrocer	*froo-tee-**ven**-do-lo*	fruttivendolo
grocery store	*ne-**gho**-tsee-o dee*	negozio di
	*ah-lee-men-**tah**-ree*	alimentari

laundry	*lah-vahn-dair-**ree**-ah*	lavanderia
market	*mair-**kah**-to*	mercato
newsagency/ stationers	*e-**dee**-ko-lah/kahr-to-**lah**-yo*	edicola/cartolaio
supermarket	*soo-pair-mair-**kah**-to*	supermercato

I would like to buy …
*vo-rrei kom-**prah**-rei …* — Vorrei comprare …

Do you have others?
*chee so-no **ahl**-trei/ee?* — Ci sono altre/i?

I don't like it.
*non mee pee-**ah**-chei* — Non mi piace.

Can I look at it?
*pos-so dah-rei oon o-kee-**ah**-tah?* — Posso dare un'occhiata?

I'm just looking.
*(sto) so-lo ghwahr-**dahn**-do* — Sto solo guardando.

Can you write down the price?
pwo skree-vair-rei eel pre-tso? — Può scrivere il prezzo?

Do you accept credit cards?
*ah-**chet**-tah lah **kahr**-tah dee **kre**-dee-to?* — Accetta la carta di credito?

Could you lower the price?
*pwo **fahr**-mee lo **skon**-to?* — Può farmi lo sconto?

You May Hear

Can I help you?
*pos-so ah-yoo-**tahr**-lah?* — Posso aiutarla?
*ko-zah dei-**zee**-dair-rah?* — Cosa desidera?

Will that be all?
*nee-ent-**ahl**-tro?* Nient'altro?
How much/many do you want?
***kwahn**-to/ee nei vwo-lei?* Quanto/i ne vuole?

Essential Groceries

batteries	*bah-tair-**ree**-e*	batterie
bread	***pah**-nei*	pane
butter	***boo**-rroh*	burro
cheese	*for-mah-joh*	formaggio
chocolate	*choh-ko-**lah**-to*	cioccolato
coffee	*kahf-**fei***	caffè
gas cylinder	***bom**-bo-lah dee **gahs***	bombola di gas
matches	*fee-ahm-**mee**-fair-ee*	fiammiferi
milk	***laht**-tei*	latte
mineral water	*ah-kwah meen-air-**ah**-lei*	acqua minerale
shampoo	*shahm-**poo***	shampoo
soap	*sah-**po**-nei*	sapone
sugar	***tsoo**-kair-oh*	zucchero
toilet paper	***kahr**-tah ee-je-nee-kah*	carta igienica
toothpaste	*den-tee-**free**-cho*	dentifricio
tea	*te*	tè
washing powder	*de-tair-**see**-vo*	detersivo
yoghurt	*yo-goort*	iogurt

Souvenirs

blown glass	*ve-tro so-fee-**ah**-to*	vetro soffiato
earrings	*o-re-**kee**-nee*	orecchini
handicrafts	*lah-**vor**-ro ahr-tee-jah-**nah**-lei*	lavoro artigianale

jewellery	*joy-**el**-lee*	gioielli
leather handbag, bag	*bor-**set**-tah/**bor**-sah dee **kwoy**-o/een pel-lei*	borsetta/borsa di cuoio/in pelle
miniature statue	*stah-**too**-ah een mee-nee-ah-**too**-rah*	statua in miniatura
necklace	*kol-**lah**-nah*	collana
pottery	*oj-**jet**-tee een chair-**ah**-mee-kah*	oggetti in ceramica
ring	*ah-**nel**-lo*	anello
rug	*tah-**pet**-to*	tappetto

Clothing

coat	*kah-**pot**-to*	cappotto
jacket	*jah-kah*	giacca
shirt	*kah-**mee**-chah*	camicia
shoes	*skar-pei*	scarpe
trousers	*pahn-tah-**lo**-nee*	pantaloni

It is too …/They are too …

	*ei **trop**-po …/so-no trop-pei/ee …*	È troppo …/Sono troppe/i …
tight	*stret-**tah**/o*	stretta/o
	stret-tei/ee	strette/i (pl)
loose	*lahr-**gha**/o,*	larga/o,
	lahr-ghei/ee	larghe/i (pl)

Toiletries

condoms	*prei-zair-vah-**tee**-vee*	preservativi
deodorant	*dei-o-dor-**rahn**-tei*	deodorante
hairbrush	*spah-tso-lah (pair ee kah-**pel**-lee)*	spazzola (per i capelli)

razor	*rah-**zoy**-o*	rasoio
sanitary napkins	*ahs-sor-**ben**-tee ee-je-nee-chee*	assorbenti igienici
shampoo	*shahm-**poo***	shampoo
shaving cream	*krei-mah dah **bahr**-bah*	crema da barba
soap	*sah-**po**-nei*	sapone
sunblock cream	*krei-mah so-**lah**-rei*	crema solare
tampons	*tahm-**po**-nee*	tamponi
tissues	*fah-tso-**let**-tee dee **kahr**-tah*	fazzoletti di carta
toilet paper	*kahr-tah ee-je-nee-kah*	carta igienica
toothbrush	*spah-tso-**lee**-no dah **den**-tee*	spazzolino da denti
toothpaste	*den-tee-**free**-cho*	dentifricio

Photography

How much is it to process this film?

*kwahn-to **kos**-dah pair svee-loo-**pah**-rei kwes-dah pel-**lee**-ko-lah?*

Quanto costa per sviluppare questa pellicola?

When will it be ready?

*kwahn-do sah-**rahn**-no **pron**-tei, lei fo-to?*

Quando saranno pronte le foto?

I'd like a film for this camera.

*vo-**rrei** oo-nah pel-**lee**-ko-lah/oon rol-**lee**-no pair kwes-dah **mah**-kee-nah fo-to-**grah**-fee-kah*

Vorrei una pellicola/un rollino per questa macchina fotografica.

ITALIAN

B&W (film)	*bee-**ahn**-ko ei **nair**-ro*	bianco e nero
camera	*mah-kee-nah*	macchina
	*fo-to-**grah**-fee-kah*	fotografica
colour (film)	*ko-**lor**-rei*	colore
film	*pel-**lee**-ko-lah/ rol-**lee**-no*	pellicola/rollino
flash	*flahsh*	flash
lens	*o-bee-e-**tee**-vo*	obiettivo
light meter	*e-spo-**zee**-me-tro*	esposimetro

Smoking

A packet of cigarettes, please.
  *oon pah-**ket**-to dee see-ghah-ret-tei, pair fah-**vor**-rei*
  Un pachetto di sigarette, per favore.

Are these cigarettes strong/mild?
  *kwes-dei see-ghah-**ret**-tei (non) so-no for-tee?*
  Queste sigarette (non) sono forti?

Do you have a light?
  *ah dah-**chen**-dair-rei?*
  Ha d'accendere?

Do you mind if I smoke?
  *lei dees-**toor**-bo se **foo**-mo?*
  Lei disturbo se fumo?

Please don't smoke.
  *pair fah-**vor**-rei, non **foo**-mah*
  Per favore, non fuma.

cigarettes	*see-ghah-**ret**-tei*	sigarette
cigarette papers	*kahr-**tee**-nei (pair see-ghah-**ret**-tei)*	cartine (per cigarette)
filtered	*kon **feel**-tro*	con filtro
lighter	*ah-chen-**dee**-no*	accendino

matches	*fee-ahm-**mee**-fair-ree*	fiammiferi
menthol	*ah-lah **men**-tah*	alla menta
pipe	***pee**-pah*	pipa
tobacco (pipe)	*tah-**bah**-ko dah pee-pah*	tabacco da pipa

Health

Where is ...?	*do-**vei** ...?*	Dov'è...?
the doctor	*eel dot-**tor**-rei/ eel me-dee-ko*	il dottore/ il medico
the hospital	*lo-spe-**dah**-lei*	l'ospedale
the chemist	*eel fahr-mah-**chee**-stah*	il farmacista
the dentist	*eel den-**tee**-stah*	il dentista

I am sick
*mee sen-to **mah**-lei*   Mi sento male.

What's the matter?
ko-zah chei?   Cosa c'è?

My ... hurts.
*mee fah **mah**-lei lah/eel ...*   Mi fa male la/il ...

Parts of the Body

arm	***brah**-cho*	braccio
back	*skee-**eh**-nah/**dor**-soh*	schiena/dorso
eye	*o-**kee**-o*	occhio
foot	*pee-e-dei*	piede
hand	***mah**-no*	mano
heart	***kwor**-rei*	cuore
leg	***ghahm**-bah*	gamba

ITALIAN

Ailments

I have … | | Ho …

an allergy	*oo-nah-lair-jee-ah*	un'allergia
a burn	*skot-tah-too-rah*	scottatura
a cold	*rahf-fre-dor-rei*	raffreddore
constipation	*stee-tee-ke-tsah*	stitichezza
a cough	*tos-sei*	tosse
diarrhoea	*dee-ah-rei-ah*	diarrea
fever	*feb-brei*	febbre
a headache	*mahl dee tes-tah*	mal di testa
hepatitis	*e-pah-tee-tei*	epatite
an infection	*een-fe-tsee-o-nei*	infezione
influenza	*een-floo-en-zah*	influenza
low/high blood pressure	*pres-see-o-nei bahs-sah/ahl-tah (dee sahn-ghwei)*	pressione bassa/alta (di sangue)
pain	*do-lor-rei*	dolore
sore throat	*mahl dee gho-lah*	mal di gola
sprain	*strah-po moo-sko-lahr-rei*	strappo muscolare
stomachache	*mahl dee sto-mah-ko*	mal di stomaco
sunburn	*sko-tah-too-rah (dahl so-lei)*	scottatura (dal sole)
venereal disease	*mah-laht-tee-ah ve-nair-ree-ah*	malattia venerea

Women's Health

Could I see a female doctor?
pos-so ve-dair-rei oo-nah dot-tor-res-sah? Posso vedere una dottoressa?

I'm pregnant.
so-no een-cheen-tah Sono incinta.

I'm on the pill.
pren-do lah peel-lo-lah

Prendo la pillola.

I haven't had my period for … weeks.
non o ah-voo-to lei
mes-troo-ah-tsee-o-nee
pair … se-tee-mah-ne

Non ho avuto le mestruazioni per … settimane.

(unusual) bleeding	*pair-dee-tah dee sahn-gwei (strah-na)*	perdita di sangue (strana)
cramps	*krahm-pee*	crampi
cystitis	*chee-stee-tei*	cistite
thrush	*kahn-dee-dah*	candida

Specific Needs

I'm …	*so-no …*	Sono …
asthmatic	*ahs-mah-tee-kah/o*	asmatica/o
diabetic	*dee-ah-be-tee-kah/o*	diabetica/o
epileptic	*e-pee-let-tee-kah/o*	epilettica/o

I'm allergic to antibiotics.
so-no ah-lair-jee-kah/o ah-lyee ahn-tee-bee-o-tee-chee

Sono allergica/o agli antibiotici.

I'm allergic to penicillin.
so-no ah-lair-jee-kah/o ah-lah pe-nee-chee-lee-nah

Sono allergica/o alla penicillina.

I have been vaccinated.
so-no stah-tah/o vah-chee-nah-tah/o

Sono stata/o vaccinata/o.

I have my own syringe.
o con mei lah mee-ah see-reeng-ghah

Ho con me la mia siringa.

ITALIAN

Useful Words & Phrases

I feel better/worse.
mee sen-to me-lyo/pej-jo   Mi sento meglio/peggio.

accident	*een-chee-**den**-tei*	incidente
addiction	*to-sse-ko-mah-**nee**-ah*	tossicomania
antibiotics	*ahn-tee-bee-o-tee-chee*	antibiotici
antiseptic	*ahn-tee-**set**-tee-ko*	antisettico
blood test	*ah-**nah**-lee-zee del **sahng**-ghwei*	analisi del sangue
contraceptive	*ahn-tee-kon-che-tsee-o-**nahl**-lei*	anticoncezionale
injection	*een-eeye-tsee-o-nei*	iniezione
injury	*fair-**ree**-tah*	ferita
medicine	*me-dee-**chee**-nah*	medicina
vitamins	*vee-tah-**mee**-nei*	vitamine

At the Chemist

I need medication for …
o bee-zo-nyah/o dee oo-nah   Ho bisogna/o di una
me-dee-cah-tsee-o-nei   medicazione per …
pair …
I have a prescription.
*o oo-nah ree-**chet**-tah*   Ho una ricetta.

At the Dentist

I have a toothache.
*o oon mahl dee **den**-tee*   Ho un mal di denti.
I've lost a filling.
o pair-so oon o-too-ra-tsee-o-nei   Ho perso un otturazione.

I've broken a tooth.
*mee see ei **rot**-to oon **den**-tei*   Mi si è rotto un dente.

I don't want it extracted.
*non lo **vo**-lyo **to**-lyair-rei*   Non lo voglio togliere.

Please give me an anaesthetic.
mee dee-ah oon ahn-e-ste-   Mi dia un anestetico, per
*tee-ko, pair fah-**vor**-fei*   favore.

Time & Dates

What date is it today?
*kei **jor**-no ei **oj**-jee?*   Che giorno è oggi?
*kwahn-tee nei ahb-bee-**ah**-*   Quanti ne abbiamo oggi?
*mo **oj**-jee?*

What time is it?
*kei **or**-rei **so**-no?*   Che ore sono?

It is …   *so-no lei …*   Sono le …
  in the morning   *dee maht-**tee**-nah*   di mattina
  in the afternoon   *dee po-mair-**ree**-jo*   di pomeriggio
  in the evening   *dee **sair**-rah*   di sera

Days of the Week

Monday	*loo-nei-**dee***	lunedì
Tuesday	*mahr-te-**dee***	martedì
Wednesday	*mair-ko-lei-**dee***	mercoledì
Thursday	*jo-ve-**dee***	giovedì
Friday	*ve-nair-**dee***	venerdì
Saturday	*sah-bah-to*	sabato
Sunday	*do-**me**-nee-kah*	domenica

ITALIAN

Months

January	*jen-**nah**-ee-o*	gennaio
February	*feb-**brah**-ee-o*	febbraio
March	***mahr**-tso*	marzo
April	*ah-**pree**-lei*	aprile
May	***mahj**-jo*	maggio
June	***joo**-nyo*	giugno
July	***loo**-lyo*	luglio
August	*ah-**ghos**-to*	agosto
September	*set-**tem**-brei*	settembre
October	*ot-**to**-brei*	ottobre
November	*no-**vem**-brei*	novembre
December	*dee-**chem**-brei*	dicembre

Seasons

summer	*e-**stah**-tei*	estate
autumn	*ahw-**toon**-no*	autunno
winter	*een-**vair**-no*	inverno
spring	*pree-mah-**vair**-rah*	primavera

Present

today	***oj**-jee*	oggi
this morning	*stah-maht-**tee**-nah*	stamattina
tonight	*stah-**sair**-rah*	stasera
this week/year	*kwes-dah set-tee-**mah**-nah/kwes-**dahn**-no*	questa settimana/quest'anno
now	*ah-**des**-so*	adesso

Past

yesterday	*ee-**air**-ree*	ieri
day before yesterday	*lahl-tro ee-**air**-ree*	l'altro ieri

yesterday morning	*ee-**air**-ree **maht-tee**-nah*	ieri mattina
last night	*ee-**air**-ree **sair**-rah*	ieri sera
last week/year	*lah set-tee-**mah**-nah skor-sah/**lahn**-no pahs-**sah**-to/**skor**-so*	la settimana scorsa/l'anno passato/scorso

Future

tomorrow	*do-**mah**-nee*	domani
day after tomorrow	*do-po-do-**mah**-nee*	dopodomani
tomorrow morning	*do-**mah**-nee **maht-tee**-nah*	domani mattina
tomorrow afternoon/evening	*do-**mah**-nee po-mair-**reej**-jo/**sair**-rah*	domani pomeriggio/sera
next week	*lah set-tee-**mah**-nah **pros**-see-mah*	la settimana prossima
next year	*lahn-no pros-**see**-mo*	l'anno prossimo

During the Day

afternoon	*po-mair-**reej**-jo*	pomeriggio
dawn, very early morning	*ahl-bah*	alba
day	*jor-no*	giorno
early	*pres-do*	presto
midnight	*me-tsah-**not**-tei*	mezzanotte
morning	*maht-**tee**-nah*	mattina
night	*not-tei*	notte
noon	*me-tso-**jor**-no*	mezzogiorno
sundown	*trah-**mon**-to*	tramonto

ITALIAN

Numbers & Amounts

0	*tsair-ro*	zero
1	*oo-no*	uno
2	*doo-ei*	due
3	*trei*	tre
4	*kwaht-tro*	quattro
5	*cheen-kwei*	cinque
6	*sei*	sei
7	*set-tei*	sette
8	*ot-to*	otto
9	*no-vei*	nove
10	*dee-ei-chee*	dieci
11	*oon-dee-chee*	undici
12	*do-dee-chee*	dodici
13	*trei-dee-chee*	tredici
14	*kwah-tor-dee-chee*	quattordici
15	*kween-dee-chee*	quindici
16	*sei-dee-chee*	sedici
17	*dee-chah-set-tei*	diciassette
18	*dee-chot-to*	diciotto
19	*dee-chah-no-vei*	diciannove
20	*ven-tee*	venti
21	*ven-too-no*	ventuno
22	*ven-tee-doo-ei*	ventidue
30	*tren-tah*	trenta
40	*kwah-rahn-tah*	quaranta
50	*cheen-kwahn-tah*	cinquanta
60	*ses-sahn-tah*	sessanta
70	*set-tahn-tah*	settanta
80	*ot-tahn-tah*	ottanta
90	*no-vahn-tah*	novanta

100	**chen**-*to*	cento
1000	**meel**-*lei*	mille
one million	*oon mee-lee-o-nei*	un milione

1st	**pree**-*mo*	primo
2nd	*se-**kon**-do*	secondo
3rd	**tair**-*tso*	terzo

¼	*oon **kwar**-to*	un quarto
⅓	*oon **tair**-tso*	un terzo
½	*oon me-**tso**/*	un mezzo/la metà
	*lah me-**tah***	
¾	*trei **kwahr**-tee*	tre quarti

Amounts

small	**pee**-*ko-lah/o*	piccola/o
big	**ghrahn**-*dei*	grande
a little (amount)	*(oon)* **po**-*ko, oon po'*	(un) poco, un po'
double	**dop**-*pee-ah*	doppio
dozen	*oo-nah do-**tsee**-nah*	una dozzina
Enough!	**bahs**-*dah!*	Basta!
few	**po**-*kei/**po**-kee*	poche/pochi
less	**me**-*no*	meno
many	**tahn**-*tei/ee*	tante/i
more	*pyoo*	più
once	*oo-nah **vol**-tah*	una volta
a pair	*oon **pah**-ee-o*	un paio
per cent	*pair-**chen**-to*	percento
some	**kwal**-*kei*	qualche
too much	**trop**-*po*	troppo
twice	*doo-ei **vol**-tei*	due volte

Abbreviations

ANSA	Italian News Agency
C.C. – Carabinieri	police
ENIT	Tourist Information Office
ferr.	railway
F.S. – Ferrovia dello Stato	National Railway
S.	Saint
SS. – Santi/Santissimi	very holy
sec.	century
v/v.le – via/viale	street/boulevard

Paperwork

form	*moh-doo-loh*	modulo
name	*no-mei*	nome
address	*een-dee-reets-o*	indirizzo
date of birth	*dah-tah dee nah-shee-tah*	data di nascita
place of birth	*lwo-gho dee nah-shee-tah*	luogo di nascita
age	*e-tah*	età
sex	*ses-so*	sesso
nationality	*nah-tsee-o-nah-lee-tah*	nazionalità
religion	*rei-lee-jo-nei*	religione
reason for travel	*mo-tee-vee dee vee-ahj-jo*	motivi di viaggio
profession	*pro-fes-see-o-nei*	professione
married	*spo-zah-tah/o*	sposata/o
divorced	*dee-vor-tsee-ah-tah/o*	divorziata/o

single	**noo**-bee-lei	nubile (f)
	che-lee-bei	celibe (m)
passport	pahs-sah-**por**-to	passaporto
passport number	noo-mair-ro del	numero del
	pahs-sah-**por**-to	passaporto
visa	**vee**-zah kon-so-**lah**-rei	visto consolare
identification (card)	(kahr-tah d)ee-den-tee-fee-kah-tsee-**o**-nei	(carta d') identificazione
birth certificate	chair-tee-fee-**kah**-to dee nah-shee-**tah**	certificato di nascita
driver's licence	pah-**ten**-tei	patente
car owner's title	**tee**-to-lo dee ro-pree-e-**tah**	titolo di proprietà
car registration	re-jee-strah-tsee-o-**nei**	registrazione
customs	do-**ghah**-nah	dogana
immigration	ee-mee-ghrah-tsee-o-**nei**	immigrazione
border	fron-tee-**air**-rah	frontiera

Emergencies

| POLICE | POLIZIA/CARABINIERI |
| POLICE STATION | QUESTURA |

Help!
    ah-**yoo**-to!   Aiuto!
It's an emergency!
    ei oon e-mer-**jen**-tsah!   È un emergenza!
Thief!
    ahl **lah**-dro!   Al ladro!

ITALIAN

There's been an accident!
*chei **stah**-to un een-chee-**den**-tei!*

C'è stato un incidente!

Call a doctor!
*kee-**ah**-mah un dot-**tor**-rei/un me-**dee**-ko!*

Chiama un dottore/
un medico!

Call an ambulance!
*kee-**ah**-mah un ahm-bu-**lahn**-tsah!*

Chiama una ambulanza!

I've been raped.
*so-no stah-tah vee-o-len-**tah**-tah/o*

Sono stata/o violentata/o.

I've been robbed!
*mee **ahn**-no de-roo-**bah**-tah/o*

Mi hanno derubata/o.

Call the police!
*kee-**ah**-mah lah po-lee-**tsee**-ah!*

Chiama la polizia!

Go away!
*vah-ee **vee**-ah! mee **lah**-shee een pah-chei!*

Vai via! Mi lasci in pace!

I'll call the police!
*kee-ah-**mair**-ro lah po-lee-**tsee**-ah!*

Chiamerò la polizia!

I am ill.
*so-no mah-**lah**-ta/o*

Sono malata/o.

My friend is ill.
*lah mee-ah ah-**mee**-kah ei mah-**lah**-tah*

La mia amica è malata. (f)

*eel mee-o ah-**mee**-ko ei mah-**lah**-to*

Il mio amico è malato. (m)

Where is the police station?
do-vei lah kwes-doo-rah?

Dov'è la questura?

Where are the toilets?
*do-ve so-no ee
ghah-bee-net-tee?*

Dove sono i gabinetti?

I am lost.
mee so-no pair-so

Mi sono perso.

Could you help me please?
mee pwo ah-yoo-tah-rei?
mee ah-yoo-tee, pair fah-vor-rei

Mi può aiutare?
Mi aiuti, per favore.

Could I please use the telephone?
*pos-so fah-rei oo-nah
te-lei-fo-nah-tah?*

Posso fare una telefonata?

I'm sorry. I apologise.
*mee skoo-zee. mee
dee-spee-ah-chei*

Mi scusi. Mi dispiace.

I didn't realise I was doing anything wrong.
non sah-pei-vo kei fah-chei-vo kwahl-ko-za dee mah-lei

Non sapevo che facevo qualcosa di male.

I didn't do it.
non lo faht-to

Non l'ho fatto.

I wish to contact my embassy/consulate.
*vo-rrei met-tair-mee een
kon-taht-to kon lah mee-ah
ahm-bah-shah-tah/eel
mee-o kon-so-lah-to*

Vorrei mettermi in contatto con la mia ambasciata/ il mio consolato.

ITALIAN

I speak English.
*pahr-lo eeng-**ghlei**-zei*

Parlo inglese.

I have medical insurance.
*o lahs-see-koo-rah-tsee-o-nei (lah-sees-**den**-tsah) me-dee-kah*

Ho l'assicurazione (l'assistenza) medica.

My possessions are insured.
*lah mee-ah **ro**-bah ei ahs-see-koo-**rah**-tah*

La mia roba è assicurata.

My … was stolen.
*mee ahn-no roo-**bah**-to …*

Mi hanno rubato …

I've lost …
*o **pair**-so …*

Ho perso …

my bags	*ee mee-**ei**-ee bah-**ghah**-lyee*	i miei bagagli
my handbag	*lah mee-ah **bor**-sah*	la mia borsa
my money	*ee mee-**ei**-ee **sol**-dee/ eel mee-o de-**nahr**-ro*	i miei soldi/il mio denaro
my travellers' cheques	*ee mee-**ei**-ee 'travellers' cheques'*	i miei travellers' cheques
my passport	*eel mee-o pahs-sah-**por**-to*	il mio passaporto
my wallet	*eel mee-o por-tah-**fo**-lyo*	il mio portafoglio

Portuguese

Introduction

Like French, Italian, Spanish and Romanian, Portuguese is a Romance language, that is, one closely derived from Latin. It is spoken by over 10 million in Portugal, 130 million in Brazil, and it is also the official language of five African nations (Angola, Mozambique, Guinea-Bissau, Cape Verde and São Tomé & Príncipe). In Asia it is still spoken in the former Portuguese territory of East Timor, and in enclaves around Malacca, Goa, Damão and Diu. Visitors to Portugal are often struck by the strangeness of the language, which some say sounds like Arabic. However, those who understand French or Spanish are often surprised to see how similar written Portuguese is to the other Romance languages.

The obscure indigenous people who inhabited the Iberian Peninsula before the arrival of the Romans are considered responsible for the most striking traits of the Portuguese language. The first Roman troops arrived in the Peninsula in the 3rd century BC, with the invasion proper beginning in 197 BC. By 27 BC it was totally under Roman domination. Roman soldiers and merchants brought their language with them: Vulgar Latin soon took over the indigenous languages, more slowly so in the west of the Peninsula, the Lusitanian territory that is now Portugal.

From 409 AD the Iberian Peninsula was successively invaded by Barbarians of Teutonic origin, and from the 6th to the 8th century by the Visigoths, who all left their imprint on the language, but their influence was not strong enough to change its by then well-established neo-Latin character.

The Arab invasion began in 711 AD, and Arabic soon became the prestige cultural language in the Peninsula. Portugal became an independent kingdom in 1139, Lisbon being reconquered from the Moors in 1147. The Moors were finally expelled from the south of Portugal in 1249, and that was the end of the last significant influence on the formation of the Portuguese language. During the Middle Ages, Portuguese underwent mostly French and Provençal influences; later, in the 16th and 17th centuries, Italian and Spanish were above all responsible for innovations in vocabulary.

Portuguese is the language of a very rich literature, which begins in the dark medieval period. In the 16th century Luis Vaz de Camões wrote the epic poem *The Lusiads*, which many foreigners know in translation. Twentieth-century Portuguese literature has not been widely read abroad, due to the lack of good translations. However, since the 1974 democratic revolution in Portugal, Europe has begun to pay more attention to Portuguese literature, and, though not always easily available, there are now good translations into English of at least the best Portuguese poet of the 20th century, Fernando Pessoa, and of some outstanding contemporary novelists, namely José Cardoso Pires and José Saramago.

Gender

Portuguese, like the other Romance languages, has masculine and feminine word forms. In this chapter, the masculine word is indicated first, the feminine word or variant syllable after and separated by a slash. When using a verb or adjectival form in the first person, remember that the masculine and feminine forms vary according to you, the speaker. Thus, if you are a male, you will say 'thank you', obriga**do**; if you are female, say 'thank you', obriga**da**.

PORTUGUESE

PORTUGUESE

Pronunciation

Pronunciation of Portuguese is difficult, given that, as in English, vowels and consonants have more than one sound, depending on position in the syllable and word stress. Moreover, there are nasal vowels and diphthongs in Portuguese which have no equivalent in English. It is therefore important to become familiar with the following simplified phonetic symbols, which are used in the pronunciation guide in this book.

Vowels

Letters	Pronunciation Guide	Sounds
a	*ah*	open **a**, as in 'cut'
a	*ă*	closed **a**, as in 'courtesy', 'her'
e	*eh*	open **e**, as in 'bet', 'bury'
e	*e*	closed **e**, as in French *été*, and similar to 'laird'
e	*'*	silent final **e**, as in 'these'. Also silent in unstressed syllables.
i	*ee*	stressed **i**, as in 'see'
o	*oh*	open **o**, as in 'pot', 'sorry'
o	*o*	closed **o**, as in 'caught', 'awful'
o, u	*u*	an 'oo' sound, as in 'good', 'pull'

Nasal Vowels

Nasalisation can be represented in Portuguese by an **n** or an **m** after the vowel, or by a tilde, ~, over it. The nasal **i** exists in English, as the 'ing' sound in 'sing'. For other vowels, try to pronounce a long **a** or **e** *(ah, eh)* holding your nose, as if you had a head cold. In this book nasal vowels are represented as: *ã, ẽ, ing* (nasal **i**), *oong* (nasal **u**).

Diphthongs

au	*ow*	as in 'now', 'out'
ai	*ay*	as in 'pie', 'dive', 'eye'
ei	*ey*	as in 'day', 'pay'
eu	*e-w*	pronounced together
oi	*oy*	similar to 'boy'

Nasal Diphthongs

Try the same technique as for nasal vowels. To say 'no', *não*, pronounce English 'now' through your nose.

ão	*ōw*	nasal 'now' (*nowng*)
ãe	*ēy*	nasal 'day' (*eing*)
õe	*õy*	nasal 'boy' (*oing*)
ui	*ūy*	similar to 'ens*uing*', 'iss*uing*'.

Consonants

The letters **b**, **d**, **f**, **l**, **m**, **n**, **p**, **s**, **t**, **v** and **z** are similar enough to their English counterparts.

c	*k*	before **a**, **o** or **u**
c	*s*	before **e** or **i**, as in 'see'
ç	*s*	as in 'see'
g	*g*	before **a**, **o** or **u**, as in 'garden'
g	*zh*	before **e** or **i**, as in 'treasure'
gu	*g*	before **e** or **i**, as in 'get'
h		never pronounced at the beginning of a word
nh	*ny*	as in 'onion'
lh	*ly*	as in 'million'
j	*zh*	as the 's' in 'treasure'
m	*m*	in final position is not pronounced, it simply nasalises the previous vowel: um (*oong*), bom (*bō*)

PORTUGUESE

qu	*k*	before **e** or **i**
qu	*kw*	before **a** or **o**, as in 'quack'
r (**rr** in the middle of a word)	*rr*	is a harsh, guttural sound similar to the French *rue*, Scottish *loch*, or German *Bach*. In some areas of Portugal this **r** is not guttural, but strongly rolled.
r	*r*	in the middle or at the end of a word it's a rolled sound, stronger than the English 'r'
s (**ss** in the middle of a word)	*s*	at the beginning of a word is pronounced like the 's' in 'send'
s	*z*	between vowels is pronounced 'z' as in 'zeal'
s	*sh*	before another consonant or at the end of a word is pronounced 'sh', as in 'she'
x	*sh*	as in 'ship': taxa *(tah-shă)*
x	*z*	as in 'zeal': exame *(ee-ză-m')*
x	*ks*	'ks', as in 'taxi'

Stress

Word stress is important in Portuguese, as it can change the meaning of the word. Many Portuguese words have a written accent. The stress must fall on that syllable when you pronounce it. Stressed syllables are in bold print in this chapter, for example: 'thanks' – obrigado, *o-bree-**gah**-du*.

Greetings & Civilities
Top Useful Phrases

Hello.	*oh-**lah***	Olá.
Goodbye.	*ă-**dewsh***	Adeus.
Yes.	*sing*	Sim.
No.	*nõw*	Não.

Excuse me.	*d'sh-**kul**-p'/kō lee-sē-să*	Desculpe/Com licença.
May I? Do you mind?	*poh-su?*	Posso?
Please.	*s'**fahsh** făvor*	Se faz favor.
Thank you.	*o-bree-**gah**-du/dă*	Obrigado/a.
That's fine./ You're welcome.	*d' **nah**-dă*	De nada.

PORTUGUESE

Greetings

Good morning.	*bō **dee**-ă*	Bom dia.
Good afternoon.	*bo-ă **tahr**-d'*	Boa tarde.
Good evening.	*bo-ă **tahr**-d'*	Boa tarde.
Goodnight.	*bo-ă **noy**-t'*	Boa noite.
How are you?	*ko-moo **shtah**?*	Como está?
Well, thanks.	*bēy, o-bree-**gah**-du/da*	Bem, obrigado/a.

Forms of Address

Madam/Mrs	*mee-nyă s'**nyo**-ră/ s'**nyo**-ră **do**-nă*	Minha senhora/ Senhora Dona
Sir/Mr	*s'**nyor***	Senhor
Miss	*m'-**nee**-nă*	Menina
companion	*kō-pă-**nyey**-ru/-ră*	companheiro/a
friend	*ă-**mee**-gu/-gă*	amigo/a

Language Difficulties

Do you speak English?
fah-lă ing-glesh?   Fala Inglês?

Does anyone speak English?
*ah ă-**kee** ahl-gēy k'fahl' ing-glesh?*   Há aqui alguém que fale Inglês?

PORTUGUESE

I speak a little Portuguese.
fah-lu oong bu-kǎ-dee-nyu d'pur-tu-gesh

Falo um bocadinho de Português.

I (don't) speak …
(nõw) fah-lu …

(Não) Falo …

I (don't) understand.
(nõw) p'r-se-bu/ē-tē-du

(Não) Percebo/Entendo.

Could you speak more slowly please?
pu-dee-ǎ fǎ-lahr maysh d'-vǎ-gahr, s'fash fǎ-vor?

Podia falar mais devagar, se faz favor?

Could you repeat that?
pu-dee-ǎ rr'-p'-teer?

Podia repetir?

How do you say …?
ko-mu eh k's'deesh …?

Como é que se diz …?

What does … mean?
k' see-gnee-fee-kǎ …?

Que significa …?

Small Talk
Meeting People

What is your name?
ko-mu s'shǎ-mǎ?

Como se chama?

My name is …
shǎ-mu-m' …

Chamo-me …

I'm pleased to meet you.
mūy-tu prǎ-zer

Muito prazer.

Nationalities

Where are you from?
dy ō dy eh?

De onde é?

Many country names, when written in Portuguese, are very similar to English. But the pronunciation can often be quite different. We've listed a few places that differ more considerably, if you can grab hold of a dictionary it might be wise to memorise the name of your country – ask a local how to say it.

PORTUGUESE

I'm from …	so …	Sou …
Australia	*dă owsh-**trah**-lee-ă*	da Austrália
England	*d'ing-glă-**teh**-rră*	de Inglaterra
Germany	*d'ahl-ee-**mah**-nya*	de Alemanha
Ireland	*dă eer-**lã**-dă*	da Irlanda
Latin America	*d'ah-**meh**-ree-kah lă-**tee**-nah*	de América Latina
Middle East	*du **meh**-diu oh-ree-**ent***	do Médio-Oriente
New Zealand	*dă **noh**-vă z'-**lã**-dee-ă*	da Nova Zelândia
Scotland	*dă sh-**koh**-see-ă*	da Escócia
West Indies	*dăsh ahn-teel-yăsh*	das Antilhas
the USA	*duz'sh-**tah**-du-zu-**nee**-dush*	dos Estados Unidos
Wales	*du pă-**eesh** d'**gah**-l'sh*	do País de Gales

Age

How old are you?
   *kwã-tu-ză-nush-**tēy**?*   Quantos anos tem?
I am … years old.
   te-nyu … ă-nush   Tenho … anos.

PORTUGUESE

Occupations

What (work) do you do?
*ēy ky **eh** k' trǎ-**bah**-lya?*   Em que é que trabalha?

I am (a/an) …   *so …*   Sou …

business person	*ee-z'-ku-**tee**-vu,*	executivo/a,
	*ē-pr'-**zah**-ree-u/-ǎ*	empresário/a
farmer	*ǎ-gree-kul-**tor**/-ǎ*	agricultor/a
journalist	*zhur-nǎ-**leesh**-tǎ*	jornalista
labourer	*o-p'-**rah**-ree-u/-ǎ*	operário/a
nurse	*ē-f'r-**mey**-ru/-rǎ*	enfermeiro/a
office worker	*ē-pr'-**gah**-du/-dǎ*	empregado/a de
	*d'sh-kree-**toh**-ree-u*	escritório
scientist	*see-ē-**teesh**-tǎ*	cientista
student	*shtu-**dā**-t'*	estudante
teacher	*pru-f'-**sor**/-ǎ*	professor/a
waiter	*ē-pr'-**gah**-du/-dǎ d'*	empregado/a de
	***me**-zǎ*	mesa
writer	*shkree-**tor**/-rǎ*	escritor/a

Religion

What is your religion?
*kwah-**leh** ǎ su-ǎ*   Qual é a sua religião?
rr'lee-zhee-õw?

I am not religious.
***nõw** so rr'-lee-zhee-*   Não sou religioso/a.
o-zu/-zǎ

I am …   *so …*   Sou …

Buddhist	*bu-**deesh**-tǎ*	budista
Catholic	*kǎ-**toh**-lee-ku/-kǎ*	católico/a
Christian	*kreesh-**tõw**/kreesh-**tā***	cristão/cristã

Hindu	*ing-**du***	hindu
Jewish	*zhu-**de**-w/zhu-**dee**-ă*	judeu/judia
Muslim	*mu-sul-**mă**-nu/-nă*	muçulmano/a

Family

Are you married?
  *eh kă-**zah**-du/-dă?*   É casado/a?
I am single.
  *so sol-**tey**-ru/-ră*   Sou solteiro/a.
I am married.
  *so kă-**zah**-du/-dă*   Sou casado/a.
How many children do you
have?
  kwā-tush fee-lyush tēy?   Quantos filhos tem?
I don't have any children.
  nōw te-nyu fee-lyush   Não tenho filhos.
Is your husband/wife here?
  *u se-w mă-**ree**-du/ă su-ă*   O seu marido/A sua mulher
  mu-lyehr shtah ă-kee   está aqui consigo?
  *kō-**see**-gu?*
Do you have a boyfriend/
girlfriend?
  *tēy nă-mu-**rah**-du/-dă?*   Tem namorado/a?

brother	*eer-**mōw***	irmão
children	*fee-lyush*	filhos
daughter	*fee-**lyă***	filha
family	*fă-**mee**-lee-ă*	família
father	*pay*	pai
grandfather	*ă-**vo***	avô
grandmother	*ă-**voh***	avó
husband	*mă-**ree**-du*	marido

PORTUGUESE

PORTUGUESE

mother	*mēy*	mãe
sister	*eer-mã*	irmã
son	*fee-lyu*	filho
wife	*mu-lyehr/shpo-ză*	mulher/esposa

Useful Phrases

Sorry. (excuse me, forgive me)
  d'sh-kul-p' Desculpe.
Sure.
  kõ s'r-te-ză/klah-ru (k' sing) Com certeza/Claro (que sim)!
Just a minute.
  oong mu-mē-tu Um momento.
Good luck!
  bo-ă sohr-t' Boa sorte.

Signs

EMERGENCY EXIT	*SAÍDA DE EMERGÊNCIA*
ENTRANCE	*ENTRADA*
EXIT	*SAÍDA*
FREE ADMISSION	*ENTRADA GRATIS*
HOT/COLD	*QUENTE/FRIO*
INFORMATION	*INFORMAÇÕES*
NO ENTRY	*PROIBIDA A ENTRADA*
NO SMOKING	*PROIBIDO FUMAR*
OPEN	*ABERTO*
CLOSED	*ENCERRADO/FECHADO*
PROHIBITED	*PROIBIDO*
TOILETS	*WC*

Getting Around

What time does ... arrive/
leave?
ă ky oh-răsh she-gă/
pahr-t' ...?

A que horas chega/parte ...?

the (air)plane	*u ă-vee-ōw*	o avião
the boat	*u bahr-ku*	o barco
the bus	*u ow-toh-kah-rru*	o autocarro
the intercity bus	*ă kah-mee-u-neh-tă*	a camioneta
the train	*u kō-boy-u*	o comboio
the tram	*u ee-leh-tree-ku*	o eléctrico

Finding Your Way

Do you have a guidebook/
local map?
tēy oong gee-ă/oong
mah-pă du see-tee-u?

Tem um guia/um mapa do
sítio?

Where is ...?
ō-dy eh ...?/ō-d'fee-kă ...?

Onde é ...?/Onde fica ...?

How do I get to ...?
ko-mu vo pă-ră ...?

Como vou para ...?

Is it far from/near here?
eh lō-zh'/pehr-tu dăkee?

É longe/perto daqui?

Can I walk there?
poh-su eer ă peh?

Posso ir a pé?

Can you show me (on the map)?
poh-d'-m' mush-trahr nu
mah-pă?

Pode-me mostrar (no mapa)?

What street is this?
k'-rru-ă eh ehsh-tă?

Que rua é esta?

What suburb is this?
k'-bay-rru eh esh-t'?

Que bairro é este?

PORTUGUESE

PORTUGUESE

Directions

Go straight ahead.
  see-gă sĕ-pr' ă dee-rey-tu/sĕ-pr' ĕy frĕ-t'
Siga sempre a direito/sempre em frente.

It's two blocks down.
  eh ă doysh kwăr-tey-rõysh dă-kee
É a dois quarteirões daqui.

Turn left …
  vee-rahsh-ker-dă …
Vire à esquerda …

Turn right …
  vee-rah dee-rey-tă …
Vire à direita …

at the next corner
  nă proh-see-măsh-kee-nă
na próxima esquina

at the traffic lights
  nu s'mah-fu-ru/nush see-naysh d' tră-see-tu
no sem foro/nos sinais de trânsito

behind	*ă-trahsh d'*	atrás de
in front of	*ĕy frĕ-t' d'*	em frente de
far	*lõ-zh'*	longe
near	*pehr-tu*	perto
opposite	*du o-tru lah-du/ ĕy frĕ-t'-d'*	do outro lado/ em frente de

Buying Tickets

TICKET OFFICE	BILHETEIRA

Where is the ticket office?
  fahsh fă-vor, õ-dy eh ă bee-ly'tey-ră?
Faz favor, onde é a bilheteira?

Where can I buy a ticket?
*õ-dy **eh** k'**kõ**-pru u
bee-**lye**-t'?*

Onde é que compro o
bilhete?

I want to go to ...
keh-ru **eer** pă-**ră** ...

Quero ir para ...

Do I need to book?
*eh pr'-**see**-zu rr'-z'r-**vahr**?*

É preciso reservar?

You need to book.
*tẽy d'fă-**zer** rr'-**zehr**-vă*

Tem de fazer reserva.

I'd like to book a seat to ...
*k'-**ree**-ă rr'-z'r-**vahr**
lu-**gahr** pă-**ră** ...*

Queria reservar lugar
para ...

It is full.
*shtah **shey**-u*

Está cheio.

Is it completely full?
*shtah shgu-**tah**-du?*

Está esgotado?

Can I have a refund?
*poh-**dẽ**-m' rree-ẽ-bol-**sahr**/
d'-vol-**ver** u dee-**nyey**-ru?*

Podem-me reembolsar/
devolver o dinheiro?

PORTUGUESE

I would like ...		
*k'-**ree**-ă ...*		Queria ...
a one-way ticket	*oong bee-**lye**-t' d' ee-dă/**sing**-pl'sh*	um bilhete de ida/simples
a return ticket	*oong bee-**lye**-t' d' ee-dă ee **vohl**-tă*	um bilhete de ida e volta
two tickets	*doysh bee-**lye**-t'sh*	dois bilhetes
a student's fare	*bee-**lye**-t' d' shtu-**dã**-t'*	bilhete de estudante
1st class	*pree-**mey**-ră **klah**-s'*	primeira classe
2nd class	*s'-**gū**-dă **klah**-s'*	segunda classe

Air

ARRIVALS	*CHEGADAS*
DEPARTURES	*PARTIDAS*
BAGGAGE COUNTER	*BALCÃO DE BAGAGENS*
CHECK-IN COUNTER	*ENTREGA DE BAGAGENS/*
	CHECK-IN
CUSTOMS	*ALFÂNDEGA*

Is there a flight to ...?
  *ah oong **voh**-u pah-ră ...?*   Há um voo para ...?
When is the next flight
to ...?
  *ă ky **oh**-ră **pahr**-t' u **proh**-*   A que hora parte o próximo
  see-mu voh-u pah-ră ...?   voo para ...?
How long does the flight take?
  *kwã-tu **doo**-ră u voh-u?*   Quanto dura o voo?
You must check in at ...
  *tẽy de ă-pre-zen-**tăr**-se ă ...*   Tem de apersentarse a ...

Bus & Tram

BUS STOP	*PARAGEM DE AUTOCARRO*
TRAM STOP	*PARAGEM DE ELÉCTRICO*

Where is the bus/tram stop?
  *õ-dy eh ă pă-**rah**-gẽy du*   Onde é a paragem do
  *ow-toh-**kah**-rru/du ee-**leh**-*   autocarro/do eléctrico?
  tree-ku?
Which bus goes to ...?
  *kwah-**leh** u ow-toh-**kah**-rru*   Qual é o autocarro para ...?
  pă-ră ...?

Does this bus go to …?
esh-*tow-toh-***kah**-*rru* **vay**
*pă-*ră …?

Este autocarro vai para …?

How often do buses pass by?
*u ow-toh-***kah**-*rru* **pah**-*să*
*kõ fr'-***kwē**-*see-ă*?

O autocarro passa com frequência?

Could you let me know when
we get to …?
poh-*d'-ma-vee-***zahr** *kwă-du*
*sh'-***gahr**-*mush ă …*?

Pode-me avisar quando
chegarmos a …?

I want to get off!
keh-*ru d'sh-***ser**!

Quero descer!

What time is the … bus?
ă ky **oh**-*ră eh u … ow-toh-*
kah-*rru*?

A que hora é o … autocarro?

next	**proh**-*see-mu*	próximo
first	*pree-***mey**-*ru*	primeiro
last	**ool**-*tee-mu*	último

Train

TIMETABLE	*HORÁRIO*
TRAIN STATION	*ESTAÇÃO FERROVIÁRIA/*
	ESTAÇÃO DE COMBÓIOS
PLATFORM NO	*PLATAFORMA No.*

Is this the right platform for …?
*eh dehsh-*tă *plah-tă-***fohr**-
*mă k' say u kõ-***boy**-*u*
pă-ra …?

É desta plataforma que sai o
combóio para …?

PORTUGUESE

The train leaves from platform …
*u kõ-**boy**-u say/pahr-t' dǎ plah-tǎ-**fohr**-mǎ nu-m'ru …*
O combóio sai/parte da plataforma número …

Passengers must …
*ush pǎ-sǎ-**zhey**-rush **deh**-vẽy …*
Os passageiros devem …

change trains	*mu-**dahr** d' kõ-**boy**-u*	mudar de combóio
change platforms	*mu-**dahr** d' plah-tǎ-**fohr**-mǎ*	mudar de plataforma

The train is delayed/cancelled.
*u kõ-**boy**-u shtah ǎ-trǎ-**zah**-du/foy ǎ-nu-**lah**-du*
O combóio está atrasado/foi anulado.

How long will it be delayed?
*u ǎ-**trah**-zu eh d' **kwā**-tu **tẽ**-pu?*
O atraso é de quanto tempo?

There is a delay of … hours.
*u ǎ-**trah**-zu eh d' … oh-rash*
O atraso é de … horas.

dining car	*vah-**gõw** rr'sh-tow-**rã**-t'*	vagão-restaurante
express	*shpreh-su*	expresso
local	*lu-**kahl**/rr'-zhee-u-nahl*	local/regional
sleeping car	*vah-**gõw** kǎ-mǎ*	vagão-cama

Metro

Which line takes me to …?
*kwah-**leh** ǎ **lee**-nyǎ pǎ-rǎ …?*
Qual é a linha para …?

What is the next station?
*kwah-**leh** ǎ **proh**-see-mǎ shtǎ-**sõw**?*
Qual é próxima estação?

Taxi

Please take me to …
leh-v'-m ă …, s' fahsh fă-vor
    Leve-me a …, se faz favor.

How much does it cost to go to …?
kwă-tu kush-tă eer ă …?
    Quanto custa ir a …?

PORTUGUESE

Instructions

Here is fine, thank you.
ă-kee shtah bēy, o-bree-gah-du/-ă
    Aqui está bem, obrigado/a.

Continue!
vah ă-dă-du/see-gă!
    Vá andando/Siga!

The next corner, please.
*nă **proh-see-mă** shkee-nă, s' fahsh fă-vor*
    Na próxima esquina, se faz favor.

The next street to the left/right.
*ă **proh-see-mă** rru-ă ah shker-dă/ah dee-rey-tă*
    A próxima rua à esquerda/ à direita.

Stop here!
pah-r' a-kee!
    Pare aqui!

Car & Bicycle

DETOUR	*DESVIO*
GARAGE	*GARAGEM*
GIVE WAY	*DAR PRIORIDADE*
MECHANIC	*MECÂNICO*
NO ENTRY	*PROIBIDA A ENTRADA*
NO PARKING	*PROIBIDO ESTACIONAR*

ONE WAY	SENTIDO ÚNICO
REPAIRS	CONSERTOS/
	REPARAÇÕES
SELF SERVICE	AUTO-SERVIÇO
UNLEADED	SEM CHUMBO

PORTUGUESE

I'd like to hire a car.
*k'ree-ă ă-lu-gahr oong
kah-rru*
Queria alugar um carro.

I'd like to hire a bicycle.
*k'ree-ă ă-lu-gahr u-mă bee-
see-kleht-ă*
Queria alugar uma bicicleta.

daily/weekly
pur dee-ă/pur s'-mă-nă
por dia/por semana

Where's the next petrol station?
*õ-dy eh ă proh-see-mă
shtă-sõw d' s'r-vee-su?*
Onde é a próxima estação
de serviço?

Please fill the tank.
*ē-shă u d'-poh-see-tu,
s' fahsh fă-vor*
Encha o depósito, se faz
favor.

I want … litres of petrol (gas).
*keh-ru … lee-trush
d' gă-zu-lee-nă*
Quero … litros de gasolina.

Please check the oil and water.
*v'-ree-fee-ku oh-lee-u ee ă
ah-gwă, s' fahsh fă-vor*
Verifique o óleo e a água,
se faz favor.

air (for tyres)	*ahr (pă-ră p-ne-wsh)*	ar (para pneus)
battery	*bă-t'-ree-ă*	bateria
brakes	*tră-võysh*	travões

clutch	*ē-bray-**ah**-zhĕy*	embraiagem
driving licence	***kahr**-tă d' kō-du-sõw*	carta de condução
engine	*mu-**tor***	motor
lights	*fă-**roysh***	faróis
oil	*oh-lee-u*	óleo
puncture	*oong **fu**-ru*	um furo
radiator	*rră-dee-ă-**dor***	radiador
road map	***mah**-pă dăz'- sh-**trah**-dăsh*	mapa das estradas
tyres	*p-**ne**-wsh*	pneus
windscreen	***pah**-ră **bree**-zăsh*	pára-brisas

PORTUGUESE

Car Problems

The battery is flat.
  *ă bă-t'-**ree**-ă **shtah** d'sh-kă-rr'-**gah**-dă*
  A bateria está descarregada.

The radiator is leaking.
  *u rră-dee-ă-**dor** shtah ă p'r-**der** ah-gwă*
  O radiador está a perder água.

I have a flat tyre.
  *te-nyu oong p'**ne**-w fu-**rah**-du*
  Tenho um pneu furado.

It's overheating.
  *shtah ah-keh-**ser** d'-**maysh***
  Está a aquecer demais.

It's not working.
  nõw fŭ-see-o-nă
  Não funciona.

Accommodation

CAMPING GROUND	*PARQUE DE CAMPISMO*
GUESTHOUSE	*PENSÃO*
YOUTH HOSTEL	*ALBERGUE DE JUVENTUDE*

PORTUGUESE

Finding Accommodation

I am looking for ...
ã-du ah pro-ku-ră d'...   Ando à procura de ...

Where is a ... hotel?
õ-dy ah oong oh-tehl ...?   Onde há um hotel ...?

cheap	*bă-rah-tu*	barato
nearby	*pehr-tu*	perto
clean	*ling-pu*	limpo

What is the address?
kwah-leh ă mu-rah-dă/   Qual é a morada/direcção?
dee-reh-sõw

Could you write the address,
please?
pu-dee-ă shkr'-ver ă   Podia escrever a
mu-rah-dă/dee-reh-sõw?   morada/direcção?

Booking a Room

Do you have any rooms
available?
tẽy kwahr-tush lee-vr'sh?   Tem quartos livres?

I'd like to book a room.
k'-ree-ă reh-zer-vahr oong   Queria reservar um quarto.
kwahr-tu

for one night/four nights
pur u-mă noy-t'/kwah-tru   por uma noite/quatro noites
noy-t'sh

from tonight/Tuesday
ah pah-teer dehsh-tă noy-   a partir desta noite/de terça
t'/d' ter-să fay-ră   feira

I'd like …	k'-ree-ă …	Queria …
a single room	oong **kwahr**-tu ing-dee-vee-du-**ahl**	um quarto individual
a double room	oong **kwahr**-tu du-plu/ oong **kwahr**-tu d' kă-**zahl**	um quarto duplo/um quarto de casal
a room with a bathroom	oong **kwahr**-tu kõ **kah**-ză d' bă-nyu	um quarto com casa de banho
to share a dorm	fee-**kahr** noong dur-mee-**toh**-ree-u	ficar num dormitório

I'm going to stay for …	vo fee-**kahr** …	Vou ficar …
one day	oong dee-ă	um dia
two days	doysh dee-ăsh	dois dias
one week	u-mă s'mă-nă	uma semana

PORTUGUESE

At the Hotel

How much is it per night/ per person?

kwă-tu eh pur **noy**-t'/ pur p'-**so**-ă?

Quanto é por noite/ por pessoa?

Can I see it?

poh-su ver?

Posso ver?

Are there any others?

ah o-trush **kwahr**-tush?

Há outros quartos?

Are there any cheaper rooms?

ah **kwahr**-tush **mayzh** bă-**rah**-tush?

Há quartos mais baratos?

Can I see the bathroom?

poh-su ver ă **kah**-ză d'bă-nyu?

Posso ver a casa de banho?

PORTUGUESE

Is there a reduction for
students/children?
> *ah d'sh-kõ-tu pǎ-rǎ
> shtu-dā-t'sh/kree-ā-sǎsh?*

Há desconto para
estudantes/crianças?

Does it include breakfast?
> *u p'ke-nu ahl-mo-su shtah
> ing-klu-ee-du?*

O pequeno almoço est
incluído?

It's fine, I'll take it.
> *shtah bēy fee-ku kõ e-l'*

Está bem, fico com ele.

I'm not sure how long I'm
staying.
> *nõw te-nyu ǎ s'r-te-zǎ d'
> kwā-tu tē-pu vo fee-kahr*

Não tenho a certeza de
quanto tempo vou ficar.

Where is the bathroom?
> *õ-dy eh ǎ kah-zǎ d' bǎ-nyu?*

Onde é a casa de banho?

Is there hot water all day?
> *ah ah-gwǎ kē-t' du-rā-t'
> to-du u dee-ǎ?*

Há água quente durante
todo o dia?

You May Hear

Do you have identification?
> *tēy ahl-goong du-ku-mē-tu
> dee-dē-tee-dah-d'?*

Tem algum documento de
identidade?

Sorry, we're full.
> *d'sh-kul-p', shtǎ-mush
> shey-ush*

Desculpe, estamos cheios.

How long will you be staying?
> *kwā-tu tē-pu vay fee-kahr?*

Quanto tempo vai ficar?

It's … per day/per person.
> *sõw … pur dee-ǎ/pur
> p'-so-ǎ*

São … por dia/por pessoa.

PORTUGUESE

Requests & Complaints

Do you have a safe where I
can leave my valuables?
tēy oong koh-fr'õ-d'
poh-să dey-shahr koy-săsh
d'vă-lor?

Tem um cofre onde possa
deixar coisas de valor?

Is there somewhere to wash
clothes?
ah õ-d'lă-vahr rro-pă?

Há onde lavar roupa?

Can I use the telephone/
kitchen?
poh-su t'l'fu-nahr/ă
ku-zee-nyă?

Posso telefonar/a cozinha?

I can't open/close the window.
năw poh-su ă-breer/feh-
shar ă zhă-neh-lă

Não posso abrir/fechar a
janela.

I've locked myself out of my
room.
dey-sh'ă shah-v'nu
kwahr-tu

Deixe a chave no quarto.

I don't like this room.
năw gohsh-tu esh-t'
kwahr-tu

Não gosto este quarto.

It's too noisy.
ah moy-t' bah-ru-lyu

Há muito barulho.

It's too dark.
eh moy-t' shkoo-ru

É muito escuro.

Checking Out

I am/We are leaving (now).
vo-m'/vă-mu-nush ē-boh-ră

Vou-me/Vamo-nos embora.

I would like to pay the bill.
  k'-ree-ă d' pă-gahr ă kŏ-tă　　Queria pagar a conta.

address	*en-dehr-eh-su*	endereço
name	*nohm*	nome
surname	*soh-br' nohm*	sobrenome
room number	*noo-mehr-u du kwahr-tu*	número do quarto

Useful Words

bathroom	*kah-ză d' bă-nyu*	casa de banho
bed	*kă-mă*	cama
blanket	*ku-b'r-tor*	cobertor
double bed	*kă-mă d' kă-zahl*	cama de casal
electricity	*ee-leh-tree-cee-dah-d'*	electricidade
excluded	*nŏw (shtah) ing-klu-ee-du*	não (está) incluído
fan	*vĕ-tu-ee-nyă*	ventoinha
included	*ing-klu-ee-du*	incluído
key	*shah-v'*	chave
quiet	*su-s'-gah-du*	sossegado
sheet	*lĕ-sohl*	lençol
shower	*shu-vey-ru/du-sh'*	chuveiro/duche
soap	*să-bu-ne-t'*	sabonete
toilet	*rr'-treh-t'*	retrete
toilet paper	*pă-pehl ee-zhee-eh-nee-ku*	papel higiénico
towel	*tu-ah-lyă*	toalha
water	*ah-gwă*	água
cold water	*ah-gwă free-ă*	água fria
hot water	*ah-gwă kĕ-t'*	água quente
window	*ză-neh-lă*	janela

Around Town

I'm looking for …
*ã-du ah pro-**ku**-ră* …

	Ando à procura …	

a bank — *doong **bā**-ku* — dum banco

the city centre — *du **cẽ**-tru dă see-**dah**-d'/dă **bay**-shă* — do centro da cidade/da baixa

the … embassy — *dă ẽ-bay-**shah**-dă d' …* — da embaixada de …

my hotel — *du **me**-w oh-**tehl*** — do meu hotel

the market — *du m'r-**kah**-du/dă **prah**-să* — do mercado/da praça

the post office — *dush ku-**rrey**-ush* — dos correios

a public toilet — *du-mă **kah**-ză d' bă-nyu pu-**blee**-kă* — duma casa de banho pública

the telephone centre — *dă sẽ-**trahl** d' t'l'-**foh**-n'sh* — da central de telefones

the tourist information office — *du tu-**reesh**-mu/du s'r-**vee**-su ding-fur-mă-**sõysh** pă-ră tu-**reesh**-tăsh* — do turismo/do serviço de informações para turistas

What time does it open?
*ă ky **oh**-răsh **ah**-br'?*

A que horas abre?

What time does it close?
*ă ky **oh**-răsh **fey**-shă?*

A que horas fecha?

At the Bank

I want to exchange some money/travellers' cheques.
*k'-**ree**-ă tru-**kahr** dee-**nyey**-ru/oongsh **sheh**-k'sh d' vee-**ah**-gẽy*

Queria trocar dinheiro/uns cheques de viagem.

PORTUGUESE

What is the exchange rate?		
kwah-leh *ă tah-shă d'*		Qual é a taxa de câmbio?
kā-bee-u?		
How many escudos per dollar?		
kwā-tuz' shku-dush **vah**-l'		Quantos escudos vale um
oong **doh**-lar?		dólar?

banknotes	**noh**-tăsh d' **bā**-ku	notas de banco
cashier	**kay**-shă	caixa
coins	mu-**eh**-dăsh	moedas
credit card	kăr-**tōw** d' **kreh**-dee-tu	cartão de crédito
exchange	**kā**-bee-u	câmbio
loose change	**troh**-kush	trocos
signature	ă-see-nă-**tu**-ră	assinatura

At the Post Office

I'd like to send …	k'-**ree**-ă mā-**dahr** …	Queria mandar …
an aerogram	oong ă-eh-roh-**gră**-	um aerograma
	mă	
a letter	u-mă **kahr**-tă	uma carta
a postcard	oong push-**tahl**	um postal
a parcel	u-mă ē-ku-mē-dă	uma encomenda
a telegram	oong t'l'-**gră**-mă	um telegrama

I would like some stamps.		
k'-**ree**-ă se-lush		Queria selos.
How much is the postage?		
kwā-tu eh ă frā-**kee**-ă?		Quanto é a franquia?
How much does it cost to		
send this to …?		
kwā-tu kush-tă mā-**dahr**		Quanto custa mandar isto
eesh-tu pă-ră …?		para …?

airmail	*ku-rrey-u ă-eh-ree-u*	correio aéreo
envelope	*ē-v'loh-p'*	envelope
mailbox	*kay-shă du ku-rrey-u*	caixa do correio
parcel	*ē-ku-mē-dă*	encomenda
registered mail	*rr'geesh-tah-du*	registado
surface mail	*vee-ă su-p'r-fee-cee*	via superfície

PORTUGUESE

Telephone

I want to call …
  k'-ree-ă t'l'-fu-nahr
  pă-ră …
                  Queria telefonar para …

The number is …
  u nu-m'ru eh …
                  O número é …

I want to speak for three
minutes.
  keh-ru fă-lahr du-ră-t'
  tresh mee-nu-tush
                  Quero falar durante três
                  minutos.

How much does a three-
minute call cost?
  kwă-tu kush-tă oong
  t'l'-fu-ne-mă d' tresh
  mee-nu-tush?
                  Quanto custa um
                  telefonema de três minutos?

How much does each extra
minute cost?
  kwă-tu kush-tă kă-dă
  mee-nu-tu ă maysh?
                  Quanto custa cada minuto a
                  mais?

It's engaged.
  shtah ing-p'-dee-du/shtah
  ă fă-lahr
                  Está impedido/Está a falar.

I've been cut off.
  d'sh-lee-go-s'
                  Desligou-se.

I want to make a reverse-charges (collect) call.

keh-ru fă-zer oong t'l'-fu-ne-mă pă-ră pă-gahr lah/u-mă shă-mah-dă pah-gă nu d'sh-tee-nu

Quero fazer um telefonema para pagar lá/uma chamada paga no destino.

Hello?

oh-lah

Olá.

I'd like to speak to Mrs Evora.

k'-ree-ă fă-lahr kō ă s'nyora e-vo-ră

Queria falar com a Senhora Evora.

Sightseeing

What are the main attractions?

kwaysh sõw ăz ă-trah-sõysh pring-see-paysh?

Quais são as atracções principais?

How old is it?

eh ă-tee-gu? d'kwă-du eh?

É antigo/De quando é?

Can I take photographs?

poh-su tee-rahr fu-tu-gră-fee-ăsh?

Posso tirar fotografias?

What time does it open/close?

ăa ky oh-răsh ah-br'/fey-shă?

A que horas abre/fecha?

library	*bee-blee-u-tek-ă*	biblioteca
church	*ee-grey-zhă*	igreja
monastery	*mosh-tey-ru*	mosteiro
museum	*moo-zay-u*	museu
cathedral	*kah-teh-drăl*	catedral
tower	*tor-re*	torre
zoo	*zhar-deeng zo-o-lo-zhee-ku*	jardim zoológico

In the Country
Weather

What's the weather like?
ko-mu shtah u tē-pu? — Como está o tempo?

The weather is … today.
u tē-pu shtah … o-zh' — O tempo está … hoje.

Will it be … tomorrow?
ah-mǎ-nyā shtǎ-rah …? — Amanhã estará …?

cloudy	*nu-blah-du*	nublado
cold	*free-u*	frio
hot	*kǎ-lor*	calor
raining	*ǎ shu-ver*	a chover
snowing	*ǎ n'vahr*	a nevar
sunny	*sohl*	sol
windy	*vē-tu*	vento

Camping

Am I allowed to camp here?
poh-su ǎ-kā-pahr ǎ-kee? — Posso acampar aqui?

Is there a campsite nearby?
ah oong pahrk' d' kā-peesh-mu ǎ-kee pehr-tu? — Há um parque de campismo aqui perto?

backpack	*mu-shee-lǎ*	mochila
can opener	*ah-br' lah-tǎsh*	abre-latas
compass	*bu-su-lǎ*	bússola
firewood	*le-nyǎ*	lenha
gas cartridge	*bu-tee-zhǎ d' gahsh*	botija de gás
mattress	*kol-shōw*	colchão
penknife	*kǎ-nee-veh-t'*	canivete
rope	*kohr-dǎ*	corda

PORTUGUESE

tent	*tē-dă*	tenda
tent pegs	*shtah-kăsh*	estacas
torch (flashlight)	*lā-tehr-nă*	lanterna
sleeping bag	*sah-ku kă-mă*	saco-cama
stove	*fu-gōw/fu-ga-rey-ru*	fogão/fogareiro
water bottle	*gă-rrah-fă dah-gwă*	garrafa de água

Food

breakfast	*p'ke-nu ahl-mo-su*	pequeno almoço
lunch	*ahl-mo-su*	almoço
afternoon tea	*lā-sh'*	lanche
dinner	*jā-tahr*	jantar

Eating Out

Table for ..., please.
  u-mă me-ză pă-ră ...,
  s'fahsh fă-vor

Uma mesa para ..., se faz favor.

Can I see the menu please?
  k'-ree-ă ver ă leesh-tă

Queria ver a lista.

I'd like the set lunch, please.
  k'-ree-a u ahl-mo-su dă kah-ză/u ahl-mo-su ă pre-su fee-ksu, s'fahsh fă-vor

Queria o almoço da casa/o almoço a preço fixo, se faz favor.

What does it include?
  ing-kluy u ke?

Inclui o quê?

Is service included in the bill?
  u s'r-vee-su shtah ing-klu-ee-du nă kō-tă?

O serviço está incluído na conta?

Not too spicy please.
  po-ku pee-kā-t', s'fahsh fă-vor

Pouco picante, se faz favor.

ashtray	*sing-**zey**-ru*	cinzeiro
the bill	*ă **kō**-tă*	a conta
a cup	*u-mă **shah**-v'nă*	uma chávena
a drink	*u-mă b'-**bee**-dă*	uma bebida
a fork	*oong **gahr**-fu*	um garfo
a glass	*oong **koh**-pu*	um copo
a knife	*u-mă **fah**-kă*	uma faca
a plate	*oong **prah**-tu*	um prato
a spoon	*u-mă ku-**lyehr***	uma colher

Making Your Own Meal

For some key essentials for sandwich-making, etc, see page 400.

Vegetarian Meals

I am a vegetarian.

   *so v'zh'-tă-**ree**-ă-nu/-nă*   Sou vegetariano/a.

I don't eat meat.

   *nõw ko-mu **kahr**-n'*   Não como carne.

Staples & Condiments

bread	*pão*	garlic	*alho*
butter	*manteiga*	oil	*olho*
cheese	*queijo*	pepper	*pimenta*
eggs	*ovos*	salt	*sal*

Soups & Staple Dishes

Arroz	Rice. Typical Portuguese dishes made with rice are *arroz de cabidela* (with duck or chicken) and *arroz de pato* (with duck and several local spicy sausages). *Arroz de polvo* (octopus) is characteristic of the Algarve. *Arroz de marisco* (shellfish) can be found all along the coast.

PORTUGUESE

Caldo verde	Potato and green cabbage soup with spicy sausage *(chouriço)*.
Canja de galinha	Chicken broth.
Caril	Curry – relatively common in Portugal since the days of the spice trade. Most common are *caril de camarão* (seafood curry) and *caril de galinha* (chicken curry). Often more spicy than hot.
Creme de camarão	Shrimp soup.
Sopa de legumes	Mixed vegetable soup.
Sopa de tomate com ovo	Fresh tomato soup, served with a whole poached egg, or with an egg stirred into it at the end.

Meat

Bifes de cebolada	Beef slices stewed with onions, garlic, tomatoes and parsley.
Bife com ovo a cavalo/Bitoque	Portuguese steaks are usually thinly cut and well done. These are fried and served with a fried egg and chips. If you want a thick steak, you must ask for *um bife alto*.
Cabrito assado	Kid is widely eaten in Portugal, usually roasted in wine with garlic and laurel.
Carne de porco com amêijoas	Pork casserole with clams and fresh coriander.
Coelho à caçadora	Rabbit casserole in red wine and tomato sauce.
Cozido à portuguesa	A stew of beef, pork and chicken, spicy sausages (*chouriço, linguiça, farinheira, morcelas,* etc) and vegetables (potatoes, turnips, carrots, cabbages).

Croquetes	Fried patties made from minced roast beef and *chouriço* sausage with bechamel sauce.
Ervilhas com ovos	A stew of fresh peas, spicy sausages and fresh herbs, with poached eggs.
Favada	Similar to the above, but made with broad beans instead of peas. No eggs added.
Febras de porco	Grilled, thinly cut pork steaks.
Frango	Chicken. *Frango assado* (roast chicken) is available everywhere. More exotic are *frango na púcara*, where chicken portions are cooked in an earthenware pot with tomato, onion, Port wine and sultanas; and *frango de churrasco*, spiced charcoal-grilled chicken.
Iscas à portuguesa	Beef liver steaks cooked with onion slices.
Leitão da Bairrada	Suckling pig, roasted in wall ovens.
Lombo de porco assado	Pork loin roasted in white wine. In the Alentejo province it is often served with clams *(amêijoas)*, elsewhere with a variety of sauces.
Rojões	Marinated, then fried, pork cubes, served together with fried pieces of pork liver and tripe.
Sarrabulho	Lean pork cubes, pieces of pork liver and tripe cooked in the pig's previously cooked blood.
Torresmos	Fatty pork cubes, fried in pig's fat, then braised in white wine. Served with potatoes fried in the pig's fat.
Vitela assada	Roast veal.

beef	*bife*	rabbit	*coelho*
chicken	*frango*	ribs	*costelas*
kid	*cabrito*	salami	*chouriço*
lamb	*carne de cordeiro*	sausage	*salsicha*
liver	*fígado*	veal	*vitella*

Seafood

Açorda de mariscos	A main course that resembles a very thick soup, made with shellfish (or sometimes fish) and soaked bread and eggs.
Bacalhau	Codfish, the dried, salted, non-smoked variety, that must be soaked before cooking. It is the traditional Portuguese dish for Christmas Eve, served with boiled potatoes and chick-peas: *bacalhau com grão* or *bacalhau da consoada*. It is often served in *bolinhos* or *pastéis de bacalhau*, small fried potato, codfish and parsley patties. It can be prepared in hundreds of other ways. Best known are:
Bacalhau assado	Charcoal-grilled.
Bacalhau à Brás	With finely-cut potato chips (French fries), scrambled eggs and olives.
Bacalhau no forno	Cooked in the oven, either with cream or tomatoes.
Bacalhau à Gomes de Sá	With slices of boiled potato and egg.
Bacalhau à Zé do Pipo	With mayonnaise and potato purée.
Caldeirada	A fish stew, with several different types of fish and sometimes also shellfish, cooked with olive oil, wine, tomatoes and onions.

Filetes de pescada/ de tamboril	Lightly battered, fried fillets of fish. *Pescada* and *tamboril* make good, large fish fillets, usually bone-free.
Rissóis	Rissoles of shellfish (*rissóis de camarão*) or fish (*rissóis de peixe*).
Sardinhas assadas	Fresh sardines, traditionally charcoal-grilled in the open air. Served with charcoal-grilled green peppers and boiled potatoes.

PORTUGUESE

anchovies	*enchovas*	mussels	*mexilhões*
clams	*ameijoas*	octopus	*polvo*
cockles	*berbigões*	oysters	*ostras*
cod	*bacalhau*	prawns	*langostins*
crab	*caranguejo*	sardines	*sardinhas*
eel	*enguia*	shrimps	*camarões*
fish	*peixe*	squid	*lula*
herring	*arenque*	sea bream	*pargo*
lobster	*lagostim*	whiting	*pescadinha*

Vegetables

artichoke	*ahl-kǎ-**shoh**-frǎ*	alcachofra
asparagus	***shpahr**-gush*	espargos
beetroot	*b'-t'-**rrah**-bǎ*	beterraba
broad beans	***fah**-vǎsh*	favas
broccoli	***broh**-ku-lush*	brócolos
Brussel sprouts	*ko-v'sh d' bru-**sheh**-lǎsh*	couves de Bruxelas
cabbage	***ko-v'***	couve
capsicum	*pee-**mē**-tu*	pimento
carrot	*s'-**no**-rǎ*	cenoura
cauliflower	***ko-v'** flor*	couve-flor
celery	***ah**-pee-u*	ápio

PORTUGUESE

chick peas	*grõw*	grão
cucumber	*p'-pee-nu*	pepino
eggplant	*b'-ring-zheh-lă*	beringela
garlic	*ah-lyu*	alho
green beans	*fey-zhõw ver-d'*	feijão verde
green peas	*er-vee-lyăsh*	ervilhas
leeks	***ah**-lyu po-**rru**/frã-**sesh***	alho porro/francês
lentils	*lē-**tee**-lyăsh*	lentilhas
lettuce	*ahl-**fah**-s'*	alface
mushroom	*ku-gu-**meh**-lu*	cogumelo
onion	*s'-**bo**-lă*	cebola
parsley	***sahl**-să*	salsa
potato	*bă-**tah**-tă*	batata
pumpkin	*ă-**boh**-bu-ră*	abóbora
radish	*rră-bă-**ne**-t'*	rabanete
spinach	*sh-pee-**nah**-fr'sh*	espinafres
(often spinach purée – *esparre-gado*)		
sweet potato	*bă-**tah**-tă **do**-s'*	batata doce
tomato	*tu-**mah**-t'*	tomate
turnip	***nah**-bu*	nabo
zucchini	*kur-**zheh**-t'*	courgette

Fruit

apple	*mă-**sā***	maçã
apricot	*ahl-**pehr**-s'/* *dă-**mahsh**-ku*	alperce/damasco
canteloupe	*m'-**lo**-ă*	meloa
cherry	*s'-**rey**-zhă*	cereja
currants	*gro-ze-lyă*	groselha
date	*tă-mă-ră*	tâmara

fig	*fee-gu*	figo
grapes	*u-văsh*	uvas
grapefruit	*tu-rō-zha*	toronja
lemon	*lee-mōw*	limão
loquat	*nesh-p'-răsh*	nêsperas
mandarin	*tă-zh'-ree-nă*	tangerina
melon	*m'-lōw*	melão
mulberries	*ă-moh-răsh*	amoras
orange	*lă-rā-zhă*	laranja
pear	*pe-ră*	pera
plum	*ă-mey-shă*	ameixa
pineapple	*ă-nă-nahsh*	ananás
pomegranate	*rru-mā*	romã
raspberries	*frā-bu-e-săsh*	framboesas
strawberries	*mu-rā-gush*	morangos
watermelon	*m'-lā-see-ă*	melancia

PORTUGUESE

Desserts & Sweets

Arroz-doce	Cinnamon-flavoured rice pudding.
Bolo de amêndoa	Almond cake.
Bolo-rei	A dry, light cake, with dry and crystalised fruits, especially made for Christmas.
Barriga-de-freira, *Encharcada,* *Seric*	These are different types of egg-yolk & sugar-syrup sweets.
Farófias	Egg-white sweet with milk-based sauce.
Leite-creme	Milk-&-egg-yolk sweet with burnt-sugar crust.
Ovos-moles	Egg-yolk-&-sugar sweet, traditionally served in small wooden barrels or in paper-like pastry.
Papos de anjo	Small egg cakes in sugar syrup.

Pastéis de nata	Small custard tarts in puff pastry.	
Pudim flan	Creme caramel.	
Queijadas	Cheese tartlets. Texture and taste vary from region to region.	
Rabanadas	Sweet egg-yolk-and-bread slices, traditionally served with syrup at Christmas.	
Torta de laranja	Light, moist, almost flourless, orange 'Swiss' roll.	
Toucinho do céu	Moist almond and cinnamon cake.	
Trouxas de ovos	Small egg-yolk-and-sugar rolls, cooked and served in syrup.	

Drinks – Nonalcoholic

coffee	*kă-feh*	café
small black	*bee-kă*	bica
long white (cup)	*kă-feh kõ ley-t'*	café com leite
long white (glass)	*gă-lõw*	galão
fruit juice	*su-mu d' fru-tă*	sumo de fruta
milk	*lay-t'*	leite
mineral water	*ah-gwă mee-n'-rahl*	água mineral
sparkling	*kõ gahsh*	com gás
still	*sē gahsh*	sem gás
soft drinks	*rre-fresh-kush*	refrescos
coffee-flavoured syrup & water	*kă-pee-leh*	capilé
tea	*shah*	chá
water	*ah-gwă*	água

Drinks – Alcoholic

beer	*s'r-vey-zhă*	cerveja
port	*vee-nyu du por-tu*	vinho do Porto
wine	*vee-nyu*	vinho

dry	*se-ku*	seco
sparkling	*shpu-mā-t'*	espumante
sweet	*do-s'*	doce

Shopping

How much does it cost?
  kwā-tu kush-tă?   Quanto custa?

general store,	*m'r-see-ă-ree-ă/*	mercearia/
shop	*shahr-ku-tă-ree-ă*	charcutaria
laundry	*lă-vă-dă-ree-ă*	lavandaria
market	*m'r-kah-du/prah-să*	mercado/praça
newsagency/	*pă-p'-lă-ree-ă/*	papelaria/tabacaria
stationers	*tă-bă-kă-ree-ă*	
pharmacy	*făr-mah-see-ă*	farmácia
supermarket	*su-pehr-m'r-kah-du*	supermercado
vegetable shop	*lu-gahr/fru-tă-ree-ă*	lugar/frutaria

I'd like to buy … *k'-ree-ă kõ-prahr …*   Queria comprar …

Do you have others?	*tẽy o-trush?*	Tem outros?
I don't like it.	*nõw gohsh-tu*	Não gosto.
I'm just looking.	*shto soh a ver*	Estou só a ver.

Can you write down the price?
  pu-dee-ă shkr-ver u pre-su?   Podia escrever o preço?

Do you accept credit cards?
  ă-sey-tõw kăr-tõysh d' kreh-dee-tu?   Aceitam cartões de crédito?

PORTUGUESE

PORTUGUESE

You May Hear

Can I help you?

*zhah **shtah** ă-tē-**dee**-du/dă?*	Já está atendido/da?
*d'-**zey**-zhă ahl-**gu**-mă **koy**-ză?*	Deseja alguma coisa?

Will that be all?

*eh **tu**-du?*	É tudo?
*may-zahl-**gu**-mă **koy**-ză?*	Mais alguma coisa?

How much/many do you want?

*kwă-tu/kwă-tush k'-**ree**-ă?*	Quanto/Quantos queria?

Essential Groceries

breakfast cereal	*se-r'-ahl*	cereal
bread	*pōw*	pão
butter	*mahn-tey-gă*	manteiga
cheese	*kay-zhu*	queijo
chocolate	*sho-ko-**lah**-t'*	chocolate
coffee	*kah-**fay***	café
gas cylinder	*bu-zhōw d'gahs*	bujão de gás
ham (cooked/ smoked)	*fiăm-br'/pr's-un-tu*	fiambre/presunto
matches	*fosh-for-osh*	fósforos
milk	*ley-t'*	leite
mineral water	*ah-gwă mee-n'**rahl***	água mineral
shampoo	*shă-**po***	shampô
soap	*să-bu-**ne**-t'*	sabonete
toilet paper	*pă-**pehl** ee-zhee-**eh**-nee-ku*	papel higiénico
toothpaste	*pahsh-tă d' dē-t'sh*	pasta de dentes
sugar	*ă-**soo**-kăr*	açúcar
tea	*shah*	chá
washing powder	*să-**bōw** eng **poh***	sabão em pó
yoghurt	*yoh-**gurt***	iogurte

Souvenirs

cork souvenirs	*ăr-tee-gush d' kur-tee-să*	artigos de cortiça
earthenware	*lo-să d' bah-rru*	louça de barro
hand woven carpets	*tă-pe-t'sh dă-rray-oh-lush*	tapetes de Arraiolos
embroidery from Madeira	*bur-dah-dush dă mă-dey-ră*	bordados da Madeira
'fado' cassettes & records	*kah-seh-t'sh ee deesh-kush d' fah-du*	cassettes e discos de fado
filigree jewellery	*fee-lee-gră-nă*	filigrana
handpainted pottery	*lo-să dahl-ku-bah-să/d'sh-tr'-mosh*	louça de Alcobaça/de Estremoz, etc
lace	*rrē-dăsh*	rendas
leathergoods	*ăr-tee-gush d' kă-b'-dahl*	artigos de cabedal
linen, napery	*ă-tu-ă-lyăh-dush/tu-ah-lyăsh d' me-ză*	atoalhados/toalhas de mesa
painted porcelain roosters	*gah-lush d' băr-seh-lush*	galos de Barcelos
shoes & handbags	*să-pah-tush ee mah-lăsh*	sapatos e malas
tiles	*ă-zu-ley-zhush*	azulejos
windmills	*mu-ee-nyush d'vē-tu*	moinhos de vento

Clothing

clothing	*rro-pă*	roupa
coat (women's)	*kă-zah-ku kō-pree-du*	casaco comprido
coat (men's)	*su-br'-tu-du*	sobretudo
shirt	*kă-mee-ză*	camisa
shoes	*să-pah-tush*	sapatos
trousers	*kahl-săsh*	calças

It is too …
*eh d'mă-zee-**ah**-du* …   É demasiado …

big	*grã-d'*	grande
small	*p'**ke**-nu*	pequeno

PORTUGUESE

Toiletries

condoms	*pr'-z'r-vă-**tee**-vush*	preservativos
deodorant	*d'zo-du-ree-**zā**-t'*	desodorizante
razor	*mah-kee-nă/lă-mee-nă d' băr-bee-**ahr***	máquina/lâmina de barbear
sanitary napkins	*pē-sush ee-zhee-**eh**-nee-kush*	pensos higiénicos
shampoo	*shã-**po***	shampô
shaving cream	*kreh-m'/shpu-mă d' băr-bee-**ahr***	creme/espuma de barbear
soap	*să-bu-**ne**-t'*	sabonete
tissues	*lē-sush d' pă-**pehl***	lenços de papel
toilet paper	*pă-**pehl** ee-zhee-**eh**-nee-ku*	papel higiénico
toothbrush	*shko-vă d' dē-t'sh*	escova de dentes
toothpaste	*pahsh-tă d' dē-t'sh*	pasta de dentes

Photography

How much is it to process this film?
*kwă-tu kush-tă rr'v'-**lahr** esh-t' **rro**-lu?*   Quanto custa revelar este rolo?

When will it be ready?
kwă-du eh k' fee-kă prō-tu?   Quando é que fica pronto?

I'd like a film for this camera.
*k'-**ree**-ă oong **rro**-lu pă-ră ehsh-tă mah-**kee**-nă*   Queria um rolo para esta máquina.

B&W (film)	*ă pre-tu ee brā-ku*	a preto e branco
camera	*mah-kee-nă*	máquina
	fu-tu-grah-fee-kă	fotográfica
colour (film)	*ă ko-r'sh*	a cores
film	*rro-lu*	rolo
flash	*flahsh*	flash
lens	*lē-t'*	lente
light meter	*ing-dee-kă-dor dă lush*	indicador da luz

PORTUGUESE

Smoking

A packet of cigarettes, please.
oong mah-su d' see-gah-rrush, s'fahsh fă-vor
Um maço de cigarros, se faz favor.

Do you have a light?
tēy lu-m'?
Tem lume?

Are these cigarettes strong/ mild?
esh-t'sh see-gah-rrush sõw fohr-t'sh/su-ah-v'sh
Estes cigarros são fortes/ suaves?

Do you mind if I smoke?
vo-sey s'een-ko-mo-dă se e-w fu-mo?
Você si incomoda se eu fumo?

Please don't smoke here.
s'fash fă-vor, nõw fu-mă ă-kee
Se faz favor, não fuma aqui.

cigarettes	*see-gah-rrush*	cigarros
cigarette papers	*pă-pehl dē-rru-lahr*	papel de enrolar
	see-gah-rrush	cigarros
filtered	*kõ feel-tru*	com filtro
lighter	*eesh-key-ru*	isqueiro
matches	*fohsh-fu-rush*	fósforos
menthol	*d' mē-tohl*	de mentol
tobacco	*tă-bah-ku*	tabaco

Health

Where is …?	õ-deh ky ah …?	Onde é que há …?
a doctor	oong **meh**-dee-ku	um médico
a hospital	oong osh-pee-**tahl**	um hospital
a chemist	u-mǎ fǎr-**mah**-see-ǎ	uma farmácia
a dentist	oong dě-**teesh**-tǎ	um dentista

What's the matter?
d' k' s'key-shǎ?
De que se queixa?

I am ill.
shto du-ē-t'
Estou doente.

My friend is ill.
u **me-w** ǎ-**mee**-gu/ǎ **mee**-nyǎ ǎ-**mee**-gǎ **shtah** du-ē-t'
O meu amigo/A minha amiga está doente.

Where does it hurt?
õ-**deh** k' ly' **doy**?
Onde é que lhe dói?

It hurts here.
doy-m' ǎ-**kee**
Dói-me aqui.

Parts of the Body

arm	**brah**-su	braço
back	**kohsh**-tǎsh	costas
ear	o-**re**-lyǎ	orelha
eye	**o**-lyu	olho
foot	peh	pé
hand	**mõw**	mão
head	kǎ-**be**-sǎ	cabeça
heart	ku-rǎ-**sõw**	coração
leg	**pehr**-nǎ	perna
mouth	**bo**-kǎ	boca
nose	nǎ-**reesh**	nariz
stomach	**shto**-mǎ-gu	estômago

Ailments

I have …
te-nyu …   Tenho …

an allergy	*u-mah-lehr-**gee**-ă*	uma alergia
a cold	*u-mă kōsh-tee-pă-sōw*	uma constipação
constipation	*pree-zōw d' vē-tr'*	prisão de ventre
diarrhoea	*dee-ă-**rrey**-ă*	diarreia
fever	*feh-br'*	febre
a headache	*u-mă dor d' kă-be-să*	uma dor de cabeça
indigestion	*ing-dee-zh'sh-tōw*	indigestão
influenza	*gree-p'*	gripe
low/high blood pressure	*ă tē-sōw bay-shă/ ahl-tă*	a tensão baixa/alta
nausea	*now-zee-ă/voh-mee-tush*	náusea/vómitos
a pain	*u-mă dor*	uma dor
sore throat	*dor d' găr-gā-tă*	dor de garganta
sprain	*u-ma tur-sōw mush-ku-lahr*	uma torsão muscular
a stomachache	*dor d'sh-to-mă-gu*	dor de estômago
sunburn	*u-mă key-mă-du-ră du sohl*	uma queimadura do sol
a toothache	*dor d' dē-t'sh*	dor de dentes
a venereal disease	*u-mă du-»e-să v'-neh-ree-ă*	uma doença venérea

PORTUGUESE

Women's Health

Could I see a female doctor?
*pr'-f'-**ree**-ă u-mă **meh**-dee-kă*   Preferia uma médica.

PORTUGUESE

I'm pregnant.
   shto grah-vee-dǎ   Estou grávida.
I'm on the pill.
   e-w toh-mu ǎ pee-lu-lǎ   Eu tomo a pílula.
I haven't had my period for
… weeks.
   ah … s'-mǎ-nǎsh k'nõw m'   Há … semanas que não me
   vẽy ǎ mẽsh-tru-ǎ-sõw   vem a menstruação.

(unusual) bleeding	*sǎn-gree-ǎ*	sangria
	ex-sep-see-o-nǎl	(excepcional)
cramps	*kǎ-ee-brǎsh*	cãibras
cystitis	*si-stee-te*	cistite
thrush	*in-fek-sõw va-jin-ǎl*	infecção vaginal

Specific Needs
I'm …
   so …   Sou …

asthmatic	*azh-mah-tee-ku/ǎ*	asmático/a
diabetic	*dee-ǎ-beh-tee-ku/ǎ*	diabético/a
epileptic	*e-pee-leh-tee-ku/ǎ*	epiléptico/a

I'm allergic to …
   so ǎ-lehr-gee-ku/-ǎ ǎ …   Sou alérgico/a a …

antibiotics	*ǎ-tee-bee-oh-tee-kush*	antibióticos
penicillin	*ah peh-nee-see-lee-nǎa*	à penicilina

I have been vaccinated.
   fuy vǎ-cee-nah-du/ǎ-a   Fui vacinado/a.
I have my own syringe.
   te-nyu ǎ mee-nyǎ proh-   Tenho a minha própria
   pree-ǎ s'-ring-gǎ   seringa.

Useful Words & Phrases

I feel better/worse.

sing-tu-m' m'-lyohr/pee-ohr Sinto-me melhor/pior.

accident	*ă-see-dē-t'*	acidente
addiction	*vee-see-u*	vício
antiseptic	*ā-tee-seh-tee-ku*	antisséptico
blood test	*ă-nah-lee-z' d' sā-g'*	análise de sangue
contraceptive	*ā-tee-kō-seh-see-u-nahl*	anticoncepcional
medicine	*rr'-meh-dee-u/*	remédio/
	m'-dee-kă-mē-tu	medicamento
vitamins	*vee-tă-mee-năsh*	vitaminas

PORTUGUESE

At the Chemist

I need medication for …

pr'-see-zu doong m'-dee-kă- Preciso dum medicamento
mē-tu pă-ră … para …

I have a prescription.

te-nyu rr'-sey-tă Tenho receita médica.
meh-dee-kă

At the Dentist

I have a toothache.

doy-m' oong dē-t' Dói-me um dente.

I've lost a filling.

kă-eew-m' oong shoong-bu Caiu-me um chumbo.

I've broken a tooth.

păr-tee oong dē-t' Parti um dente.

I don't want it extracted.

nōw keh-ru k' mu ă-rrā-k' Não quero que mo arranque.

Please give me an anaesthetic.

de-mă-n'sh-t'-zee-ă, Dê-me anestesia, se faz
s' fahsh fă-vor favor.

PORTUGUESE

Time & Dates

What time is it?
ky-oh-răsh sōw?
                                         Que horas são?

What date is it today?
k' dee-ă eh o-zh?
                                         Que dia é hoje?

It is … am/pm.
sōw … oh-răsh dă   São … horas da manhã/da
mă-nyā/dă tahr-d'   tarde.

in the morning	*d' ma-nyā*	de manhã
in the afternoon	*d' tahr-d'/ah tahr-d'*	de tarde/à tarde
in the evening	*ow fing dă tahr-d'/*	ao fim da tarde/
	ah noy-t'	à noite

Days of the Week

Monday	*s'-goong-dă fey-ră*	Segunda-feira
Tuesday	*ter-să fey-ră*	Terça-feira
Wednesday	*kwahr-tă fey-ră*	Quarta-feira
Thursday	*king-tă fey-ră*	Quinta-feira
Friday	*seysh-tă fey-ră*	Sexta-feira
Saturday	*sah-bă-du*	Sábado
Sunday	*du-ming-gu*	Domingo

Months

January	*zhă-ney-ru*	Janeiro
February	*f'-v'-rey-ru*	Fevereiro
March	*mahr-su*	Março
April	*ă-breel*	Abril
May	*may-u*	Maio
June	*zhu-nyu*	Junho
July	*zhu-lyu*	Julho
August	*ă-gosh-tu*	Agosto
September	*s'-tē-bru*	Setembro

October	*o-**tu**-bru*	Outubro
November	*nu-**vē**-bru*	Novembro
December	*d'-**zē**-bru*	Dezembro

Seasons

summer	*v'-**rõw***	verão
autumn	*o-**to**-nu*	outono
winter	*ing-**vehr**-nu*	inverno
spring	*pree-mă-**veh**-ră*	primavera

Present

today	*o-zh*	hoje
this morning	*o-zh d' mă-**nyã***	hoje de manhã
tonight	*o-zh ah **noy**-t'*	hoje à noite
this week	*ehsh-tă s'-**mă**-nă*	esta semana
this year	*esh-ty ănu*	este ano
now	*ă-**goh**-ră*	agora

Past

yesterday	*õ-tēy*	ontem
day before yesterday	*ā-tee-õ-tēy*	anteontem
last night	*õ-tēy ah **noy**-t'*	ontem à noite
(two) days ago	***ah (doysh) dee**-ăsh*	há (dois) dias

Future

tomorrow	*ah-mă-**nyã***	amanhã
day after tomorrow	*d'-**poysh** dah-mă-**nyã***	depois de amanhã
in (two) days	*dē-tru d' (**doysh**) dee-ăsh*	dentro de (dois) dias
next week	*nă **proh**-see-mă s'-**mă**-nă*	na próxima semana

PORTUGUESE

During the Day

afternoon	*tahr*-d'	tarde
day	*dee*-ă	dia
midnight	*mey*-ă *noy*-t'	meia-noite
morning	mă-*nyă*	manhã
night	*noy*-t'	noite
noon	*mey*-u *dee*-ă	meio-dia
sundown	*por* du *sohl*	pôr do sol
sunrise	năsh-ser du *sohl*/	nascer do sol/
	mă-dru-*gah*-dă	madrugada

Numbers & Amounts

1	*oong*/*u*-mă	um/uma
2	*doysh*/*du*-ăsh	dois/duas
3	tresh	três
4	*kwah*-tru	quatro
5	*sing*-ku	cinco
6	seysh	seis
7	*seh*-t'	sete
8	*oy*-tu	oito
9	*noh*-v'	nove
10	dehsh	dez
11	* õ*-z'	onze
12	*do*-z'	doze
13	*tre*-z'	treze
14	kă-*tor*-z'	catorze
15	*king*-z'	quinze
16	d'-ză-*seysh*	dezasseis
17	d'-ză-*seh*-t'	dezassete
18	d'-*zoy*-tu	dezoito
19	d'-ză-*noh*-v'	dezanove
20	*ving*-t'	vinte

100	*sēy*	cem
1000	*meel*	mil
one million	*oong mee-lyōw d'*	um milhão de

Amounts

small	*p'ke-nu*	pequeno
big	*grã-d'*	grande
more	*maysh*	mais
less	*me-nush*	menos
few	*po-kush/po-kăsh*	poucos/as
some	*ahl-goongsh/ahl-gu-măsh*	alguns/algumas
too much/ many	*d'-maysh/d'-mă-zee-ah-dush*	demais/demasiados
a little (amount)	*oong po-ku/oong bu-kă-dee-nyu*	um pouco/um bocadinho
Enough!	*bahsh-tă! she-gă!*	Basta! Chega!

PORTUGESE

Abbreviations

AD/a.C.	AD/BC
AE (auto-estrada)	freeway
B.I. (Bilhete de Identidade)	ID (Identity card)
B.T.	Traffic Police
CP	Portuguese Trains
D°	right-hand side (used in flat addresses)
Esq°	left-hand side (used in flat addresses)
IVA	VAT (value-added tax)
Pr.	town square (used in adresses)
PSP	Police (cities)
R.	Street (used in addresses)
r/c	ground floor

PORTUGUESE

Paperwork

name/surname	nome/apelido
address	morada/direcção
date of birth	data de nascimento
place of birth	lugar de nascimento
age	idade
nationality	nacionalidade
religion	religião
reason for travel	motivo da viagem
profession	profissão
marital status	estado civil
passport	passaporte
passport number	número do passaporte
visa	visa/visto
tourist card	cartão de turista
identification	documento/bilhete de identidade
birth certificate	certidão de nascimento
driver's licence	carta de condução
car owner's title	livrete/documentos do carro
car registration	matrícula do carro
customs	alfândega
immigration	imigração
border	fronteira

Emergencies

POLICE	*POLÍCIA*
POLICE STATION	*ESQUADRA DA POLÍCIA*

Help!	*su-ko-rru!*	Socorro!
Go away!	*dey-sh'-mĕ pahsh!*	Deixe-me em paz!
Thief!	*lă-drŏw!*	Ladrão!

Call the police!
shă-mă pu-lee-see-ă!
Chame a polícia!

Call a doctor!
shă-m' oong meh-dee-ku!
Chame um médico!

Call an ambulance!
shă-mu-mă-bu-lă-see-ă!
Chame uma ambulância!

There's been an accident!
o-v' oong ă-see-dē-t'!
Houve um acidente!

I've been raped.
fuy vee-u-lah-dă/vee-u-lah-rŏw-m'
Fui violada/Violaram-me.

I've been robbed.
fuy rro-bah-du/-dă
Fui roubado/a.

I am ill.
shto du-ē-t'
Estou doente.

I am lost.
shto p'r-dee-du/-dă
Estou perdido/a.

Where is the police station?
õ-dy eh ă sh-kwah-dră dă pu-lee-see-ă?
Onde é a esquadra da polícia?

Where are the toilets?
õ-dy eh ă kah-ză d' bă-nyu?
Onde é a casa de banho?

Could you help me please?
ing-pohr-tă-s' d' mă-zhu-dahr?
Importa-se de me ajudar?

Could I please use the telephone?
poh-su t'l'fu-nahr?
Posso telefonar?

I'm sorry. I apologise.
  *d'sh-**kul**-p' . p'r-**dõw***

Desculpe. Perdão.

I didn't realise I was doing anything wrong.
  *nõw să-**bee**-ă k'**shtah**-vă ă fă-**zer** mahl*

Não sabia que estava a fazer mal.

I didn't do it.
  *e-w nõw fee-**zee**-su*

Eu não fiz isso.

I wish to contact my embassy/consulate.
  keh-ru fă-**lahr** kõ ă **mee**-nya ẽ-bay-**shah**-dă/kõ u **me**-w kõ-su-**lah**-du*

Quero falar com a minha embaixada/o meu consulado.

I speak English.
  fah-lu ing-**glesh***

Falo Inglês.

I have medical insurance.
  *te-nyu s'**gu**-ru meh-**dee**-ku*

Tenho seguro médico.

My possessions are insured.
  *te-nyu s'**gu**-ru (kõ-tră **rro**-bu)*

Tenho seguro (contra roubo).

My … was stolen.
  *rro-bah-**rõw**-m' u/ă …*

Roubaram-me o/a …

I've lost …
  *p'r-**dee** …*

Perdi …

my bags	*ăsh **mah**-lăsh*	as malas
my handbag	*ă **mah**-lăă/ăă kăr-**tey**-ră*	a mala/a carteira
my money	*u dee-**nyey**-ru*	o dinheiro
my travellers' cheques	*ush me-w-sh sheh-k'sh d' vee-**ah**-gẽy*	os meus cheques de viagem
my passport	*u pah-să-**pohr**-t'*	o passaporte

SCOTTISH

SCOTTISH

Scottish Gaelic

Introduction

Scottish Gaelic (Gàidhlig) is spoken by about 80,000 people in Scotland, mainly in the Highlands and Islands, and by many native speakers and learners overseas. It is a member of the Celtic branch of the Indo–European family of languages which has given us Gaelic, Irish, Manx, Welsh, Cornish and Breton. Although it is the Celtic language most closely associated with Scotland it was quite a latecomer to those shores. Other Celtic languages in the form of Pictish and Brittonic had existed prior to the arrival and settlement by Gaelic–speaking Celts (Gaels) from Ireland from the fourth to the sixth centuries AD. These Irish settlers, known to the Romans as Scotti, were eventually to give their name to the entire country. Initially they settled in the area on the west coast of Scotland in which their name is perpetuated, Earra Ghaidheal (Argyll). As their territorial influence extended so did their language and from the ninth to the 11th centuries Gaelic was spoken throughout the country. For many centuries the language was the same as the language of Ireland; there is little evidence of much divergence before the 13th century. Even up to the 18th century the bards adhered to the strict literary standards of Old Irish.

The Viking invasions from 800 AD brought linguistic influences which are evident in many of the coastal placenames of the Highlands.

Gaelic culture flourished in the Highlands until the 18th century and the Jacobite rebellions. After the Battle of Culloden in 1746 many Gaelic speakers were forced from their ancestral lands; this 'ethnic cleansing' by landlords and governments culminating in the Highland Clearances of the 19th century. Although still studied at the academic level, the spoken language declined, being regarded as a mere 'peasant' language of no modern significance.

It was only in the 1970s that Gaelic began to make a come-back with a new generation of young enthusiasts who were determined that it should not be allowed to die. People from all over Scotland, and indeed worldwide, are beginning to appreciate their Gaelic heritage.

After two centuries of decline, the language is now being encouraged with financial help from government agencies and the EU. Gaelic education is flourishing from playgroups to tertiary levels. This renaissance flows out into the field of music, literature, cultural activities, and broadcasting.

The Gaelic language has a vital role to play in the life of modern Scotland.

The usual word order in Gaelic is verb–subject–object. There are two forms of the pronoun 'you' in Gaelic – the singular *thu*, and the plural form *sibh* which is also used as a formal singular. We use the informal *thu* in these phrases.

Some English Words Borrowed from Gaelic

bard	*baard*	bard – a poet
ben	*beh–een*	beinn – a hill
bog	*bohk*	bog – soft, wet
brogue	*bro–ck*	bròg – a shoe
caber	*cap–er*	cabar – a pole
claymore	*cly–af mor*	claidheamh mòr – a big sword
dune	*doo–n*	dùn – a heap

galore	*gu lyor*	gu leòr – plenty
loch	*loch*	loch
Sassenach	*Sasunach*	Sasannach – an Englishman
sporran	*sporan*	sporan – a purse
strath	*strah*	strath – a mountain valley

Pronunciation

Stress usually falls on the first syllable of a word. The Gaelic alphabet has only 18 letters:

Vowels

There are five vowels: a, e, i, o and u.

a, o, u are known as broad vowels
e, i are known as slender vowels

Vowel sounds can be lengthened by being marked with a grave accent.

bata (a stick) *bàta* (a boat)

Consonants

There are 12 consonants: b, c, d, f, g, l, m, n, p, r, s, t, and the letter h (only used to change other sounds).

Consonants may be pronounced in different ways depending on the vowel beside them. The spelling rule in Gaelic is 'broad to broad and slender to slender'. This means that if, in a word, a consonant is preceded by a broad vowel it must be followed by a broad vowel, and if it is preceded by a slender vowel it must be followed by a slender vowel. Consequently, we speak about broad consonants and slender consonants.

balach (a boy) *caileag* (a girl)

- Broad consonants sound approximately as in English.
- Slender consonants are often followed by a 'y' sound.

c	always a hard 'k' sound ; never an 's' sound
d	when broad, thicker than English 'd'; when slender, sound as 'j' in 'jet'
l, ll	when slender, as 'l' in 'value'
n, nn	when slender, as 'n' in 'new'
s	when slender, as 'sh'
t	when broad, thicker than English 't'; when slender as 'ch' in 'chin'

When consonants are followed by 'h', a change of sound occurs:

bh mh	as 'v'
ch	when broad, as 'loch' (not lock!)
	when slender, as the German 'ich'
dh gh	when broad, it is voiced at back of the throat
	when slender, as 'y' – there is no English equivalent
fh	silent
ph	as 'f'
sh	as 'h' before a broad vowel
th	as 'h'

There are a number of Gaelic sounds, especially vowel combinations and consonantal changes brought about by the addition of the letter **h**, which cannot be reproduced satisfactorily in English. The help of a native speaker is invaluable for these.

Greetings & Civilities

Good morning.	*madding va*	Madainn mhath.
Good afternoon/ evening.	*fesskurr ma*	Feasgar math.
Good night.	*uh–eech–uh va*	Oidhche mhath.

SCOTTISH GAELIC

How are you?	*kimmer uh ha oo?*	Ciamar a tha thu?
Very well, thank you.	*gley va, tappuh let*	Glè mhath, tapadh leat.
I'm well, thank you.	*ha mee goo ma, tappuh let*	Tha mi gu math, tapadh leat.
That's good.	*sma shin*	'S math sin.

Please.	*mahs eh doh hawl eh*	Mas e do thoil e.
Thank you.	*tappuh let*	Tapadh leat.
Many thanks.	*moe–ran ta–eeng*	Mòran taing.
You're welcome.	*sheh doh veh–huh*	'Se do bheatha.
I beg you pardon.	*baaluv*	B'àill leibh.
Excuse me.	*gav mo lishk–yal*	Gabh mo leisgeul.
I'm sorry.	*ha mee dooleech*	Tha mi duilich.

Small Talk

Do you speak (have) Gaelic?	*uh vil ga–lick ackut*	A bheil Gàidhlig agad?
Yes, a little.	*ha, beg–an*	Tha, beagan.
Not much.	*chan yil moe–ran*	Chan eil mòran.

What is your name?	*jae an tannam uh ha orsht?*	De an t-ainm a tha ort?
Who are you?	*coe oosuh?*	Co thusa?
I am ...	*is meeshuh ..*	Is mise ...
Good health! (Cheers!)	*slahntchuh va*	Slàinte mhath!

SCOTTISH GAELIC

Goodbye. (lit: Blessings go
with you)
   B–yan–achd let   Beannachd leat.
Goodbye. (The same with you)
   mar shin let   Mar sin leat.

Signs & Placenames

TOURIST INFORMATION CENTRE	*IONAD–FIOSRACHAIDH LUCHD–TURAIS*
WELCOME!	*FAILTE!*
A HUNDRED THOUSAND WELCOMES!	*CEUD MILE FAILTE!*
WELCOME TO ...	*FAILTE GU ...*
INVERNESS	*INBHIR NIS*
PORTREE	*PORTRIGH*
STORNOWAY	*STEORNABHAGH*
WESTERN ISLES COUNCIL	*COMHAIRLE NAN EILEAN*
STREET	*SRAID*
BANK STREET	*SRAID A' BHANCA*
CHURCH STREET	*SRAID NA H–EAGLAISE*
THE BANK	*AM BANCA*
BANK OF SCOTLAND	*BANCA NA H–ALBA*
TELEPHONE	*FON*
CINEMA	*TAIGH–DHEALBH*
TOILET	*TAIGH BEAG*
THE SHOPS	*NA BUTHAN*
TOWN CENTRE	*MEADHAN A ' BHAILE*
SCHOOL	*SGOIL*
THE NEWSAGENT'S	*BUTH NAM PAIPEARAN*

SCOTTISH GAELIC

SCOTTISH GAELIC

THE BAKER	AM FUINEADAIR
THE CHURCH	AN EAGLAIS
THE CHURCH OF SCOTLAND	EAGLAIS NA H–ALBA
LIBRARY	LEABHAR LANN
SWIMMING POOL	AMAR SNAMH

Useful Phrases

Weather

It's warm today.	*ha eh blah un joo*	Tha e blàth an diugh.
It's cold today.	*ha eh foo–ur un joo*	Tha e fuar an diugh.
The day is beautiful.	*ha un la bree–a–uh*	Tha an latha brèagha.
It's wet.	*ha e flooch*	Tha e fliuch.
It's raining.	*ha un tooshku a–woon*	Tha an t–uisge ann.
It's misty.	*ha k–yaw a–woon*	Tha ceò ann.
Has the rain stopped?	*un daw skoor un tooshku*	An do sguir an t–uisge?

Travel & Accommodation

Can you tell me ...?
 un yee–ish oo ghoe ...?   An innis thu dhomh ...?

I want to go to ...
 ha mee ug–ee–urry uh gholl goo ...   Tha mi ag iarraidh a dhol gu ...

How do I get to ...?
 kimmer uh yaev mee goo ...?   Ciamar a gheibh mi gu ...?

by bus	*ir uh vuss*	air a' bhus
by train	*ir un tren*	air an trean
by car	*a–woon un car*	ann an car

THE STATION	AN STEISEAN
THE BUS	AM BUS
THE TRAIN	AN TREANA
THE PLANE	AM PLEAN
TAXI	TACSAIDH
THE AIRPORT	AM PORT ADHAR
THE FERRY	AN AISEAG
THE BOAT	AM BATA

a hotel	*tuh–ee awstu*	taigh òsda
a bedroom	*roowm caddil*	rùm cadail
a toilet	*tuh–ee beck*	taigh beag

| BED & BREAKFAST | LEABAIDH 'S BRACAIST |
| HOTEL | TAIGH–OSDA |

SCOTTISH GAELIC

Food

food & drink	*bee–ugh agus joch*	biadh agus deoch
I'm hungry.	*ha an tac–russ orrom*	Tha an t–acras orm.
I'm thirsty.	*ha am pah–ugh orrom*	Tha am pathadh orm.
I want ...	*ha mee ug ee–uhree*	Tha mi ag iarraidh ...
I'd like ...	*boo tawl lehum*	Bu toigh leam ...
I don't like ...	*chah tawl lehum*	Cha toigh leam ...
That was good.	*va shood ma*	Bha siud math.
Very good.	*gley va*	Glè mhath.

a biscuit	*briskatch*	brioscaid
apple juice	*sooh ooh–al*	sùgh ubhal
bread	*aran*	aran
broth, soup	*broht*	brot
butter	*eem*	ìm

SCOTTISH GAELIC

cheese	*kashuh*	càise
cream	*baahrr*	bàrr
dessert	*meehlshuhn*	mìlsean
fish	*eeusk*	iasg
meat	*fehyawl*	feòil
oatcakes	*aran korkuh*	aran coirce
orange juice	*sooh awhrinsh*	sùgh orains
peas	*pessir*	peasair
porridge	*lee–chuh*	lite
potatoes	*boontahtuh*	buntàta
salmon	*brahdan*	bradan
vegetables	*glasreech*	glasraich

Drinks

a cup of coffee	*coopa cawfee*	cupa cofaidh
a cup of tea	*coopa tee*	cupa tì
black coffee	*cawfee dooh*	cofaidh dubh
black tea	*tee dhooh*	tì dhubh
with milk	*le bainne*	leh bahnyuh
with sugar	*leh shooh–car*	le siùcar
a drink of milk	*joch vahnyuh*	deoch bhainne
a glass of water	*glahnyuh ooshkuy*	glainne uisge
a glass of wine	*glahnyuh feeuhn*	glainne fìon
beer	*lyawn*	leann
red wine	*feeuhn jerrack*	fìon dearg
white wine	*feeuhn gyahl*	fìon geal
whisky	*ooshkuy–beh–huh*	uisge–beatha

SPANISH

SPANISH

Spanish

Introduction

Spanish, or Castilian, as it is often and more precisely called, is the most widely spoken of the Romance languages. Outside Spain, it is the language of all of South America, except Brazil and the Guianas; of Mexico, Central America, and most of the West Indies; and, to some extent, of the Philippines and Guam, as well as of some areas of the African coast and in the USA. In Spain itself, three Romance languages are spoken: Castilian (the main one) in the north, centre and south; Catalan, in the east and south-east; and Galician (a dialect of Portuguese), in the north-west. There is another language, of obscure, non-Latin origin: Basque, spoken in the north-east. Castilian, or Spanish, covers the largest territory. Within Spanish there are yet three dialectal divisions (Castilian-Andalusian, Leonese-Asturian, and Navarro-Aragonese), but these involve mainly differences in pronunciation and need not be considered separately here. The other main Romance language in the Peninsula is, of course, Portuguese.

Spanish is the neo-Latin language derived from the Vulgar Latin which Roman soldiers and merchants brought to the Iberian Peninsula during the period of the Roman conquest (3rd to 1st century BC). By 19 BC Spain had become totally Roman, and popular Latin became the language of the Peninsula in the four centuries of Romanisation which followed. Latin completely obliterated the languages of the Celtic and Iberian indigenous tribes.

In 711 AD an African Berber army invaded the Peninsula.

Soon many more Arabs came from the African Maghreb, and it was not until the 9th century that the reconquest of Spain began, led by the Christians who had taken refuge in the mountains of the north. As the reconquest advanced southwards, the Latin spoken by those Christians was progressively brought back to central and, eventually, southern Spain. Although the Arabs were not completely driven from the south for centuries yet, and although many people spoke Arabic as well as Vulgar Latin during that period, the influence of the Arabic language on Spanish is limited to vocabulary innovations.

With Columbus's discovery of the New World in 1492 began an era of Spanish expansion in America, which is reflected in the language. *Patata, tomate, cacao* and *chocolate* are a few examples of accretions from the American Indian languages. But fundamentally Spanish lexicon, syntax, phonology and morphology has always remained neo-Latin.

Spanish literature begins in the 12th century with the famous epic poem *Cantar de mío Cid*. Cervantes's 17th century *Don Quijote* is universally known. Nowadays Spain has an equally thriving literature, some of which is available in English translation – although not as much as that of the celebrated Latin American boom. Novelists such as Ana María Matute, Carmen Martín Gaite, Juan Goytisolo, Miguel Delibes and the 1989 Nobel Prize winner, José Camilo Cela, have had some of their works translated into English, and these will give visitors a valuable insight into contemporary Spanish society.

Gender

In this chapter the masculine form of a word appears first, separated from the feminine ending by a slash.

SPANISH

Pronunciation

Pronunciation of Spanish is not difficult, given that many Spanish sounds are similar to their English counterparts, and there is a clear and consistent relationship between pronunciation and spelling. If you stick to the following rules you should have very few problems being understood.

Vowels

Unlike English, each of the vowels in Spanish has a uniform pronunciation which does not vary. For example, the Spanish 'a' has one pronunciation rather than the numerous pronunciations in English, such as the 'a's in 'cake', 'art' and 'all'. Vowels are pronounced clearly even in unstressed positions or at the end of a word.

a	as the 'u' in 'nut', or a shorter sound than the 'a' in 'art'; represented in our pronunciation guide by *ah*
e	as the 'e' in 'met'
i	similar to the 'i' sound in 'marine' but not so drawn out or strong; between that sound and that of the 'i' in 'flip'
o	similar to the 'o' in 'hot'
u	as the 'oo' in 'fool'

Consonants

Some Spanish consonants are the same as their English counterparts. Pronunciation of other consonants varies according to which vowel follows, and also according to what part of Spain you're in. The Spanish alphabet also contains three consonants which are not found in the English alphabet: **ch**, **ll** and **ñ**.

b	when initial, or preceded by a nasal, as the 'b' in 'book'; elsewhere, and most often in Spanish, a much softer **b** than the English one

SPANISH

c	a hard 'c' as in 'cat' when followed by **a**, **o**, **u** or a consonant; as the 'th' in 'thin' before **e** or **i**
ch	as the 'ch' in 'choose'
d	in an initial position, as the 'd' in 'dog'; elsewhere as the 'th' in 'then', represented here by *TH*
g	in an initial position, as the 'g' in 'gate' before **a**, **o** and **u**; everywhere else, the Spanish **g** is much softer than the English one. Before **e** or **i** it is a harsh, breathy sound, similar to the 'h' in 'hit'.
h	never pronounced, silent
j	a harsh, guttural sound similar to the 'ch' in the Scottish 'loch', represented here by *h*.
ll	as the 'lli' in 'million'; some people pronounce it rather like the 'y' in 'yellow'; represented here by *ly*
ñ	this is a nasal sound like the 'ni' in 'onion', represented here by *ny*
q	as the 'k' in 'kick'; **q** is always followed by a silent **u** and is only combined with **e** as in *que* and **i** as in *qui*
r	a rolled 'r' sound; a longer and stronger sound when it is a double **rr** or when a word begins with **r**
s	as the 's' in 'send'
v	the same sound as **b**
x	as the 'ks' in 'taxi',when between two vowels; as the 's' in 'say' when the **x** precedes a consonant
z	as the 'th' in 'thin'

Semiconsonant

y	pronounced as the Spanish **i** when it is at the end of a word or when it stands alone as a conjunction. As a consonant, its sound is somewhere between 'y' in 'yonder' and 'g' in 'beige', depending on the region.

SPANISH

Stress

Words stress usually falls on the second-last syllable of a word. An acute accent in a syllable, however, indicates that the stress falls on that syllable.

Greetings & Civilities

Top Useful Phrases

Hello.	*o-lah!*	¡Hola!
Goodbye.	*ah-THios!*	¡Adiós!
Yes/No.	*si/no*	Sí/No.
Excuse me.	*per-**mi**-so*	Permiso.
Please.	*por fah-**bor***	Por favor.
Thank you.	*grah-thiahs*	Gracias.
Many thanks.	*moo-chahs/*	Muchas/
	*moo-**chi**-si-mahs*	Muchísimas
	grah-thi-ahs	gracias.
That's fine.	*de **nah**-THah*	De nada.
You're welcome.		

May I? Do you mind?
  *pwe-THo?/me per-**mi**-te?* ¿Puedo?/¿Me permite?
Sorry. (excuse me, forgive me)
  *lo **sien**-to/dis-**kool**-pe-me/* Lo siento. Discúlpeme.
  *per-**THo**-ne-me* Perdóneme.

Greetings

Good morning.	*bwe-nos **THi**-ahs*	Buenos días.
Good afternoon.	*bwe-nahs **tahr**-THes*	Buenas tardes.
Good evening/	*bwe-nahs **no**-ches*	Buenas noches.
night.		
How are you?	*ko-mo es-**tah**?*	¿Cómo está?
	ke tahl?	¿Qué tal?
Well, thanks.	*bien, grah-thiahs*	Bien, gracias.

Forms of Address

Madam/Mrs	se-**nyo**-rah/**do**-nya	Señora/Doña
Sir/Mr	se-**nyor**/don	Señor/Don
Miss	se-nyo-**ri**-tah	Señorita
companion	kom-pah-**nye**-ro/ah	compañero/a
friend	ah-**mi**-go/ah	amigo/a

Language Difficulties

Do you speak English?
*ah-blah in-**gles**?*
¿Habla inglés?

Does anyone speak English?
*ahy **ahl**-gien ke ah-**ble** in-**gles**?*
¿Hay alguien que hable inglés?

I speak a little Spanish.
*ah-blo oon po-**ki**-to de kahs-te-**lyah**-no/es-pah-**nyol***
Hablo un poquito de castellano/español.

I don't speak …
*no ah-**blo** …*
No hablo …

I (don't) understand.
*(no) en-**tien**-do*
(No) Entiendo.

Could you speak more slowly please?
*pwe-THe ah-**blahr** mahs des-**pah**-thio, por fah-**bor**?*
¿Puede hablar más despacio, por favor?

Could you repeat that?
*pwe-THe rre-pe-**tir**-lo?*
¿Puede repetirlo?

How do you say …?
*ko-mo se **di**-the …?*
¿Cómo se dice …?

What does … mean?
*ke si-gni-**fi**-kah …?*
¿Qué significa …?

Small Talk
Meeting People

What is your name?
*ko-mo se **lyah**-mah
oos-te**TH**?*

¿Cómo se llama usted?

My name is …
*me **lyah**-mo …*

Me llamo …

I'd like to introduce you to …
*ki-sie-rah pre-sen-**tahr**-le
ah …*

Quisiera presentarle a …

I'm pleased to meet you.
***moo**-cho **goos**-to*

Mucho gusto.

Where are you from?
*de **THon**-de es oos-te**TH**?*

¿De dónde es usted?

Nationalities

Many country names in Spanish are very similar to English, and
you should be OK if you say your country according to Spanish
pronunciation (eg Japan; *hah-pon*). Here a few that differ.

I am from …	*soy THe …*	Soy de …
England	*in-glah-**te**-rrah*	Inglaterra
Germany	*ah-le-**mah**-niah*	Alemania
Holland	*los pah-is-es **ba**-hos*	los Paises Bajos
Ireland	*ir-**lahn**-dah*	Irlanda
New Zealand	*nwe-bah the-**lahn**-diah/the-**lahn**-dah*	Nueva Zelandia/ Zelanda
Scotland	*es-**ko**-thiah*	Escocia
South America	*soo-THah-**me**-ri-kah*	Sudamérica
the USA	*los es-**tah**-THos oo-ni-**THos***	Los Estados Unidos
Wales	*pah-is THe **gah**-les*	País de Gales

SPANISH

Age

How old are you?
   kwahn-tos ah-nyos tie-ne? ¿Cuántos años tiene?
I am … years old.
   ten-go … ah-nyos Tengo … años.

Occupations

What do you do?
   ke ah-the oos-teTH? ¿Qué hace usted?

I am a/an …	*soy …*	Soy …
artist	*ahr-tis-tah*	artista
business person	*ko-mer-thi-ahn-te*	comerciante
doctor	*dok-tor/-ah,*	doctor/a,
	me-di-ko/-ah	médico/a
engineer	*in-he-nie-ro/-ah*	ingeniero/a
factory worker	*o-bre-ro/-ah*	obrero/a
farmer	*ah-gri-cool-tor/-ah,*	agricultor/a,
	grahn-he-ro/-ah	granjero/a
journalist	*pe-ri-o-THis-tah*	periodista
lawyer	*ah-bo-gah-THo/-ah*	abogado/a
manual worker	*o-bre-ro/ah,*	obrero/a,
	trah-bah-hah-dor/-ah	trabajador/a
mechanic	*me-kah-ni-ko/-ah*	mecánico/a
nurse	*en-fer-me-ro/-ah*	enfermero/a
office worker	*o-fi-thi-nis-tah,*	oficinista,
	em-ple-ah-do/-ah	empleado/a
scientist	*thien-ti-fi-ko/-ah*	científico/a
student	*es-tu-THi-ahn-te*	estudiante
teacher	*pro-fe-sor/-ah*	profesor/a
waiter	*kah-mah-re-ro/-ah*	camarero/a
writer	*es-kri-tor/-ah*	escritor/a

SPANISH

Religion

What is your religion?
kwahl es soo rre-li-hion?   ¿Cuál es su religión?

I am not religious.
no soy rre-li-hi-o-so/ah   No soy religioso/a.

I am …	*soy …*	Soy …
Buddhist	*bu-THis-tah*	budista
Catholic	*kah-to-li-ko/-ah*	católico/a
Christian	*kris-ti-ah-no/-ah*	cristiano/a
Hindu	*in-doo*	hindú
Jewish	*hoo-THi-o/-ah*	judío/a
Muslim	*moo-sool-mahn/-ah*	musulm n/a

Family

Are you married?
es kah-sah-THo/-ah?   ¿Es casado/a?

I am single.
soy sol-te-ro/-ah   Soy soltero/a.

I am married.
soy kah-sah-THo/-ah   Soy casado/a.

How many children do you have?
kwahn-tos i-hos tie-ne?   ¿Cuántos hijos tiene?

I don't have any children.
no ten-go i-hos   No tengo hijos.

I have a daughter/a son.
ten-go oo-nah i-hah/oon i-ho   Tengo una hija/un hijo.

How many brothers/sisters do you have?
kwahn-tos/-ahs er-mah-nos/-ahs tie-ne?   ¿Cuántos/as hermanos/as tiene?

Is your husband here?
*su es-**po**-so/mah-ri-**THo** es-**tah** ah-**ki**?*   ¿Su esposo/marido está aquí?

Is your wife here?
*su es-**po**-sah/mu-**her** es-**tah** ah-**ki**?*   ¿Su esposa/mujer está aquí?

Do you have a boyfriend/ girlfriend?
*tie-ne **no**-bio/-ah?*   ¿Tiene novio/a?

brother	er-**mah**-no	hermano
children	i-hos	hijos
daughter	i-hah	hija
family	fah-**mi**-liah	familia
father	pah-**THre**/pah-**pah**	padre/papá
grandfather	ah-**bwe**-lo	abuelo
grandmother	ah-**bwe**-lah	abuela
husband	es-**po**-so/mah-ri-**THo**	esposo/marido
mother	mah-**THre**/mah-**mah**	madre/mamá
sister	er-**mah**-nah	hermana
son	i-ho	hijo
wife	es-**po**-sah/mu-**her**	esposa/mujer

Useful Phrases

Sure.
*por su-**pwes**-to!/**ko**-mo no!/ **klah**-ro!*   ¡Por supuesto!/¡Cómo no!/ ¡Claro!

Just a minute.
*oon mo-**men**-to*   Un momento.

It's (not) important.
*(no) es im-por-**tahn**-te*   (No) Es importante.

It's (not) possible.
*(no) es po-**si**-ble*   (No) Es posible.

Wait!
es-pe-re! ¡Espere!
Good luck!
bwe-nah swer-te!/swer-te! ¡Buena suerte!/¡Suerte!

Signs

EMERGENCY EXIT	*SALIDA DE EMERGENCIA*
ENTRANCE	*ENTRADA*
EXIT	*SALIDA*
FREE ADMISSION	*ENTRADA GRATIS*
HOT/COLD	*CALIENTE/FRIO*
INFORMATION	*INFORMACION*
NO ENTRY	*PROHIBIDO EL PASO*
NO SMOKING	*PROHIBIDO FUMAR*
OPEN/CLOSED	*ABIERTO/CERRADO*
PROHIBITED	*PROHIBIDO*
RESERVED	*RESERVADO*
TELEPHONE	*TELEFONO*
TOILETS	*SERVICIOS/ASEOS*

Getting Around

What time does … leave/
arrive?
   ah ke o-rah sah-le/
   lye-gah …? ¿A qué hora sale/llega …?

the (air)plane	*el bwe-lo*	el vuelo
the boat	*el boo-ke/bahr-ko*	el buque/barco
the bus (city)	*el ahoo-to-boos*	el autobús
	el boos	el bus
the bus (intercity)	*el ahoo-to-kahr*	el autocar

| the train | *el **tren*** | el tren |
| the tram | *el **trahm**-bi-ah* | el tranvía |

Finding Your Way

Do you have a guidebook/
local map?

*tie-ne oo-nah **gi**-ah/oon
plahn de lah thiu-**THahTH**?* ¿Tiene una guía/un plan de
la ciudad?

Where is …?

*don-de es-tah …?/don-de
ke-THah …?* ¿Dónde está …?/¿Dónde
queda …?

How do I get to …?

*ko-mo pwe-THo lye-**gahr**
ah …?* ¿Cómo puedo llegar a …?

Is it far from/near here?

*es-**tah** le-hos/ther-kah de
ah-**ki**?* ¿Está lejos/cerca de aquí?

Can I walk there?

*se pwe-THe kah-mi-**nahr**
ahs-tah ah-**lyi**/ah-**lyah**?* ¿Se puede caminar hasta
allí/allá?

Can you show me (on the map)?

*me pwe-THe mos-**trahr**/
indi-**kahr** en el **mah**-pah?* ¿Me puede mostrar/indicar
(en el mapa)?

Are there other means of
getting there?

*ahy o-tros me-**THios**
pah-rah ir ah-**lyi**/ah-**lyah**?* ¿Hay otros medios para ir
allí/allá?

What … is this?

*ke … es es-**tah**/es-te?* ¿Qué … es ésta/éste?
street ***kah**-lye* calle
suburb ***bah**-rrio, soo-**boor**-bio* barrio, suburbio

Directions

Turn left …	**do-**ble ah lah ith-**kier-**THah …	Doble a la izquierda …
Turn right …	**do-**ble ah lah THe-**re-**chah …	Doble a la derecha …
at the next corner	en lah **pro-**ksi-mah es-**ki-**nah	en la próxima esquina
at the traffic lights	en el se-**mah-**fo-ro	en el semáforo

Go straight ahead.
   si-gah/**bahy-**ah **to-**THo THe-**re-**cho

Siga/Vaya todo derecho.

It's two streets down.
   es-**tah** ah THos **kah-**lyes THe ah-**ki**

Está a dos calles de aquí.

behind	de-**trahs** THe	detrás de
near	**ther-**kah	cerca
far	le-**hos**	lejos
in front of	en-**fren-**te THe/ de-**lahn-**te THe	enfrente de/ delante de
opposite	**fren-**te ah	frente a

Buying Tickets

| TICKET OFFICE | *TAQUILLA* |

Excuse me, where is the ticket office?
   per-**THon don-**de ke-**THah** lah tah-**ki-**lyah?

¿Perdón, dónde queda la taquilla?

Where can I buy a ticket?
  *don-de pwe-THo kom-prahr
  el bi-lye-te/pah-sah-he?*

¿Dónde puedo comprar el billete/pasaje?

I want to go to …
  kie-ro ir ah …

Quiero ir a…

Can I reserve a place?
  *pwe-THo rre-ser-bahr
  oo-nah plah-thah/oon
  ah-sien-to?*

¿Puedo reservar una plaza/un asiento?

Do I need to book?
  ten-go ke rre-ser-bahr?

¿Tengo que reservar?

You need to book.
  tie-ne/ahy ke rre-ser-bahr

Tiene/Hay que reservar.

I would like to book a seat to …
  *ki-sie-rah rre-ser-bahr
  oo-nah plah-thah pah-rah …*

Quisiera reservar una plaza para …

I would like …
  ki-sie-rah …

Quisiera …

a one-way ticket	*oon bi-lye-te sen-thi-lyo*	un billete sencillo
a return ticket	*oon bi-lye-te de i-THah i bwel-tah*	un billete de ida y vuelta
two tickets	*dos bi-lye-tes*	dos billetes
a student fare	*oon bi-lye-te THe es-tu-THi-ahn-te*	un billete de estudiante
a child's/ pensioner's fare	*oon bi-lye-te THe ni-nyo/pen-si-o-nis-tah*	un billete de niño/pensionista
1st class	*pri-me-rah klah-se*	primera clase
2nd class	*se-goon-dah klah-se*	segunda clase

It is full.
es-ta kom-ple-to   Está completo.
Is it completely full?
es-tah kom-ple-tah-men-te   ¿Está completamente lleno?
lye-no?
Can I get a stand-by ticket?
pwe-THo kom-prahr oon   ¿Puedo comprar un
es-tahnd-bahy ti-ket   'standby ticket' (pasaje
(pah-sah-he soo-he-to ah   sujeto a espacio)?
es-pah-thio)?

Air

ARRIVALS	*LLEGADAS*
DEPARTURES	*PARTIDAS*
CHECKING IN	*FACTURACION/*
	CHECK-IN
CUSTOMS	*ADUANA*
LUGGAGE PICKUP	*RECOGIDA DE EQUIPAJE*
REGISTRATION	*REGISTRO*

Is there a flight to …?
ahy oon bwe-lo pah-rah …?   ¿Hay un vuelo para …?
When is the next flight to …?
kwahn-do sah-le el pro-ksi-   ¿Cuándo sale el próximo
mo bwe-lo pah-rah …?   vuelo para …?
How long does the flight take?
kwahn-to tiem-po   ¿Cuánto tiempo dura el
THoo-rah el bwe-lo?   vuelo?
What is the flight number?
kwahl es el noo-me-ro THel   ¿Cuál es el número del
bwe-lo?   vuelo?

You must check in at …
*tie-ne ke fahk-too-rahr el
e-ki-pah-he/pre-sen-tahr-se
en …*

Tiene que facturar el equi-
paje/presentarse en …

airport tax	*tah-sah ah-e-ro-por-too-ah-riah*	tasa aeroportuaria
boarding pass	*tahr-he-tah THe em-bahr-ke*	tarjeta de embarque

Bus & Tram

BUS STOP	*PARADA DE AUTOBUS*
TRAM STOP	*PARADA DETRANVIA*

Where is the bus/tram stop?
*don-de es-tah lah pah-rah-
THah THe aoo-to-boos/
trahm-bi-ah*

¿Dónde está la parada de
autobús/tranvía?

Which bus goes to …?
*kwahl es el aoo-to-boos ke
bah ah …?*

¿Cuál es el autobús que
va a …?

Does this bus go to …?
es-te aoo-to-boos bah ah …?

¿Este autobus va a …?

How often do buses pass by?
*kwahn-tahs be-thes
pah-sah el aoo-to-boos?*

¿Cuántas veces pasa el
autobus?

Could you let me know when
we get to …?
*pwe-THe ah-bi-sahr-me/
in-di-kahr-me kwahn-do
lye-ge-mos ah …?*

¿Puede avisarme/indicarme
cuando lleguemos a …?

I want to get off!
   *kie-ro bah-**hahr**-me!*   ¡Quiero bajarme!

What time is the … bus?
   *ah ke **o**-rah **sah**-le el …*
   *ahoo-to-**boos**/boos?*   ¿A qué hora sale el …
                                autobús/bus?

next	***pro**-ksi-mo*	próximo
first	*pri-**mer***	primer
last	***ool**-ti-mo*	último

Train

TRAIN STATION	*ESTACION DE TRENES/FERROCARRIL*
PLATFORM NO	*ANDEN Nº*
TIMETABLE	*HORARIO*

Is this the right platform for …?
   *el tren **pah**-rah … **sah**-le*
   *THe **es**-te ahn-**den**?*   ¿El tren para … sale de este andén?

The train leaves from platform …
   *el tren **sah**-le THel ahn-**den***
   ***noo**-me-ro …*   El tren sale del andén número …

Passengers must change trains/platforms.
   *los pah-sah-**he**-ros*
   ***THe**-ben kahm-bi-**ahr** THe*
   *tren/ahn-**den***   Los pasajeros deben cambiar de tren/andén.

SPANISH

dining car	*ko-che ko-me-THor/ bah-gon res-tahoo-rahn-te*	coche-comedor/ vagón restaurante
express	*es-pre-so/ra-pi-do*	expreso/rapido
local	*de ther-kah-ni-ahs*	de cercanías
sleeping car	*ko-che kah-mah*	coche-cama

Metro

CHANGE (for coins) THIS WAY TO ...	*CAMBIO (MONEDA SUELTA) DIRECCION ...*

Which line goes to ...?
   ke li-neah ko-ho pah-rah ...?
        ¿Qué línea cojo para ...?

What is the next station?
   kwahl es lah pro-ksi-mah es-tah-thion?
        ¿Cuál es la próxima estación?

Taxi

Please take me to ...
   por fah-bor lye-be-me ah ...
        Por favor, lléveme a ...

How much is it to go to ...?
   kwahn-to kwes-tah/bah-le ir ah ...?
        ¿Cuánto cuesta/vale ir a ...?

Instructions

Here is fine, thank you.
   ah-ki es-tah bien, grah-thiahs
        Aquí está bien, gracias.

Stop here!
   pah-re ah-ki
        ¡Pare aquí!

SPANISH

Please wait here.
por fah-bor es-pe-re ah-ki

Por favor espere aquí.

The next corner, please.
lah pro-ksi-mah es-ki-nah, por fah-bor

La próxima esquina, por favor.

The next street to the left/right.
lah pro-ksi-mah cah-lye ah lah ith-kier-THah/THe-re-chah

La próxima calle a la izquierda/derecha.

Useful Phrases

The train is delayed/cancelled.
el tren tie-ne rre-trah-so/ fu-e kahn-the-lah-THo

El tren tiene retraso/fue cancelado.

How long will it be delayed?
kwahn-to lye-bah THe rre-trah-so?

¿Cuánto lleva de retraso?

There is a delay of … hours.
lye-bah … o-rahs THe rre-trah-so

Lleva … horas de retraso.

How long does the trip take?
kwahn-to tiem-po THoo-rah el biah-he?

¿Cuánto tiempo dura el viaje?

Is it a direct route?
biah-hah THi-rek-to?

¿Viaja directo?

Is that seat taken?
es-tah o-koo-pah-THo es-te ah-sien-to?

¿Está ocupado este asiento?

I want to get off at …
kie-ro ah-pe-ahr-me en …

Quiero apearme en …

Excuse me.
per-mi-so

Permiso.

Car & Bicycle

DETOUR	*DESVIO*
FREEWAY	*AUTOPISTA*
GARAGE	*GARAJE/TALLER*
GIVE WAY	*CEDA EL PASO*
MECHANIC	*MECANICO*
NO ENTRY	*DIRECCION PROHIBIDA*
NO PARKING	*PROHIBIDO ESTACIONAR*
ONE WAY	*SENTIDO UNICO*
REPAIRS	*REPARACIONES*
SELF SERVICE	*AUTOSERVICIO*
STOP	*STOP/PARE*
UNLEADED	*SIN PLOMO*

Where can I hire a car?
don-de pwe-THo ahl-ki-lahr oon ko-che/aoo-to?

¿Dónde puedo alquilar un coche/auto?

Where can I hire a bicycle?
don-de pwe-THo ahl-ki-lahr oo-nah bi-thi-kle-tah?

¿Dónde puedo alquilar una bicicleta?

How much is it daily/weekly?
kwahn-to kwes-tah por THi-ah/por se-mah-nah?

¿Cuánto cuesta por día/por semana?

Does that include insurance/mileage?
in-kluy-e el se-goo-ro/el ki-lo-me-trah-he?

¿Incluye el seguro/el kilometraje?

Where's the next petrol station?
ahy oo-nah gah-so-li-ne-rah por ah-ki?

¿Hay una gasolinera por aquí?

Please fill the tank.
por fah-bor, lye-ne-me el de-po-si-to
Por favor, lléneme el depósito.

I want … litres of petrol (gas).
kie-ro … li-tros THe gah-so-li-nah
Quiero … litros de gasolina.

Please check the oil and water.
por fah-bor, rre-bi-se el ni-bel THel ah-thei-te i THel ah-gwah
Por favor, revise el nivel del aceite y del agua.

How long can I park here?
kwahn-to tiem-po pwe-THo es-tah-thio-nahr ah-ki?
¿Cuánto tiempo puedo estacionar aquí?

Does this road lead to?
se bah ah … por es-tah kah-rre-te-rah?
¿Se va a … por esta carretera?

air	*ahi-re*	aire
battery	*bah-te-ri-ah*	batería
brakes	*fre-nos*	frenos
clutch	*em-brah-ge*	embrague
driver's licence	*kahr-ne/per-mi-so THe kon-doo-thir*	carnet/permiso de conducir
engine	*mo-tor*	motor
lights	*fah-ros*	faros
oil	*ah-thei-te*	aceite
puncture	*pin-chah-tho*	pinchazo
radiator	*rrah-THi-ah-THor*	radiador
road map	*mah-pah THe cah-rre-te-rahs*	mapa de carreteras
tyres	*neoo-mah-ti-kos*	neumáticos/llantas
windscreen	*pah-rah-bri-sahs*	parabrisas

Car Problems

I need a mechanic.
*ne-the-si-to oon
me-kah-ni-ko*   Necesito un mecánico.

What make is it?
de ke mahr-kah es?   ¿De qué marca es?

The battery is flat.
*lah bah-te-ri-ah es-tah
des-kahr-gah-THah*   La batería está descargada.

The radiator is leaking.
*el rrah-THi-ah-THor tie-ne
oo-nah foo-gah*   El radiador tiene una fuga.

I have a flat tyre.
ten-go oon pin-chah-tho   Tengo un pinchazo.

It's overheating.
*es-tah re-kah-len-tahn-
do-se*   Está recalentándose.

It's not working.
no foon-thi-o-nah   No funciona.

Accommodation

CAMPING GROUND	TERRENO DE CAMPING
GUEST HOUSE	PENSION/CASA DE
	HUESPEDES
YOUTH HOSTEL	ALBERGUE PARA
	JOVENES

SPANISH

Finding Accommodation

I'm looking for a …
ahn-do boos-kahn-do oon …   Ando buscando un …

cheap hotel	*o-tel bah-rah-to*	hotel barato
good hotel	*bwen o-tel*	buen hotel
nearby hotel	*o-tel ther-kah-no*	hotel cercano
clean hotel	*o-tel-lim-pio*	hotel limpio

What is the address?
kwahl es lah di-rek-thion?   ¿Cuál es la dirección?

Could you write the address, please?
pwe-THe es-kri-bir lah di-rek-thion por fah-bor?   ¿Puede escribir la dirección, por favor?

Booking a Room

Do you have any rooms available?
tie-ne ah-bi-tah-thi-o-nes li-bres?   ¿Tiene habitaciones libres?

I'd like to book a room.
kie-ro rre-ser-bahr oo-nah ah-bi-tah-thion   Quiero reservar una habitación.

for one night/four nights
por oo-nah no-che/ kwah-tro no-ches   por una noche/cuatro noches

from tonight/Tuesday
pah-rah es-te no-che/ pah-rah mahr-tes   para este noche/para Martes

I'd like ...	*ki-sie-rah* ...	Quisiera ...
a single room	*oo-nah ah-bi-tah-thion in-di-bi-THoo-ahl*	una habitación individual
a double room	*oo-nah ah-bi-tah-thion do-ble*	una habitación doble

SPANISH

| a room with a bathroom | ***oo*-nah ah-bi-tah-thion kon bah-nyo** | una habitación con baño |
| to share a dorm | **kom-pahr-*tir* oon dor-mi-*to*-rio** | compartir un dormitorio |

I'm going to stay for …
  me boy ah ke-THahr …   Me voy a quedar …

one day	*oon di-ah*	un día
two days	*dos THi-ahs*	dos días
one week	*oo-nah se-mah-nah*	una semana

At the Hotel

How much is it per night/
per person?
  **kwahn-*to* kwes-tah por
  no-che/por per-*so*-nah?**   ¿Cuánto cuesta por noche/
  por persona?

Can I see it?
  pwe-THo ber-lah?   ¿Puedo verla?

Are there any others?
  ahy o-trahs?   ¿Hay otras?

Are there any cheaper rooms?
  *ahy ah-bi-tah-thi-o-nes
  mahs bah-rah-tahs?*   ¿Hay habitaciones más
  baratas?

Is there a reduction for
students/children?
  *ahy ahl-goon des-kwen-to/
  pre-thio es-pe-thi-ahl
  pah-rah es-too-THi-ahn-tes/
  ni-nyos?*   ¿Hay algún descuento/
  precio especial para
  estudiantes/niños?

Does it include breakfast?
  in-kluy-e el de-sahy-oo-no?   ¿Incluye el desayuno?

Can I see the bathroom?
  pwe-THo ber el bah-nyo?   ¿Puedo ver el baño?

It's fine, I'll take it.
bah-le, lah ahl-ki-lo

Vale, la alquilo.

I'm not sure how long I'm staying.
no es-toy se-goo-ro
kwahn-to tiem-po me boy
ah ke-THahr

No estoy seguro cuánto tiempo me voy a quedar.

You May Hear

Do you have identification?
tie-ne kahr-ne THe i-THen-ti-THahTH?

¿Tiene carnet de identidad?

Your membership card, please.
su tahr-he-tah de so-thio, por fah-bor

Su tarjeta de socio, por favor.

Sorry, we're full.
lo sien-to, no te-ne-mos nah-THah li-bre

Lo siento, no tenemos nada libre.

How long will you be staying?
kwahn-to tiem-po se ke-THah?

¿Cuánto tiempo se queda?

How many nights?
kwahn-tahs no-ches?

¿Cuántas noches?

It's … per day/per person.
son … por THi-ah/por per-so-nah

Son … por día/por persona.

Requests & Complaints

Can I use the kitchen/telephone?
pwe-THo oo-sahr lah ko-thi-nah/el te-le-fo-no?

¿Puedo usar la cocina/el teléfono?

Is there hot water all day?
ahy ah-gwah kah-lien-te to-THo el di-ah?

¿Hay agua caliente todo el día?

Is there somewhere to wash clothes?
ahy ahl-goon loo-gahr THon-de pwe-THah lah-bahr lah rro-pah?

¿Hay algún lugar donde pueda lavar la ropa?

Do you have a safe where I can leave my valuables?
tie-ne oo-nah kah-hah fwer-te THon-de pwe-THah de-hahr mis ko-sahs THe bah-lor?

¿Tiene una caja fuerte donde pueda dejar mis cosas de valor?

Please wake me up at …
por fah-bor, des-pier-te-me ah lahs …

Por favor, despiérteme a las …

The room needs to be cleaned.
ahy ke lim-pi-ahr lah ah-bi-tah-thion

Hay que limpiar la habitación.

Please change the sheets.
por fah-bor, kahm-bie lahs sah-bah-nahs

Por favor, cambie las sábanas.

I can't open/close the window.
no pwe-THo ah-brir/ the-rrahr lah ben-tah-nah

No puedo abrir/cerrar la ventana.

I've locked myself out of my room.
the-rre lah pwer-tah i se me ol-bi-dah-ron lahs lyah-bes THen-tro

Cerré la puerta y se me olvidaron las llaves dentro.

The toilet won't flush.
*lah THes-**kahr**-gah THe lah*
*rre-**tre**-te no foon-thi-o-nah*
La descarga de la retrete no funciona.

I don't like this room.
*no me **goos**-tah es-tah*
*ah-bi-tah-**thion***
No me gusta esta habitación.

It's ...	*es ...*	Es ...
too small	*de-mah-si-**ah**-THo*	demasiado
	*chi-**ki**-tah/pe-**ke**-nyah*	chiquita/ pequeña
noisy	*rrwi-**THo**-sah*	ruidosa
too dark	*de-mah-si-**ah**-TH*	demasiado oscura
	*os-**koo**-rah*	
expensive	*kah-rah*	cara

Checking Out

I am/We are leaving now.
*me boy/nos **bah**-mos*
ah-o-rah
Me voy/Nos vamos ahora.

I'd like to pay the bill.
*kie-ro pah-**gahr** lah*
kwen-tah
Quiero pagar la cuenta.

address	*di-rek-**thion***	dirección
name	***nom**-bre*	nombre
surname	*ah-pe-**lyi**-THo*	apellido
room number	***noo**-me-ro THe lah*	número de la
	*ah-bi-tah-**thion***	habitación

Useful Words

air-con	***ahi**-re ah-kon-di-thi-*	aire
	*o-**nah**-THo*	acondicionado
bathroom	***bah**-nyo*	baño
bed	***kah**-mah*	cama

clean	*lim*-pio/ah	limpio/a
dark	os-*koo*-ro/ah	oscuro/a
dirty	*soo*-thio/ah	sucio/a
double bed	*kah*-mah THe	cama de
	mah-tri-mo-nio	matrimonio
electricity	e-lek-tri-thi-*THahTH*	electricidad
excluded	no in-kloo-i-*THo*	no incluido
fan	ben-ti-lah-*THor*	ventilador
included	in-kloo-i-*THo*	incluido
key	*lyah*-be	llave
quiet	trahn-*ki*-lo/ah	tranquilo/a
sheet	sah-*bah*-nah	sábana
shower	*doo*-chah	ducha
swimming pool	pis-*thi*-nah	piscina
toilet	rre-*tre*-te/*bah*-ter	retrete/wáter
toilet paper	pah-*pel* i-hi-e-ni-ko	papel higiénico
towel	to-*ah*-lyah	toalla
water	*ah*-gwah	agua
cold water	*ah*-gwah *fri*-ah	agua fría
hot water	*ah*-gwah kah-*lien*-te	agua caliente
window	ben-*tah*-nah	ventana

Around Town

I'm looking for …
ahn-do boos-*kahn*-do …	Ando buscando …
a bank	oon *bahn*-ko	un banco
the city centre	el *then*-tro THe lah thiu-*THahTH*	el centro de la ciudad
the … embassy	lah em-bah-*hah*-THah …	la embajada …
the post office	ko-*rre*-os	Correos

a public toilet	*ser-bi-thios/ah-se-os* *poo-bli-kos*	servicios/aseos públicos
the telephone centre	*lah then-trahl te-le-fo-ni-kah*	la central telefónica
the tourist information office	*lah o-fi-thi-nah THe too-riz-mo*	la oficina de turismo

What time does it open?
ah ke o-rah ah-bren? ¿A qué hora abren?

What time does it close?
ah ke o-rah thie-rrahn? ¿A qué hora cierran?

At the Bank

I want to exchange some money/travellers' cheques.
kie-ro *kahm-bi-ahr* THi-*ne*-ro/ *che*-kes THe *biah-he* Quiero cambiar dinero/ cheques de viaje.

What is the exchange rate?
kwahl es el ti-po THe kahm-bio? ¿Cuál es el tipo de cambio?

How many pesetas per dollar?
kwahn-tahs *pe-se-tahs por* **THo**-lahr? ¿Cuántas pesetas por dólar?

Can I have money transferred here from my bank?
pwe-THen trahns-fe-rir-me THi-**ne**-ro THe mi **bahn**-ko ah *es-te?* ¿Pueden transferirme dinero de mi banco a éste?

How long will it take to arrive?
kwahn-to *tiem-po tar-THa-rah en lye-gahr?* ¿Cuánto tiempo tardará en llegar?

Has my money arrived yet?

*yah ah lye-**gah**-THo mi THi-ne-ro?*   ¿Ya ha llegado mi dinero?

banknotes	*bi-**lye**-tes THe **bahn**-ko*	billetes (de banco)
cashier	***kah**-hah*	caja
coins	*mo-ne-THahs*	monedas
credit card	*tahr-he-tah THe **kre**-THi-to*	tarjeta de crédito
exchange	***kahm**-bio*	cambio
loose change	*mo-**ne**-THahs swel-tahs*	monedas sueltas
signature	***fir**-mah*	firma

At the Post Office

I'd like to send …	*ki-**sie**-rah em-bi-**ahr** …*	Quisiera enviar …
an aerogram	*oon ah-e-ro-**grah**-mah*	un aerograma
a letter	*oo-nah **kahr**-tah*	una carta
a postcard	*oo-nah tahr-**he**-tah pos-**tahl***	una tarjeta postal
a parcel	*oon pah-**ke**-te*	un paquete
a telegram	*oon te-le-**grah**-mah*	un telegrama

I would like some stamps.

*ki-**sie**-rah **oo**-nos se-lyos*   Quisiera unos sellos

How much is the postage?

*kwahn-to **bah**-le el frahn-**ke**-o?*   ¿Cúanto vale el franqueo?

How much does it cost to send this to …?

*kwahn-to kwes-tah em-bi-**ahr** es-to ah …?*   ¿Cuánto cuesta enviar esto a …?

SPANISH

airmail	*por bi-ah ah-e-re-ah*	por vía aérea
envelope	*so-bre*	sobre
mail box	*boo-thon*	buzón
parcel	*pah-ke-te*	paquete
registered mail	*ko-rre-o ther-ti-fi-kah-THo*	correo certificado
surface mail	*por bi-ah te-rres-tre/ mah-ri-ti-mah*	por vía terrestre/ marítima

Telephone

I want to ring …
   kie-ro lyah-mahr ah …   Quiero llamar a …

The number is …
   el noo-me-ro es …   El número es …

I want to speak for three minutes.
   kie-ro ah-blahr tres mi-noo-tos   Quiero hablar tres minutos.

How much does a three-minute call cost?
   kwahn-to kwes-tah/bah-le oo-nah lyah-mah-THah THe tres mi-noo-tos?   ¿Cuánto cuesta/vale una llamada de tres minutos?

How much does each extra minute cost?
   kwahn-to kwes-tah cah-THah mi-noo-to ah-THi-thi-o-nahl?   ¿Cuánto cuesta cada minuto adicional?

I want to make a reverse-charges (collect) call.
   kie-ro ah-ther oo-nah lyah-mah-THah ah ko-bro rre-ber-ti-THo   Quiero hacer una llamada a cobro revertido.

It's engaged.
*es-**tah** ok-ooh- pah-**THah*** — Está ocupada.

I've been cut off.
*me ahn kor-**tah**-THo (lah ko-moo-ni-kah-**thion**)* — Me han cortado (la comunicación).

Hello? *o-**lah**?* — Hola?

I would like to
speak to Mr Perez.
*ki-sie-rah ah-**blahr** kon el se-**nyor** pe-reth* — Quisiera hablar con el señor Pérez.

Sightseeing

What are the main attractions?
*kwah-les son lahs ah-trahk-thi-o-nes prin-thi-**pah**-les?* — ¿Cuáles son las atracciones principales?

How old is it?
*es ahn-**ti**-gwo?/de **kwahn**-do es?* — ¿Es antiguo?/¿Dé cuándo es?

Can I take photographs?
*pwe-**THo** to-**mahr** fo-tos?* — ¿Puedo tomar fotos?

What time does it open/close?
*ah ke o-rah ah-bren/**thie**-rrahn?* — ¿A qué hora abren/cierran?

ancient	*ahn-**ti**-gwo/-ah*	antiguo/a
archaeological	*ahr-ke-o-**lo**-hi-co/-ah*	arqueológico/a
beach	*plahy-ah*	playa
building	*e-THi-**fi**-thi-o*	edificio
castle	*kahs-**ti**-lyo*	castillo
cathedral	*kah-te-**THrahl***	catedral
church	*i-**gle**-siah*	iglesia

SPANISH

concert hall	*sah-lah THe kon-**thier**-tos/te-**ah**-tro*	sala de conciertos/teatro
library	*bi-bli-o-te-kah*	biblioteca
main square	***plah**-thah mahy-**or***	Plaza Mayor
monastery	*mo-nahs-te-rio*	monasterio
old city	*thiu-**THahTH** ahn-ti-gwah/**bah**-rrio **bie**-ho*	ciudad antigua/barrio viejo
palace	*pah-**lah**-thio*	palacio
opera house	*lah o-pe-rah*	la Opera
ruins	*rroo-i-nahs*	ruinas
stadium	*es-tah-THio*	estadio
statues	*es-tah-twahs*	estatuas
university	*oo-ni-ber-si-**THahTH***	universidad

Entertainment

What's there to do in the evenings?

| *ke se pwe-THe ah-**ther** por lah **no**-che?* | ¿Qué se puede hacer por la noche? |

Are there any nightclubs?

| *ahy dis-ko-**te**-kahs?* | ¿Hay discotecas? |

Are there places where you can hear local music?

| *ahy loo-**gah**-res **THon**-de se pwe-**THah** o-**ir** moo-sik-ah?* | ¿Hay lugares donde se pueda oír música? |

How much is it to get in?

| ***kwahn**-to kwes-tah lah en-**trah**-THah?* | ¿Cuánto cuesta la entrada? |

| cinema | ***thi**-ne* | cine |

In the Country
Weather

What's the weather like?
  ko-mo es-tah el tiem-po?   ¿Cómo está el tiempo?

The weather is fine/bad today.
  ah-the bwen/mahl tiem-po hoy   Hace buen/mal tiempo hoy.

Will it be … tomorrow?
  es-tah-rah/ah-rah/ah-brah … mah-nyah-nah?   ¿Estará/Hará/Habrá … mañana?

cloudy	*(es-tah-rah) noo-blah-THo*	(Estará) nublado
cold	*(ah-rah) fri-o*	(Hará) frío
foggy	*(ah-brah) ne-bli-nah/nie-blah*	(Habrá) neblina/niebla
frosty	*(ah-brah) es-kahr-chah*	(Habrá) escarcha
hot	*(ah-rah) kah-lor*	(Hará) calor
raining	*lyo-be-rah*	Lloverá
snowing	*ne-bah-rah/(ah-brah) nie-be*	Nevará/(Habrá) nieve
sunny	*(ah-rah) sol*	(Hará) sol
windy	*(ah-rah) bien-to*	(Hará) viento

Camping

Am I allowed to camp here?
  es-tah per-mi-ti-THo ah-kahm-pahr ah-ki?   ¿Está permitido acampar aquí?

Is there a campsite nearby?
  ahy oon te-rre-no THe kahm-ping ther-kah?   ¿Hay un terreno de camping cerca?

backpack	*mo-chi-lah/mo-rrahl*	mochila/morral
can opener	*ah-bre-lah-tahs*	abrelatas

SPANISH

compass	**broo**-hoo-lah	brújula
crampons	krahm-**po**-nes	crampones
firewood	**le**-nyah	leña
gas cartridge	kahr-**too**-cho THe gahs	cartucho de gas
ice axe	**pi**-ko/**pi**-kah	pico/pica
penknife	nah-**bah**-hah	navaja
rope	**kwer**-dah	cuerda
tent	**tien**-dah (THe kahm-**pah**-nyah)	tienda (de campaña)
tent pegs	es-**tah**-kahs	estacas
torch (flashlight)	lin-**ter**-nah	linterna
sleeping bag	**sah**-ko THe THor-**mir**	saco de dormir
stove	es-**too**-fah/ko-**thi**-nah	estufa/cocina
water bottle	kahn-tim-**plo**-rah	cantimplora

Food

breakfast	de-sahy-**oo**-no	desayuno
lunch	ahl-**mwer**-tho/ko-**mi**-THah	almuerzo/comida
dinner	**the**-nah	cena

Eating Out

Table for …, please.
oo-nah me-**sah** pah-**rah** …, por fah-**bor**

Una mesa para …, por favor.

Can I see the menu please?
pwe-THo ber lah **lis**-tah/el me-**noo** por fah-**bor**?

¿Puedo ver la lista/el menú, por favor?

Is service included in the bill?
el ser-**bi**-thio es-**tah** in-**kloo**-i-THo en lah **kwen**-tah?

¿El servicio está incluido en la cuenta?

I'd like the set lunch, please.

*ki-sie-rah el ahl-**mwer**-tho ah **pre**-thio fi-ho/ahl-**mwer**-tho ko-**rrien**-te por fah-**bor***	Quisiera el almuerzo a precio fijo/almuerzo corriente, por favor.

What does it include?

*ke es-**tah** in-kloo-i-THo?/ ke in-**kluy**-e?*	¿Qué está incluido? ¿Qué incluye?

Not too spicy please.

*no mooy pi-**kahn**-te, por fah-**bor***	No muy picante, por favor.

ashtray	*the-ni-**the**-ro*	cenicero
the bill	*lah **kwen**-tah*	la cuenta
a cup	*oo-nah **tah**-thah*	una taza
dessert	***pos**-tre*	postre
a drink	*oo-nah be-bi-THah*	una bebida
a fork	*oon te-ne-**THor***	un tenedor
fresh	***fres**-ko/ah*	fresco/a
a glass	*oon **bah**-so (oo-nah **ko**-pah)*	un vaso (una copa for wine or spirits)
a knife	*oon ku-**chi**-lyo*	un cuchillo
a plate	*oon **plah**-to*	un plato
spicy	*pi-**kahn**-te*	picante
a spoon	*oo-nah koo-**chah**-rah*	una cuchara
stale	*pah-sah-**THo**/rrahn-thio*	pasado/rancio

Making Your Own Meal

For some key essentials for sandwich-making, etc, see page 469.

Vegetarian Meals

Vegetables are normally listed (and served) separately in Spanish menus, so you can always order them as separate courses. Look under *Legumbres* or *Entremeses* on the menu.

SPANISH

I don't eat meat.
   *no ko-mo **kahr**-ne*   No como carne.

Judías verdes con salsa de tomate
   Green beans in tomato sauce.

Pisto manchego
   Stewed zucchini, peppers, tomatoes and onions.

Revuelto de huevos a la riojana
   Eggs scrambled in an onion and tomato sauce.

Tortilla de patata
   Fried potato and onion omelette. This is the basic tortilla, but other ingredients can be added: chorizo (sausage), ham, mushrooms, eggplant, prawns, peppers or tuna.

Fruit & Vegetables

apple	*manzana*	lentils	*lentejas*
apricot	*albaricoque*	lettuce	*lechuga*
artichoke	*alcachofa*	mushroom	*champiñon*
beetroot	*remolacha*	olives	*aceitunas*
blackberries	*moras*	onion	*cebolla*
cabbage	*repollo*	orange	*naranja*
capsicum	*pimentón*	parsley	*perejil*
carrot	*zanahoria*	peach	*melocotón*
celery	*apio*	pear	*pera*
cherries	*cerezas*	peas	*arvejas*
chick peas	*garbanzos*	pineapple	*piña*
cucumber	*pepino*	plum	*ciruela*
eggplant	*berenjena*	pumpkin	*calabaza*
figs	*brevas*	rasberries	*frambuesas*
grapefruit	*pomelo*	spinach	*espinacas*
grapes	*uvas*	strawberries	*fresas*
green beans	*judias verdes*	sultanas	*uvas pasas*
leek	*puerro*	turnip	*nabo*

Staples & Condiments

bread	*pan*	garlic	*ajo*
butter	*mantequilla*	oil	*aceite*
cheese	*queso*	pepper	*pimienta*
eggs	*huevos*	salt	*sal*

Soups

Caldo gallego	White bean and potato soup with turnip greens and chorizo sausage.
Fabada asturiana	Broad bean (*fava*) soup with Spanish sausages (chorizos, *morcillas*) and *serrano* ham.
Garbanzos con carne	A chick-pea, pork, chorizo and vegetable soup that can be served as a main course.
Gazpacho	A chilled soup made from tomato, onion, green pepper and garlic.
Olla podrida	A soup/main course made with vegetables (chick-peas, carrots, potatoes, turnips), meats (pork, beef, chorizos) and broth, served with fried slices of bread.
Sopa al cuarto de hora	Clam, shrimp, ham and rice soup, served with chopped hard-boiled egg.

Meat

Albóndigas	Meatballs in onion and chicken sauce.
Callos a la madrileña	Tripe stew with ham, chorizo, and sometimes calf's feet.
Cochifrito	Lamb fricassee in lemon and garlic sauce.
Cordero asado	Roast lamb (often in white wine and garlic).
Chorizos al horno	Spanish spicy sausages, fried in their own fat, and then baked in the oven.
Chuletas de cordero a la navarra	Lamb chops and chorizo sausage, baked with onion, garlic and tomato.

SPANISH

Filete de termera
　Veal steak.
Habas a la catalana
　A casserole of broad bean *(fava)* with chorizo sausage, parsley and mint.
Lomo de cerdo a la zaragozana
　Pork loin chops with tomato sauce and black olives.
Paella
　See the Seafood section.
Tortilla
　See Vegetarian Meals, page 461.

beef	*carne de vaca*	rabbit	*conejo*
chicken	*pollo*	ribs	*costillas*
hare	*liebre*	salami	*chorizo*
kid	*cabrito*	sausage	*salchicha*
lamb	*cordero*	tripe	*callos*
liver	*hígado*	veal	*ternera*

Seafood

Almejas a la marinera
　Clams in white wine with garlic, onions and parsley.
Bacalao al ajo arriero
　Salt cod cooked in olive oil with tomatoes, onions and garlic.
Besugo al horno
　Red snapper, baked with sliced potatoes in olive oil, onions and tomatoes.
Calamares en su tinta
　Squid fried with onions, garlic and parsley, with a sauce made from the squid's ink.
Crema de cangrejos de Segovia
　Freshwater crab and fish soup.

Changurro
  Crabmeat with sherry and brandy, baked and served in individual ramekins.

Merluza/Mero en salsa verde
  Hake/Pollock cutlets fried in olive oil, with parsley and green pea sauce.

Merluza a la madrileña
  Tail piece of hake, baked in a wine, mustard, tomato and crushed black olive sauce.

Paella
  Spain's best-known dish: saffron rice with seafood, chicken pieces, chorizos and vegetables. In the Valencian paella the shellfish may be lobster, shrimps, prawns, clams and/or mussels. The Castilian paella is likely to have only clams, but veal, beef or pork cubes may be added as well as chicken. The vegetables are normally peas and peppers. The paella is traditionally cooked out-of-doors on wood fires.

Salpicón de mariscos
  Shrimp and lobster salad.

Truchas a la española
  Grilled trout with onion and parsley.

Truchas a la navarra
  Marinated trout, baked with red wine and herbs.

Zarzuela de mariscos
  A shellfish stew from Catalonia. The elaborate version will include lobster, shrimps, mussels, clams, scallops, *serrano* ham, ground almonds, tomato and white wine.

SPANISH

anchovies	*anchoas*	prawns	*gambas*
clams	*almejas*	sea bream	*besugo*
cod	*bacalao*	shellfish	*mariscada*
crab	*cangrejo*	shrimps	*mariscos*

fish	*pescado*	sole	*lenguado*
hake	*merluza*	squid	*calamares*
herring	*arenque*	trout	*trucha*

Poultry & Game

Cocido madrileño
Boiled chicken, meats, chorizos and vegetables (usually chick-peas, potatoes, carrots and leeks).

Codornices a la cazadora
Quail stew with onions, leeks, tomatoes, turnips and carrots.

Liebre a la cazadora
A hare casserole in red wine and garlic.

Perdices estofadas
Partridges braised in white wine with vegetables and garlic.

Pollo a la chilindrón
Sautéed chicken, with green and red peppers, tomatoes, *serrano* ham, and green and black olives.

Pollo en pepitoria
Casserole of chicken pieces braised in white wine, with ground almonds, garlic and saffron.

Desserts & Sweets

Bartolillos de Madrid	Small pastry fritters with custard filling.
Bizcocho borracho	Squares of sponge cake soaked in a syrup of sweet wine and cinnamon.
Brazo de gitano	Sponge cake roll with rum cream filling.
Buñuelos de pl tano	Banana fritters.
Buñuelos de viento	Pastry fritters sprinkled with sugar and cinnamon.
Churros madrileños	Crisp-fried crullers, sprinkled with sugar (similar to doughnuts).

SPANISH

Flan de huevos	Spanish version of creme caramel.
Flan de naranja	Orange creme caramel.
Leche frita	Custard squares fried in olive oil and sprinkled with sugar and cinnamon. Served hot or cold.
Mantecados de Astorga	Plain or cinnamon muffins.
Natillas	Soft custard served in individual dishes, topped with egg white or with a ladyfinger biscuit.

Drinks – Nonalcoholic

coffee	*café*
with milk	*café con leche*
iced	*café helado*
fruit juice	*zumo/jugo*
soft drinks	*refrescos*
almond	*horchata*
water	*agua*
mineral water	*agua mineral*
natural (no gas)	*sin gaz*
plain	*agua natural*
tea	*té*

Drinks – Alcoholic

beer	*cerveza*		
champagne	*cava*		
sherry	*jerez*		
wine	*vino*		
red	*tinto*	red wine punch	*sangría*
rosé	*rosado*	sparkling	*espumoso*
white	*blanco*		

SPANISH

Shopping

bookshop	*li-bre-**ri**-ah*	librería
camera shop	***tien**-dah THe ahr-ti-koo-los fo-to-**grah**-fi-kos*	tienda de artículos fotográficos
delicatessen	***tien**-dah THe em-boo-ti-THos/sahl-chi-che-**ri**-ah*	tienda de embutidos/salchichería
general store, shop	***tien**-dah THe ah-li-men-tah-**thion**/ahl-mah-**then***	tienda de alimen-tación/almacén
laundry	*lah-bahn-de-**ri**-ah*	lavandería
market	*mer-**kah**-THo*	mercado
newsagency/stationers	*pah-pe-le-**ri**-ah*	papelería
supermarket	*su-per-mer-**kah**-THo*	supermercado
vegetable shop	*ber-THoo-le-**ri**-ah/froo-te-**ri**-ah*	verdulería/frutería

How much is it?
  kwahn-to kwes-tah? ¿Cuánto cuesta?
  kwahn-to bah-le? ¿Cuánto vale?
I'd like to buy …
  *ki-**sie**-rah kom-**prahr** …* Quisiera comprar …
Do you have others?
  tie-ne o-tros? ¿Tiene otros?
I don't like it.
  *no me **goos**-tah* No me gusta.
Can I look at it?
  *pwe-THo mi-**rahr**-lo/ah* ¿Puedo mirarlo/a?
I'm just looking.
  *so-lo es-toy mi-**rahn**-do* Sólo estoy mirando.

Can you write down the price?
pwe-THe es-kri-bir el
pre-thio?
¿Puede escribir el precio?

Do you accept credit cards?
ah-thep-tahn tahr-he-tahs
THe kre-THi-to?
¿Aceptan tarjetas de crédito?

Could you lower the price?
po-THri-ah bah-hahr oon
po-ko el pre-thio?
¿Podría bajar un poco el precio?

I don't have much money.
no ten-go moo-cho THi-ne-ro
No tengo mucho dinero.

You May Hear

Can I help you?
en ke pwe-THo ser-bir-le?
¿En qué puedo servirle?

Will that be all?
ahl-go mahs?
¿Algo más?

Would you like it wrapped?
se lo em-bwel-bo?
¿Se lo envuelvo?

Sorry, this is the only one.
lo sien-to, es el oo-ni-ko ke
te-ne-mos
Lo siento, es el único que tenemos.

How much/many do you want?
kwahn-to/s kie-re?
¿Cuánto/s quiere?

Essential Groceries

batteries	*pi-las*	pilas
bread	*pahn*	pan
butter	*man-teh-ki-yah*	mantequilla
cereal	*seh-reh-ahl*	cereal
cheese	*ke-soh*	queso
chocolate	*cho-koh-lah-teh*	chocolate

coffee	*kah-**fey***	café
gas cylinder	*si-lin-droh THe gas*	cilindro de gas
matches	*fos-fo-ros/the-ri-lyahs*	fósforos/cerillas
milk	*leh-che*	leche
fruit	*fru-ta*	fruta
shampoo	*chahm-**poo***	champú
soap	*hah-**bon***	jabón
sugar	*ah-zuh-karr*	azucar
tea	*teh*	té
toilet paper	*pah-**pel** i-hi-e-ni-ko*	papel higiénico
toothpaste	*pahs-tah THen-ti-fri-kah*	pasta dentífrica
washing powder	*hah-**bon** de lah-**vahr***	jabón de lavar
yoghurt	*yo-**goor***	yogur

Souvenirs

earrings	*pen-**dien**-tes/ ah-**re**-tes*	pendientes/ aretes
fans	*ah-bah-**ni**-kos*	abanicos
handicraft	*ahr-te-sah-**ni**-ah*	artesanía
leather wine bottle	*bo-tahs de **bi**-no*	botas de vino
leathergoods	*ah-ti-koo-los de **kwe**-ro*	artículos de cuero
mantillas	*mahn-**ti**-lyahs*	mantillas
necklace	*ko-**lyahr***	collar
nougat (Spanish)	*too-**rron***	turrón
pottery	*ahl-fah-re-**ri**-ah/ the-**rah**-mi-kah*	alfarería/cerámica
ring	*ah-**ni**-lyo/sor-**ti**-hah*	anillo/sortija
rug	*ahl-**fom**-brah/ tah-**pe**-te*	alfombra/tapete
scarves	*pah-**nywe**-los*	pañuelos

Clothing

jacket	*chah-**ke**-tah*	chaqueta
shirt	*kah-**mi**-sah*	camisa
shoes	*thah-**pah**-tos*	zapatos
trousers	*pahn-tah-**lo**-nes*	pantalones

It is too big/small.
  *es de-mah-si-**ah**-THo*   Es demasiado
  ***grahn**-de/pe-ke-nyo*   grande/pequeño

Toiletries

condoms	*pre-ser-bah-**ti**-bos/* *kon-**do**-nes*	preservativos/ condones
deodorant	*de-so-THo-**rahn**-te*	desodorante
hairbrush	*the-**pi**-lyo (**pah**-rah el kah-**be**-lyo/**pe**-lo)*	cepillo (para el cabello/pelo)
razor	*nah-**bah**-hah THe ah-fey-**tahr***	navaja de afeitar
sanitary napkins	*kom-**pre**-sahs i-hi-**e**-ni-kahs*	compresas higiénicas
shampoo	*chahm-**poo***	champú
shaving cream	*kre-mah THe ah-fey-**tahr***	crema de afeitar
soap	*hah-**bon***	jabón
sunblock	***kre**-mah pro-tek-**to**-rah kon-trah el sol*	crema protectora contra el sol
tissues	*pah-**nywe**-los THe pah-**pel***	pañuelos de papel
toilet paper	*pah-**pel** i-hi-**e**-ni-ko*	papel higiénico
toothbrush	*the-**pi**-lyo THe **THien**-tes*	cepillo de dientes
toothpaste	*pahs-tah THen-**ti**-fri-kah/ pahs-tah THen-**tahl***	pasta dentífrica/ pasta dental

Photography

How much is it to process this film?

> *kwahn-to kwes-tah rre-be-lahr es-te rro-lyo/es-tah pe-li-koo-lah?*

¿Cuánto cuesta revelar este rollo/esta película?

When will it be ready?

> *kwahn-do es-tah-rah lis-to?*

¿Cuándo estará listo?

I'd like a film for this camera.

> *kie-ro oon rro-lyo pah-rah es-tah kah-mah-rah fo-to-grah-fi-kah*

Quiero un rollo para esta cámara fotográfica.

B&W (film)	*blahn-ko i ne-gro*	blanco y negro
camera	*kah-mah-rah fo-to-grah-fi-kah*	cámara (fotográfica)
colour (film)	*pe-li-koo-lah en ko-lo-res*	(película) en colores
film	*pe-li-koo-lah/rro-lyo fo-to-grah-fi-ko*	película/rollo (fotográfico)
flash	*bom-bi-lyah/flahsh*	bombilla/flash
lens	*len-te*	lente
light meter	*me-THi-THor THe looth*	medidor de luz

Smoking

A packet of cigarettes, please.

> *oon pah-ke-te THe thi-gah-rri-lyos, por fah-bor*

Un paquete de cigarrillos, por favor.

Are these cigarettes strong/mild?

> *son fwer-tes o swah-bes es-tos thi-gah-rri-lyos?*

¿Son fuertes o suaves estos cigarrillos?

Do you have a light?
tie-ne fwe-go?   ¿Tiene fuego?
Do you mind if I smoke?
le mohl-es-tah si fuh-mo?   ¿Le molesta si fumo?
Please don't smoke here.
poor-fah-vorr no fu-meh   Por favor, no fume aqui.
ah-ki

cigarettes	*thi-gah-rri-lyos*	cigarrillos
cigarette	*pah-pel THe*	papel de fumar
papers	*foo-mahr*	
filtered	*kon fil-tro*	con filtro
lighter	*en-then-de-THor/*	encendedor/
	me-che-ro	me-chero
matches	*fos-fo-ros/the-ri-lyahs*	fósforos/cerillas
menthol	*men-to-lah-THo*	mentolado
pipe	*pi-pah*	pipa
tobacco (pipe)	*pi-kah-THoo-rah*	picadura (para
	(*pah-rah pi-pah*)	pipa)

Health

Where is …?	*don-de es-tah …?*	¿Dónde está …?
the doctor	*el dok-tor/el*	el doctor/el
	me-THi-ko	médico
the hospital	*el os-pi-tahl*	el hospital
the chemist	*lah fahr-mah-thiah*	la farmacia
the dentist	*el den-tis-tah*	el dentista

I'm sick.
es-toy en-fer-mo/-ah   Estoy enfermo/a.
My friend is sick.
mi ah-mi-go/-ah es-tah   Mi amigo/a está enfermo/a.
en-fer-mo/-ah

SPANISH

What's the matter?
   *de ke se **ke**-hah?*   ¿De qué se queja?
It hurts here.
   *me **THwe**-le ah-**ki***   Me duele aquí.
My … hurts.
   *me **THwe**-le*   Me duele … (sg)

Parts of the Body

arm	*el **brah**-tho*	el brazo
back	*lah es-**pahl**-dah*	la espalda
ear	*lah o-**re**-hah*	la oreja
eye	*el **o**-ho*	el ojo
foot	*el **pie***	el pie
hand	*lah **mah**-no*	la mano
head	*lah kah-**be**-thah*	la cabeza
heart	*el ko-rah-**thon***	el corazón
leg	*lah **pier**-nah*	la pierna

Ailments

I have …
   ***ten**-go* …   Tengo …

an allergy	*ah-**ler**-hiah*	alergia
anaemia	*ah-**ne**-miah*	anemia
a burn	*oo-nah ke-mah-**THoo**-rah*	una quemadura
a cold	*oon res-fri-**ah**-THo/ kah-**tah**-rro*	un resfriado/ catarro
constipation	*es-tre-nyi-**mien**-to*	estreñimiento
a cough	*tos*	tos
diarrhoea	*di-ah-**rre**-ah*	diarrea
fever	***fie**-bre*	fiebre
glandular fever	*mo-no-noo-kle-**o**-sis*	mononucleosis
a headache	*do-**lor** THe kah-**be**-thah*	dolor de cabeza

indigestion	*in-di-hes-**tion***	indigestión
influenza	***gri**-pe*	gripe
itch	*ko-me-**thon**/pi-kah-**thon***	comezón/picazón
low/high blood pressure	*pre-**sion** bah-hah/**ahl**-tah*	presión baja/alta
sore throat	*do-**lor** THe gahr-**gahn**-tah*	dolor de garganta
sprain	*oo-nah tor-the-**THoo**-rah*	una torcedura
a stomachache	*do-**lor** THe es-to-mah-go*	dolor de estómago
sunburn	*oo-nah ke-mah-**THoo**-rah THe sol*	una quemadura de sol
a venereal disease	*oo-nah en-fer-me-**THahTH** be-**ne**-re-ah*	una enfermedad venérea

Women's Health

Could I see a female doctor?
*me po-**THri**-ah ah-ten-**der** oo-nah THok-to-rah*
¿Me podría atender una doctora?

I'm pregnant.
*es-**toy** em-bah-rah-**thah**-THah/en-**thin**-tah*
Estoy embarazada/encinta.

I'm on the pill.
*to-mo lah **pil**-do-rah ahn-ti-kon-thep-ti-bah*
Tomo la píldora anticonceptiva.

I haven't had my period for … weeks.
*ah-the … se-**ma**-nas ke no me bie-ne/lye-ga la **rre**-glah*
Hace … semanas que no me viene/llega la regla.

(unusual) bleeding	*san-**grant**-eh rah-rah*	sangrante (rara)
cramps	*cah-lahm-brehs*	calambres
cystitis	*sis-teet-is*	cistitis
thrush	*af-**tah***	afta

SPANISH

Specific Needs

I'm …	*soy …*	Soy …
asthmatic	*ahz-**mah**-ti-ko/-ah*	asmático/a
diabetic	*THi-ah-**be**-ti-ko/-ah*	diabético/a
epileptic	*e-pi-**lep**-ti-ko/-ah*	epiléptico/a

I'm allergic to antibiotics/
penicillin
*soy ah-**ler**-hi-ko/-ah ah los* Soy alérgico/a a los
*ahn-ti-bi-**o**-ti-kos/lah pe-ni-* antibióticos/la penicilina.
thi-li-nah

I've been vaccinated.
*es-**toy** bah-ku-**nah**-THo/-ah* Estoy vacunado/a.

I have my own syringe.
***ten**-go mi **pro**-piah* Tengo mi propia jeringa.
*he-**rin**-gah*

Useful Words

I feel better/worse.
*me **sien**-to me-**hor**/pe-**or*** Me siento mejor/peor.

accident	*ahk-thi-**THen**-te*	accidente
addiction	*bi-thio/dro-gah-THik-**thion**/de-pen-**den**-thiah*	vicio/drogadicción/dependencia
blood test	*ah-**nah**-li-sis THe **sahn**-gre*	análisis de sangre
injection	*in-yek-**thion***	inyección
injury	***dah**-nyo*	daño
oxygen	*ok-**si**-he-no*	oxígeno
vitamins	*bi-tah-**mi**-nahs*	vitaminas

At the Chemist

I need medication for …
ne-the-si-to oon me-THi-kah-men-to pah-rah …
Necesito un medicamento para …

I have a prescription.
ten-go rre-**the**-ta **me**-THi-ka
Tengo receta médica.

antibiotics	*ahn-ti-bi-o-ti-kos*	antibióticos
antiseptic	*ahn-ti-sep-ti-ko*	antiséptico

At the Dentist

I have a toothache.
me THwe-le oo-nah mwe-lah
Me duele una muela.

I've lost a filling.
se me kahy-o oon em-pahs-te
Se me cayó un empaste.

I've broken a tooth.
se me rrom-pi-o oon dien-te
Se me rompió un diente.

I don't want it extracted.
no kie-ro ke me lo ah-rrahn-ke
No quiero que me lo arranque.

Please give me an anaesthetic.
por fah-bor THe-me oon ah-nes-te-si-ko
Por favor, deme un anestésico.

Time & Dates

What date is it today?
ke THi-ah es oy/ah kwahn-tos es-tah-mos?
¿Qué día es hoy?/ ¿A cuántos estamos?

What time is it?
ke o-rah es/ke o-rahs son?
¿Qué hora es?/¿Qué horas son?

It is one o'clock.
  es lah oo-nah   Es la una.
It is (two o'clock).
  son lahs (dos)   Son las (dos).

in the morning   *de lah mah-nyah-nah* de la mañana
in the afternoon   *de lah tahr-THe*   de la tarde
in the evening   *de lah no-che*   de la noche

Days of the Week

Monday	*loo-nes*	lunes
Tuesday	*mahr-tes*	martes
Wednesday	*mier-ko-les*	miércoles
Thursday	*hwe-bes*	jueves
Friday	*bier-nes*	viernes
Saturday	*sah-bah-THo*	sábado
Sunday	*do-min-go*	domingo

Months

January	*e-ne-ro*	enero
February	*fe-bre-ro*	febrero
March	*mahr-tho*	marzo
April	*ah-bril*	abril
May	*mahy-o*	mayo
June	*hoo-nio*	junio
July	*hoo-lio*	julio
August	*ah-gos-to*	agosto
September	*sep-tiem-bre*	septiembre
October	*ok-tu-bre*	octubre
November	*no-biem-bre*	noviembre
December	*di-thiem-bre*	diciembre

SPANISH

Seasons

summer	*be-**rah**-no*	verano
autumn	*o-**to**-nyo*	otoño
winter	*in-**bier**-no*	invierno
spring	*pri-mah-**be**-rah*	primavera

Present

today	*oy*	hoy
this morning	*es-tah mah-**nyah**-nah*	esta mañana
this afternoon	*es-tah **tahr**-THe*	esta tarde
tonight	*es-tah **no**-che*	esta noche
this week/year	*es-tah se-**mah**-nah/es-te **ah**-nyo*	esta semana/este año
now	*ah-o-rah*	ahora

Past

yesterday	*ahy-**er***	ayer
day before yesterday	*ahn-te-ahy-**er***	anteayer
yesterday morning	*ahy-**er** por lah mah-**nyah**-nah*	ayer por la mañana
yesterday afternoon/evening	*ahy-**er** por lah **tahr**-THe/**no**-che*	ayer por la tarde/noche
last night	*ah-**no**-che*	anoche
last week/year	*lah se-**mah**-nah pah-**sah**-THah/el **ah**-nyo pah-**sah**-THo*	la semana pasada/el año pasado

Future

tomorrow	*mah-**nyah**-nah*	mañana
day after tomorrow	*pah-**sah**-THo mah-**nyah**-nah*	pasado mañana

tomorrow morning	mah-**nyah**-nah por lah mah-**nyah**-nah	mañana por la mañana
tomorrow afternoon/evening	mah-**nyah**-nah por lah **tahr**-THe/**no**-che	mañana por la tarde/noche
next week	lah se-**mah**-nah ke **bie**-ne	la semana que viene
next year	el **ah**-nyo ke **bie**-ne	el año que viene

During the Day

afternoon	**tahr**-THe	tarde
dawn, very early morning	mah-THroo-**gah**-THah	madrugada
day	**di**-ah	día
early	tem-**prah**-no	temprano
midnight	me-THiah-**no**-che	medianoche
morning	mah-**nyah**-nah	mañana
night	**no**-che	noche
noon	me-THio-**THi**-ah	mediodía
sundown	**pwes**-tah THel sol/-ah-**tahr**-THe-**ther**	puesta del sol/ atardecer
sunrise	ah-**mah**-ne-**ther**	amanecer

Numbers & Amounts

0	**the**-ro	cero
1	**oo**-no/**oo**-nah	uno, una
2	dos	dos
3	tres	tres
4	**kwah**-tro	cuatro
5	**thin**-ko	cinco
6	seis	seis
7	**sie**-te	siete

8	*o*-cho	ocho
9	*nwe*-be	nueve
10	*dieth*	diez
11	*on*-the	once
12	*do*-the	doce
13	*tre*-the	trece
14	kah-*tor*-the	catorce
15	*kin*-the	quince
16	die-thi-*seis*	dieciséis
17	die-thi-*sie*-te	diecisiete
18	die-thi-*o*-cho	dieciocho
19	die-thi-*nwe*-be	diecinueve
20	*bein*-te	veinte
30	*trein*-tah	treinta
40	kwah-*ren*-tah	cuarenta
50	thin-*kwen*-tah	cincuenta
60	se-*sen*-tah	sesenta
70	se-*ten*-tah	setenta
80	o-*chen*-tah	ochenta
90	no-*ben*-tah	noventa
100	*thien/thien*-to	cien/ciento
1000	mil	mil
one million	oon mi-*lyon*	un millón
1st	pri-*me*-ro	primero (1ro)
2nd	se-*goon*-do	segundo (2do)
3rd	ter-*the*-ro	tercero (3ro)
¼	oon **kwahr**-to	un cuarto
⅓	oon *ter*-thio	un tercio
½	me-*THio/ah*	medio/a
¾	tres **kwahr**-tos	tres cuartos

Amounts

small	*pe-**ke**-nyo/-ah,* *chi-ko/-ah*	pequeño/a, chico/a
big	***grahn**-de*	grande
a little (amount)	*oon po-**ki**-to*	un poquito
double	*el **do**-ble*	(el) doble
a dozen	*oo-nah THo-**the**-nah*	una docena
Enough!	***bahs**-tah*	¡Basta!
few	*(oo-nos) **po**-kos* *(oo-nahs) **po**-kahs*	(unos) pocos (m) (unas) pocas (f)
less	***me**-nos*	menos
many	***moo**-chos/ahs*	muchos/as
more	*mahs*	más
once	*oo-nah beth*	una vez
a pair	*oon pahr*	un par
percent	*por **thien**-to*	por ciento
some	*ahl-**goo**-nos/ahs*	algunos/as
too much	*de-mah-si-**ah**-THo*	demasiado
twice	*dos **be**-thes*	dos veces

Abbreviations

A.C. *or* d.de J.C.	AD
a.de J.C.	BC
C/Av., Avda./Pza.	St, Rd/Ave/Square
C.I.	ID
Cia	Co. (company)
Depto./Sede	Dept/HQ
IVA	VAT
PVP	RRP (recommended retail price)
SIDA	AIDS
Sr./Sra./Srta.	Mr/Mrs/Ms
Talgo	inter-city train

Paperwork

name and surname	nombre y apellido
address	dirección
date of birth	fecha de nacimiento
place of birth	lugar de nacimiento
age	edad
sex	sexo
nationality	nacionalidad
religion	religión
reason for travel	motivo del viaje
profession	profesión
marital status	estado civil
passport	pasaporte
passport number	número del pasaporte
visa	visado
tourist card	tarjeta de turismo
identification	carnet de identidad
birth certificate	partida de nacimiento
driver's licence	carnet de conducir
car owner's title	título de propiedad
car registration	matrícula
customs	aduana
immigration	inmigración
border	frontera

Emergencies

POLICE	*POLICIA*
POLICE STATION	*ESTACION DE POLICIA*

Help!
*so-**ko**-rro! ahoo-si-lio!* ¡Socorro! ¡Auxilio!

It's an emergency!
*es oo-nah e-mer-**hen**-thiah!* ¡Es una emergencia!

There's been an accident!
***oo**-bo oon ahk-thi-**THen**-te!* ¡Hubo un accidente!

Call a doctor!
***lyah**-me ah oon dok-**tor**!* ¡Llame a un doctor!

Call an ambulance!
***lyah**-me **oo**-nah ahm-boo-**lahn**-thiah!* ¡Llame una ambulancia!

I've been raped.
*e si-do bio-**lah**-THah/me bio-**lah**-ron* He sido violada./Me violaron.

I've been robbed!
*me ahn rro-**bah**-THo!* ¡Me han robado!

Call the police!
***lyah**-me ah lah po-li-**thi**-ah!* ¡Llame a la policía!

Where is the police station?
***don**-de ke-**THah** lah es-tah-**thion** de po-li-**thi**-ah?* ¿Dónde queda la estación de policía?

Go away!
***bah**-yah-se!* ¡Váyase!

I'll call the police!
*boy ah lyah-**mahr** ah lah po-li-**thi**-ah!* ¡Voy a llamar a la policía!

Thief!
*oon lah-**THron**!* ¡Un ladrón!

I am ill.
*es-**toy** en-**fer**-mo/-ah* Estoy enfermo/a.

I am lost.
   *es-**toy** per-**THi**-**THo**/-ah*   Estoy perdido/a.

Where are the toilets?
   ***don**-de **ke**-**THahn** los
   ser-**bi**-thios?*   ¿Dónde quedan los
                                            servicios?
Could you help me please?
   *pwe-**THe** ahy-oo-**THahr**-
   me por fah-**bor**?*   ¿Puede ayudarme, por
                                            favor?
Could I please use the telephone?
   *pwe-**THo** oo-**sahr** el te-le-
   fo-no, por fah-**vor**?*   ¿Puedo usar el teléfono, por
                                            favor?

I'm sorry. (I apologise)
   *lo **sien**-to/dis-**kool**-pe-me*   Lo siento./Discúlpeme.
I didn't realise I was doing
anything wrong.
   *no sah-**bi**-ah ke no es-**tah**-
   bah per-mi-**ti**-THo*   No sabía que no estaba
                                            permitido.
I didn't do it.
   *no lo **i**-the*   No lo hice.
I wish to contact my embassy/
consulate.
   *de-**se**-o ko-moo-ni-**kahr**-me
   con mi em-bah-**hah**-dah/
   kon-soo-**lah**-THo*   Deseo comunicarme con mi
                                            embajada/consulado.

I speak English.
   ah**-blo in-**gles   Hablo inglés.
I have medical insurance.
   ***ten**-go se-**goo**-ro **me**-THi-ko*   Tengo seguro médico.

My … was stolen.
*me rro-**bah**-ron mi …* Me robaron mi …

I've lost … *e per-**THi**-THo …/* He perdido …/
  *per-**THi** …* Perdí …

my bags	*mis mah-**le**-tahs*	mis maletas
my handbag	*mi **bol**-so*	mi bolso
my money	*mi **THi**-ne-ro*	mi dinero
my travellers' cheques	*mis **che**-kes biah-**he**-ros, **che**-kes de **biah**-he*	mis cheques viajeros, cheques de viaje
my passport	*mi pah-sah-**por**-te*	mi pasaporte

My possessions are insured.
***ten**-go se-**goo**-ro **kon**-trah **rro**-bo* Tengo seguro contra robo.

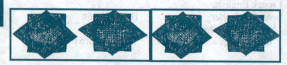

WELSH

WELSH

Welsh

Introduction

The Welsh language, *yr iaith Gymraeg,* (pronounced *uhr yaith gome-raig)*, belongs to the Celtic branch of the Indo-European language family. Closely related to Breton and Cornish, and more distantly to Irish, Scottish Gaelic and Manx, it is the strongest Celtic language both in terms of numbers of regular speakers (508,000 in the 1991 Census) and place in society. It was once spoken throughout the island of Britain south of a line between modern Glasgow and Edinburgh, but was gradually pushed westwards by the invading Angles and Saxons, following the retreat of the Roman legions in the fifth century. Its earliest literature was written towards the end of the sixth century in what is now southern Scotland, by the court poets Taliesin and Aneirin, who pioneered a continuous literary tradition of some 14 centuries.

The basis of the Acts of Union with England 1536 and 1542 was that the Welsh would acquire equal rights with the English only when they abandoned their language. Decline set in at that point but it was not rapid, for some 50% still spoke Welsh in 1900. Thereafter the language retreated more rapidly, so that by 1961 only 26% were Welsh-speaking and there was general alarm that the language might disappear. However, the 1960s saw the emergence of a popular movement in support of the language, galvanised by the Saunders Lewis BBC lecture, *Tynged yr Iaith* ('The Fate of the Language'). It was spearheaded by university students and inspired by pop singers like Dafydd Iwan, and succeeded through campaigns of civil disobedience in winning equal recognition for Welsh in one domain of society after another. Recent figures would suggest that the decline has been halted. The language has reasserted its position in the educational system, with Welsh-medium schools growing ever more popular. There has been a Welsh-language TV channel, S4C, since 1983 and recent years have seen the resurgence of Welsh as a badge of national identity, particularly among the young.

The usual word order in Welsh, as in the other Celtic languages and unlike most European languages, is verb–subject–object. The initial consonant of feminine nouns changes after the definite article, for example 'girl: the girl', *merch: y ferch* (pronounced *merrkh: uh verrkh*).

Pronunciation

All letters are pronounced and stress is usually on the second-last syllable. Letters may be pronounced as in English, except:

c	always as 'k'
ch	as in Scottish 'loch'
dd	always as 'th' in 'the', never as in 'thin'
f	'v'
ff	'f'
g	always as 'g' in 'garden'
ng	as 'ng' in 'sing'
ll	'hl', or voiceless 'l' – does not occur in English
ph	'f'
r	trilled with the tip of the tongue, as in Spanish
rh	'hr' (voiceless 'r')
s	always as in 'sit', never as in 'rose'
si	'sh'

th	always as 'th' in 'thin', never as in 'the'
u	'ee'
w	'oo'
y	as 'ee' in words of one syllable, and in the last syllable of a word of many syllables;
	as the 'a' in 'about' in other syllables of a word of many syllables, and in the definite article y, yr; in yn, yng, ym, fy, dy, syr and nyrs

ae, ai, au	as in 'aye'
aw	'ow' in 'cow'
ei, eu	'ey', similar to 'I'
iw, uw, yw	as 'yoo'
oe, oi	as the 'oy' in 'boy'
ei, eu	as 'oo + ee'

Greetings & Civilities

Hi!	Helo!
Good morning.	
boh-reh dah	Bore da.
Good afternoon.	
pruhn-hown dah	Prynhawn da.
Good evening.	
nohs-wyth thah	Noswaith dda.
Good night.	
nohs dah	Nos da.
How are you?	
shuh my?	Shwmae?
Well.	
uhn-thah	Yn dda.
Very well, thanks.	
uhn-thah yown, dee-olkh	Yn dda iawn, diolch.

WELSH

What's new?
   beth seen neh-with?   Beth sy'n newydd?
Have fun!
   hoo-il vowrr   Hwyl fawr.

Civilities
Please.
   ohss gwel-ookh-uhn-thah   Os gwelwch yn dda.
Thank you.
   dee-olkh   Diolch.
Thank you very much.
   dee-olkh uhn-vowrr   Diolch yn fawr.
You're welcome.
   kroy-soh   Croeso.
I'd like to present you to ...
   duh-nah ...   Dyna ...
I'm pleased to meet you.
   mayn thah ghen ee goorrth   Mae'n dda gen i gwrdd â
   ah khee   chi.

Forms of Address
Sir/Mr ...   Syr/Mr
Madame/Mrs ...   Mrs

Small Talk
What's your name?
   beth yoo'kh en-oo khee?   Beth yw eich enw chi?
I'm ...
   ... uhd-oo ee   ... ydw i.
Who is he/she?
   poo-ee yoo eh/hee   Pwy yw ef/hi?

WELSH

I don't know.
oon ee thim Wn i ddim.
Where are you from?
oh blay ruhd-ukh kheen dohd? O ble rydych chi'n dod?

I'm from … *oh …* O …

Australia	*ow-stral-ee-ah*	Awstralia
Canada	*gahn-ada*	Ganada
England	*loy-gr*	Loegr
New Zealand	*zeh-land neh-with*	Zeland Newydd
Scotland	*uhr ahl-ban*	Yr Alban
Wales	*gome-ree*	Gymru
the USA	*uhr ee-nol dal-AYE-thee-igh*	Yr Unol Daleithiau

NB For other countries, see the note in the Irish chapter.

Useful Phrases

How do you say that in Welsh?
beth you hoon uhn gome-rayg? Beth yw hwn yn Gymraeg?
Are you learning Welsh?
uhd-ukh khi uhn duhss-kee come-rayg? Ydych chi yn dysgu Cymraeg?
Yes./No.
uhd-oo/nag-uhd-oo Ydw/Nag ydw.
Excuse me.
ehs-ghess-ohd-ookh vee Esgusodwchfi.
Where's the toilet, please?
blay mayrr tee bakh? Ble mae'r tý bach?

On the left.	*arr uh khweeth*	Ar y chwith.
On the right.	*arr uh day*	Ar y de.
Straight on.	*uhm-LAYN*	Ymlaen.

Food

Waiter!
  gwayn-eeth! Gweinydd!

What will you drink/eat?
  beth vuh-thukh khee uhn Beth fyddych chi yn
  boo-ee-tah/uhv-ehd? bwyta/yfed?

Cheers!
  yekh-eed dah! Iechyd da!

I'd like ...	*ruhd-oo ee*	Rydw i eisiau ...
	ish-yigh ...	
a little bread, please	*tipp-in oh-vah-rah, ohss gwel-ookh-uhn-thah*	typyn o fara, os gwelwch yn dda.
a beer	*goo-roo*	gwrw
a drop of ...	*uh-khu-ig oh ...*	ychydig o ...
apple juice	*seethe aval*	sudd afal
orange juice	*seethe ohr-en*	sudd oren
water	*thoor*	ddwr
wine	*ween*	win
fish	*bus-god*	bysgod
meat	*gheeg*	gig
potatoes	*dah-tooss*	datws

Quick Reference
Basque

Hello.	*kai-sho*	Kaixo.
Good morning.	*e-goo-non*	Egun On.
Goodbye.	*a-goor*	Agur.

| Please. | *me-se-des* | Mesedez. |
| Thank you. | *es-ke-rree-kahs-ko* | Eskerrik asko. |

| Excuse me. | *barr-kah-too* | Barkatu. |
| You're welcome. | *es o-rre-gah-teek* | Ez horregatik. |

Where's the toilet, please?
ko-moo-nah, non dah-gho?　Komuna non dago?

At the end.
　ahs-ke-ne-ahn　　　　　　Azkenean.
On the left.
　es-kairr-tah-rah　　　　　Ezkertara.
On the right.
　es-koo-bee-tah-rah/　　　Eskubitara/
　es-koo-mah-tah-rah　　　Eskumatara. (Biscay Basque)
Straight ahead.
　soo-sen soo-sen-e-ahn　Zuzen-zuzenean.

495

ERRETZEA DEBEKATUA	NO SMOKING
HIRIAREN ERDIALDEA	CITY CENTRE (on buses)
ANDREAK/JAUNAK	LADIES/GENTLEMEN
EDARITEGIA	BAR
EMAN BIDEA	YIELD (GIVE WAY)
ERTZAINTZA	BASQUE POLICE
IRTEERA	EXIT
KONTUZ!	CAUTION!
LURSAIL JABEDUNA	PRIVATE PROPERTY
SARRERA	ENTRANCE
SARTZEA DEBEKATURIK	NO ENTRY
UDALTZAINGOA	MUNICIPAL POLICE

Quick Reference
Catalan

Hello.	Hola!
Good morning.	Bon dia.
Goodbye.	Adéu/Adéu-siau.
Please.	Sisplau/Si us plau.
Thank you (very much).	(Moltes) Gràcies.
That's fine/You're welcome.	De res.
Yes/No.	Sí/No.
Excuse me.	Perdoni.
Do you speak English?	Parla anglès?
I (don't) understand.	(No) ho entenc.
Excuse me, where is ...?	Perdoni, on és...?
How much is it ?	Quant val?
Do you have any rooms available?	Hi ha habitacions lliures?
How much is it per night/ per person?	Quant val per nit/persona?
I'd like a single/double room.	Voldria una habitació individual/doble.
I'd like to pay the bill.	Voldria pagar el compte.

OPEN/CLOSED	OBERT/TANCAT
BUDGET HOTEL	HOSTAL (Hs)
CUSTOMS	DUANA
INFORMATION	INFORMACIO
DO NOT TOUCH	NO TOCAR
EXIT	SORTIDA
EMERGENCY EXIT	SALIDA D'EMERGENCIA
GUESTHOUSE	PENSIO (P)
TOILETS	SERVEIS
YOUTH HOSTEL	ALBERG JUVENIL
MOUNTAIN LODGE	REFUGI DE MUNTANYA

Quick Reference
Dutch

Hello.	*dahkh/hah-loh*	Dag/Hallo.
Good morning.	***khoo**-der **mor**-khern*	Goede morgen.
Goodbye.	*dahkh*	Dag.
Please.	*ahls-tü-**bleeft**/ ahls-yer-**bleeft***	Alstublieft/ Alsjeblieft.
Thank you.	*dahnk ü/yer (wehl)*	Dank U/je (wel).

| Excuse me. | *pahr-**don*** | Pardon. |
| Yes/No. | *yaa/nay* | Ja/Nee. |

Do you speak English?
*spraykt ü/sprayk yer **ehng**-erls?* — Spreekt U/spreek je Engels?

I (don't) understand.
*ik ber-**khreyp** heht (neet)* — Ik begrijp het (niet).

I am lost.	*ik behn der wehkh kweyt*	Ik ben de weg kwijt.
Where is …?	*waar is …?*	Waar is …?
Go straight ahead.	*khaa rehkht-**dor***	Ga rechtdoor.
Turn left …	*khaa links-ahf …*	Ga linksaf …
Turn right …	*khaa rehkhts-ahf …*	Ga rechtsaf …

499

Dutch *Quick Reference*

| How much is it …? | **hoo**-*vayl kost heht …?* | Hoeveel kost het …? |
| What time is it? | *hoo laat is heht?* | Hoe laat is het? |

Where are the toilets?
*waar zeyn de twah-**leht**-tern/way-**says**?*   Waar zijn de toiletten/WC's?

| today | *vahn-**daakh*** | vandaag |
| tomorrow | **mor**-*khern* | morgen |

EMERGENCY EXIT	NOODUITGANG
ENTRANCE	INGANG
EXIT	UITGANG
THIS WAY TO	RICHTING
FREE ADMISSION	GRATIS TOEGANG
HOT/COLD	WARM/KOUD
INFORMATION	INFORMATIE, INLICHTINGEN
NO ENTRY	VERBODEN TOEGANG
NO SMOKING	VERBODEN TE ROKEN
OPEN/CLOSED	OPEN/GESLOTEN
PROHIBITED	VERBODEN
RESERVED	GERESERVEERD
TELEPHONE	TELEFOON
TOILETS	WC's/TOILETTEN
MEN	HEREN/MANNEN
WOMEN	DAMES/VROUWEN

Quick Reference
French

Hello.	*bõ-zhoor*	Bonjour.
Good morning.	*bõ-zhoor*	Bonjour.
Goodbye.	*oh rer-vwahr*	Au revoir.
Please.	*seel voo plei*	S'il vous plaît.
Thank you.	*mehr-see*	Merci.
Many thanks.	*mehr-see boh-koo*	Merci beaucoup.
Yes/No.	*wee/nõ*	Oui/Non.
Excuse me.	*ehk-skü-zei mwah*	Excusez-moi.

Do you speak English?
| *voo pahr-lei ã-glei?* | Vous parlez anglais? |

I (don't) understand.
| *zher (ner) kõ-prã (pah)* | Je (ne) comprends (pas). |

I am lost.	*zher mer swee ei-gah-rei*	Je me suis égaré/-ée.
Where is …?	*oo ei …?*	Où est …?
Go straight ahead.	*kõ-teen-wei too drwah*	Continuez tout droit.
Turn left …	*toor-nei ah gohsh …*	Tournez à gauche …
Turn right …	*toor-nei ah drwaht …*	Tournez à droite …

| How much is it? | *sei kõ-byẽ?* | C'est combien ? |
| What time is it? | *kehl err ei teel?* | Quelle heure est-il? |

I want to go to …	*zher ver ah-lei ah …*	Je veux aller à …
I would like …	*zher voo-drei …*	Je voudrais …
a one-way ticket	*ē bee-yei ah-lei sēpl*	un billet aller simple
a return ticket	*ē bee-yei ah-lei ei rertoor*	un billet aller et retour

I'd like a single/double room.

| *zher voo-drei ün shābr ah ē lee/doobl* | Je voudrais une chambre à un lit/double. |

Can I see it?

| *zher per lah vwahr?* | Je peux la voir? |

| today | *oh-zhoor-dwee* | aujourd'hui |
| tomorrow | *der-mē* | demain |

EMERGENCY EXIT	ISSUE DE SECOURS
ENTRANCE	ENTRÉE
EXIT	SORTIE
FREE ADMISSION	ENTRÉE GRATUITE
HOT/COLD	CHAUDE/FROIDE
INFORMATION	RENSEIGNEMENTS
NO ENTRY	ENTRÉE INTERDITE
NO SMOKING	DÉFENSE DE FUMER
OPEN/CLOSED	OUVERT/FERMÉ
PROHIBITED	INTERDIT
RESERVED	RÉSERVÉ
TOILETS	TOILETTES

Quick Reference
German

English	Pronunciation	German
Hello. (Good day)	*ghu-tehn taak*	Guten Tag.
Good morning.	*ghu-tehn mor-ghehn*	Guten Morgen.
Goodbye.	*owf vee-dehr-zayn*	Auf Wiedersehen.
Please.	*bi-teh*	Bitte.
Thank you.	*dahng-keh*	Danke.
Yes/No.	*yaa/nain*	Ja/Nein.
Excuse me.	*ehnt-shul-di-ghung*	Entschuldigung.

Do you speak English?
  shpreh-khehn zee ehng-lish? — Sprechen Sie Englisch?
I (don't) understand.
  ikh fehr-shtay-eh (nikht) — Ich verstehe (nicht).

I am lost.
  ikh haa-beh mikh fehr-irt — Ich habe mich verirrt.
Where is …?
  voh ist …? — Wo ist …?
Go straight ahead.
  ghay-ehn zee gheh-raa-deh-ows — Gehen Sie geradeaus.
Turn left …
  bee-ghehn zee … lingks ahp — Biegen Sie … links ab.
Turn right …
  bee-ghehn zee … rehkhts ahp — Biegen Sie … rechts ab.

How much is it?
  *vee-**feel** ko-steht ehs?*   Wieviel kostet es?
What time is it?   *vee shpayt ist ehs?*   Wie spät ist es?

I want to go to …
  *ikh **merkh**-teh nahkh …*   Ich möchte nach … fahren.
  fah-rehn
Do you have any rooms available?
  *haa-behn zee nokh **frai**-yeh*   Haben Sie noch freie
  tsi-mehr?   Zimmer?

I'd like a …   *ikh **merkh**-teh …*   Ich möchte …
one-way/return   *ain-tsehl-kahr-teh/*   Einzelkarte/
  ticket   *rük-fahr-kahr-teh*   Rückfahrkarte.
single/double room   *ain-tsehl-tsi-mehr/*   Einzelzimmer/
                     do-pehl-tsi-mehr   Doppelzimmer

today   *hoy-teh*   heute
tomorrow   *mor-ghehn*   morgen

EMERGENCY EXIT	NOTAUSGANG
ENTRANCE	EINGANG
EXIT	AUSGANG
FREE ADMISSION	EINTRITT FREI
HOT/COLD	HEIß/KALT
INFORMATION	AUSKUNFT
NO ENTRY	KEIN ZUTRITT
NO SMOKING	RAUCHEN VERBOTEN
OPEN/CLOSED	OFFEN/GESCHLOSSEN
PROHIBITED	VERBOTEN
RESERVED	RESERVIERT
TOILETS	TOILETTEN (WC)

Quick Reference
Greek

Hello.	*ya sas*	Γεια σας
Good morning.	*kalimera*	Καλημέρα.
Goodbye.	*andio*	Αντίο.

| Please. | *parakalo* | Παρακαλώ. |
| Thank you. | *efharisto* | Ευχαριστώ. |

Excuse me/sorry!	*me sinhorite/*	Με συγχωρείτε/
	sighnomi!	συγγνώμη!
Yes./No.	*ne/ohi*	Ναι/Όχι.

Do you speak English?
mi-la-te angli-ka?	Μιλάτε Αγγλικά;
I don't understand.	
den katalaveno	Δεν καταλαβαίνω.

I am lost.	*eho hathi*	Έχω χαθεί.
Where is ...?	*pou ine ...?*	Πού είναι ...;
Go straight ahead.	*piyenete katefthian*	Πηγαίνετε κατ'ευθείαν.

| Turn left ... | *stripste aristera ...* | Στρίψτε αριστερά ... |
| Turn right ... | *stripste dexia ...* | Στρίψτε δεξιά ... |

| I want to go to ... | *the-lo na pa-o sto/* | Θέλω να πάω στο/ |
| | *sti ...* | στη ... |

Greek *Quick Reference*

| single (ticket) | *ablo (isitirio)* | απλό (εισιτήριο) |
| return (ticket) | *(isitirio) me epistrofi* | (εισιτήριο) με επιστροφή |

Do you have any rooms available?
e-hete dhia-the-sima dho-ma-tia? — Έχετε διαθέσιμα δωμάτια;

I'd like a …	*thelo ena …*	Θέλω ένα …
single room	*mono dhomatio*	μονό δωμάτιο
double room	*dhiplo dhomatio*	διπλό δωμάτιο

| today | *simera* | σήμερα |
| tomorrow | *avrio* | αύριο |

CASH DESK (in banks & shops)	*ΤΑΜΕΙΟ*
CUSTOMS	*ΤΕΛΩΝΕΙΟΝ*
DOCTOR'S SURGERY	*ΙΑΤΡΕΙΟ*
ENTRY	*ΕΙΣΟΔΟΣ*
EXIT	*ΕΞΟΔΟΣ*
FROM …	*ΑΠΟ …*
HOSPITAL	*ΝΟΣΟΚΟΜΕΙΟ*
INFORMATION	*ΠΛΗΡΟΦΟΡΙΕΣ*
MEN (toilets)	*ΑΝΔΡΩΝ*
NO SMOKING	*ΑΠΑΓΟΡΕΥΕΤΑΙ ΤΟ ΚΑΠΝΙΣΜΑ*
POLICE	*ΑΣΤΥΝΟΜΙΑ*
PROHIBITED	*ΑΠΑΓΟΡΕΥΕΤΑΙ*
TO …	*ΠΡΟΣ …*
WOMEN (toilets)	*ΓΥΝΑΙΚΩΝ*

Quick Reference
Irish

Hi/Good morning/ Good afternoon.	*dee-a gwit*	Dia duit. (lit. 'God to you')
Goodbye.	*slaan*	Slán.

Please.
lyeh do hull — Le do thoil.

Thank you.
go-ra mo ogot — Gura maith agat.

You're welcome.
taa faa-il-tyeh roht — Tá fáilte romhat.

Excuse me.
gov mo lyeh-shkay-al — Gabh mo leithscéal.

I understand.	*tig-im*	Tuigim thú.
I don't understand.	*nyee hig-im hoo.*	Ní thuigim thú.

Say it again, please.
obb-ir a-reesh ay, lyeh do hull — Abair arís é, le do thoil.

Write it down, please.
shkreev sheess ay, lyeh do hull — Scríobh síos é, le do thoil.

Where's the toilet, please?
kaa will on lyeh-aras, lyeh do hull? — Cá bhfuil an leithreas, le do thoil?

On the left.	*ehr klay*	Ar clé.
On the right.	*ehr yesh*	Ar dheis.
Straight on.	*dyee-rokh ehr ay*	Díreach ar aghaidh.

NO SMOKING	NÁ CAITEAR TOBAC
CITY CENTRE (on buses)	AN LÁR
LADIES/GENTLEMEN	MNÁ/FIR

Quick Reference
Italian

Hello.	*chahw*	Ciao.
Good morning.	*bwon-**jor**-no*	Buongiorno.
Goodbye.	*ah-rree-ve-**dair**-chee/chahw*	Arrivederci/Ciao.
Please.	*per fah-**vor**-rei/per pee-ah-**chair**-rei*	Per favore./Per piacere.
Thank you.	*ghrah-tsee-e*	Grazie.
You're welcome.	*prei-gho*	Prego.
Yes./No.	*see/no*	Sì./No.
Excuse me.	*mee **skoo**-zee*	Mi scusi.

Do you speak English?
  *pahr-lah (pahr-lee) eng-**ghlei**-zei?*   Parla (Parli) inglese?
I (don't) understand.
  *(non) kah-**pees**-ko*   (Non) Capisco.

I am lost.	*mee so-no **pair**-so*	Mi sono perso.
Where is …?	*do-**vei** …?*	Dov'è …?
Go straight ahead.	*see vah (vah-ee) **sem**-prei dee-**reet**-to*	Si va sempre diritto.
Turn left …	*jee-rah ah see-**nee**-strah …*	Gira a sinistra …
Turn right …	*jee-rah ah **de**-strah …*	Gira a destra …

Italian *Quick Reference*

How much is it?	*kwahn-to kos-dah?*	Quanto costa?
What time is it?	*kei **or**-rei so-no?*	Che ore sono?

I want to go to …
  *vor-rei ahn-**dah**-rei ah …*   Vorrei andare a …
I'd like …
  *vo-**rrei** …*   Vorrei …
one-way/return ticket
  *(oon bee-**lyet**-to dee) so-lo*   (Un biglietto di) Solo
  *ahn-**dah**-tah/ahn-**dah**-tah*   andata/Andata e ritorno.
  *ei ree-**tor**-no*
Do you have any rooms available?
  *ah **del**-lei kah-**mair**-rei*   Ha delle camere libere?
  lee-bair-rei?

today	*oj-jee*	oggi
tomorrow	*do-**mah**-nee*	domani

CUSTOMS	DOGANA
EMERGENCY EXIT	USCITA DI SICUREZZA
ENTRANCE	INGRESSO/ENTRATA
EXIT	USCITA
FREE ADMISSION	INGRESSO GRATUITO
HOT/COLD	CALDO/FREDDO
NO ENTRY	VIETATO ENTRARE
NO SMOKING	VIETATO FUMARE
OPEN/CLOSED	APERTO/CHIUSO
PROHIBITED	PROIBITO/VIETATO
TOILETS	GABINETTI
POLICE	POLIZIA/CARABINIERI
POLICE STATION	QUESTURA/CASERMA

Quick Reference
Portuguese

English	Pronunciation	Portuguese
Hello.	*oh-lah*	Olá.
Good morning.	*bõ dee-ă*	Bom dia.
Goodbye.	*ă-dewsh*	Adeus.
Please.	*s'fahsh făvor*	Se faz favor.
Thank you.	*o-bree-gah-du/dă*	Obrigado/a.
That's fine./ You're welcome.	*d'nah-dă*	De nada.
Excuse me.	*d'sh-kul-p'/kõ lee-sē-să*	Desculpe/Com licença.
Yes/No.	*sing/nõw*	Sim/Não

Do you speak English?
fah-lă ing-glesh?   Fala Inglês?

I (don't) understand.
(nõw) p'r-se-bu/ē-tē-du   (Não) Percebo/Entendo.

Where are the toilets?
õ-dy eh ă kah-ză d' bă-nyu?   Onde é a casa de banho?

Where is …?
õ-dy eh …?/õ-d' fee-kă …?   Onde é …?/Onde fica …?

Go straight ahead.
see-gă sē-pr' ă dee-rey-tu/sē-pr' ēy frē-t'   Siga sempre a direito/ sempre em frente.

Turn left …
vee-rahsh-ker-dă …   Vire à esquerda …

Turn right …
vee-rah dee-rey-tă …   Vire à direita …

How much does it cost?
   kwã-tu kush-tă?   Quanto custa?
What time is it?
   ky-oh-răsh sõw?   Que horas são?

I want to go to …	*keh-ru eer pă-ră* …	Quero ir para …
one-way ticket	*oong bee-lye-t' d' ee-dă/sing-pl'sh*	um bilhete de ida/ simples
return ticket	*oong bee-lye-t' d' ee-dă ee vohl-tă*	um bilhete de ida e volta

Do you have any rooms available?
   tẽy kwahr-tush lee-vr'sh?   Tem quartos livres?
I'd like …
   k'-ree-¢ …   Queria …
a single/double room
   oong kwahr-tu ing-dee-vee- um quarto individual/de casal.
   du-ahl/d'kă-zahl

today	*o-zh*	hoje
tomorrow	*ah-mă-nyã*	amanhã

EMERGENCY EXIT	SAÍDA DE EMERGÊNCIA
ENTRANCE	ENTRADA
EXIT	SAÍDA
FREE ADMISSION	ENTRADA GRATIS
HOT/COLD	QUENTE/FRIO
INFORMATION	INFORMAÇÕES
NO ENTRY	PROIBIDA A ENTRADA
NO SMOKING	PROIBIDO FUMAR
OPEN	ABERTO
CLOSED	ENCERRADO/FECHADO

Quick Reference
Scottish Gaelic

Good morning.	*madding va*	Madainn mhath.
Goodbye.	*b–yan–achd let*	Beannachd leat.
Goodbye. (The same with you)	*mar shin let*	Mar sin leat.
Please.	*mahs eh doh hawl eh*	Mas e do thoil e.
Thank you.	*tappuh let*	Tapadh leat.
You're welcome.	*sheh doh veh–huh*	'Se do bheatha.
Excuse me.	*gav mo lishk–yal*	Gabh mo leisgeul.
I'd like ...	*boo tawl lehum*	Bu toigh leam ...
I want to go to ...		
ha mee ug–ee–urry uh gholl goo ...		Tha mi ag iarraidh a dhol gu ...
How do I get to ...?		
kimmer uh yaev mee goo ...?		Ciamar a gheibh mi gu ...?

THE STATION	AN STEISEAN
THE BUS	AM BUS
THE TRAIN	AN TREANA
THE PLANE	AM PLEAN
TAXI	TACSAIDH
THE AIRPORT	AM PORT ADHAR
THE FERRY	AN AISEAG
THE BOAT	AM BATA

TOURIST INFORMATION CENTRE	IONAD–FIOSRACHAIDH LUCHD–TURAIS
WELCOME TO ... INVERNESS PORTREE STORNOWAY WESTERN ISLES COUNCIL	FAILTE GU ... INBHIR NIS PORTRIGH STEORNABHAGH COMHAIRLE NAN EILEAN
STREET BANK STREET CHURCH STREET	SRAID SRAID A' BHANCA SRAID NA H–EAGLAISE
THE BANK BANK OF SCOTLAND	AM BANCA BANCA NA H–ALBA
BED & BREAKFAST HOTEL	LEABAIDH 'S BRACAIST TAIGH–OSDA
TELEPHONE CINEMA TOILET THE SHOPS TOWN CENTRE SCHOOL THE NEWSAGENT'S	FON TAIGH–DHEALBH TAIGH BEAG NA BUTHAN MEADHAN A ' BHAILE SGOIL BUTH NAM PAIPEARAN

Quick Reference
Spanish

Hello.	*o-lah!*	¡Hola!
Good morning.	*bwe-nos THi-ahs*	Buenos días.
Goodbye.	*ah-THios!*	¡Adiós!
Please.	*por fah-bor*	Por favor.
Thank you.	*grah-thiahs*	Gracias.
Many thanks.	*moo-chahs/* *moo-chi-si-mahs* *grah-thi-ahs*	Muchas/ Muchísimas gracias.
Excuse me.	*per-mi-so*	Permiso.
Yes/No.	*si/no*	Sí/No.

Do you speak English?
ah-blah in-gles?   ¿Habla inglés?

I (don't) understand.
(no) en-tien-do   (No) Entiendo.

Where are the toilets?
don-de ke-THahn los ser-bi-thios?   ¿Dónde quedan los servicios?

Where is …?	*don-de es-tah …?*	¿Dónde está …?
Turn left …	*do-ble ah lah ith-kier-THah …*	Doble a la izquierda …
Turn right …	*do-ble ah lah THe-re-chah …*	Doble a la derecha …
Go straight ahead.	*si-gah/bahy-ah to-THo THe-re-cho*	Siga/Vaya todo derecho.

515

Spanish *Quick Reference*

How much is it?
   kwahn-to kwes-tah?   ¿Cuánto cuesta?
What time is it?
   ke o-rah es/ke o-rahs son?   ¿Qué hora es?

I want to go to …	*kie-ro ir ah …*	Quiero ir a…
a one-way ticket	*oon bi-lye-te sen-thi-lyo*	un billete sencillo
a return ticket	*oon bi-lye-te de i-THah i bwel-tah*	un billete de ida y vuelta

Do you have any rooms available?
   tie-ne ah-bi-tah-thi-o-nes li-bres?   ¿Tiene habitaciones libres?
Can I see it?
   pwe-THo ber-lah?   ¿Puedo verla?

today	*oy*	hoy
tomorrow	*mah-nyah-nah*	mañana

EMERGENCY EXIT	SALIDA DE EMERGENCIA
ENTRANCE	ENTRADA
EXIT	SALIDA
FREE ADMISSION	ENTRADA GRATIS
HOT/COLD	CALIENTE/FRIO
NO ENTRY	PROHIBIDO EL PASO
NO SMOKING	PROHIBIDO FUMAR
OPEN/CLOSED	ABIERTO/CERRADO
TOILETS	SERVICIOS/ASEOS

Quick Reference
Welsh

Hi!	Helo!
Good morning.	
boh-reh dah	Bore da.
Good night.	
nohs dah	Nos da.
Please.	
ohss gwel-ookh-uhn-thah	Os gwelwch yn dda.
Thank you.	
dee-olkh	Diolch.
You're welcome.	
kroy-soh	Croeso.
How do you say that in Welsh?	
beth you hoon uhn gome-rayg?	Beth yw hwn yn Gymraeg?
Yes./No.	
uhd-oo/nag-uhd-oo	Ydw/Nag ydw.
Excuse me.	
ehs-ghess-ohd-ookh vee	Esgusodwchfi.
Where's the toilet, please?	
blay mayrr tee bakh?	Ble mae'r ty bach?

Appendix

Esperanto: A Global Language

The international language Esperanto was initiated in 1887 by a Warsaw oculist, Dr L.Zamenhof, as a neutral, easily learned means of communication between speakers of different languages. Today it has become a language used by a community of at least three million worldwide. Radio stations from Warsaw to Beijing, Brazil to the Vatican, broadcast in Esperanto and it is becoming increasingly popular in Asia.

Esperanto vocabulary derives predominantly from Western Europe languages, though words from other sources are constantly being added. Its word order and morphology (word structure) have Slavic influences, and its grammar has much in common with such languages as Chinese, Arabic, Turkish, Swahili and Japanese.

Why Use Esperanto?

English is widely used as a language for global communication, particularly in the areas of tourism, trade, science, transport communications and on the Net. However, English is seen by some as the language of an old colonial empire and a recently arrived super power, and its global usage may therefore be interpreted as a cultural monopoly, or even threat. The use of English on a global scale also means that many words, particularly new ones, have entered into the vocabulary of other languages, thus changing the nature of each language. Of course, this has always been how languages develop, and every language contains many borrowed words. But the heavy influence of English this century has resulted in resistence from some, while others who welcome the widespread use of one language such as English, still recognise the potential of a neutral language that could be used alongside or in its place.

So, why should an artificially created language such as Esperanto become a global language? Supporters of the language give the following reasons:

- Esperanto enables people of diverse linguistic backgrounds to communicate on the basis of equality – no native speakers correcting you, and nobody imposing their language on others. It thus favours linguistic diversity, as each speaker is free to retain their own language while still being able to converse across cultures.

- It is estimated as 12 times easier than any other language to learn, due to its regular grammar and lack of exceptions. Speakers say you can become fluent within 100 hours, less if you are familiar with a second language, especially a Romance language.

- Esperanto provides opportunities to meet other speakers through well-organised networks in over 120 countries. *Pasporta Servo*, for instance, has over a thousand addresses in 74 countries where free overnight accommodation is offered to Esperanto speakers, thus providing an opportunity for travellers and locals to meet.

- The use of Esperanto as a conference language for the EU, UN and other organisations would cut translation costs enormously. For instance, in 1995 the addition of Swedish and Finnish to the EU increased the number of working pairs of languages required from 72 to 110. These costs add pressure to the EU, and other international groups, to limit the number of working languages used, but it is argued that this would lead to more inequality. When the French Minister Lamassoure proposed limiting the number of working languages for the EU to the 'big 5' (English, French, German, Spanish and Italian), he faced almost unanimous condemnation in the European Parliament, some MEPs calling his proposal a 'crime'.

One argument against Esperanto is that, as a language artificially created, and one that sprang up initially as a written language (unlike other languages which grow and develop from verbal roots long before they are written), Esperanto cannot continue to develop as other 'living' languages do. Esperantists argue that Esperanto is, in fact, in a unique position to develop very broadly, as the grammar of the language (the 'sixteen rules') allows words from any language to be incorporated. The vocabulary has changed and expanded over time as any other language does. The system of the language can also handle many idiomatic phrases from other languages, and it has been argued that translations into Esperanto capture more accurately the original meaning of the work than other languages are able to.

The Alphabet
Vowels

The vowels *a*, *e*, *i*, *o* and *u* sound like are there three or two.

Consonants

The letters *b*, *d*, *f*, *h*, *k*, *l*, *m*, *n*, *p*, *s*, *t*, *v* and *z* are all as in English. The following sounds, except the *h*, are all found in English, but written differently. The letter *r* is always trilled, as in Italian.

Letter	Pronunciation Guide
c	'ts' as in 'bits'
c	as 'ch'
g	hard, as in 'go'
g	soft, as in 'Joe'
h	as in the Scottish '*loch*' or standard German '*ich*'
j	as 'y'
j	as the 's' in 'pleasure'
s	as 'sh'
u	as 'w'

The Sixteen Rules of Esperanto

It is important to note that Esperanto has no irregularities or exceptions.

1) There is no indefinite article ('a/an'), which means that the same word applies for 'a bird' and 'bird'. If you need to single the bird out, you say 'one bird'. There is only one definite article: *la*, and like 'the' in English, it never changes.

child/a child   *infano*   the child   *la infano*

2) All nouns have the same ending: *o*, in the singular, and *oj* in the plural.

friend (male or female) *amiko*   friends   *amikoj*

3) All adjectives end in a.

4) The numbers are built on the basic numerals of one to ten, a hundred and a thousand. Thus 12 is translated as 'ten two'; 22 is 'two ten two'; 102 is '100 two'. See the list of numbers on page 525.

5) Personal pronouns are:

mi	I	*ni*	we
vi	you	*vi*	you (plural)
li, si, gi	he, she, it	*oni*	one, people
si	himself, herself, themselves	*ili*	they

6) Verbs do not change with person (I, you, we, etc) or number. The tense is created by changing the ending of the root verb:

infinitive (root)	*-i*	to learn	*lerni*
present	*-as*	learn/s	*lernas*
past	*-is*	learnt	*lernis*
future	*-os*	will learn	*lernos*
conditional (if...would, could, should)	*-us*	would learn, etc	*lernus*
imperative (command)	*--u*	Learn!	*lernu*

7) Adverbs end in *e*.

8) Prepositions go before the noun.

9) Every word is read as it is written.

10) Stress is always on the second-last syllable (each vowel counts as a syllable).

11) Compound words are formed by adding words together, with no changes.

12) The word *ne* is used for negatives, but is dropped if a word in the sentence already expresses the negative. When two negatives *(ne ... ne)* are used, it emphasises the negation (unlike English, which turns the meaning into a positive)

13) To indicate direction (going to, travelling to, walking to, etc), nouns involved have the letter *n* added to them. This also applies to direct objects.

'... in the room' is *en la cambro*; '... into the room' is *en la cambron*'
'He built the house' is *Ili konstruis la domon.* ('house' on its own is *domo)*

14) Every preposition has a specific meaning, but if there is a possibility of ambiguity the word *je* is used as a general preposition.

15) Foreign words, when introduced into the language, take on the spelling of Esperanto.

telephone	*telefono*	physics	*fiziko*
electronics	*elektroniko*	computer	*komputilo*

16) The final vowel of the noun and the article may be replaced by an apostrophe, for instance, when preceding a vowel sound.

Esperanto vocabulary always develops from a root word:

varma	warm		
varmega	hot	*malvarma*	cold
varmeta	lukewarm	*malvarmeta*	cool
varmigi	to warm something		

amo	love		
ami	to love	*malami*	to hate
ameti	to like	*ekami*	to begin to love
amindumi	to court	*aminda*	worthy of love
amori	to make love	*amadi*	to continue to love
amebla	capable of love	*ame*	lovingly

Greetings & Civilities

Hi!	*sal-oot-on!*	Saluton!
Good morning.	*boh-nan ma-tay-non*	Bonan matenon.
Good afternoon.	*boh-nan ta-gon*	Bonan tagon.
Good evening.	*boh-nan veh-spehrr-on*	Bonan vesperon.
Good night.	*boh-nan nok-ton*	Bonan nokton.
How are you?	*kee-el vee farr-tas?*	Kiel vi fartas?
Well.	*boh-neh*	Bone.
Very well, thanks.	*treh boh-neh, dang-kon*	Tre bone, dankon.
Please.	*mee peh-tass*	Mi petas.
Thankyou.	*dang-kon*	Dankon.
You're welcome.	*neh dang-kin-deh*	Ne dankinde.

Goodbyes

Goodbye.	*jeess reh-vee-doh*	Gis revido.
See you later.	*jeess poh-steh*	Gis poste.

Useful Phrases

What's your name?	*kee-oh est-ass vee-ah noh-moh?*	Kio estas via nome?
I'm ...	*mee est-ass ...*	Mi estas ...
Where are you from?	*deh kee-eh vee veh-nass?*	De kie vi venas?
I'm from ...	*mee veh-nass deh ...*	Mi venas de ...

Do you speak Esperanto?
*choo vee parr-**ohl**-ass esp-err-**ant**-on?*
Cu vi parolas Esperanton?

I'm a beginner but I'd like to meet some Esperanto speakers.
*mee **est**-ass kom-ent-**san**-tol, said mee **shat**-oos ren-**kon**-tee esp-err-an-**tist**-oyn*
Mi estas komencanto, sed mi satus renkonti Esperantis-tojn.

How do you say that in Esperanto?
*kee-el vee deer-ass tee-on es-perr-**ant**-eh?*
Kiel vi diras tion Esperante?

When did you learn Esperanto?
*kee-am vee lerr-niss es-perr-**ant**-on?*
Kiam vi lernis Esperanton?

Yes/No.	*yes/neh*	Jes/Ne.
Where is ...	*kee-eh est-ass ...?*	Kie estas ...?
On the right.	*dek-streh*	Dekstre.
On the left.	*mal-**dek**-streh*	Maldekstre.
Straight on.	*rek-teh*	Rekte.

Numbers

1	unu	5	kvin	9	nau/u	20	dudek
2	du	6	ses	10	dek	21	dudek unu
3	tri	7	sep	11	dek unu	100	cent
4	kvar	8	ok	12	dek du	1000	mil

Further Information

Dictionaries are available from well-stocked bookstores. With a dictionary alongside the 16 rules laid out here, you should be able to communicate easily at a basic level. For reading material, try David Richardson's *Esperanto: Learning and Using the International Language* (1988, Eastsound, Wa; Orcas).

If you want to pursue the language further while in Europe, or to meet locals who speak it, try contacting the following groups.

Belgium: *Belga Esperanto-Federacio*, 21 rue du Brillant, BE-1170 Bruxelles; ph 03-234 34 00

England: *Esperanto-Asocio de Britio*, 140 Holland Park Avenue, London W11 4UF; ph 0171-727 7821

France: *Unulgo Franca por Esperanto*, 4bis, rue de la Cerisaie, FR-75004 Paris; ph 1-42 78 68 86

Germany: *Germana Esperanto-Asocio*, Immentalstr.3, DE-79104 Freiburg; ph 0761-28 92 99

Greece: *Helena Esperanto-Asocio*, Aristidu 9, GR-105 59 Athina; ph 01-33 13 917

Holland: *Esperanto Nederland*, Ineke Emmelkamp, Arubastraat 12, NL-9715 RW Groningen; ph 050-571 88 40

Ireland: *Esperanto-Asocio de Irlando*, 9 Templeogue Wood, Dublin 6W; ph 01-490 29 19

Italy: *Itala Esperanto-Federacio*, vai Villoresi 38, IT-20143 Milan; ph 02-58 100 857

Portugal: *Portugala Esperanto-Asocio*, Rua Dr João couto 6 r/c A, PT-1500 Lisboa; ph 01-714 13 59

Spain: *Hispana Esperanto-Federacio*, Rodriguez San Pedro 13 3° 7, ES-280 15 Madrid; ph 91-446 80 79
Euska Esperanto-Asocio, Zapatería 29, ES-01001 Vitoria-Gasteiz, Basque Country
Katalun Esperanto-Asocio, Apariat 290, ES-08200 Sabadell, Catalonia; ph 93-7163633

Index

French 90

German 152

Irish... 286

Italian...296

Portuguese 360

Scottish Gaelic 416

Spanish 426

Welsh...488

Quick Reference Sheets..495–518

Appendix...519

LONELY PLANET PHRASEBOOKS

Complete your travel experience with a Lonely Planet phrasebook. Developed for the independent traveller, the phrasebooks enable you to communicate confidently in any practical situation – and get to know the local people and their culture.

Skipping lengthy details on where to get your drycleaning ironed, information in the phrasebooks covers bargaining, customs and protocol, how to address people and introduce yourself, explanations of local ways of telling the time, dealing with bureaucracy and bargaining, plus plenty of ways to share your interests and learn from locals.

Arabic (Egyptian)
Arabic (Moroccan)
Australian
  Introduction to Australian English,
  Aboriginal and Torres Strait languages
Baltic States
  Estonian, Latvian and Lithuanian
Bengali
Brazilian
Burmese
Cantonese
Central Asia
Central Europe
  Czech, French, German,
  Hungarian, Italian and Slovak
Eastern Europe
  Bulgarian, Czech, Hungarian, Polish,
  Romanian and Slovak
Ethiopian (Amharic)
Fijian
French
German
Greek
Hill Tribes
Hindi/Urdu
Indonesian
Italian
Japanese
Korean
Lao
Malay
Mandarin
Mediterranean Europe
  Albanian, Croatian, Greek, Italian,
  Macedonian, Maltese, Serbian and
  Slovene

Mongolian
Nepali
Papua New Guinea (Pidgin)
Pilipino (Tagalog)
Quechua
Russian
Scandinavian Europe
  Danish, Finnish, Icelandic,
  Norwegian and Swedish
South-East Asia
  Burmese, Indonesian, Khmer, Lao,
  Malay, Pilipino (Tagalog), Thai and
  Vietnamese
Spanish (Castilian)
  Also includes Basque, Catalan and Gali-
  cian
Spanish (Latin American)
Sri Lanka
Swahili
Thai
Tibetan
Turkish
Ukrainian
USA
  Introduction to US English,
  Vernacular, Native American
  languages and Hawaiian
Vietnamese
Western Europe
  Useful words and phrases in Basque,
  Catalan, Dutch, French, German,
  Greek, Irish, Italian, Portuguese, Scott-
  ish Gaelic, Spanish (Castilian) and
  Welsh

COMPLETE LIST OF LONELY PLANET BOOKS

AFRICA
Africa - the South • Africa on a shoestring • Arabic (Moroccan) phrasebook • Cairo • Cape Town • Central Africa • East Africa • Egypt • Egypt travel atlas • Ethiopian (Amharic) phrasebook • The Gambia & Senegal • Kenya • Kenya travel atlas • Malawi, Mozambique & Zambia • Morocco • North Africa • South Africa, Lesotho & Swaziland • South Africa, Lesotho & Swaziland travel atlas • Swahili phrasebook • Tunisia • Trekking in East Africa• West Africa • Zimbabwe, Botswana & Namibia • Zimbabwe, Botswana & Namibia travel atlas

Travel Literature: The Rainbird: A Central African Journey • Songs to an African Sunset: A Zimbabwean Story

ANTARCTICA
Antarctica

AUSTRALIA & THE PACIFIC
Australia • Australian phrasebook • Bushwalking in Australia • Bushwalking in Papua New Guinea • Fiji • Fijian phrasebook • Islands of Australia's Great Barrier Reef • Melbourne • Micronesia • New Caledonia • New South Wales • New Zealand • Northern Territory • Outback Australia • Papua New Guinea • Papua New Guinea phrasebook • Queensland • Rarotonga & the Cook Islands • Samoa • Solomon Islands • South Australia • Sydney • Tahiti & French Polynesia • Tasmania • Tonga • Tramping in New Zealand • Vanuatu • Victoria • Western Australia

Travel Literature: Islands in the Clouds • Sean & David's Long Drive

CENTRAL AMERICA & THE CARIBBEAN
Bahamas, Turks & Caicos • Bermuda • Central America on a shoestring • Costa Rica • Cuba • Eastern Caribbean • Guatemala, Belize & Yucatán: La Ruta Maya • Jamaica

Travel Literature: Green Dreams: Travels in Central America

EUROPE
Amsterdam • Andalucia • Austria • Baltics States phrasebook • Berlin • Britain • Canary Islands • Central Europe on a shoestring • Central Europe phrasebook • Czech & Slovak Republics • Denmark • Dublin • Eastern Europe on a shoestring • Eastern Europe phrasebook • Estonia, Latvia & Lithuania • Finland • France •French phrasebook • Germany • German phrasebook • Greece • Greek phrasebook • Hungary • Iceland, Greenland & the Faroe Islands • Ireland • Italian phrasebook • Italy • Lisbon • London • Mediterranean Europe on a shoestring • Mediterranean Europe phrasebook • Paris • Poland • Portugal • Portugal travel atlas • Prague • Romania & Moldova • Russia, Ukraine & Belarus • Russian phrasebook • Scandinavian & Baltic Europe on a shoestring • Scandinavian Europe phrasebook • Slovenia • Spain • Spanish phrasebook • St Petersburg • Switzerland • Trekking in Spain • Ukrainian phrasebook • Vienna • Walking in Britain • Walking in Italy • Walking in Switzerland • Western Europe on a shoestring • Western Europe phrasebook

Travel Literature: The Olive Grove: Travels in Greece

INDIAN SUBCONTINENT
Bangladesh • Bengali phrasebook • Bhutan • Delhi • Goa • Hindi/Urdu phrasebook • India • India & Bangladesh travel atlas • Indian Himalaya • Karakoram Highway • Nepal • Nepali phrasebook • Pakistan • Rajasthan • Sri Lanka • Sri Lankan phrasebook • Trekking in the Indian Himalaya •

COMPLETE LIST OF LONELY PLANET BOOKS

ISLANDS OF THE INDIAN OCEAN
Madagascar & Comoros • Maldives • Mauritius, Réunion & Seychelles

NORTH AMERICA
Alaska • Backpacking in Alaska • Baja California • California & Nevada • Canada • Chicago • Deep South • Florida • Hawaii • Honolulu • Los Angeles • Mexico • Mexico City • Miami • New England • New Orleans • New York City • New York, New Jersey & Pennsylvania • Pacific Northwest USA • Rocky Mountain States • San Francisco • Seattle • Southwest USA • USA phrasebook • Washington, DC & the Capital Region
Travel Literature: Drive thru America

NORTH-EAST ASIA
Beijing • Cantonese phrasebook • China • Hong Kong • Hong Kong, Macau & Guangzhou • Japan • Japanese phrasebook • Japanese audio pack • Korea • Korean phrasebook • Kyoto • Mandarin phrasebook • Mongolia • Mongolian phrasebook • North-East Asia on a shoestring • Seoul • Southwest China • Taiwan • Tibet • Tibet phrasebook • Tokyo
Travel Literature: Lost Japan

MIDDLE EAST & CENTRAL ASIA
Arab Gulf States • Arabic (Egyptian) phrasebook • Central Asia • Central Asia phrasebook • Iran • Israel & the Palestinian Territories • Israel & the Palestinian Territories travel atlas • Istanbul • Jerusalem • Jordan & Syria • Jordan, Syria & Lebanon travel atlas • Lebanon • Middle East • Turkey • Turkish phrasebook • Turkey travel atlas • Yemen
Travel Literature: The Gates of Damascus • Kingdom of the Film Stars: Journey into Jordan

SOUTH AMERICA
Argentina, Uruguay & Paraguay • Bolivia • Brazil • Brazilian phrasebook • Buenos Aires • Chile & Easter Island • Chile & Easter Island travel atlas • Colombia • Ecuador & the Galápagos Islands • Latin American Spanish phrasebook • Peru • Quechua phrasebook • Rio de Janeiro • South America on a shoestring • Trekking in the Patagonian Andes • Venezuela
Travel Literature: Full Circle: A South American Journey

SOUTH-EAST ASIA
Bali & Lombok • Bangkok • Burmese phrasebook • Cambodia • Ho Chi Minh City • Indonesia • Indonesian phrasebook • Indonesian audio pack • Jakarta • Java • Laos • Laos travel atlas • Lao phrasebook • Malay phrasebook • Malaysia, Singapore & Brunei • Myanmar (Burma) • Philippines • Pilipino phrasebook • Singapore • South-East Asia on a shoestring • South-East Asia phrasebook • Thailand • Thailand's Islands & Beaches • Thailand travel atlas • Thai phrasebook • Thai Hill Tribes phrasebook • Thai audio pack • Vietnam • Vietnamese phrasebook • Vietnam travel atlas

ALSO AVAILABLE: Brief Encounters •Travel with Children • Traveller's Tales

For ordering information contact your nearest Lonely Planet office.

PLANET TALK
Lonely Planet's FREE quarterly newsletter

Every issue is packed with up-to-date travel news
and advice including:

- a letter from Lonely Planet co-founders Tony and
  Maureen Wheeler
- go behind the scenes on the road with a Lonely
  Planet author
- feature article on an important and topical travel
  issue
- a selection of recent letters from travellers
- details on forthcoming Lonely Planet promotions
- complete list of Lonely Planet products

To join our mailing list contact any Lonely Planet office.

LONELY PLANET PUBLICATIONS

AUSTRALIA
PO Box 617, Hawthorn 3122, Victoria
tel: (03) 9819 1877 fax: (03) 9819 6459
e-mail: talk2us@lonelyplanet.com.au

UK
10a Spring Place,
London NW5 3BH
tel: (0171) 428 4800 fax: (0171) 428 4828
e-mail: go@lonelyplanet.co.uk

USA
150 Linden Street,
Oakland, CA 94607
tel: (510) 893 8555
TOLL FREE: 800 275-8555
fax: (510) 893 8572
e-mail: info@lonelyplanet.com

FRANCE:
1 rue de Dahomey,
75011 Paris
tel: 01 55 25 33 00 fax: 01 55 25 33 01
e-mail: bip@lonelyplanet.tr

**World Wide Web: http://www.lonelyplanet.com
or AOL keyword: lp**